THE EARL OF ESSEX AND LATE ELIZABETHAN POLITICAL CULTURE

OXFORD HISTORICAL MONOGRAPHS

The Earl of Essex
and Late Elizabethan
Political Culture

ALEXANDRA GAJDA

OXFORD
UNIVERSITY PRESS

*This book has been printed digitally and produced in a standard specification
in order to ensure its continuing availability*

OXFORD
UNIVERSITY PRESS

Great Clarendon Street, Oxford OX2 6DP
United Kingdom

Oxford University Press is a department of the University of Oxford.
It furthers the University's objective of excellence in research, scholarship,
and education by publishing worldwide.

Oxford is a registered trade mark of Oxford University Press in the UK
and in certain other countries

© Alexandra Gajda 2012

The moral rights of the author have been asserted

Reprinted 2013

British Library Cataloguing in Publication Data
Data available

Library of Congress Cataloging in Publication Data
Data available

ISBN 978-0-19-969968-1

For my family

Preface and Acknowledgements

'Essex? He was a fool!' This remark, delivered by an eminent professor of early modern history, greeted a paper that I had just delivered on Essex and popular politics in Oxford in 2007. It was intended (though did not succeed) to close down a discussion of how historians might evaluate the significance of Essex's appeal on 8 February 1601 to the citizens of London to rise and join with him to defend his life, and reform the government of the realm. Despite the efforts of recent scholars to rehabilitate Essex's reputation as a serious statesman, the extraordinary implosion of Essex's later career, which plummeted from the heights of popularity, favour, and praise, remains more notorious than understood. A tendency to dismiss the earl as a petulant butterfly, who pranced and sulked his way to the scaffold, still persists in academic scholarship as well as in the popular imagination. In fact, in sixteenth-century England, Robert Devereux, 2nd earl of Essex, was a nobleman of unparalleled domestic and international renown: a soldier, statesman, and hereditary noble of exceptionally powerful ambition, who generated a huge response from his contemporaries, but who also divided and polarized opinion. This widespread acclaim for the earl, and his sensational fall from grace, rising, and death, spanned and defined the politics of the final decade of Elizabeth's rule, which has been seen as the darkest, and most turbulent of the Queen's reign—an era of severe economic hardship, exacerbated by the immense burdens of continental war, and underscored by profound anxieties about the unsettled succession to the crown.

This study attempts to understand Essex as contemporaries saw him, and as he saw himself, through an analysis of the ideological frameworks that gave shape to his political mentality. It examines the attitudes of the earl and his closest followers and political advisors to war, religion, and domestic politics, and the literary and historical frameworks that both influenced and gave meaning to Essex's increasingly fractured relationship with the Elizabethan regime. This work is also a study of Essex's reverberating impact on Elizabethan politics, and of the ways that contemporaries responded to Essex and his example in positive and negative senses. It analyses the agency of texts and ideas in real political contexts: the decline of Essex's career, and his downfall and death in 1601. More broadly, it is an exploration of the interface between ideas and politics in late sixteenth-century England. In short, it is a study of how late Elizabethan political culture both shaped—and was shaped by—the earl of Essex.

I am very grateful for permission to cite from manuscripts owned or controlled by the marquis of Salisbury; the Henry E. Huntington Library, California; the Masters of the Bench of the Inner Temple, the Warwickshire Record Office; and Durham University Library. I would also like to thank the Arts & Humanities Research Council (AHRC) (formerly AHRB) for funding the thesis upon which this book is based.

Perhaps unlike the earl of Essex, I have been exceptionally fortunate in the counsel that I have received from friends and fellow scholars over the years. My first thanks must go to Susan Brigden, matchless supervisor of my DPhil thesis. I have been sustained by her teaching, friendship, and advice through the bleakest and best of times. The examiners of my thesis, Jenny Wormald and Blair Worden, provided extremely helpful encouragement and criticism in my viva, and much support since. Pauline Croft has been a great mentor and friend. I have also learned a great deal from other scholars working on Elizabethan political culture, Essex, and the 1590s. In particular, Paul Hammer, Essex's exemplary biographer, has been exceptionally generous with his time and the exchange of ideas. Paulina Kewes, Peter Lake, and Malcolm Smuts have offered inspiration and advice, while I have enjoyed many stimulating exchanges about Essex with Janet Dickinson, Neil Younger, and Hugh Gazzard.

The development of my thought also owes a great deal to friendships with my peers, in particular Anna Bayman, Leif Dixon, and George Southcombe. I must also thank Paul Cavill, Nancy Durrant, Ella Heeks, Sophie Lazar, Paul Miller, Danielle Moon, Tom Porter, Cath Rothon, Amy Scott, Tracey Sowerby, Grant Tapsell, Andrea Walkden, and Catherine Wright. I owe a great deal to Chris Joy and Diane Troth, my sixth-form history teachers, who first taught me about the sixteenth century. While I was an undergraduate and graduate at New College, Oxford, Eric Christiansen, Ruth Harris, and David Parrott provided an excellent education. I must thank Gareth Davies, Tim Gardam, Peter Ghosh, and Howard Hotson, for electing me to a Junior Research Fellowship at St Anne's College, Oxford, and providing such a welcoming and scholarly atmosphere. The same applies to my colleagues at the University of Birmingham, especially Hugh Adlington, Elaine Fulton, Tara Hamling, Simone Laqua-O'Donnell, Tom Lockwood, George Lukowski, and Gillian Wright. I must single out Richard Cust for his great support, and Margaret Small, upon whom I have depended entirely for shelter and sustenance. For uncountable reasons, many of them related to the competitive reading in which we indulged as children, everything I do owes an enormous amount to Susie Cogan. Christopher Gort has mended my computer on more occasions than he would have wished: I really have always appreciated it. Any flaws in this book are, of course, entirely my own.

The boundless love and support that I have always received from my parents, Ann and Norbert Gajda, have maintained me in everything that I have done. Finally, I cannot really express the depth of my gratitude and love for James Phythian-Adams—for everything, for always.

Contents

Abbreviations

APC	*Acts of the privy council of England,* new series, J. R. Dasent, E. G. Atkinson et al. eds, 46 vols (London, 1890–1964).
Apologie	Robert Devereux, 2nd earl of Essex, *To Maister Anthonie Bacon. An apologie of the Earle of Essex, against those which fasly* [falsly] *and maliciously taxe him to be the onely hinderer of the peace, and quiet of his countrey* (1600).
BIHR	*Bulletin of the Institute of Historical Research.*
Birch, *Memoirs*	T. Birch, *Memoirs of the reign of Queen Elizabeth, from the year 1581 till her death, from the original papers of Anthony Bacon*... 2 vols (London, 1754).
BL	British Library, London.
Bod	Bodleian Library, Oxford.
Camden, *Annales*	William Camden, *Annales rerum Anglicarum et Hibernicarum regnante Elizabetha*, ed. Thomas Hearne (Oxford, 1717).
Cecil MS	Cecil manuscript, Hatfield House, Hertfordshire.
Collins, *Letters and memorials*	A. Collins, *Letters and memorials of state*... *[of theSidney family]*... *from the originals at* Penshurst Place *in* Kent, 2 vols (London, 1746).
Calendar of Carew manuscripts	*A Calendar of the Carew manuscripts, preserved in the Archiepiscopal library at Lambeth (1515–1624)*, ed. J. S. Brewer and W. Bullen, 6 vols, (London, 1867–73).
CSPD	*Calendar of state papers, domestic series, preserved in Her Majesty's Public Record Office, Edward VI, Mary I, Elizabeth, James I*, R. Lemon and M. A. E. Green eds, 12 vols (London, 1865–72).
CSPI	*Calendar of state papers, relating to Ireland, of the reign of Elizabeth*, H. C. Hamilton, E. G. Atkinson et al. eds, 11 vols (London, 1860–1912).
CSP Spanish	*Calendar of letters and state papers, relating to English affairs, preserved principally in the archives of Simancas, Elizabeth*, M. A. S. Hume ed., 4 vols (London, 1896–99).
CSP	*Calendar of state papers, relating to Scotland and Mary, Queen of Scots, 1547–1603, preserved in the Public Record*

	Office, and elsewhere in England, J. Bain, W. K. Boyd et al. eds, 13 vols (Edinburgh and Glasgow, 1898–1969).
EHR	*English Historical Review.*
HL	Henry E. Huntington Library, San Marino, CA, USA.
Howell, *State Trials*	Thomas Bayley Howell ed., *Cobbett's complete collection of state trials and proceedings for high treason and other crimes and misdemeanours* . . . 33 vols (London: T. C. Hansard, 1809–26).
HJ	*Historical Journal.*
HLQ	*Huntington Library Quarterly.*
HMC	Historical Manuscripts Commission.
HMC Bath	HMC. *Calendar of the manuscripts of the Most Honorable the Marquis of Bath preserved at Longleat, Wiltshire*, 5 vols (London, 1904–80).
HMC de L'Isle and Dudley	HMC. *Report on the manuscripts of Lord de L'Isle and Dudley, preserved at Penshurst Place*, 6 vols (London, 1925–66)
HMC Salisbury	HMC. *A calendar of the manuscripts of the Most Hon. the marquis of Salisbury, KG, &c., preserved at Hatfield House, Hertfordshire*, 24 vols (London, 1883–1976).
ITL	Inner Temple Library.
LPL	Lambeth Palace Library.
JBS	*Journal of British Studies.*
LMA	London Metropolitan Archives.
Manning, *Hayward's Life and raigne*	John J. Manning ed., *First and second parts of John Hayward's The life and raigne of King Henrie IIII* Camden Society, 4th ser., 42 (London, 1991).
McClure, *Letters of John Chamberlain*	N. E. McClure, *The letters of John Chamberlain*, 2 vols (Philadelphia, PA: American Philosophical Society, 1939).
MS	Manuscript.
TNA	The National Archives, London.
ODNB	*Oxford Dictionary of National Biography*, ed. H. C. G. Matthew and Brian Harrison (Oxford: Oxford University Press, 2004), online edn, Oct. 2008.
PMLA	*Publications of the Modern Language Association of America.*
Spedding, *L&L*	James Spedding ed., *The letters and the life of Francis Bacon* . . . *set forth in chronological order, with a commentary* . . . 7 vols (London: Longmans, 1861–74).

Strype, *Annals*	John Strype ed., *Annals of the reformation and establishment of religion, and other various occurrences in the Church of England, during Queen Elizabeth's happy reign* ... 4 vols in 7, (Oxford, 1824).
TRHS	*Transactions of the Royal Historical Society.*
WRO	Warwickshire Record Office.

A NOTE ON THE TEXT

Abbreviations have been expanded in quotations. Where appropriate the usage of 'u' and 'i' has been modernised to 'v' and 'j'. It is assumed that all works printed before 1700 were published in London unless otherwise stated. Dates are Old Style, but it is assumed that the year begins on 1 January.

Introduction

I

In 1604, in the hopeful dawn of the reign of James VI and I, Robert Pricket, soldier and author of anti-Catholic polemic, published a posthumous tribute to Robert Devereux, 2nd earl of Essex, 'Natures pride, Vertues bulwarke' 'the whole worlds wonder'. His eulogy was acutely purposeful. Essex, the personification of 'Honour's fame', had ended his life in the most ignominious of violent deaths, beheaded for treason on 25 February 1601. Pricket wrote to redeem his hero by immortalizing his character and deeds; above all, to blot out 'the name of traytor' from historical memory.[1]

In *Honors fame in triumph riding* Pricket tilted with the dark assessments of Essex's character that had appeared in government propaganda after the earl's disastrous rising on 8 February 1601. After his arrest Essex had been likened in sermon, speech, and printed pamphlet to the most famous traitorous rebels—an overweening noble, who would have harnessed the latent violence of the commons to realize his vaunting ambition: to usurp the throne and 'sett the crowne of England upon his owne head'.[2]

Essex, whose career was the ultimate illustration of the turning of fortune's wheel, had an important afterlife in the seventeenth century, as a serious didactic example to those who would ascend the slippery top of the court.[3] Thomas Scott's incendiary pamphlet of 1624, *Robert earle of Essex his ghost, sent from Elizian to the nobility, gentry and communaltie*

---

[1] *Honors fame in triumph riding. Or, the life and death of the late honorable Earle of Essex* (1604), sigs. A4ʳ⁻ᵛ, [B3ᵛ], Eʳ.

[2] TNA, SP 12/278/63, f. 108ʳ, 'A direction for the preachers', 14 February 1601.

[3] See covert allusions to Essex in Samuel Daniel's *Philotas* (1600–5) and Ben Jonson's *Sejanus his fall* (1603):Hugh Gazzard, '"Those Graue Presentments of Antiquitie": Samuel Daniel's *Philotas* and the earl of Essex', *Review of English Studies*, 51/203 (2000), 423–50; Peter Lake, 'From *Leicester his commonwealth* to *Sejanus his fall*: Ben Jonson and the politics of Roman (Catholic) virtue', in Ethan H. Shagan ed., *Catholics and the 'protestant nation': religious politics and identity in early modern Britain* (Manchester: Manchester University Press, 2005), 128–61; Maureen King, 'The Essex myth in Jacobean England', in Glenn

of England, revived Pricket's assessment of the earl as a sage and godly
Protestant warrior, the terror of Spain, whose heroic exploits shamed the
Jacobean peace. Neither hero nor villain, William Camden's Essex is an
Elizabethan Coriolanus, whose archaic fixation with military virtue
renders him a woeful politician. 'Slow to wickedness', Essex 'seemed
not made for the court'.[4] Isaac Casaubon, the great classical scholar,
saw the earl's history as an *exemplum* of the perils of dangerous reading.
In a pale anticipation of Hobbes's argument that the intemperate
influence of classical authors was a fundamental cause of the English
civil war, he singled out the agent of Essex's downfall to be Henry
Cuffe, Essex's learned secretary, who had goaded his master to arms
with inflammatory quotations from Lucan's *Pharsalia*.[5]

Over-mighty subject and traitor? Protestant hero, unjustly slandered
and destroyed? Or a man whose adherence to an ethical code was too
absolute for the murky world of the Elizabethan court, or whose actions
were informed by an ill-directed faith in the application of ancient literature to contemporary times? These are very different—frequently
conflicting—narratives of the history of the same man. These interpretations of Essex's career and rising enshrine competing definitions of political virtue, the nature of obedience, and the distinctions between treachery,
rebellion, and legitimate protest.

Despite their variant appraisals of Essex, the authors of all of these
seventeenth-century accounts, approbatory or otherwise, assume that the
earl presented an important challenge to the values underpinning the
sixteenth-century monarchy. For Jacobean minds Robert Devereux was
significant above all for the ideas that shaped his attitude to war, religion,
virtue, and court politics—ideas that structured his political conduct and
defined his career.

Scholars of modern times have not always afforded Essex such serious
appraisal. The evocation of Gloriana's candlelit romance with her last
doomed favourite in the most melodramatic of Lytton Strachey's psychological sketches tends to trigger scholars' ascetic distaste for the romanti-
cizing of Elizabethan political history. Essex's martial ambitions have often
been dismissed as swaggering glory-hunting, while his tempestuous personal relationships with courtiers and the queen herself have been defined

Burgess, Wymer Roland and Jason Lawrence eds, *The accession of James I: historical and
cultural consequences* (Basingstoke: Palgrave MacMillan, 2006), 177–86.

⁴ 'Nec ille certe ad aulam factus videbatur, qui ad scelera segnis…Nemo gloriam, ex
virtute magis concupivit, & cetera omnia minus curavit', Camden, *Annales*, 863.

⁵ Bod, Casaubon MS 28, f. 127ʳ; see Lisa Jardine and Anthony Grafton, '"Studied for
Action": How Gabriel Harvey read his Livy', *Past and Present*, 129/1 (1990), 75.

as products of his abrasive character.[6] For Wallace MacCaffrey, Essex's turbulent impact on Elizabethan politics was caused by his unstable personality; for Lacey Baldwin Smith, the earl was consumed by a deadly paranoia.[7]

The shadows that hang over all evaluations of Essex are the disastrously un-epic dimensions of his rising in 1601. Essex's strange foray into the city of London on 8 February with a few hundred men at most was a desperate attempt to assert political ascendancy over Elizabeth, and to remove his enemies from the court. A spectacular failure, the revolt was quickly contained with great ease by the government's forces; a pathetic coda to the grand sequence of 'Tudor rebellions'.[8] To later generations, this disastrous end to such a glamorous career has seemed to be the inevitable outcome of Essex's deluded political myopia.

Contemporaries did not adopt a dismissive attitude toward the earl's weight as a soldier and a statesman, or his impact on Elizabethan politics. No other nobleman living under a sixteenth-century monarch was so rapturously acclaimed in his lifetime for his great qualities.[9] Robert Pricket's workmanlike eulogy for Essex borrows deliberately from the glittering tribute of Edmund Spenser, written in 1596, when extraordinary feats were expected from this 'noble Peer/Great *Englands* glory and

[6] Lytton Strachey, *Elizabeth and Essex: a tragic history* (London: Chatto and Windus, 1928); Essex's frivolity is assumed in the popular biography of Robert Lacey, *Robert, earl of Essex: an Elizabethan Icarus* (London: Weidenfeld and Nicolson, 1971). The classic biography is G. B. Harrison, *The life and death of Robert Devereux, earl of Essex* (London: Cassell, 1937). See also volumes VII–XII of E. M. Tenison's documentary history of Elizabeth's reign, *Elizabethan England: being the history of this country 'in relation to all foreign princes'*, 12 vols (Leamington Spa, 1933–61); W. B. Devereux ed., *Lives and Letters of the Devereux, earls of Essex, in the reigns of Elizabeth, James I and Charles I, 1540–1646*, 3 vols (London: John Murray, 1853). For Essex's military career see R. B. Wernham, *After the armada: Elizabethan England and the struggle for Western Europe, 1588–1595* (Oxford: Clarendon Press, 1984) and idem, *The return of the armadas: the last years of the Elizabethan war against Spain, 1595–1603* (Oxford: Clarendon Press, 1994). The definitive biography of Essex's early career is P. E. J. Hammer, *The polarisation of Elizabethan politics: the political career of Robert Devereux, 2nd earl of Essex, 1585–1597* (Cambridge: Cambridge University Press, 1999); also see idem,'Devereux, Robert, second earl of Essex (1565–1601)', *ODNB*.
[7] Wallace T. MacCaffrey, *Elizabeth I: war and politics* (Princeton, NJ: Princeton University Press, 1992), 453–536; Lacey Baldwin Smith, *Treason in Tudor England: politics and paranoia* (London: Jonathan Cape, 1986), 192–276.
[8] Anthony Fletcher and Diarmaid MacCulloch, *Tudor rebellions*, 5th edn (Harlow: Pearson Longman, 2004), 118–19.
[9] Essex was the recipient of more literary dedications than any other figure in the 1590s: Alistair Fox, 'The complaint of poetry for the death of liberality: the decline of literary patronage in the 1590s', in John Guy ed., *The Reign of Elizabeth I: court and culture in the last decade* (Cambridge: Cambridge University Press, 1995), 229–57; Hugh Gazzard, 'The patronage of Robert Devereux, 2nd earl of Essex c.1577–1596', unpublished DPhil thesis (University of Oxford, 2000).

the Worlds wide wonder' (145–6).[10] If the nineties were 'nasty', to paraphrase Patrick Collinson, Essex embodied the glamorous hope of a brighter future—after the long-awaited death of the ageing queen.[11]

Other scholars, affording the earl the weight that contemporaries hailed, have illuminated a career that was both more substantial and multidimensional than previously realized. Above all, Paul Hammer's acutely scholarly biographical studies have given much sharper clarity to the range and reach of Essex's significance in Elizabethan politics.[12] Born in 1565, Essex's political career commenced as England entered into open enmity with Spain. On the unhappy death of his father, Walter Devereux, in Ireland in September 1576, Essex succeeded to the earldom, but a dreadfully indebted estate. As a royal ward, his education was supervised by William Cecil, Lord Burghley; at Trinity College Cambridge the earl proceeded to the MA degree, an exceptionally rare qualification in a young nobleman, indicating Essex's fondness for the company of scholars, and his future interest in intellectual pursuits.

It was under the influence of Robert Dudley, earl of Leicester, however, that Essex's political career took shape. Dudley, who had married Essex's mother Lettice Knollys in 1578, took the young earl to the Netherlands, appointing him colonel-general of the cavalry, his first military office.[13] After the skirmish at Zutphen in September 1586, Leicester knighted his stepson (and godson), thus releasing him from wardship. More famously, Essex inherited one of the swords of the dying Sir Philip Sidney, a gesture which had a profound impact on the young nobleman's self-image. Essex's entry into adulthood, then, was inspired by martial ideals, and his career would be defined by war.

It was rather as a courtier than a soldier, though, that Essex's career took flight on his return to England. Young, handsome, and articulate, the earl caught the eye and favour of the queen, again in part through the powerful patronage of Leicester.[14] By the summer of 1587, Essex was established as Elizabeth's new favourite and master of the horse (which Leicester resigned to advantage him), and a threatening rival to Sir Walter Ralegh,

---

[10] Edmund Spenser, *Prothalamion, or, a spousall verse* in *The shorter poems*, ed. Richard A. MacCabe (London and New York: Penguin, 1999), 496.

[11] Patrick Collinson, 'Ecclesiastical vitriol: religious satire in the 1590s and the invention of Puritanism', in Guy, *Reign of Elizabeth I*, 154.

[12] This is intended as a brief introductory sketch of Essex's career, derived from the works cited above.

[13] Simon Adams, *Leicester and the court: essays on Elizabethan politics*, (Manchester: Manchester University Press, 2002).

[14] P. E. J. Hammer, '"Absolute sovereign and mistress of her grace"? queen Elizabeth and her favourites, 1581–1592', in J. H. Elliott and Laurence W. B. Brockliss eds, *The world of the favourite* (New Haven, CT and London: Yale University Press, 1999), 38–53.

whose career would be fatally entwined with his own. Leicester's death in September 1588 removed his chief patron, but Essex's favour with the queen persisted. Elizabeth showered the impoverished earl with honours and grants, the most important of which would be Leicester's farm of the customs on sweet wines: this lucrative revenue would come to dominate both Essex's finances and his fate.

The earl's ardent expectations of martial honour, whetted in the Netherlands, were never dampened by life at court. Ignoring Elizabeth's prohibition, Essex secretly joined Sir Francis Drake and Sir John Norris's ill-fated naval expedition to Portugal in 1589, where his chivalrous conduct was widely praised.[15] The earl's public career could have ended with this escapade, especially when Elizabeth discovered that he had made a clandestine marriage to Frances, widow of Sir Philip Sidney and daughter of Sir Francis Walsingham. Instead, in a form of behaviour that became a characteristic pattern, Essex charmed his way back into the queen's favour, and, with the support of Burghley and Sir Christopher Hatton, was rewarded in 1591 with formal military command over Elizabeth's army in Normandy.[16] The campaign was rendered a failure by the conflicting strategic interests of Elizabeth and Henry IV; but Essex's career as England's senior aristocratic soldier had commenced.

However, Essex's desire for military glory was the crest of much deeper ambitions. Thanks to his earldom, ancestry, and swiftly established favour with Elizabeth, Essex entrenched himself as a much more substantial political heavyweight, gaining elevation to the privy council on 25 February 1593 (a position that his courtly rival Ralegh would never achieve). The most aggressive proponent of military interventionism against Spain on the council, Essex would cement his position as the foremost military expert, recognized by his appointments as master of the ordnance in March 1597, and earl marshal in December later that year. To underpin his expertise in foreign policy he also sought to replicate the omniscient networks of intelligence controlled by his father-in-law, Francis Walsingham, through the aegis of Anthony Bacon, who entered his service late in 1592.[17] By 1595, Essex and his associates were confidently building the earl to be the chief statesman in the land after Burghley's death.

The extent of Essex's ambition is reflected too in the scope, range, and depth of his political interests. Scholars working in very different fields

[15] R. B. Wernham, *The expedition of Sir John Norris and Sir Francis Drake to Spain and Portugal, 1589* (Navy Records Society, 127: Aldershot, 1988).

[16] H. A. Lloyd, *The Rouen campaign 1590–1592: politics, warfare and the early-modern state* (Oxford: Clarendon Press, 1973).

[17] See Gustav Ungerer, *A Spaniard in Elizabethan England: the correspondence of Antonio Pérez's exile*, 2 vols (London: Tamesis, 1974–6) and Hammer, *Polarisation*, Chapter 5.

have argued that the earl's cultivation of a widespread clientele and following outside the confines of his limited ancestral estates was zealous and highly aggressive—in local politics, parliament, and especially the patronage of soldiers.[18] So too was Essex's development of a religious following. In defiance of Thomas Scott's heroic international Protestant emerges an Essex who was a strenuous ecumenical religious patron, a notable friend and protector of Puritans, Catholics, and Conformist clerics.[19] The earl's engagement with intellectual culture, through his patronage of scholars, also derived from his professed faith in the utility of learning for understanding the contemporary world. Most famously, but mysteriously, the earl's association with histories of Richard II—Sir John Hayward's *The first parte of the life and raigne of King Henrie IIII*, dedicated to the earl on its publication in 1599, and the play watched by the earl's supporters on the eve of his rising in 1601—have placed Essex at the centre of fervent speculation that his revolt was the perverse and tragic outcome of the belief that historical patterns provided a model for future political action.[20]

As the earl's star rose in the domestic and international scene, he finally claimed the glory that he craved. In June 1596, he and the lord admiral, Charles Howard, co-commanded the glorious English strike on Spanish soil. Essex captured the laurels, leading the storm of Cadiz, and winning widespread renown throughout Christendom for his chivalrous soldiery—Spenser's 'whole world's wonder'.

[18] On Essex's following see Hammer, *Polarisation*, Chapter 7; A. H. Dodd, 'North Wales in the Essex revolt of 1601', *EHR*, 59 (1944), 348–70; idem, 'The earl of Essex's faction in north Wales, c.1593–1601: supplementary notes', *National Library of Wales Journal*, 6 (1949–59), 190–1; Penry Williams, *The Council in the Marches of Wales under Elizabeth I* (Cardiff: University of Wales Press, 1958) 281–97; R. Reid, 'The political influence of the north parts under the Tudors', in R. W. Seton-Watson ed., *Tudor studies* (London: Longmans, 1924), 228–9; J. E. Neale, *The Elizabethan House of Commons* (London: Jonathan Cape, 1949 [1961]), especially Chapter 11; G. L. Hutson, 'The military following of Robert Devereux, 2nd earl of Essex and the rising of 1601', unpublished MLitt thesis (Oxford, 1987).
[19] Patrick Collinson, *The Elizabethan puritan movement* (London: Jonathan Cape, 1967), 444–7; P.E.J. Hammer, 'An Elizabethan spy who came in from the cold: the return of Anthony Standen to England in 1593', *Historical Research*, 65 (1992), 277–95. See further discussion in Chapter 3.
[20] R. Malcolm Smuts, 'Court-centred politics and the uses of Roman historians, c.1590–c.1630', in Kevin Sharpe and Peter Lake eds, *Culture and politics in early Stuart England* (Basingstoke: Macmillan, 1994), 21–30; David Womersley, 'Sir Henry Savile's Translation of Tacitus and the Political Interpretation of Elizabethan Texts', *Review of English Studies*, 17/167 (1991), 313–42; J. H. M. Salmon, 'Stoicism and Roman example: Seneca and Tacitus in Jacobean England', *Journal of the History of Ideas*, 50/2 (1989), 207–8; Blair Worden, 'Which play was performed at the Globe Theatre on 7 February 1601?', *London Review of Books*, 25/13 (2003), 22–4; P. E. J. Hammer, 'Shakespeare's *Richard II*, the Play of 7 February 1601, and the Essex Rising', *Shakespeare Quarterly*, 59/1 (2008), 1–35.

From this glorious zenith, Essex's fortune unravelled. Weather, incoherent strategy, and the internal divisions of the commanders doomed the planned assaults on the Spanish coast, navy, and treasure fleets in the summer and autumn of 1597, the so-called 'Islands Voyage', occasioning the final breach between Essex and his old rival, Ralegh. Their sorry failure also convinced the queen that ambitious naval and military incursions would never achieve any tangible goal.[21]

In the aftermath of the Islands Voyage, the earl's position in domestic politics also grew unstable. The dominant patterns of Essex's thinking became overwhelmed by the intensifying conviction that his ambitions were thwarted by domestic political enemies on the council and at court. These included, of course, Ralegh and Charles Howard, the lord admiral, Essex's rivals for military *gloire*, and Henry Brooke, 11th Baron Cobham, the newest favourite of Elizabeth, and Ralegh's closest ally.[22] But most importantly, they encompassed Essex's growing animosity to Sir Robert Cecil.[23] Essex had not foreseen Burghley's son as an immediate rival to his own ambitions, as he forged a working relationship with both Cecils throughout the early- and mid-1590s. But Cecil's appointment as secretary of state in July 1596 gave him wide-ranging powers of access to the queen and political knowledge while Essex was so frequently absent on military campaign. Low-level animosity, fuelled by the mocking culture of his friends, had long existed beneath the surface of cordial relations that Essex enjoyed with Burghley's son. The death of the lord treasurer on 4 August 1598 released a brake on Essex's relations with rivals on the council and at court. Increasingly, Essex would come to imagine Cecil as the spidery architect of a web spun to destroy him, and to ensnare the Elizabethan polity within its threads.

The next years then witnessed what Hammer has defined as the 'polarisation' of Elizabethan politics, when the harmony of the regime was openly fractured by Essex's enmities.[24] In the spring and summer of 1598, Essex's opposition to propositions that England make peace with Spain brought him into intense and aggressive conflict with other councillors. But the earl's antagonism extended also to the queen. Essex was

---

[21] Samuel Purchas, *Hakluytus Posthumus or Purchas his Pilgrimes*, 20 vols (Glasgow, 1905–7), XX, 44–5, 69–70; Wernham, *Return of the armadas*, Chs. X–XII.

[22] Robert W. Kenny, *Elizabeth's admiral: the political career of Charles Howard, Earl of Nottingham, 1536–1642* (Baltimore, MD and London: Johns Hopkins Press, 1970). The best account of Brooke's Elizabethan career is in the biography of his father: David McKeen, *A memory of honour: the life of William Brooke, Lord Cobham*, 2 vols (Salzburg: Institut für Anglistik und Amerikanistik, 1986), II, Chs. 20–24.

[23] Pauline Croft, 'Cecil, Robert, first earl of Salisbury (1563–1612)', *ODNB*.

[24] P. E. J. Hammer, 'Patronage at court, faction and the earl of Essex', in Guy, *Reign of Elizabeth I*, 65–86.

driven from court when he quarrelled spectacularly with Elizabeth at the end of June, apparently in a dispute over the appointment of the new lord deputy of Ireland. Exiled from court until September, Essex's extended period of retreat was a forerunner of deeper disgrace to come.

1599 was the climacteric year in Essex's life. As the crisis of the rebellion of Hugh O'Neill, earl of Tyrone, deepened, the earl had been summoned back to court. On 27 March 1599 Essex departed from London in command of the largest Tudor expeditionary force ever sent to Ireland, with a mandate to crush Tyrone. Convinced that his resources were inadequate, the earl abandoned the planned assault on Tyrone's power base in Ulster, directing his troops instead to a protracted campaign in Leinster and Munster. Though initially successful, Essex found his army weakened, his campaign floundering, and the queen furious that her instructions were being ignored.[25] Fearful that his enemies at court were grievously wounding his influence with Elizabeth, Essex took the fateful decision on 15 September to make a truce with the enemy. Eight days before, Essex had infamously conducted a private conversation with Tyrone at Bellaclinthe Ford. As Elizabeth dispatched commands fiercely forbidding conciliation, Essex swooped back to England with a small band of followers, and forced his way into the queen's bedchamber—her intimate privy apartment—to give explanation for his behaviour.

This desperate action resulted in disgrace rather than reconciliation. Essex was placed under house arrest, and was stripped of office at a tribunal at York House on 5 June 1600. Although released in August, he remained estranged from the court, in agonized hope of return to public life. Alienated and humiliated, the earl generated the same divided response that would greet his execution for treason in 1601. As he sweated in exile, the earl's admirers mourned him as a victim of the workings of the court, a virtuous figure struck low by the machinations of dreadful enemies, in a corrupt political environment. His critics, in powerful positions in the government, increasingly suspected him to be a dangerous, destabilizing malcontent, who might aspire to more than the role of a subject, and who enjoyed a highly dangerous degree of public sympathy.[26] As the events that precipitated his rising were set in motion, Essex sharply divided opinion; these divisions directly affected his fate.

Bringing together a rich analysis of all the very disparate elements of Essex's career is Mervyn James's brilliant account of Essex's revolt, which

[25] MacCaffrey, *Elizabeth I*, 418–30; Cyril Falls, *Elizabeth's Irish wars*, 2nd edn. (London: Constable, 1996), 230–52; J. McGurk, *The Elizabethan conquest of Ireland: the 1590s crisis* (Manchester: Manchester University Press, 1997).
[26] See below, Chapter 6.

remains unsurpassed as a study of the cultural contexts of Essex's rising. For James, Essex's downfall and death exemplify the changing role of the English nobility, and the anachronism of the chivalric culture that united his followers. As strong as the ties of friendship and honour were between Essex and his friends, they were ultimately no match for a contemporary ethic of obedience to the monarch that cut across all other forms of allegiance.[27] Anyone writing about Essex owes a particular debt to James's work and its breadth of insight. This study offers a different analysis of the political ideas that informed the earl and his circle. One of its broader aims is to qualify James's understanding of the all-pervasive 'orthodoxy' of the sixteenth-century doctrine of absolute obedience.

While drawing extensively on this rich body of scholarship, the following study takes a different approach to Essex and the rising of 1601. Most importantly, this is not a biographical work; the place to turn to for a new narrative of political events. Instead, this work aims to deepen our understanding of the earl's career by thematic analysis of the expression of political and religious ideas within but also outside of Essex's circle, roughly from the middle of the 1590s until his downfall in 1601.

This book is an attempt to examine, as far as is possible to do so, the extent to which ideas gave shape to the political events of the late 1590s. Rather than defining Essex's fate as the product of his unstable temperament or psychology, I will follow a line of analysis more similar to Camden or Casaubon's: Essex's career was shaped by the dominant ideologies that influenced discussion of politics in Elizabeth's reign; by assumptions and expectations about the intentions and behavioural patterns of political actors living in a monarchical state at war, riven by confessional division, and on the brink of succession to a new monarchy. The earl's actions in 1601 can only be understood if that particular dynamic—the interface between ideas and politics—can be recovered.

As such, this work is as much about the thought of those close acquaintances of the earl, the nearest friends and likeminded associates who exercised direct influence on Essex's mentality, as it is a study of the earl's own thought. The definition of this map is necessarily complex. Essex frequently insisted that the man in politics should seek wisdom in books, and take counsel from learned advisors. This book will particularly analyse texts produced by and for the earl, to further his career, or to furnish him with advice and reflect on his political behaviour. As Hammer

---

[27] Mervyn James, 'At a crossroads of the political culture: the Essex revolt, 1601', in *Society, politics and culture: studies in early modern England* (Cambridge: Cambridge University Press, 1986), 416–65.

has shown, many men in Essex's secretariat—which included the infamous Henry Cuffe—were highly-trained scholars, who actively contributed to literary and political compositions intended to promote the earl's political goals.[28]

Neither 'secretary' nor 'patron', though, properly describes Essex's relationship with closer friends and advisors. While Essex's attempts to procure for him the positions of attorney-general and solicitor-general were a famous failure, Francis Bacon contributed to several literary compositions publicized under Essex's name. He acted as a consistent, often critical advisor to the earl, and would turn dramatically against his former patron when he played a starring role at Essex's trial in February 1601. As such Bacon chronicled the rise and fortunes of Essex's career; his critiques of the earl's behaviour are as revealing as the 'scholarly services' that he performed for his patron.[29]

Other clients of Essex provided similar scholarly and political services in more partisan ways. The closest of these lived at Essex House itself: Antonio Pérez, the Tacitean scholar and former secretary of Philip II of Spain, was an enticingly glamorous source of information about foreign affairs, whose escape from imprisonment in Aragon in 1591 brought him to England and Essex's patronage and hospitality. Living at Essex House from March 1594 to July 1595, Pérez attached himself passionately to the earl's rising star, seeing in Essex the man who could bring Spanish power to its knees. His writings on kingship and tyranny had a deeper significance in shaping political discussion between Essex and his associates.[30]

Anthony Bacon, the closest of all Essex's friends (moving into Essex House soon after Pérez's departure), was perhaps most influential. With Pérez he established the earl's intelligence service in Europe, and the massive bulk of his surviving papers at Lambeth Palace Library physically documents the extensive nature of his work for Essex, and the mutual

---

[28] P. E. J. Hammer, 'The uses of scholarship: the secretariat of Robert Devereux, second earl of Essex, *c*.1585–1601', *EHR*, 109 (1994), 26–51; idem, 'Essex and Europe: evidence from confidential instructions by the earl of Essex, 1595–6', *EHR*, 111 (1996), 357–81.

[29] For Francis Bacon's political career and his relationship with Essex see Lisa Jardine and Alan Stewart, *Hostage to fortune: the troubled life of Francis Bacon* (London: Gollancz, 1998), 146–262; E. A. Abbott, *Bacon and Essex: a sketch of Bacon's earlier life* (London, 1877).

[30] Gregorio Marañón, trans. Charles David Ley, *Antonio Pérez, 'Spanish traitor'* (London: Hollis and Carter, 1954); Pérez's time in England and his relationship with the earl of Essex is superbly documented by Gustav Ungerer's edition of his correspondence, n. 17, above.

affection and respect that he and the earl acknowledged in each other.[31] Fulke Greville transferred much of his former admiration for Philip Sidney to this new paragon of chivalric militarism: Greville's literary works were influenced by the values and political ideas that formed discussion in Essex House, where he also lodged from September 1596.[32]

More shadowy, but highly influential in this in this network of Essex's close friends and clients was Lord Henry Howard (later earl of Northampton), whose Elizabethan career, blighted by association with radical Catholicism, gained a new lease of legitimacy in the twilight years of Elizabeth's reign, as he moved into Essex's orbit. Howard too fostered close friendship with Anthony Bacon, so close that it won the formidable opprobrium of Lady Anne Bacon, the redoubtable mother of the Bacon brothers.[33] In the realm of formal scholarship Henry Savile, warden of Merton College, Oxford, and the queen's tutor in Greek, was a weighty intellectual mentor to the earl; while the writings and friendship of Alberico Gentili, regius professor of civil law at Oxford, were important to Essex, who was godfather to his son.[34]

It has been less easy to analyse the influence of other important associates on Essex's own mentality and political thinking. Henry Wriothesley, 3rd earl of Southampton, joint leader of the rising in 1601, was certainly dazzled by Essex's militaristic glamour. Despite reams of speculative scholarship on his relationship with Shakespeare, only small quantities of Southampton's own writings survive from this period in his life.[35] Charles Blount, 8th Baron Mountjoy, an

---

[31] Bacon had been resident at Bishopsgate Street, close to Essex House, since May 1594. The best account of Bacon's life is in Jardine and Stewart, *Hostage to fortune*, 146–252.

[32] For Greville's career, literature, and political thought see especially Ronald A. Rebholz, *The life of Fulke Greville, first Lord Brooke* (Oxford: Clarendon Press, 1971). Greville and Anthony Bacon were required by the government to vacate Essex House in March 1600 with the rest of Essex's household.

[33] For Howard's Elizabethan career see D. C. Andersson, *Lord Henry Howard (1540–1614): an Elizabethan life* (Cambridge: D. S. Brewer, 2009); Linda Levy Peck, *Northampton: patronage and policy at the court of James I* (London: Allen and Unwin, 1982), 6–22; for his relationship with Essex see P. E. J. Hammer, 'How to become an Elizabethan statesman: Lord Henry Howard, the Earl of Essex, and the politics of friendship', *English Manuscript Studies, 1100–1700*, 13 (2007), 1–34.

[34] Essex and Sir Robert Cecil petitioned successfully for Savile's appointment as provost of Eton in 1596, despite the fact that he was not in religious orders: HMC *Salisbury*, V, 188–9, 291. Essex's son, the third earl, was educated under Savile at Merton; John M. Fletcher ed., *Registrum annalium Collegii Mertonensis 1567–1603* (Oxford: Clarendon Press, 1976), 352. For Gentili and Essex see G. H. J. van der Molen, *Alberico Gentili and the development of international law: his life, work and times*, 2nd edn (Leyden: A.W.Sijthoff, 1968), 57–8.

[35] Southampton seems to have moved in Essex's orbit since joining the Islands Voyage of 1597: C. C. Stopes, *The life of Henry, third earl of Southampton, Shakespeare's patron*, (Cambridge: Cambridge University Press, 1922); G. P. V. Akrigg, *Shakespeare and the earl*

early rival of Essex as a favourite of Elizabeth, was the paramour of Essex's sister Penelope. By the end of the 1590s, these lovers were Essex's most powerful domestic political allies, when Mountjoy replaced Essex as lord deputy of Ireland.[36] Sir Robert Sidney, Philip's brother, and a politically engaged poet in his own right, sought through Essex's patronage to gain political advancement that would take him from his hated position as governor of Flushing.[37] None of these figures have left extensive surviving evidence, though, of their influence over Essex's own thought about politics and religion; as such, they appear more peripherally in the following analysis.

The work is more than a study of the immediate friends and followers of the earl. It is a thematic exploration of the wider impact of Essex's career on the political culture of the 1590s. Thus responses to the earl will be examined by those who admired or criticized him but who did not necessarily enjoy a close (or, indeed, any) personal acquaintance. Competing understandings of Essex's behaviour from before and after the rising are enshrined in a great range of evidence: correspondence, treatises, plays, engravings, portraits, libels, sermons, and literary dedications. In particular, this work recognizes the role that imaginative literature played in defining contemporary political processes, and its importance for the history of ideas. It would be a task well beyond the scope of this monograph to attempt a wide-ranging analysis of Essex's influence on Elizabethan drama and poetry. The earl's importance to Edmund Spenser (whose elaborate funeral in January 1599 was paid for by Essex) and, much more opaquely, to William Shakespeare, can only be touched on very briefly, but it is hoped that the arguments posed here might contribute to our understanding of Elizabethan writers, by deepening our comprehension of the texture of political discourse in the 1590s.

More broadly, then, the example of Essex's career will be seen as a prism through which many aspects of the culture of late Elizabethan politics are refracted with colour and clarity. Those who admired the earl (particularly when he was in political disgrace) tended to ask difficult

---

of Southampton (London: H. Hamilton, 1968); Neil Cuddy, 'The conflicting loyalties of a "vulgar counselor": the third earl of Southampton, 1597–1624', in John Morrill, Paul Slack and Daniel Woolf eds, *Public duty and private conscience in seventeenth-century England. Essays presented to G. E. Aylmer* (Oxford: Clarendon Press, 1993), 121–50.

[36] F. M. H. Jones, *Mountjoy, 1563–1606: the late Elizabethan deputy* (Dublin and London: Clonmore & Reynolds and Burns Oates & Washbourne, 1958); A. Wall, 'Rich, Penelope, Lady Rich, 1563–1607', *ODNB*.

[37] Millicent V. Hay, *The life of Robert Sidney: earl of Leicester (1563–1626)* (Washington, DC: Folger Shakespeare Library, 1984); Michael Brennan, *The Sidneys of Penshurst and the monarchy, 1500–1700* (Aldershot: Ashgate, 2006).

questions of a queen and government that allowed the suffering of a virtuous hero. The language that Essex's critics used to denounce his character, though, tended to define an authoritarian concept of political authority that challenged the earl's codes of behaviour, and emphasized the sanctity of hierarchy and obedience that the earl was accused of violating. These attitudes enrich our understanding of the articulation of political ideas in the 1590s, ideas which were more varied and variously expressed than historians have previously described.

II

The 1590s occupies a discrete and somewhat disconnected niche in the miniature renaissance in the writing of Elizabethan political history. The pioneering work of Simon Adams, Patrick Collinson, and Peter Lake has transformed the landscape of late sixteenth-century historiography; scholars are commanded to integrate the history of ideas into analysis of Elizabethan politics and religion.[38] Most notoriously influential has been Collinson's famous definition of England as a 'monarchical republic', and his description of the mindset of the Protestant ruling elite—with the notable exception of the queen—that predominantly conceptualized the Elizabethan polity as a mixed monarchy: a 'common weal'—the *'res publica'*—where the monarch's authority was bound, both by constitutional limitations of laws and parliament, but also by the more general duty to listen to the counsel of her virtuous subjects.[39]

While analyses of endemic factionalism within Elizabethan politics before 1585 have largely been replaced by a far more consensual understanding of the workings of the regime, recently scholars have argued that the real fractures and anxiety-ridden tensions were between the queen and her subjects—including her own councillors and bishops—over religion and the direction of foreign policy. Above all, Elizabeth's relentlessly answerless response to the question of succession caused the most significant crises of

[38] S. L. Adams, 'The Protestant cause: religious alliance with the West European Calvinist communities as a political issue in England, 1585–1630', unpublished DPhil thesis (University of Oxford, 1973); P. Lake, *Anglicans and Puritans? Presbyterian and conformist thought from Whitgift to Hooker* (London: Allen and Unwin, 1988); Patrick Collinson, *'De Republica Anglorum*: or, history with the politics put back', and 'The monarchical republic of queen Elizabeth I' printed in *Elizabethan Essays* (London: Hambledon, 1994), 1–29, 31–57.
[39] Simon Adams, 'Eliza enthroned? The court and its politics', in C. Haigh ed., *The reign of Elizabeth I* (Basingstoke: MacMillan, 1984), 55–77. See John F. McDiarmid ed., *The monarchical republic of early modern England: essays in response to Patrick Collinson* (Aldershot: Ashgate, 2007), especially McDiarmid's introduction, 1–18.

conscience among her godly 'citizens', provoking conflict between their personal allegiance to the queen, and their separate duty to the Protestant commonwealth, which Elizabeth appeared to imperil through her refusal to provide or name an heir. Stalking the nightmares of godly Protestants was the dreaded spectre of the accession of the Catholic Mary, queen of Scots.[40] Famously, Collinson defined as quasi-republican William Cecil's plans for a council to convene a parliament to appoint a successor in the event of Elizabeth's sudden death, as well as the Bond of Association of 1584, in which a broad scion of the 'political nation' swore to bring to justice perpetrators of the queen's assassination, as well as the figure for whose benefit the crime had been committed.

Recent scholarship has emphasized the foundations, expositions, and ubiquity of theories of mixed monarchy as articulated by these governing elites when expressing their own vision—so often at odds with Elizabeth's —of how commonwealth and church should be governed. Stephen Alford's distinguished studies of William Cecil have illuminated the significant variance between the political creed of Elizabeth's chief minis- ter and the queen in the 1560s.[41] A. N. McLaren strongly argues that Elizabeth's gender encouraged members of the regime to defend the legitimacy of her rule in terms of their own masculine contribution to political decision making, as godly counsellors and through male institu- tions: privy council, parliament, and the clerical establishment.[42] Markku Peltonen has demonstrated the importance for Elizabethan elites of the classical–humanist ideal of the *vita activa*, as filtered through the renais- sance Ciceroneanism that was the basis of all formal education.[43] Blair Worden, also demonstrating the centrality of active and martial virtue in the mentality of Philip Sidney, has shown that Elizabeth's contrasting reluctance to intervene for the cause of the Calvinist Dutch in the 1570s and early 1580s was interpreted by 'forward Protestants' as a woeful dereliction of duty to the international Protestant cause, and prompted Sidney's sensitive literary explorations of the legitimacy of coercing neglectful monarchs who govern wilfully and shun godly counsel.[44]

[40] Patrick Collinson, 'The Elizabethan exclusion crisis and the Elizabethan polity', *Proceedings of the British Academy*, 84 (1994), 51–92.

[41] Stephen Alford, *The early Elizabethan polity: William Cecil and the British succession crisis, 1558–1569* (Cambridge: Cambridge University Press, 1998) and idem, *Burghley: William Cecil at the court of Elizabeth I* (New Haven, CT and London: Yale University Press, 2008).

[42] A. N. McLaren, *Political culture in the reign of Elizabeth I: queen and commonwealth, 1558–1585* (Cambridge: Cambridge University Press, 1999).

[43] Markku Peltonen, *Classical humanism and republicanism in English political thought, 1570–1640* (Cambridge: Cambridge University Press, 1995).

[44] Blair Worden, *The sound of virtue: Philip Sidney's* Arcadia *and Elizabethan politics* (New Haven, CT and London: Yale University Press, 1996).

Peter Lake, though, issues an important warning: the expression by 'godly citizens' of theories of mixed monarchy—advanced in attempts to compel Elizabeth into actions that she felt disinclined to follow—prompted the opposite response from other quarters. Elizabeth herself, as well as a growing body of 'quintessentially monarchical' (usually anti-Puritan) thinkers, increasingly articulated 'absolute' and 'imperial' ideas of kingship, which laid strong emphasis on the divine origins of monarchy, the inviolability of Elizabeth's powers and prerogative, and her *unaccountability* to any but God for her actions, whatever the virtuous credentials of her counsellors. The tendency for these dichotomies to emerge in moments of particular tension had great significance for the ways in which Essex's career would be interpreted in life and death.[45]

Other recent historiographical trends have particular importance for this study of Elizabethan political culture. First, following the pioneering work of Michael Questier, Alexandra Walsham, Peter Lake, and Ethan Shagan, Catholic voices are being integrated into mainstream narratives of Elizabethan politics and religion.[46] The ideological positions adopted by elites and the regime itself were shaped in a dynamic response to the writings and experiences of Elizabethan Catholics, whether living in England, or in continental exile. In the hands of gifted Catholic polemicists, the credibility of the godly polity was mocked and undermined in 'anti-commonwealth' tracts that described England as a toxic realm oppressed by the queen's atheistical (read Protestant) counsellors.[47] In the erastian Elizabethan state, it was Catholics who were most compulsively forced to choose between loyalty to the queen and religious conscience. No less than their Protestant counterparts, the political

[45] Peter Lake, '"The monarchical republic of queen Elizabeth I" (and the fall of Archbishop Grindal) revisited', in McDiarmid, *Monarchical republic*, 129–48.

[46] In particular see the essays in Shagan, *Catholics and the 'Protestant nation'*; Peter Lake and Michael Questier, *The Antichrist's lewd hat: Protestants, papists and players in post-Reformation England* (New Haven, CT and London: Yale University Press, 2002); Michael Questier, *Catholicism and community in early modern England: politics, aristocratic patronage, and religion, c.1550–1640* (Cambridge: Cambridge University Press, 2006); for Walsham, see most recently '"This newe army of Satan": the Jesuit mission and the formation of public opinion in Elizabethan England', in David Lemmings and Claire Walker eds, *Moral panics, the media and the law in early modern England* (Basingstoke and New York: Palgrave Macmillan, 2009), 41–62.

[47] Simon Adams, 'Favourites and factions at the Elizabethan court', in *Leicester and the court*, 46–67; Peter Lake, '"The monarchical republic of Elizabeth I" revisited (by its victims) as a conspiracy', in Barry Coward and Julian Swann eds, *Conspiracies and conspiracy theory in early modern Europe: from the Waldensians to the French Revolution* (Aldershot: Ashgate, 2004), 87–111; Michael Questier, 'Elizabeth and the Catholics', in Shagan, *Catholics and the 'Protestant nation'*, 69–94.

identity of Elizabethan Catholics was defined and shaped by their attitude to the unsettled succession.

Historians of Elizabeth's reign have also begun fruitfully to interrogate the social depth of participation in political culture. The enforcement of the sixteenth-century reformations, and the (not unconnected) rise in literacy, as well as the growth of both print and manuscript culture, necessarily expanded the ways in which the regime itself, as well as particular groups and individuals within the polity, appealed to and engaged with wider audiences, through oral and written media. Natalie Mears, Peter Lake, and Steven Pincus in particular have absorbingly argued that the enriched political discourse of the Elizabethan period is proof of the existence of an Elizabethan public sphere, that was energized sporadically and at key moments of political crisis or interest, especially engaging those politically astute subjects/citizens who emerged from the new grammar schools and the expanding universities.[48]

Nearly all of the historiography described above, however, has focused on the first three decades of Elizabeth's reign. There is a venerable tradition of defining the politics and political culture of the 'long' 1590s—usually more profitably described as the period from England's entry into the war with Spain—as discrete and separate. The death of key personnel: the earl of Leicester in 1588 and Francis Walsingham in 1590, and the rise of John Whitgift, archbishop of Canterbury (the first Elizabethan bishop to sit on the privy council, appointed in 1586), marked a decisive change in conciliar politics, especially diminishing the protection that Puritans had enjoyed from powerful statesmen. A state at war, the regime imposed unprecedented fiscal burdens on the English populace during the worst decade of harvest failure and economic crisis since the reigns of Edward VI and Mary I. The interminable 'Elizabethan exclusion crisis', meanwhile, had been solved in the most dramatic way, the council acting to outmanoeuvre Elizabeth to force the execution in 1587 of Mary, Queen of Scots. The 1590s, argues John Guy, can be defined as Elizabeth's 'second reign', with a very different political culture and climate from the 'first'.[49]

Although Guy's formulation is intended to 'tease', there is a significant core to his argument that has found wide support from other historians. Guy has robustly argued that the political culture of the 1590s was

---

[48] Natalie Mears, *Queenship and political discourse in the Elizabethan realms* (Cambridge: Cambridge University Press, 2005); Peter Lake and Steven Pincus, *The politics of the public sphere in early modern England* (Manchester: Manchester University Press, 2007).
[49] John Guy, 'Introduction: the 1590s? the second reign of Elizabeth I', in Guy, *Reign of Elizabeth I*, 1–19; Ian W. Archer, 'The 1590s: apotheosis or nemesis of the Elizabethan regime?', in A. Briggs and D. Snowman eds, *Fins de siècle: how centuries end 1400–2000* (New Haven, CT and London: Yale University Press, 1996), 65–98.

characterized by a 'swing to the right'. Partly as a reaction to the radical implications of Mary's execution, but also to the extremes of Presbyterian agitation for reform of church government, the theory of the mixed polity came to be widely discredited. From the court and the clerical establishment, where Conformist clerics swept to prominence, concepts of divine kingship yoked to theories of unlimited monarchy were more stridently expressed. Elizabeth's lawyers argued that common law could be overridden by the High Commission empowered by the royal supremacy, implying that the monarch's powers were superior to the common law and by implication the more general limits of positive laws and institutions. Outside of the realm of ecclesiastical politics, greater emphasis was laid on the obedience of subjects and the sinfulness of subjects' resistance under all circumstances.

Concepts of mixed or elective monarchy—which had celebrated the participatory role of political elites, and the restraints that might be placed on a monarch's exercise of power—were deliberately shunned because of their association with radical Presbyterian ecclesiological and political thought. Growing sensitivity towards theories of resistance, too, was an anxious response to radical Catholic endorsements of the papal condemnation of Elizabeth, which justified the rebellion of the queen's subjects.[50] Rather than confidently celebrating the *vita activa* and the duties of godly citizenship, elites were increasingly concerned to define the sanctity of political hierarchies because of a growing reactionary fear of disorder, and the destabilizing properties of print, literature, and radical religious culture. Meanwhile, as the mystical symbolism of the majestic portraits of the queen grew ever more elaborate, the 'cult' of Elizabeth reached a hysterical hyperbolic pitch, as competitive courtiers combed the panoply of renaissance symbolism to express their undying adoration of their immortal goddess, Gloriana.[51]

Guy's hypothesis has been strengthened by analyses of broader intellectual trends in the 1590s. Lisa Ferraro Parmelee's study of English printed translations of French pamphlet literature has persuasively shown that the fascinated dread that Elizabethans exhibited towards civil war on the

[50] Peter Holmes, *Resistance and compromise: the political thought of Elizabethan Catholics* (Cambridge: Cambridge University Press, 1982).

[51] Guy, 'Introduction: the 1590s?'; idem, 'The Elizabethan establishment and the ecclesiastical polity', in Guy, *Reign of Elizabeth I*, 126–49; also see McLaren, *Political culture*, 9–10, 195–7; Peter Lake, 'The Anglican Moment'? Richard Hooker and the ideological watershed of the 1590s', in Stephen Platten ed., *Anglicanism and the western Christian tradition: continuity, change and the search for communion* (Norwich: Canterbury Press, 2003), 90–121; McDiarmid, 'Introduction', *Monarchical republic*, 4; Lake, *Anglicans and Puritans*, 197–293; Roy Strong, *The cult of Elizabeth* (London: Thames and Hudson, 1977).

continent nurtured an atmosphere conducive to the expression of absolutist theories of monarchy in England. Thus ground was prepared for the
accession of that famous proponent of divine right monarchy, James VI of
Scotland—whose claim to the crown rested on hereditary right.[52]

The Ciceronean underpinnings of theories of active citizenship and
mixed monarchy, it is argued, were also challenged by the influence of
continental Tacitism, which, with its emphasis on the morally ambiguous
means by which great men obtained and wielded power, rendered older
languages of political virtue and participation obsolete.[53] Again, responding to the European-wide influence of Justus Lipsius, Tacitus's great
editor, it was in the 1590s that the language of 'state' was increasingly
used to define both realm and government. Continental 'reason of state'
literature described the means through which princes or rulers might
intensify their fiscal and military powers, unhindered by positive laws
and institutions, or by conventional ethical principles. In Elizabethan
England, the term did not have its recognizably modern sense, to mean
the agency and/or organs and institutions of rule, but its use notably
avoided associations with the mixed polity that inhered in the language of
'commonwealth'.[54]

Literary studies in particular, however, have argued against the homo-
geneity of any 'swing to the right' in the broader Elizabethan political
culture. Authoritarian definitions of monarchical power and the royal
supremacy emerged congruently with an increasingly complex literary
culture, where drama and poetry were used as vehicles to explore political
ideas, to scrutinize the actions of courts and courtiers, monarchs and their
greater subjects. Andrew Hadfield strongly argues that while plays about
English and Roman history certainly revealed the anxieties felt by many
Elizabethans about civil war and contested succession, dramatists—and
presumably their audiences—retained their fascination with republican
theories of government.[55]

---

[52] Lisa Ferraro Parmelee, *Good newes from Fraunce: French anti-league propaganda in late
Elizabethan England* (Rochester, NY: University of Rochester Press, 1996); Peter Lake,
'The king, (the queen) and the Jesuit: James Stuart's *True law of free monarchies* in context/s',
TRHS, sixth ser., 14 (2004), 243–60.

[53] Guy, 'Introduction: the 1590s?', in idem, *Reign of Elizabeth I*, 15–16; Gerhard
Oestreich, *Neostoicism and the early modern state* (Cambridge: Cambridge University
Press, 1982).

[54] Quentin Skinner, 'The State' in Terence Ball, James Farr, Russell L. Hanson eds,
Political innovation and conceptual change (Cambridge: Cambridge University Press, 1989),
90–131.

[55] Andrew Hadfield, *Shakespeare and republicanism* (Cambridge: Cambridge University
Press, 2005).

Ironically, theories of divine right monarchy emanating from Conformist clerical circles were articulated at a time when, it is argued, Elizabeth was increasingly marginalized by the physical effects of age, and her loss of control over a new generation of younger courtiers. Close textual analysis of poetry about the court reveals that many participants in the so-called 'cult of Elizabeth' were acutely aware that they were composing expressions of devotion to an immortal, beauteous queen who bore no recognizable resemblance to the elderly Elizabeth, whose body natural clearly displayed the ravages of time.[56]

Within the wider literary culture, debates about different forms of polity were of far less interest than schema that defined political causation in terms of the morality of political actors, the virtues and vices of rulers and elites. These frameworks were sharpened by classical influences: by Tacitus's dark accounts of the Imperial court at Rome and Senecan drama, which placed stoic notions of the conflict between reason and the passions at the centre of political tragedy.[57] But the profoundly negative images of the court that prevailed in sixteenth-century Europe—the ubiquitous literary paradigms of the evil counsellor, the maligned but virtuous courtier, and the morally ambiguous ruler susceptible to flattery and prone to sensuality—also featured in Catholic 'anti-commonwealth' discourse, which denounced the hold of Elizabeth's tyrannical ministers over a weak monarch, mourned the demise of the virtuous ancient nobility, and luridly vilified the corruption of the court.[58] Finally, there is the matter of Essex, and his profound impact on the political culture of Elizabeth's 'second reign'.

III

In the winter of 1595–6, Essex's name was attached to letters of travel advice to the earl of Rutland, then about to embark on a continental tour.[59] Written partially if not wholly by Francis Bacon, the first of these

[56] Helen Hackett, *Virgin mother, maiden queen: Elizabeth I and the cult of the virgin Mary* (Basingstoke: Palgrave MacMillan, 1995); Julia M. Walker ed., *Dissing Elizabeth: negative representations of Gloriana* (Durham, NC and London: Duke University Press, 1998).

[57] See Rebecca Bushnell, *Tragedies of tyrants: political thought and theater in the English Renaissance* (Ithaca, NY: Cornell University Press, 1990), 5–38.

[58] See Lake, '*Sejanus his Fall*'; Curtis Perry, *Literature and favouritism in early modern England* (Cambridge: Cambridge University Press, 2006).

[59] The authorship of these letters has been the subject of a projected spat between Hammer and Brian Vickers. Paul Hammer attributes their authorship to Essex, P. E. J. Hammer, 'Letters of travel advice from the earl of Essex to the earl of Rutland: some comments',

epistles was circulated scribally, intended to add *gravitas* to the earl's reputation for sagacity. Rutland is told to nurture his 'active virtues' to 'attain to knowledge, which is not only the excellentest thing in man, but the very excellency of man'. Learning is only fostered in 'flourishing states', and is liable to be ruined in countries plagued by civil war, or luxury and corruption. The study of history is of the greatest use, 'in matter moral, military and politic', but knowledge is also to be attained through 'study, conference, and observation'. In foreign climes Rutland will be able to study the 'likeness between nature and nature, force and force, action and action, state and state, time past and time present'. He will learn the geography and topography of the countries that he visits, the social structures, laws, manners of the people. He will have a unique opportunity to examine the varying political structures of different states:

> where the sovereignty is in one, as in a monarchy, in a few, or in the people; or if it be mixed, to which of these forms it most inclines. Next, what ministers of state and subalternate governors as council and magistrates.[60]

Here, encapsulated, are the attitudes that formed Essex's own creed as a statesman: faith in the practical utility of history, a comparative ecumenical interest in different kinds of Christian polities, the weighting of constitutions. He is interested in mixed monarchies where authority is inherent in its greater members.

All of these endeavours undertaken by Rutland, though, are directed to a higher cause: the strenuous pursuit of knowledge for its application to public service, essential for the virtuous citizen or the welfare of the flourishing state. The following study will demonstrate that, rather than discredited in the 1590s, aspects of the political outlook deemed central to the creed of so-called 'monarchical republicanism' can be discerned in the mentality of Essex and his associates—albeit in a form that was modified in response to the political and intellectual challenges of the 1590s, and directed above all towards defining the earl's own role in the Elizabethan polity.

Philological Quarterly, 74 (1995), 317–25. Vickers questions this attribution, 'The authenticity of Bacon's earliest writings', *Studies in Philology*, 94 (1997), 248–96. Hammer refutes Vickers's argument by demonstrating that Bacon could not possibly have written the third letter, *Polarisation*, 149, n. 200, and argues that only the first and third letters traditionally so-described were directed to Rutland. Both authors agree, though, that single authorship of documents such as these is unlikely. The letters are conveniently printed in Brian Vickers ed., *Francis Bacon: a critical edition of the major works* (Oxford: Oxford University Press, 1996), 69–80.

[60] Vickers, *Francis Bacon*, 69–80.

Possessed of an overwhelming sense of his martial and intellectual gifts, Essex found Ciceronean concepts of active citizenship, grounded in the virtue of letters and arms, to be absolutely central to his self-identity, where they fused with medieval and chivalric codes of honour and ancient nobility. As will be seen in Chapter 6, far from challenging Ciceronean-ism, the study of Tacitus in Essex's circle cohered with ideals of the *vita activa* to create a very specific form of critique of the Elizabethan monarchical polity and Essex's role within it, endowing the earl with a great sense of entitlement to play an active and dominant role in public life.

Extremely sensitive to the uses of political vocabulary, the earl and his associates certainly shunned terms that were associated with the political theories of radical Puritanism. The *language* of 'commonwealth', so strongly linked to the political ideas of Thomas Cartwright was, in the hands of Essex and the Bacons, markedly rejected in favour of the terms 'state' or 'country'.[61] But Essex was faced with the same dilemma that troubled previous generations of Elizabeth's subjects who disagreed with or opposed the religious or political decisions taken by queen or regime—the difficulty of reconciling his personal allegiance to Elizabeth's body natural with the sense of duty that he felt towards the welfare of the broader political nation.[62]

Similarly, while Puritan attempts to energize 'popular' political sentiment were widely vituperated in the rhetoric of Elizabethan elites in the 1590s, especially after the suppression of the Marprelate pamphleteers, it was Essex who most consistently attempted to galvanize popular support and public opinion, through personal display and, far more covertly, through the dissemination of texts.[63] Each of these elements of the earl's political conduct would be turned against Essex by critics and rivals as his career declined, evidencing his dangerous ambition and instability.

Essex's personal attitudes, often expressed with ferocious vitality, can be slippery and difficult to pin down. Having risen to power as a royal favourite, Essex was responsible for some of the more florid excesses of the 'cult of Elizabeth', throughout his career penning overwrought expressions of love and blind devotion to his mistress. Recognizing the stains as well as the strengths of popularity, Essex very bitterly vituperated the condemnation the traducing of his reputation in print and political gossip when this alienated him further from the queen and the court. The earl's

---

[61] Discussed in Chapter 4.

[62] McLaren, *Political culture*; Marie Axton, *The queen's two bodies: drama and the Elizabethan succession* (London: Royal Historical Society, 1977).

[63] P. E. J. Hammer, 'The smiling crocodile: the Earl of Essex and late-Elizabethan "popularity"', in Lake and Pincus, *Public sphere*, 95–115; P. E. J. Hammer, 'Myth-making: politics, propaganda and the capture of Cadiz in 1596', *HJ*, 40 (1997), 621–42.

political views must, then, be described with a sensitive understanding of the circumstances in which they were articulated, and the generic conventions of the texts in which they survive.

It would be impossible, though, to deny that the earl and his associates developed a deepening critique of the politics of the court as the decade wore on, resulting in and sharpened by Essex's fall from power in September 1599. All of those literary paradigms of court corruption, including models derived specifically from Catholic polemic, gelled to shape the earl's dark appraisal of the court, giving an ideological coherence to his certainty that those ministers and courtiers whom he perceived as his rivals were evil counsellors, corrupting the commonwealth. By 1601, the earl was convinced that the court and the slumbering queen had succumbed to the dominance of an evil faction intent on his destruction and the subversion of the succession. If we take Essex's explanations at face value, the rising of 1601 was a last-ditch attempt to rid the realm of a corrupt council and court, while protecting his own life, and allowing him to act as a kingmaker after Elizabeth's natural death.[64]

The cultural and intellectual frameworks that shaped the mental world of the earl and his associates also had profound implications for Essex's assessment of the government of the queen. The propensity of a monarch to listen to evil counsel was a manifestation of a weak tyranny, characteristic of the government of a ruler who was dominated by will and passion rather than concern for the public good. Furthermore, a nobleman who made a physical intervention in the polity in self-defence and for the health of the realm was, in the context of late sixteenth-century political thought, acting according to the principle of resistance, either through the natural law of self-preservation, or in a public capacity, to restore a sick, misgoverned state.

IV

The first chapter is a detailed study of the revolt itself. It focuses on the ways in which Essex and his followers conceived and defended the legitimacy of their actions, in contrast to the regime's denunciation of the rising as a dangerous rebellion. Essex's presentation of his rising as an attack on evil counsellors was legally interpreted as treason; his profession of absolute loyalty to the queen herself was qualified by his commitment to 'matters of state'—toleration for Catholics, but crucially the settlement of the succession in favour of James VI of Scotland. In the face of Essex's protestations to the contrary, propaganda asserted that the earl's ultimate aim was the deposition of the queen; and the qualities that he represented—faith in

---

[64] See Chapter 1.

the pre-eminence of his own nobility and virtue, his cultivation of 'popularity', his association with Catholic toleration, and his interest in the historical paradigms afforded by classical scholarship and history, were all heaped up as cumulative evidence of his long-simmering ambitions for the unlawful usurpation of authority.

The rest of the book is structured thematically around the motifs that emerged in the rising and its aftermath, so that the long roots of these competing interpretations of Essex and his career can be understood. Chapter 2 is a study of the ideological contexts of Essex's attitude towards the war with Spain, his overwhelming political preoccupation before 1599. It is argued that the justification for aggressive anti-Spanish militarism in the 1590s was couched in a language far more secular than that of the 1570s and 1580s, and was framed to encompass the broadest confessional base of support for the war. The earl's aggressive militarism encouraged, therefore, the stridently Hispanophobic condemnation of the secular tyranny of Philip II, which in itself promoted a deeper engagement with the general theoretical problem of subjects' rights to resist tyrannical rulers.

The implications of Essex's militarism for his domestic political thought are also explored. The earl's celebration of the latent strength of English arms can be contextualized within a wider classical–humanist discourse that conflated the necessity of English military preparedness with the health of the flourishing English state. Divisions over the direction of the war also contributed directly to the story of the earl's downfall. Essex's *Apologie*, written in 1598 to oppose the Cecilian-led propositions for a peace with Spain, contributed to a bitter debate about England's foreign policy. Most significantly for his later career though, the *Apologie* also contains the first sketch of Essex's burgeoning belief that his domestic rivals were warming towards a dangerous pact with Spain.

In Chapter 3 Essex's religious politics are examined. It is argued that the tolerant and ecumenical views of Francis and Anthony Bacon were particularly influential on Essex's attempts to style himself as the champion and patron of a very broad base of confessional opinion in the mid-1590s. Essex was especially encouraged to cultivate the support of 'loyalist' Catholics, who ostensibly sought religious toleration in return for political obedience to the queen. Of particular importance was Essex's relationship with Thomas Wright, an ex-Jesuit priest for whom the earl gained an unprecedented guarantee of personal toleration in 1595. But Essex's daring religious politics were to revisit him in a highly negative way: the famous dedication to Essex of the notorious Catholic treatise, *A conference about the next succession to the crowne of Ingland* (1594/5), had an immediate and reverberating impact on Essex's association with Catholic toleration: as well as dealing dangerously in matters of the succession, the treatise (published under the pseudonym R. Doleman, but assumed to be written by the Jesuit Robert Parsons) also contained a defence of the principle of popular sovereignty and the right of subjects to depose tyrannical monarchs. The *Conference*, and the earl's entanglement with Catholic succession politics, would cast a long shadow over Essex's subsequent history.

Chapter 4 examines Essex's attitudes to the Elizabethan polity, in particular in relation to the decline of his career, before and after his fall from grace in October 1599. The origins of Essex's conviction that his political rivals had created a dangerous oppositional faction are reassessed. So too are Essex's ambiguous, often contradictory attitudes towards Elizabeth herself, and his critical response to her exercise of monarchical power. This chapter also contains a more sustained analysis of the earl's powerful identification of his own welfare with the health of the Elizabethan polity. Essex's profession of concern for matters of state—denounced by his detractors as the cynical and deliberate cultivation of 'commonwealth causes'—illuminates the foundation of his claims that he acted in the interests of the realm on 8 February 1601. The earl's engagement with renaissance debates about the nature and constitutional role of the nobility are examined in a study of his pursuit and brief exercise of the office of earl marshal. Finally, Essex's opaque attempts to energize the Elizabethan 'public sphere' are reconsidered from the surviving—often ambiguous—textual evidence.

Chapter 5 examines contemporary responses to the decline of the earl's career, both positive and negative. It reconsiders the substance of his fabled popularity, and the growing divisions between those who were warily critical of the earl's behaviour and mentality, and those who adopted Essex's own concept of his sufferings. An increasing body of detractors, including his advisor Francis Bacon, was troubled by the earl's public expression of unseemly attitudes towards political obedience, and the codes of virtue and honour to which he adhered. Meanwhile, surviving evidence of the attitudes of Essex's more ardent partisans is surprisingly provocative in its defence of his rightful role in the polity, and even its description of the queen's involvement in Essex's plight. The vehement denunciation by queen and regime of Essex's popular reputation prefigured the development of deeper suspicions of the earl's instability and of his future ambitions.

Chapter 6 revisits Casaubon's explanation of the Essex rising as the product of wayward attitudes towards reading, history, and classical literature. While Roman ideals of the relationship between arms and letters and the flourishing commonwealth continued to be widely expressed in praise for Essex's militarism, the fashionable study of Tacitus fostered a parallel obsession with the likely repression of virtue, and the imminent decline of states that failed to reward virtuous conduct. Readings of Tacitus by Sir Henry Savile indicate the frameworks employed by Essex to interpret his political problems as manifestations of a corrupt polity, and products of a state governed by a weak tyranny.

This chapter also examines the connections between Essex's rising in 1601, and the fascination of writers and dramatists with medieval baronial revolts in the wider literary culture. England's late medieval past offered models of intervention to a disaffected aristocratic subject for the reformation of a diseased state on the brink of a possible crisis of succession. These solutions, though, were widely condemned in late sixteenth-century literature as sinfully rebellious, and liable to result in that most radical outcome—the deposition of the monarch. If Essex and his associates looked to 'study for action', as they professed to do, how did they reconcile their political loyalty to Elizabeth, their anointed monarch, with the historical lessons of the past?

Strong motifs weave contrapuntally through all of the ensuing discussion, a reflection of their role in shaping the political discourse of Elizabeth's 'second reign'. First is the size and scope of Essex's political ambitions. Indeed, the great difficulty in stamping out a particular version of many-faced Essex derives in part from his desire to appeal to as broad a political constituency as possible, to show his indispensability in all matters of high policy as he steeled himself to assume pre-eminence under the queen after Burghley's decline.[65]

This ambition, of course, was inextricably related to uncertainty about who that monarch would be after the demise of Elizabeth. Recent scholarship has emphasized the deep fears that continued to plague the Elizabethan regime—and James VI himself—about the Scottish king's ability to secure the throne of England.[66] These anxieties, so deviously exploited by Robert Parsons, also played a deceptively important role in nurturing the suspicions of Essex *and* his rivals about each other's unspoken intentions in the event of Elizabeth's death. The unsettled succession—and the intense paranoia that it engendered—dominated political culture in Elizabeth's 'second reign' no less than during the first three decades of her rule. It was the looming backdrop to Essex's rising of 1601.

---

[65] Joel Hurstfield, 'The succession struggle in late Elizabethan England', in S. T. Bindoff, J. Hurstfield and C. H. Williams eds, *Elizabethan government and society: essays presented to Sir John Neale* (London: Athlone Press, 1961), 369–96.

[66] See, for example, J. C. Mayer ed., *The struggle for the succession in late Elizabethan England: politics, polemics, and cultural representations* (Montpellier: Université Paul Valéry, 2004).

Amidst this claustrophobic anxiety, where printed debate about Elizabeth's heir was deemed a treasonable offence in law, Elizabethans tended to interpret their world through dramatic literary paradigms that created extremely negative expectations of the behaviour of political actors. Essex—constantly counselled to do so by friends and advisors—inclined to believe that honour and virtue were under siege in the dangerous world of the court. Models for kingship, too, were particularly un-nuanced. Elizabeth hardly embodied the moral depravity of the Roman tyrant Nero, or violated legal and constitutional proprieties in the manner of Richard II, but these were archetypes held up by her own subjects as mirrors which reflected her rule.

But Essex too was a victim of this same pessimistic literary culture. The earl's critics, including the queen, were similarly sensitized to the historical *topoi* of the over-mighty noble, or the popular demagogue—both models that seemed to fit the earl's great ambition and his political behaviour. Essex's fate was cast as competing narratives of internal threats to the realm appeared to cohere.

Finally, Essex's revolt presented an acute challenge to some of the necessary fictions that subjects and monarchs alike used to describe the operation of monarchy. In sixteenth-century England, as John Guy has so persuasively argued, potential friction between descending and ascending theories of imperial and mixed monarchy was oiled by the wonderfully flexible and universally acknowledged duty of the monarch to listen to counsel.[67] The great unspoken flaw in the model was, of course, that the monarch's inclination to heed counsellors was discretionary, and dependent on his or her choice of ministers and advisors. In the political culture of the 1590s, the dominant discourse about counsel was a negative one that emphasized the propensity of monarchs to ignore wise advice and listen to flatterers or evil, self-interested ministers. The role of counsellors was not predominantly defined as the sustaining strength of the monarchy, but, as Essex came to believe, as a poisonous source of corruption and instability.

Most significantly, the earl's rising, hopeless as it may have been, raised the intractable problem that would be writ so much larger in the seventeenth century: what was the legitimate response of virtuous subjects, denied political agency or an outlet to express grievances, when they believed that their polity, consciences, and lives were dangerously imperilled by a corrupt or ungodly monarchy?

---

[67] John Guy, 'The rhetoric of counsel in early modern England', in Dale Hoak ed., *Tudor political culture* (Cambridge: Cambridge University Press, 1995), 292–310; John Guy, 'The Tudor monarchy and its critiques', in John Guy ed., *The Tudor monarchy* (London: Arnold, 1997), 78–109.

1

The Essex rising of 1601

On Saturday 7 February 1601 the privy council gathered at the house of Lord Buckhurst, the lord treasurer, and summoned the earl of Essex to give explanation for the 'concourse of people and great resorte of Lordes and others to Essex Howse'.[1] 'In bed & all a sweat after tennis', Essex demurred. A second summons was issued: Essex refused once more.[2] Several of Essex's friends and followers had spent the afternoon watching the Lord Chamberlain's Men act a specially commissioned play at the Globe Theatre of 'Kyng Henry the iiiith, and of the kyllyng of Kyng Richard the Second'.[3] After the performance most of the theatregoers returned to Essex House. As the company assembled, Essex made an announcement: the council's summons, he explained, was a plot laid by his enemies to entice him from his home; their real aim was his death.[4]

Casting around for a plan, Essex consulted those followers who were privy to his most secret thoughts: Sir Christopher Blount, his stepfather, Sir John Davies, Sir Gelly Merrick, Sir Ferdinando Gorges, Sir Charles Danvers, Henry Cuffe, and the earl of Southampton. While flight was

[1] BL, Cotton MS Julius F VI, ff. 450ʳ, 445ʳ–452ᵛ, apology of Sir Ferdinando Gorges. According to attorney general Coke's notes on the treason of Lord Sandys, full news of Essex's plots reached the council the following Thursday: TNA, SP 12/278/73, f. 124ʳ. Eyewitness accounts are A. Wall, 'An account of the Essex revolt, February 1601', *BIHR*, 54 (1981), 131–3; the narrative by 'Vincent Hussey' (in the writing of Thomas Phelippes), *CSPD, 1598–1603*, 549–52. Accounts of the revolt are: Hammer, 'Shakespeare's *Richard II*'; James, 'At a crossroads'; Hutson, 'Military following'; Janet Dickinson, 'The Essex rebellion, 1601: subversion or supplication?', PhD thesis, (University of Southampton, 2006).
[2] BL, Cotton MS Julius F VI, f. 450ᵛ. Also see TNA, SP 12/279/12, f. 19ʳ, confession of Dr Giles Fletcher; Fletcher was told that Essex had been summoned about the sighting of Spanish ships, but heard that this was a pretext for an attack by Ralegh; another rumour was that Essex would be murdered by his servant Wiseman: SP 12/278/70, f. 120ʳ, examination of Henry Cuffe.
[3] TNA, SP 12/278/78, f. 130ʳ, examination of Sir Gelly Merrick; SP 12/278/72, 122ʳ, examination of Sir William Constable. See Worden, 'Which play was performed'; Hammer, 'Shakespeare's *Richard II*'; Jonathan Bate, *Soul of the age. The life, mind and world of William Shakespeare* (London: Viking, 2008), 257–81.
[4] TNA, SP 12/278/72, f. 122ʳ.

scorned, a direct attack on the court was deemed too risky: Gorges warned that the guard had been doubled.[5] At a critical moment a message arrived from mysterious 'friends in the Citty', alerting Essex to 'som harde measure intended against him', and promising that they 'were reddy...to defend him, agaynst the mallice of his private enemyes'. His fears of an assassination plot now confirmed, the news gave stronger substance to Essex's other half-formed plan—to 'move the Citty', and cause the 'Citizens to take armes in his behalfe'. Messages were sent into London enjoining Essex's friends to come to his aid. Essex wrote a personal letter to the queen.[6]

Throughout the night Sir Gelly Merrick, who had been stockpiling muskets, fortified the house.[7] Lord Sandys, (called at 6 or 7 a.m.), arrived to find a body of nobles assembled; the earls of Southampton and Rutland, William Parker, Lord Monteagle, and Lord Chandos as well as an assortment of other knights, gentlemen, and followers, who had been called with news of a plot laid by Sir Walter Ralegh and Lord Cobham to murder Essex.[8] Lady Rich made personal summonses to Sir Henry Bromley and the earl of Bedford.[9] Meanwhile, Essex looked to London's elite citizens. A copy of his letter to the queen was sent to Sheriff Smith, 'Collonell of 1000 men'.[10] The bearer delivered the letter to Smith's wife, in her pew at the Sunday sermon: ominously the sheriff was absent.[11]

Early on Sunday morning Gorges met Ralegh, his kinsman, on the Thames, who warned him urgently to flee. According to his later confession, Gorges staunchly refused, but thus counselled Ralegh to make haste for the court for his own safety.[12] Alert to Essex's preparations, the council organized defences, erecting a barricade of coaches between the court and Charing Cross. The lord mayor, Sir William Rider, was directed to levy the trained bands, while members of the Inns of Court were ordered to arm.[13]

[5] BL Cotton MS Julius F VI, f. 450ᵛ; TNA, SP 12/278/86, f. 140ʳ, examination of Sir Christopher Blount.
[6] BL, Cotton MS Julius F VI, f. 450ᵛ; TNA, SP 12/278/68, 86, ff. 117ʳ, 140ʳ, SP 12/279/12, f. 19ʳ.
[7] TNA, SP 12/279/3, f. 4ʳ, SP 12/278/71, f. 121ʳ, examinations of Sir Gelly Merrick and Henry Patye.
[8] TNA, SP 12/279/51, 75, 76, ff. 73ʳ, 126ʳ, 128ʳ, examinations of the earl of Rutland, Lord Sandys, Lord Monteagle.
[9] TNA, SP 12/279/10, f. 13ʳ; Cecil MS 76/67.
[10] John Bruce ed., *Correspondence of James VI with Sir Robert Cecil, and others in England, during the reign of queen Elizabeth...*, (London: Camden Society, 1861), 109, confession of Christopher Blount.
[11] TNA, SP 12/278/58, 59, ff. 96ʳ–99ᵛ, proofs against and examination of Sheriff Smith; TNA, SP 12/279/6, f. 9ʳ, examination of Captain Gregory Rigges.
[12] BL, Cotton MS Julius F VI, ff. 446ᵛ–447ʳ.
[13] *CSPD, 1598–1601*, 550; *APC*, XXXI, 147–8.

At 10 a.m. four emissaries from the court were sent to Essex House: Lord Keeper Egerton, Lord Chief Justice Popham, Essex's uncle Sir William Knollys, and the earl of Worcester.[14] In the courtyard, as Essex and Southampton explained to the lords of the council that their lives were endangered, Essex's followers formed a menacing throng. Egerton recalled that the mob urged Essex to 'kylle them', and to cast the Great Seal out of the window. Essex drew the lords into his study and placed a guard about the door: he promised to return swiftly, whence they might join his triumphant procession to Whitehall, and humbly prostrate themselves before Elizabeth.

With the arrival of the lords, Essex was forced, finally, to act. Descending to the courtyard again, he explained to the company that his enemies, Cecil, Cobham, and Ralegh, 'sought his life dyversely', setting spies to entrap him, and forging his name on treasonable documents.[15] Then he processed into London, accompanied by a band of men numbering between 150 and 300, including all of the assembled nobles.[16] Accounts of how the company were armed differ. One source claimed that they were 'only with their rapiers and daggers not drawn but their points upwards; and some with pistols and petronells'; another insisted that the rebels were armed 'only with rapiers'; a third was assured that 'most of them had Frenche pistols'.[17] Blount later confessed his great unhappiness that Essex had not waited for a supply of 120 horses.[18] The earl and his followers were certainly not yet prepared for prolonged military action.

From Essex House in the Strand the earl and his companions marched east, past St Paul's, where London's great and good attended the Sunday sermon. A few young men grabbed their cloaks and swords and joined the procession, but support *en masse* was unforthcoming.[19] Reaching Fenchurch Street, and the house of Sherriff Smith, the earl exhorted the Londoners to arms, crying out that they did both him and themselves 'harme for that they came naked'.[20] William Pickering, an armourer nearby, refused to furnish 100 pikes, despite Essex's emotional appeal— 'not for me Pickeringe?'[21]

---

[14] TNA, SP 12/278/97, ff. 155ʳ–158ᵛ, declarations of Lord Keepers Egerton, Lord Chief Justice Popham, and the earl of Worcester.

[15] Cecil MS 84/7, speeches of Christopher Dorrington.

[16] *CSPD (1598–1601)*, 550; TNA, SP 12/278/72, f. 122ᵛ.

[17] *CSPD (1598–1601)*, 550; BL, Egerton MS 2606, f. 1ʳ.

[18] Bruce, *Correspondence*, 109.

[19] *CSPD, (1598–1601)*, 550; TNA, SP 12/278/45, f. 63ʳ, examination of William Masham; SP 12/282/13, 14, 17, ff. 24ʳ–32ᵛ, indictment of William Masham, examinations of Thomas Woodhouse and William Gresham.

[20] TNA SP 12/278/51, f. 73ᵛ; SP 12/278/60, ff. 100ʳ–101ᵛ, confession of John Bargar.

[21] Cecil MS 76/91, examination of William Pickering.

Still, Essex knew that he could count upon the support of Smith who would alert the trained bands.[22] Smith had received a verbal warning from Essex while coming from the sermon at St Paul's: now at home, he found the earl and his company assembling, appealing for men and weapons. Smith's part is slightly mysterious: after the rising he would insist that he had urged Essex to seek out the protection of the lord mayor, Sir William Rider; the earl refused, insisting that Rider be summoned to him. While Smith departed, the company refreshed themselves with beer, while Essex sought more halberts and summoned armourers.[23]

Essex's behaviour appears to have baffled the majority of those who saw him. His supporters appealed for protection in the name of the queen, crying out that the earl would be murdered by his enemies, 'Lord Cobham, Sir Walter Rawley and Mr Secretarye Cissell'.[24] Their assassination plots, though, were linked to a far weightier peril to national liberty. In Fenchurch Street the earl appealed to the citizens to come 'for ayde to defend the queene, Religion and his life'—'the crowne of England was offred to be sould to the infanta' of Spain.[25] One witness remembered Essex's rousing proclamation: 'now or never is the tyme for you to pursue your liberties: which yf at this tyme you forsake, you are suer [sure] to enduer bondage'.[26]

The company left Smith's house and wandered up and down outside, their destination unclear and their intentions increasingly aimless. When the lord mayor finally approached with Smith, Essex and the sheriff had conference in Gracechurch Street at 2 p.m. which was reported differently after the rising. Essex demanded the whereabouts of the thousand men that Smith had promised; Smith claimed that he had refused, denying that he had made any such promise, and begged the earl to yield to the lord mayor. Essex, however, reported that Smith had apologized for betraying his word, explaining that in the confusion he 'could not drawe his regiment together'. John Bargar (a soldier who had once served under Essex), used by Rider as a go-between, recalled hearing the Sheriff advise Essex to take possession of Ludgate and Newgate—thither he would send arms.[27]

---

[22] SP 12/278/51, f. 73ʳ; SP 12/278/75, f. 126ᵛ.

[23] TNA, SP 12/278/57, f. 94ʳ, report by John Smith; SP 12/279/58, f. 96ʳ.

[24] *CSPD, 1598–1601*, 550; Wall, 'Essex Revolt', 132. Not all witnesses named Cecil; see eadem, 131.

[25] Cecil MS 76/91, examinations of Gabriel Tomlinson, Richard Edwards, Richard Walkett, William Pickering, Sir Richard Martin; TNA, SP 12/278/51, f. 73ᵛ; SP 12/278/45, f. 63ʳ⁻ᵛ.

[26] Cecil MS 83/57, Timothy Willis to Sir Robert Cecil.

[27] TNA, SP 12/278/58, 59, 60, ff. 96ʳ–101ᵛ.

By now the situation was desperate. When the news arrived that heralds had denounced Essex and his company as traitors, some followers deserted, the nature of their crime revealed to their supposedly unsuspecting horror.[28] Essex set off to Ludgate, now fortified by John Leveson and the forces of the bishop of London. Both sides fired pistols: leading the charge Blount was wounded; Essex's page, Henry Tracey, was killed; the earl himself shot in the hat. Around fifty of the rump of followers took boats at Queenhithe, rowing back to Essex House. Small comfort lay in the knowledge that one final bargaining token remained to the rebels: the hostages in Essex's study.[29]

To Essex's dismay, Sir Ferdinando Gorges had returned earlier to Essex House and released the lords of the council. With this act Gorges probably saved his own life, but horribly maimed his reputation. Now Essex prepared for the inevitable siege, lining the windows with heavy books, and burning secret papers.[30] Forces surrounded the house and sporadic shots were fired on both sides. Sir Robert Sidney negotiated from outside the gates in a poignant exchange with Essex and the earl of Southampton, later written up as a 'separate' and frequently copied. To Sidney's condemnation of their recourse to arms Southampton replied:

> deare cousin Sydney, to whom would you have us to yeald to, our enemies? . . . wee who have soe often ventured our lives in defence of her Majesty and the realme should nowe prove traytors to the queene and state? Noe cousin, wee detest that name and all trayterous actions.[31]

Essex and Lord Sandys were apparently alone in showing enthusiasm for a fight until the death.[32] The women within, the countess of Essex, Lady Rich, and the countess of Southampton were evacuated, but further resistance was futile. The rebels surrendered with demands for fair trials and religious solace. Essex began his final battle: fought to defend his reputation and the legality of his actions, if not his life.[33]

THE IMMEDIATE RESPONSE

This, then, was the Essex rising—shambolic, and simply confusing to most observers. On 13 February a perplexed John Thynne described

---

[28] Cecil MS 76/67; BL, Cotton MS Julius F VI, f. 447ʳ.
[29] BL, Cotton MS Julius F VI, f. 447ᵛ; BL, Egerton MS 2606, f. 1ᵛ.
[30] BL, Egerton MS 2606, f. 1ᵛ.
[31] Ibid., f. 1ʳ⁻ᵛ.
[32] TNA, SP 12/278/73, f. 124ʳ.
[33] BL, Egerton MS 2606, f. 2ʳ⁻ᵛ.

'suche a hurrle burlye in London and the courte as I never sawe'.[34] The government's ultimate reprisals seemed light: while many were fined and imprisoned, the only nobleman to be executed was Essex himself, beheaded on 25 February, in a semi-private execution within the Tower. Of the other rebels only four were to die: Sir Gelly Merrick, Henry Cuffe, Sir Christopher Blount, and Sir Charles Danvers, executed on 13 and 18 March. Did this rising—so pathetically contested—really deserve its definition as a rebellion?

In a recent article Paul Hammer argues that what appears to have been the most 'pitifully ineffective coup' was, indeed, nothing of the sort. Essex appealed to protection from the citizens so that he might process peacefully to the queen and appeal to her mercy: 'launching a *coup d'état* was precisely what Essex was trying *not* to do'.[35]

Hammer's desire to explode the conventional understanding of Essex's rising as a failed rebellion implies that the earl's actions on 8 February had legitimacy as understood by contemporaries. The complicated means and ends of Essex and his followers certainly require careful analysis. This venture into London was a panicked response to the summons from the privy council: Essex genuinely believed that his life was in danger, either from assassination, or the implications of arrest and trial for treason.

On the day of 8 February, however, Essex was not aimless. Despite making a show of their pacific intentions, Essex and his followers directly appealed to the ordinary citizens and London's ruling elite to join them against the forces that threatened the welfare of queen and country. This 'bodyguard' would be provided by the sheriff; the 'citizens' of London were also 'to take armes in his behalfe'. Ideally Essex's passage to Elizabeth would have been bloodless; but at the very least the rebels would have had to overpower the guard, of which Ralegh was the captain, whence the purgation of the court would follow: surely a *coup d'état* of sorts.

The small number of executions was most probably a symptom of the government's wariness of public sympathy for Essex, and continued anxiety about the crisis that had been avoided. A coda of worrying events confirmed the privy council's determination to obliterate public affection for the earl. On Thursday 12 February Captain Thomas Lee, a soldier close to Essex, was found loitering dangerously outside the privy chamber.[36] Contacting five former military clients of Essex, he planned to seize

[34] Wall, 'Essex Revolt', 132.
[35] Hammer, 'Shakespeare's *Richard II*', 16.
[36] Lee had returned with Essex to London in September 1599 and had been temporarily arrested: *CSPI, 1599–1600*, 390–9.

Elizabeth, and to force her to release the imprisoned nobles. This plot, though, was a nasty shock to the government: Lee had been apprehended within the heart of the court; his trial on 16 February and execution the next day were accomplished quietly, with maximum haste.[37] Just as Lee was arrested a second conspiracy was discovered that also aimed at liberating Essex. A group of London apprentices, rumoured to be 5000 strong, planned to gather by the spreading of libels to assault the court, 'surprise some honourable persons there' and 'entreat' the queen to free Essex and Southampton. Although the three ringleaders were pardoned in July, the privy council's fear of the destabilizing properties of libels and the potential violence of London apprentices lingered on throughout the year.[38] Three days after Essex's own execution a man named Woodhouse was hanged for 'speaking and libelling' against Essex's arrest.[39] The ports were closed, the trained bands of the Home Counties were levied, while the authorities tried to assess the extent of Essex's following in the provinces.[40]

The government emphatically defined the rising as an 'open action of rebellion'.[41] In Star Chamber on 13 February prominent privy councillors denounced Essex as a 'popular traytor', a 'hipocriticall traytor', who had nurtured ambitions for six long years to be king. In the slightly longer surviving account of the speeches, Sir Robert Cecil declared that Essex's ambitions had been whetted by 'the booke written of Henry 4th'—John Hayward's notorious *The first parte of the life and raigne of King Henrie IIII*, the history of Richard II's deposition, that had been published in 1599 with a famously inflammatory dedication to Essex.[42] A list of directions for preachers was circulated to disseminate the substance of the Star Chamber speeches from the pulpit; these too emphasized the 'designements of the traitorous Erle' to 'become an other Henry the 4th'.[43]

The government's denunciation of Essex as a failed usurper attempted to undermine the earl's own defences of his actions. On the day of the rising Essex and his followers had grounded their unsuccessful appeal to the citizens in emphatic vows of loyalty to Elizabeth, shouting that they acted to save queen and state from the grip of evil counsel. Upon arrest the 'rebels' were unanimously defiant: they abhorred 'all trayterous actions'.

---

[37] TNA, SP 12/278/61, ff. 104^r–106^v, examination of Thomas Lee; Howell, *State Trials*, I, 1403–15.
[38] *HMC Salisbury*, XI, 132, 156, 321–2. A proclamation against seditious libels was issued on 5 April: *APC* XXXI, 266.
[39] John Stowe, *A summarie of the chronicles of England* (1604), 433.
[40] *APC*, XXXI, 148–67.
[41] TNA, SP 12/278/35, f. 49^r.
[42] TNA, SP 12/278/54, ff. 79^r–80^r; a shorter version is SP 12/278/55, ff. 90^r–91^r.
[43] TNA, SP 12/278/63, ff. 108^r–109^v.

Typically, the instructions to preachers and Cecil's speech in Star Chamber had pre-empted this line of reasoning. Essex's protestations of loyalty to Elizabeth were a rhetorical sham: the earl 'pretendeth that his only drifte was to have removed certeyne persons from about her Majesty' to conceal his true purpose: 'to have sett the Crowne of England uppon his owne head'.[44] These competing narratives of Essex's intentions established the conceptual frameworks that supporters and detractors of the earl would use to justify or condemn the rising in the months to come. Neither interpretation told the whole of the truth.

'HIS PORPOSE OF GOINGE TO THE COURTE'

As a favourite of the queen, Essex knew that political influence was inseparable from access to her presence. He now presented his rising as a spontaneous attempt to seek personal communication with Elizabeth denied him by the ascendency of hostile counsellors. As Southampton insisted: 'if wee might but freelie declare our mindes before her she would redeem us and blame them that we most blame'.[45] But as the government began their interrogations of the earl's imprisoned followers, many of their pre-rising suspicions were confirmed. Protests of spontaneity were mendacious: the rising of 8 February was the distorted premature realization of months of scheming to effect Essex's 'porpose of goinge to the Courte'.[46]

This plan to force access to Elizabeth's presence was a pattern of desperate action that Essex had attempted before, with disastrous consequences. On 28 September 1599, he had forced his way into the queen's presence to give his own account of the disastrous Irish campaign, and the truce agreed with Tyrone.[47] Riding directly to the court and Elizabeth, his face and body covered in 'Dirt and Mire', he burst into her bedchamber. The queen 'newly up, the Hare about her Face', listened to Essex with sympathy at first; at a further interview that afternoon she had implacably soured.[48] The following day Essex was commanded to report to the council, after which he was placed under house arrest.

---

[44] TNA, SP 12/278/63, ff. 108ʳ–109ᵛ. A sermon was preached to this effect at Paul's Cross on 15 February: *HMC Salisbury*, XI, 55–6.
[45] BL, Additional MS 2606, f. 2ʳ.
[46] Bruce, *Correspondence*, 100.
[47] Essex listed the senior soldiers who accompanied him as the earl of Southampton, Sir Henry Dockwra, Sir Henry Danvers, Captain Thomas Williams, Captain Thomas Lee: TNA, SP 63/205/188, f. 357ʳ.
[48] Collins, *Letters and memorials*, II, 127–9.

Since this dramatic fall from grace, Essex had focused his energies into persistently thwarted attempts to come into Elizabeth's presence once more, convinced that face-to-face communication with the queen would restore his political fortunes. Essex's advisors—notably Lord Henry Howard and Francis Bacon—urged the earl to petition Elizabeth in a series of elaborate emotional epistles which begged the queen to renew her personal favour.[49] According to Henry Wotton's biographical account, the earl had even considered surprising Elizabeth as she walked in Greenwich, where he could 'come forthe and humble himselfe before Her in the field'.[50] The queen, though, had remained cold and impervious to most of Essex's entreaties and the pleading of his (mainly female) supporters at court.[51] Impotent and desperate, Essex fell back once more on another plan to force his way to Elizabeth's presence.

Essex defended his rising as a physical version of his epistolary campaign, a brave attempt to hazard Elizabeth's mercy. But refuge in the humble language of access bypassed the illegitimate means through which Essex had planned the restoration of his political influence; schemes which had involved the use of force in various guises. Tellingly, Gorges revealed that Essex's advisors were all too ready to 'distrust the worste' when the earl informed them on the eve of the rising of warrants signed for their arrest.[52] The conspirators were well aware—despite protestations to the contrary—that their plans would be treasonable in the eyes of the government.

WIDER SCHEMES: IRELAND AND SCOTLAND

Ireland was the Rubicon of Essex's career. During the course of that miserable campaign his hostility to Cecil became implacable, as the earl blamed military failure on the courtly enemies who stifled his lines of supply. It was also after his return from Ireland that Essex was first directly associated with seditious conduct, and with designs on the crown. Following Essex's return to England, the council recorded Irish gossip that Essex and Tyrone had agreed to divide rule of the two kingdoms between

---

[49] On 29 September 1600, Edward Reynolds wrote to Essex giving Howard's instructions on writing to the queen: Cecil MS 83/72. See Chapters 4 and 5.

[50] Sir Henry Wotton, *A parallel betweene Robert late earle of Essex, and George late duke of Buckingham* (1641), 13.

[51] Lady Scrope, Lady Walsingham, the countess of Warwick, and the earl's sisters and wife unsuccessfully lobbied for Essex; Collins, *Letters and memorials*, II, 131–2, 139.

[52] BL, Cotton MS Julius F VI, f. 450ᵛ.

them in the event of Elizabeth's death: Essex as king of England, O'Neill viceroy of Ireland.[53]

Tried for misconduct in Ireland at York House on 5 June 1600, Essex had fiercely denied—and been reprieved of—making any secret deal with Tyrone when the earls had private conference at Bellaclinthe Ford on 7 September 1599, prior to drawing up articles for a truce. Some early propaganda—the preaching instructions and the Star Chamber speeches—heavily speculated that a pact between Tyrone and Essex had been a forerunner of the earl's later treasons. At trial though, allegations of Irish conspiracy were conspicuous by their sudden absence.[54] The privy council had sharply shied away from provoking Essex himself into a public debate about events in Ireland, when it was revealed that this might throw alarming light on the activities of the current lord deputy, mandated to suppress the rebellion.

Under interrogation Sir Christopher Blount, Essex's stepfather, de-scribed a very different plan, also hatched in Ireland, to restore Essex's ailing fortunes. At Dublin Castle, just after the shattering defeat of Sir Conyers Clifford's army in the Curlew Mountains on 5 August, Essex had sought a rash solution to his weakening domestic influence. The earl proposed to take between 2000 and 3000 English troops from Ireland to land in Wales, to increase this army with Welsh followers and 'by all sortes of discontented people', and to make for the court. Blount insisted that he and Southampton had fervently dissuaded Essex from this foolhardy course, advising Essex instead to take 'a competent number of choyce men' with him to London, who would prevent his arrest 'if he had not found hir Majestie gracious' when he pleaded his case against his enemies. This was the ill-starred course that Essex would subsequently adopt.[55]

In custody, Essex lived in constant—and justifiable—fear that his enemies plotted to bring formal charges of treason against him.[56] His friends shared these anxieties: Lord Mountjoy and the earl of South-ampton hatched courses for flight or, yet again, 'by posessing the Courte with his frends to bringe him selfe agayne to her Majesties presence'.[57]

[53] TNA, SP 12/274/22, f. 34ʳ, the examination of Thomas Wood, taken before the privy council on 20 January 1600. These rumours are discussed in Chapter 5.

[54] McClure, *Letters of John Chamberlain*, I, 120. Allegations resurfaced in the indictment of Blount: Howell, *State Trials* 1432–5.

[55] Bruce, *Correspondence*, 107–8.

[56] The privy council's compilation of materials relating to Essex's 'treasons' throughout 1600 is discussed in Chapter 5.

[57] Bruce, *Correspondence*, 101, declaration of Sir Charles Danvers.

Essex dismissed the former course as cowardly, but the latter strategy remained at the heart of plans.

The conspirators' revelation of the next stage of plotting was even more dangerous to the authorities, as it involved, once again, Essex's most important English ally, Lord Mountjoy, sent as the next lord deputy to Ireland in February 1600. Mountjoy was one of the few truly powerful statesmen unequivocally of Essex's faction, and was genuinely convinced of the earl's persecution by malicious enemies. Southampton's confession revealed that Mountjoy's interrelated anxieties about Essex and 'the government of this state' had been strong throughout 1599: he had 'foreseen [Essex's] ruine' while Essex was still in Ireland.[58]

Cuffe later recalled that Mountjoy's sympathy for Essex's plight had a much deeper significance than personal affection for the earl: 'thincking the publicke to suffer with his private', Mountjoy believed that '[Essex's] retourne to her majesties former grace woulde tourne to the good of thousandes'. And it was apparently Mountjoy who made the momentous decision to write to James VI of Scotland in the summer of 1599, even before Essex's dramatic return. His purpose: to deliver to James Essex's (and his own) assurance that they supported the Scottish claim to Elizabeth's throne.[59]

With this act, Mountjoy formally related the welfare of Essex and the dominance of evil counsel at Elizabeth's court to the greatest political issue of the reign—the unsettled succession. The declaration of James's title would remain the coherent centre of all plans to restore Essex's political fortunes. Mountjoy threw himself deeper into treasonable conduct, contacting James once again before his own departure for Ireland. This time his proposals had teeth. Mountjoy suggested that if James approved, he would take between 4000 and 5000 soldiers from Elizabeth's Irish army to join with a following raised by Essex and a Scottish force 'for the healthe of those' 'which was fitt in establishinnge such a course as should be best for our contry'. Southampton also wrote to James professing his allegiance, and he and Mountjoy swore oaths to protect Elizabeth. Smelling a plot, the privy council imprisoned the messenger Henry Lee on his return from Scotland.[60]

Crucially, James was cautiously receptive to these overtures, proclaiming that he 'lyked the course well'. James was probably equivocating, and

---

[58] Ibid., 96.
[59] Bruce, *Correspondence*, 87, 95–107; Helen Georgia Stafford, *James VI and the throne of England* (New York and London: D. Appleton-Century Company, 1940), 209 and *passim*.
[60] Bruce, *Correspondence*, 96, 103; see TNA, SP 59/38/1169, ff. 298ʳ–304ʳ, declaration of Henry Lee, 12 April 1600; Cecil MS 78/26 and 26 ii.

in June the king failed to raise money for an army.[61] Mountjoy's anxiety about the prospect of a contested throne seems to have persisted after Essex's death. Tellingly, he commissioned a performance of the old succession drama *Gorboduc* at Dublin Castle in September 1601.[62] But as it became apparent that Essex would not be tried for treason, Mountjoy withdrew his support, denouncing the legitimacy of Essex's plans. In April 1600, when Southampton journeyed to Ireland with a petition from Essex for military succour, the lord deputy refused; assured of Essex's personal safety, he claimed that such a scheme 'hee could no way thinke honest'.[63] After his release from custody in August, Essex tried once again, this time sending Sir Charles Danvers to urge Mountjoy at least to write a formal letter which the earl could show to the queen, 'wherein hee should complaine of the ill gouerment of the state' and summon Essex to redress it.[64] Begging also for a bodyguard of soldiers to overcome the guard at the court, Essex insisted 'he should come in such peace as a dogge should not wagg his tongue against him'.[65] Still, Mountjoy was reluctant: he 'had sett his hart only uppon followinge of the Queen's service'.[66] Mountjoy now clearly identified the earl's courses as dangerous and treasonable, even if they were *framed* in loyalist language.

Essex, however, deepened his own direct engagement with the Scottish king. At Christmas 1600, the earl sent an extraordinary letter to James, describing an erupting plot to subvert the succession, hatched by their mutual enemies.[67] In fierce rhetoric Essex defined their common cause: the faction that sought his own destruction tyrannized over the queen, and impelled him to act to destroy those evil foes who would 'oppress innocencie, cancel merit, justify conspiracy, make lawe, inspire

---

[61] Susan Doran, 'The Relationship between Elizabeth I and James VI of Scotland', in Susan Doran and Glenn Richardson eds, *Tudor England and its Neighbours* (Basingstoke: Palgrave Macmillan, 2005), 225–6; Stafford, *James VI and the throne of England*, 213; James and Essex's shared belief in succession plot is discussed in Chapter 4.

[62] Christopher Morash, *A history of Irish theatre, 1601–2000* (Cambridge: Cambridge University Press, 2002), 2–3.

[63] Bruce, *Correspondence*, 97. Southampton travelled on to the Low Countries until his summons from Essex in the winter of 1600.

[64] Ibid., 98. See also Cecil MS 80/93, Essex to Danvers, 28 July 1600.

[65] Bruce, *Correspondence*, 89–90, examination of Henry Cuffe, and 106.

[66] Ibid., 98.

[67] Essex's friend, Peregrine Bertie, 13th Baron Willoughby of Willoughby, Beck, and Eresby, governor of Berwick, facilitated communications. In November the privy council hauled to London and imprisoned Sir William Eure, whom Willoughby had employed in various negotiations over border disputes, for meeting with James in October. Willoughby's shrill denials of all knowledge of suspicious behaviour by Eure are contradictory and hollow: TNA, SP 59/39/1293, 1294, 1298, esp. ff. 274ʳ, 278ʳ, 286ʳ; *HMC Salisbury*, X, 407–8, 418–19; below, n. 72.

Judges, overawe the people, bury freedome, usurpe sovereignty for the present, and *prepare a way for an unjust succession hereafter*' [emphasis added]—the succession of the Infanta Isabella Clara Eugenia, daughter of Philip II, and archduchess of Austria and the Netherlands.[68]

Essex then informed James that he prepared to take assertive action against their common enemies: 'Now doth reason, honor and conscience command me to be active'. His purpose, though, was to secure the declaration of James as 'the certaine and undoubted successor to this crowne'. As in his fruitless appeals to Mountjoy, Essex sealed the legitimacy of their proposed joint action with promises of fidelity to Elizabeth.

The letter fulfilled its purpose. Essex demanded that James send a 'discreet, secret and faithfull Ambassador' to negotiate with him, ideally John Erskine, eighteenth or second earl of Mar.[69] This time the king responded exactly as Essex demanded, preparing to send Mar on embassy to England with Edward Bruce, abbot of Kinloss. James' instructions for Mar candidly directed his delegate to treat all his relations with the court with the deepest suspicion and to follow 'the advice of my friends there, whose counsel *ye shall directly follow*' [emphasis added]. If Mar was convinced by Essex, James allowed that he might 'give them full assurance of my assisting them accordingly'. James's only stipulation was that 'old reservation of the safety of the queen's person'.[70]

This concern for Elizabeth's life was pragmatic: conditioned by the awareness of all parties that the 'Act for the Suretie of the Queen's Majestie's Most Royal Person' (27 Eliz. I, c. 1) debarred from the throne the claim of those in whose name assassination plots were performed. But both men were now verbally committed to supporting action: to declare the succession, and to restore the ascendency of Essex.

Essex destroyed most of his correspondence with James on the day of the rising, burning a letter kept in a black purse around his neck, as well as papers stored in a locked chest.[71] Anthony Bacon, who had brokered communication with Scotland, also destroyed much of his correspondence from after 1597, compounding the mystery of his whereabouts at the time

---

[68] BL, Additional MS 31022, ff. 107[r]–108[r]. This letter exists only in a copy in the British Library; it was transmitted to James via the bookseller, Thomas Norton, who received it from Willoughby: Bruce, *Correspondence*, 90.

[69] See the 'Instructions for the earl of Marre' as described by Henry Cuffe, Bruce, *Correspondence*, 82–4.

[70] James revised his instructions for Mar and Bruce on 12 or 13 February, in light of this 'accident', still believing that he and 'friends' might make a stand about the succession: G.V. P. Akrigg ed., *Letters of king James VI and I* (Berkeley, CA: University of California Press, 1984), 169–71.

[71] Bruce, *Correspondence*, 80–1, 90. Essex also burned an account of his own history.

of the rising by dying in May 1601.[72] The date of Mar's arrival, though, is vital. Essex asked him to come by 1 February, but James delayed his journey. Had the embassy been in London on 8 February, the nature of these dealings would surely have been revealed more publicly, precipitating a much more serious diplomatic crisis. With Essex's death—and the deliberate suppression of James's part by the authorities—a genuine succession crisis was averted.

STANDING ON HIS OWN STRENGTH

In the Tower after his trial, Essex broke down. Having refused to acknowledge his courses as treasonable, he now apparently admitted that he had been subject to relentless pressure from his followers to take seditious action.[73] The confessions of this tight-knit group, though, reveal Essex to have been at the centre of threads of schemes and intrigues in which he was the prime mover: Danvers explained that it was in the summer of 1600 that Essex *himself* first 'fell uppon this project of the courte'.[74]

On 29 July Sir Henry Bromley, a well known Puritan follower of the earl, wrote to Cuffe in exasperation that plans to spring Essex from captivity had stalled:

> '[T]he summer is halfe dunne, tyme is pressious, oportunyte may bee lost; I am and will bee as I have promised, I expect but direction, for I am wholly his that you ar.[75]

Essex's custodians were finally removed on 26 August; but the urgency of schemes to restore his fortunes heightened perilously when the earl's patent for the monopoly of sweet wines ended on Michaelmas Day. Beseiged by creditors, Essex faced financial as well as political ruin. John Littleton was dispatched to the Low Countries to summon Southampton.[76]

From December, tormented anxieties were channelled into a series of plans force access to the queen. The letter to James dispatched, Essex decided that the support he could personally mobilize was sufficient for a

---

[72] Bruce, *Correspondence*, 90–2. Of the arrested rebels, only Cuffe mentioned Anthony Bacon, noting that he handled Scottish intelligence; Francis Bacon may have kept his brother's name clean.

[73] TNA, SP 12/278/104, f. 207ʳ, 'An abstract out of the Erle of Essex confession'.

[74] Bruce, *Correspondence*, 105.

[75] Cecil MS 179/131. For Bromley see Chapter 4, 182.

[76] Bruce, *Correspondence*, 97–8; Southampton was one of a number of Elizabethan soldiers who had raced to the Netherlands after the Battle of Nieuwpoort in July; at Christmas Cuffe and Merrick had secret conference at Mountjoy's house: TNA, SP 12/278/61, f. 106ʳ.

coup before the end of the next law term. Close followers of the earl had been slowly gathering weapons and armour for months.[77] Sir Gelly Merrick and his brother Sir Francis sent into South Wales to stir support in the heartlands of their regional power; messages were also sent to North Wales, Staffordshire, and Wiltshire, bringing various military acquaintances of Essex to town after Christmas. One source reported that a contingent of Welshmen were on their way to London when they heard news of the rising.[78] Francis Bacon memorably wrote that of the earl's company on 8 February 'a man may finde almost out of every County of England some, which could not be by chance or constellation'.[79] This gives a false impression of the size of the following that Essex intended, or indeed, was able to summon: numbering only one lord lieutenant amongst his followers (Lord Sandys) Essex could not have mustered the county regiments.[80] The earl's plans focused on gathering a small but dedicated following of around 120 men, able to launch a swift and secret assault.

In early January the earl of Southampton, riding with only one servant in the London streets, was attacked unprovoked by Lord Grey and his military clients, in the course of a feud which had raged for over a year. Grey's swift release from the Fleet on 2 February convinced the earls that their enemies had complete dominion over Elizabeth.[81] Essex's final hope of access to public life was also dashed in January, when it became apparent that Elizabeth had decided not to convene parliament, which the earl had hoped to attend as a peer of the realm.[82] On 3 February members of Essex's inner sanctum, Southampton, Danvers, Gorges, Sir John Davies, and Sir John Littleton commenced talks at Drury House to discuss proposals for action, to take place perhaps the following weekend.[83] They debated

---

[77] Cecil MS 38/56, 73/112, 76/82,103, 84/14.

[78] In a seemingly connected move, Sir Gelly Merrick had conveyed all his goods in trust to Roger Vaughan, lieutenant of Radnorshire: Cecil MS 73/112, 83/97, 98; Williams, *Council in the Marches of Wales*, 288–9; John Salisbury, knighted by Essex in Ireland, received a letter from the earl two weeks before Christmas: Cecil MS 214/35, 'An information concerning Sir John Lloyd, Owen Salysbury, Peter Wynne, &c'. Also see Cecil MS 38/56, 'An information concerning some gentlemen in Staffordshire, frequenters to the Earl of Essex'.

[79] F. Bacon, *A Declaration of the practices & treasons attempted and committed by Robert late Earle of Essex and his complices . . .* (1601), sig. D4[r].

[80] James, 'At a crossroads', 424–6, 438–9.

[81] Grey and Southampton began their feud in Ireland in 1599, and continued to challenge each other in a bizarre series of encounters in the Low Countries in the summer of 1600: Cecil MS 76/25–27, 68/56–58, 81/10–11; McClure, *Letters of John Chamberlain*, I, 106–7, 115.

[82] TNA, SP 12/278/68/117[r].

[83] Details of the Drury House plots are found in the examinations and confessions of Sir Ferdinando Gorges, Sir John Davies, Sir Charles Danvers, and Sir Henry Neville: TNA, SP

whether to make directly for the queen, where the guard at court contained many of Essex's old retainers. Sir John Davies gave advice on the logistics of a prior assault on the Tower, and drew up plans to penetrate the precincts of the court. Gorges, though, voiced severe misgivings about the weakness of the following Essex proposed to use. Losing patience, Southampton, Essex's *consigliere*, railed against the dissipating momentum. According to Gorges, it was then that the appeal to London was first proposed. At some point the fates of Essex's enemies were also imagined; they would be subjected to 'honorable triall' and replaced. Sir Henry Neville—who had been courted assiduously by Cuffe and Essex since the previous August— and Sir Thomas Bodley were proposed as alternative candidates to Cecil as secretary; Ralegh was to be replaced by Sir William Russell as captain of the guard.[84] Though not at Drury House, Blount later admitted to discussion of more violent solutions, especially towards Cecil.[85]

Although he took care to distance himself physically from the talks, they were devised and orchestrated by Essex, who alone was abreast of all the various schemes, and held separate consultations with Blount, Merrick, and Cuffe. The plans had most certainly been conceptualized as a form of aggressive *coup d'état*: as Gorges explained, on 8 February 'hee had made himselfe a defendante that before was resolved to bee an assaylaunte'.[86] When asked why the supporters had thought their plans a legitimate intervention, Blount replied that he 'doeth not knowe, but that in former tymes, subjects have used force for their mediation'.[87]

DEFINING THE EARL'S TREASON

That Essex would be found guilty at his trial on 19 February was inevitable. But as the famous epigram of Sir John Harington acknowledged, treason and rebellion were subjective concepts in sixteenth-century England—never more so than in response to Essex's rising.[88] The final

12/278/84, 93, 89, ff. 137^{r-v}, 149^r–150^r, 144^r–145^r, SP 12/279/11, ff. 15^r–18^v; BL, Cotton MS Julius F VI, ff. 449^r–450^r.

[84] Bruce, *Correspondence*, 90, examination of Henry Cuffe. Neville was informed of the plotting on 2 February, but declined involvement; he was imprisoned for failing to inform the authorities of Essex's plans, and was released at James's accession with Southampton: TNA, SP 12/279/11, ff. 15^r–18^v, confession of Sir Henry Neville.

[85] Bruce, *Correspondence*, 109; BL, Cotton MS Julius F VI, f. 446^v.

[86] BL, Cotton MS Julius F VI, f. 450^v.

[87] TNA, SP 12/278/86, f. 140^v.

[88] 'Treason never prosper, what's the reason? For if it doth prosper, none dare call it treason', Sir John Harington, *The most elegant and witty epigrams of Sir John Harington, Knight* (1618), Bk 4, no. 5.

battle waged by Essex and his supporters was ideological, fought over Essex's posthumous reputation, the lines drawn by competing definitions of treason, and of public and private authority.

All the arrested rebels chorused one constant refrain: Essex had no designs on the crown, and no harm to the queen would have occurred. At trial on 5 March the lesser conspirators, Sir Christopher Blount, Sir Gelly Merrick, Henry Cuffe, and Sir Charles Danvers, who had already confessed to premeditated plots to storm the court, still pleaded not guilty of treason.[89]

The revelation, though, that his followers had confessed to pre-conceived plots horribly shattered the credibility of Essex's first narrative of the rising as a spontaneous act of self-defence.[90] On a stunned back foot, Essex steadfastly denied that they were guilty of a political crime; the ends of their conduct, and the pursuit of private vengeance justified their courses. This defence rested in an appeal to the law of nature, which allowed action for self-protection, over the pedantry of common law.[91]

The prosecution, delivering operatic thanks for their escape from the tyrannical rule of 'King Robert the First', charged the earls and lesser conspirators with compassing the throne for Essex *and the royal dignity*, exploiting the capacious ambiguity of the 1352 treason statute (25 Edw. III, st. 5, c. 2), which defined as treason the usurpation of the prince's 'regality' as well as any threatened physical assault.[92] The earls' actions were deemed treasonable regardless of harm intended to Elizabeth's person, because this autonomous intervention 'usurped upon the Kings authoritie and presumed to climbe thereunto the kings highe touer of Justice'.[93] Essex's aborted plans to use the English army in Ireland, to take the Tower—the queen's arsenal—or to levy the London militia were

---

[89] Howell, *State trials*, I, 1417–19. So too, for the same reasons, had Thomas Lee: ibid., 1403.

[90] Different accounts of the trial of Essex and Southampton survive. The text commonly used in Howell, *State trials*, 1333–60, is comparable to the manuscript account of the arraignment of Essex and Southampton in the State Papers, TNA, SP 12/278/101, ff. 166ʳ–180ᵛ; it appears to be the earliest and fullest contemporary account. The template for a second, more condensed account, is TNA, SP 12/278/102, ff. 183ʳ–198ʳ. Coke's detailed notes for the trials TNA, SP 12/278/98–100, ff. 159ʳ–165ᵛ, are contemporary, and demonstrate the lines of argument that were pursued.

[91] TNA, SP 12/278/101, f. 179ᵛ. Edward Seymour, duke of Somerset, in the mid-sixteenth century made a similar distinction between law and conscience at his trial: Lacey Baldwin Smith, 'English treason trials and confessions in the sixteenth century', *Journal of the History of Ideas*, 15/4 (1954), 479.

[92] TNA, SP 12/278/101, ff. 167ᵛ–169ᵛ, SP 12/278/102, ff. 185ʳ–186ʳ. See John Bellamy, *The Tudor law of treason: an introduction* (London: Routledge, 1979), 9–82; Alan Orr, *Treason and the state: law, politics and ideology in the English Civil War* (Cambridge: Cambridge University Press, 2002), 1–35.

[93] TNA, SP 12/278/98, f. 159ʳ.

interpretable as conspiracy to levy war; actual resistance (however pathetic) had been offered to the queen's forces at Ludgate. Even Essex's protest that he intended no harm to Elizabeth's natural body was dismissed: any subject found in 'open rebellion', Coke insisted, 'is in construction of the lawe guilty of determininge the death and destruction of the prince'.[94] Coke, the supreme ancient constitutionalist, also pre-empted Essex's defence on the grounds of necessity and the law of nature by asserting the superiority of the common law, as interpreted by generations of lawyers, over the 'singular or privat opinion or conceat' of even the wisest individual.[95]

The prosecution wore down the defiance of Southampton, who admitted guilt through ignorance, and pleaded for mercy. He would escape his sentence, to be released from the Tower on the accession of James. Essex's confession took longer to procure. In the Tower, Abdias Ashton, his chaplain, exhorted him to meditate on his sins and die a truly penitent death.[96] As Essex's gaze fixed on the afterlife, his spirit was apparently broken. He produced a verbal and longer signed confession of his crimes on 21 February, the substance of which exists only in an abstract endorsed by the privy council, and an account of his confession made on the day of his execution on 25 February, signed by three ministers: Ashton, William Barlow, and Thomas Montford. In these texts Essex confessed to pre-planning the rising, and admitted that he was 'justly spewed out of the Realme'.[97] According to the eyewitness accounts of his semi-private execution in the Tower, Essex repeated the substance of his confession on the scaffold, dying a repentant, self-confessed traitor, ruing

> last sinne, this greate, this bloodye, this crying & this infectious sinne, whereby so manye, for love of me, have ventured their lives and soules, and have bene drawen to offend God, to offend their soveraigne, & to offend the world.[98]

The substance of Essex's confession revealed nothing new in terms of evidence. The vital change was that the earl now admitted his deeds to

---

[94] TNA, SP 12/278/101, f. 168[r–v]. Robert Cecil wrote to Sir George Carew that Essex planned to use 'the shadow of [Elizabeth's] authority for changing of government': *Calendar of Carew manuscripts, 1600–1603*, 37.

[95] TNA, SP 12/278/98, f. 159[r]. Also see TNA, SP 12/278/101, f. 168[v], NA SP 12/278/102, f. 185[r–v].

[96] Beach Langston, 'Essex and the art of dying', *HLQ*, 13 (1950), 109–20; James, 'At a crossroads', 457–9.

[97] TNA, SP 12/278/104, 113, ff. 207[r–v], 222[r], abstract of the earl's confession in the tower, and the earl's confession to his ministers, printed in Bacon, *Declaration*, sigs. Q3r–[Q4[r]].

[98] TNA, SP, 12/278/112, f. 220[r], 'The manner of the earle of Essex his death'. Varied versions of the speech circulated, though they differ little in significant content; see SP 12/278/114, 115.

have been 'vylent courses' and political crimes. Essex now heaped blame on his evil advisors, especially Henry Cuffe, who was brought before the earl and charged to 'call to God for mercy and to the queene': crucially he urged Southampton to confess 'what danger shee [the queen] hath ben in'. Essex now acknowledged that his 'courses', if successful, might have imperilled the queen, with 'more dangerous and malicious ends for the disturbance of Estate'.[99]

For the government, the repentance of the traitor was essential to the reassertion of moral and political order. Essex's confession, though, was of particular importance to the council, because they were intensely fearful of public sympathy for the earl. Instructions to the constable and the lieutenant of the Tower called strongly for vigilance lest the earl's execution speech be provocatively self-justifying.[100] The earl's 'confessions' were published in Bacon's *A declaration of the practices and treasons... of the late Earle of Essex*, the official printed account of the rising. William Barlow, the queen's chaplain, whose signature confirmed the articles of Essex's confession, emphasized the nature of the earl's penitent death at Essex's funeral sermon at Paul's Cross, delivered on 1 March. This sermon, the contents of which were dictated by Cecil, was also published with the addition of Essex's confession and scaffold speech, as the privy council energetically enshrined their official narrative of Essex's treasons from press and pulpit.[101]

Contemporaries immediately challenged Essex's self-admitted guilt, especially his willingness to blame friends and followers for his actions.[102] As far away as Tuscany, Henry Wotton deeply mistrusted official accounts of Essex's final words that had reached him in Florence.[103] Bacon denounced the circulation of 'divers false and corrupt Collections and Relations' of Essex and Southampton's trial, while Barlow railed against narratives of Essex's execution, which reported that the earl had declaimed the 54th or 94th psalm on the scaffold.[104] Official versions relate that Essex conventionally recited the 51st psalm, a penitent plea for God's

---

[99] TNA, SP 12/278/104, f. 207[r]; Bacon, *Declaration*, sig. Q3v.

[100] TNA, SP 12/278/111, ff. 218[r] –19[r].

[101] William Barlow, *A Sermon preached at Paules Crosse, on the first Sunday in Lent* (1601); Bacon, *Declaration*, sig. Q3[r-v].

[102] George Carleton reported how strange it was for 'thes noble and resolute men' 'to strive who should drawe one an other in deepest': TNA, SP 12/279/35, f. 45[r].

[103] A. Crinó, 'Trenta lettere inedite di Sir Henry Wotton, nell'archivio di Stato di Firenze', *Rivista di letterature moderne e comparate*, 8 (1955), 110–11. Wotton had been in Tuscany for some months before the rising.

[104] Bacon, *Declaration*, sig. A3[v]; Barlow, *Sermon preached at Paules Crosse*, unpaginated. The sermon denigrating Essex's character preached before the trial had been so badly received that Cecil and Bancroft instructed Barlow to preach a toned down attack on Essex himself: TNA, SP 12/278/126,ff. 250[r]–251[r]; Arnold Hunt, 'Tuning the pulpits: the religious context of the Essex revolt', in Lori-Anne Ferrell and P. E. McCullough eds, *The*

mercy; the 54th psalm promises divine vengeance upon King David's enemies, and the 94th is even more inflammatory: 'who will rise up for me against the evildoers? ... he shall cut them down in their own iniquity, and shall cut them off in their own wickedness'. In other words, alternative narratives of Essex's execution in circulation suggested that he died a vengeful death, cursing his enemies.

Those closer to Essex also queried the government's account of the earl's end. Ashton, parrying fierce criticism of his behaviour, later suggested that the meaning of Essex's confession was dangerously misinterpreted: Essex's 'bloody sin' was not a revelation of plans for usurpation, only an admission of the *unwanted* anarchy that his rising might have provoked.[105] An anonymous correspondent of Anthony Bacon insisted that before Ashton churned up his soteriological guilt, Essex had planned a public defence of his actions, insisting that the ends of his conduct more than justified the means. The earl, the correspondent approvingly related, had taken action not to settle private scores, but for the weightiest of public causes: the removal of 'evil Instruments from about [the queen's] Person', the 'settling a Succession for the Crown to the Preventing of Spanish servitude'.[106]

EVIL COUNSELLORS, THE QUEEN, AND THE PATTERNS OF HISTORY

At the heart of any defence of Essex's treason—planned as well as enacted—was the belief that his ends were legitimized by the urgent necessity to purge the realm of evil counsellors, 'Mortal Enemies of this Kingdom'.[107] There was no novelty in this language of political protest: all sixteenth-century rebels attacked the monarch's servants and defended their actions with declarations of personal allegiance to the prince. In the 1640s, violent criticism of the government of Charles I would be directed at the ministers who had counselled the king to dangerous and ungodly policies.

English sermon revised: religion, literature and history, 1600–1750 (Manchester: Manchester University Press, 2000), 97–8.

[105] Folger Shakespeare Library, MS v. b. 214, ff. 266^{r}–268^{r}, 270^{r}–271^{r}. Ashton insisted that he had signed the confession reluctantly, so as not to have to preach the earl's funeral sermon: Fritz Levy, 'Theatre and court in the 1590s', in Guy, *Reign of Elizabeth I*, 287–95; Hunt, 'Tuning the pulpits', 102–5.

[106] Bod, Rawlinson MS D 1175, 198–209, 'A letter to Mr A. Bacon concerning the earl of Essex', 30 May 1600, at 204–5.

[107] BL, Egerton MS 2606, f. 1$^{r–v}$; Bod, Rawlinson MS D 1175, 204.

It seems amazing, though, that Essex believed that Cecil, Ralegh, and Cobham were ensnared in a scheme to sell the crown to Spain. A moment of the highest melodrama occurred at Essex's trial, when Cecil suddenly emerged to deliver a hand-wringing denunciation of allegations of his dealings with Spain. Unwilling to reveal his own negotiations with James VI, Essex's defence of his convictions looked weak and foolish.[108]

Inevitably, the prosecution argued that Essex's conflation of threats to his person with a Spanish succession plot was merely a cynical attempt to legitimize his actions. A broader assessment of Essex's political and ideological preoccupations, though, will prove that Essex had genuinely come to view his personal enemies as a deadly clique of evil counsellors, possessing malignant designs on the succession. Hostile critiques of a *regnum Cecilianum*, of an English realm tyrannized by the ascendancy of a Cecil, were conceptual models of the Elizabethan commonwealth that significantly predated Essex's own rise to prominence, with origins in Catholic polemical attacks on Elizabethan government from the 1570s onwards.[109] A draft of historical notes by Robert Cecil cited the parallels between Essex's rhetoric and the justifications against base evil counsellors used by the Catholic nobility in the Northern Rebellion in 1569: 'so dyd Northumberland and Westmoreland rise'.[110]

It was the deep impact, too, of a particular work of Catholic polemic that entrenched fears in England—and Scotland—that serious and underhand attempts would be made to assert the title of the Infanta Isabella Clara Eugenia, now archduchess of the Southern Netherlands, and the daughter of Philip II. At his trial, Essex sensationally imputed that Cecil had approvingly cited the Catholic treatise *A conference about the next succession to the crowne of Ingland*. This notorious book, which warmly endorsed the hereditary claim of the crown of Spain to the English throne, had scandalized the court on its appearance in 1595, churning up the deep anxieties about the succession that lurked in the minds of all politically engaged Elizabethans. More than anyone, Essex was keenly sensitive to the impression that the *Conference* had wrought on the political imaginations of Elizabeth's subjects: the author—widely assumed to be Robert Parsons, the English Jesuit—had mockingly dedicated the work to the earl, deliberately to destabilize Essex's public position.[111] By 1601, Essex was all too ready to believe that Cecil, whom he now viewed as his

---

[108] TNA, SP 12/278/101, f. 176[r].
[109] See Introduction, n. 39 and n. 40; below, Chapters 2 and 3.
[110] TNA, SP 12/278/127, f. 252[r], 'a Memoriall about the Insurrection of the Earl of Essex'.
[111] TNA, SP 12/278/101, ff. 175[r]–177[r]. The report had come from Southampton via Sir William Knollys, who was called upon to deny that Cecil had discussed the book treasonably.

mortal enemy, would approve of a treatise that had caused him such public humiliation.

Essex's suspicion of a Spanish succession plot was not, though, the product of his individual brain-sick fantasy. It was clearly entertained by Mountjoy and Southampton, but also by James VI, who had paid serious attention to the warnings of Essex and his friends, and was equally inclined to identify Robert Cecil as the Machiavellian genius behind a plot to prohibit his succession.[112] As will be shown in Chapter 2, the roots of Essex's belief in a specific succession plot at the heart of the court can also be traced back to divisions over the direction of foreign policy that emerged in 1598, when Essex bitterly opposed William and Robert Cecil's sympathetic attitude to peace with Spain.[113] Cuffe cited the secretary's willingness to negotiate with Spain and his friendly attitude towards the archdukes in the Netherlands as proof of his support of the infanta; Buckhurst, the lord treasurer, had allegedly described Archduke Albert as the 'best frend' of the queen.[114]

The context of domestic politics also confirmed to Essex and his friends that the younger Cecil had inherited the crown of the *regnum Cecilianum*, which intensified its hold over court and state. There is no doubt that Essex believed that his enemies relentlessly pursued his downfall: he held them responsible for his fall from grace, and for blocking all channels of access to the queen.

As Essex's fortunes had plummeted in 1599, he had watched the careers and wealth of his 'enemies' rise in the balance. Cuffe defined the contours of this powerful cabal, which had gained a stranglehold over the key military and fiscal resources of the kingdom so that they might place their own candidate on the throne: Lord Cobham, warden of the Cinque Ports, was ascendant in the South-east; Ralegh, governor of Jersey, in the West; Thomas Cecil, Lord Burghley, Robert's older brother, had been appointed president of the council of the north in August 1599. The finances of the realm were in the hands of the lord treasurer, Buckhurst, a noted enthusiast for peace; while the navy was controlled by Lord Admiral Howard, earl of Nottingham. The nebulous powers of the secretary placed Cecil at the heart of council and court, controlling access, information, and intelligence.[115] As will be discussed in Chapter 4, many of Essex's rivals had gained office and advancement

[112] James's attitudes are discussed below in Chapter 4.
[113] The impact of these negotiations is discussed in Chapter 2.
[114] Bruce, *Correspondence*, 82–4.
[115] Ibid., 81–2.

despite Essex's opposition, and during his absences from court on military campaign.

By conventionally contrasting their attack on this hostile faction with their absolute loyalty to queen and state, Essex and the rebels also subjected the discourse of opposition to evil counsel to searching critique. The statute of 1352 described as treason the killing of the king's ministers or justices in execution of their office. At Essex's trial, though, Coke argued much more radically that mere hostility to the servants of the monarch *itself* was an attack on sovereignty: 'he that abuseth the government hateth the governor'.[116] This extremely authoritarian formulation, if taken to its logical conclusion, would stifle any critique of royal government by a subject, utterly exploding the utility of the rhetoric of evil counsel which directed criticism of policy away from the monarch's actions. Ironically, Coke's argument anticipated the same attitude of the Stuart kings, who regarded the libelling of ministers and favourites as innately seditious.[117]

The authorities were also keen to insist that the life of the queen would have been inevitably endangered by the coup. The crucial confessions were from Blount: claiming that he had always been the first to denounce any 'projects of blood' when they were raised, he insinuated that the Drury House plots had been less innocent than the conspirators had revealed.[118] On the scaffold, preparing to meet his maker, Blount admitted that they had known the wider implications of their actions: 'rather then we should have failed of our purpose, it would have cost much bloud and perhappes have drawn some from her Majesties own person'.[119]

Most importantly Bacon, Coke, and Cecil cast Essex's treasons in a historical as well as a legal framework, hewing at the foundations of Essex's loyalism, his breast-beating vows of allegiance to Elizabeth. By 'turning their imputation upon Counsellours, and persons of credit with their Soveraigne', argued Bacon, the earl and his supporters had pursued 'the beaten path of Traytours'.[120] Historical precedent proved that Essex's attack on evil counsel evidenced his seditious intent: all rebels used this hypocritical language to dress treasonable behaviour in loyalist rhetoric;

---

[116] TNA, SP 12/278/101, f 168ᵛ. See Alastair Bellany, 'A poem on the archbishop's hearse: puritanism, libel and sedition after the Hampton Court Conference', *JBS*, 34 (1995), 137–64.

[117] Richard Cust, 'Charles I and popularity', in Thomas Cogswell, Richard Cust and Peter Lake eds, *Politics, religion and popularity in early Stuart Britain: essays in honour of Conrad Russell* (Cambridge: Cambridge University Press, 2002), 235–58.

[118] Bruce, *Correspondence*, 109.

[119] Bod, Rawlinson MS C 774, f. 34ᵛ; Bacon, *Declaration*, sig. Q2ᵛ.

[120] Bacon, *Declaration*, sig. [E4ʳ].

opposition to evil counsel was the preliminary language employed in actions that precipitated the deposition of monarchs in centuries past. Describing as treason the usurpation of the sovereignty of the prince, Coke asked 'how long liveth Richard the 2 after he was surprised in the same waie?' He invoked the precedence of 'Isabel, wife to Edward II [who] for the profit of the holy church, her lord the king and of the common-welth assembled many of the nobility the nobles and the great personnes to remove councillors'. He had no need to elaborate on Edward II's subsequent history and fate.[121]

Regardless of the authorship of the play watched by some of the 'rebels' on the eve of the rising, Essex and his followers would have been utterly aware that opposition to Richard II's evil counsellors was the justification used by Henry Bullingbrook to frame his own intention to reform the government of England. Like Essex, Bullingbrook publicly shunned any intention of harming the king: just as Essex's followers swore allegiance to Elizabeth, John Hayward had emphasized the oaths taken by Bulling-brook and the other rebellious nobles, that they 'should not procure nor permit any bodily harme to be done unto King Richard; whereupon they bound themselves upon their honours to prosecute all extremities against his mischievous counsailers'.[122]

As the government repeatedly insisted, Essex knew full well that an action initiated as an assault on evil counsel had resulted in the enforced abdication and death of this particular king.

Hammer has argued that, in fact, Essex and his circle's interest in the story of Richard II indicates the reverse of Bacon's allegations. The earl's supporters watched a play about Richard II on 7 February because of obvious parallels between Ricardian and Elizabethan England. The play, however, was intended to be a *warning* to Essex to avoid following Bullingbrook's dreadful courses. In Hammer's words, Essex and his fol-lowers hoped that the earl would emulate Bullingbrook's initial action to purge the state of evil counsel, but would this time 'do it *properly*', without the awful consequences of 1399—the deposition of the monarch.[123]

The association between Essex and histories of Richard II will be addressed more thoroughly in Chapter 6; but Hammer's interpretation rests on a particular reading of Shakespeare's *Richard II* (which he is certain was the play watched at the Globe) that implies that the dramatist meant his audience to read no ambiguity into Bullingbrook's early

[121] TNA, SP 12/278/98, f. 159ᵛ; Howell, *State Trials*, 1421–2.

[122] Manning, *Hayward's Life and raigne*, 119; also see Chapters 5 and 6 for a full discussion of the association of Essex, Hayward, and histories of Richard II.

[123] Hammer, 'Shakespeare's *Richard II*', 34 and *passim*.

refutation of designs on the crown; a reading that assumes that Richard's deposition or enforced abdication is the disastrous, but *unintentional* consequence of an ill-managed noble intervention to reform government. In fact, it is impossible to form such a definitive interpretation of the motivations of Shakespeare's Bullingbrook from the existing play-text. Bullingbrook is deliberately taciturn; the audience must itself decide if he acts at first only to claim his confiscated inheritance and to thwart the evil counsellors, Bushy, Bagot, and Green, or if he entertains ambition for higher powers from the point of his return from exile. Shakespeare also makes the impossibility in forming these kinds of judgments about historical actors and actions—and the limited extent to which political language and rhetoric itself can be trusted—a central theme of the play. And, as Coke would have pointed out if Bullingbrook had stood before him in the dock, even Henry's limited intervention in moving against evil counsellors was an action that usurped sovereignty: in the great abdication scene (only first printed in the 1608 quarto) Richard hands his crown to Henry, bitterly pointing out that his cousin already exercises *de facto* power.

It is precisely these ambiguities—this tension between rhetoric and action—that Bacon and Coke had highlighted as *evidence* of Essex's more seditious aims. All rebels, they argued, with designs on the crown or otherwise, *would* insist on their loyalty to the existing ruler to claim legitimacy. But historical example proved that the autonomous opposition of a subject against any counsellor of the monarch was an illegitimate act in itself that would almost certainly result in a much more serious 'reformation of government' than the removal of courtiers. How could Essex's own utterances be trusted?

Essex and his circle's historical interests also require us to rethink their appraisal of the queen herself. Literary accounts of the reigns of Richard II and Edward II indulged the fascination of Elizabethans with the definition of weak monarchy as the operation of tyranny. Far more explicitly than Shakespeare, whose Richard is an autonomously wilful despot, John Hayward's errant king is a tyrant *because* he governs through evil counsel. Any parallel drawn between Elizabeth and Richard II implied the same about England's queen. Essex's developing attitude to court, evil counsel, and the queen was complex and often contrary: but as will be shown, the intellectual and cultural frameworks used by Essex's circle to understand the political world of the Elizabethan court did not deepen the unspotted loyalty of Essex to his mistress. They caused him to emphasize the queen's faults of character and judgment, her arbitrary rule. The undeniable truth in the government's condemnation of Essex's rising was that there was a wide ideological chasm between the 'loyalist' protestations of the earl and his followers, their conception of legitimate political action, and their awareness of the patterns of history.

MATTERS OF STATE: SUCCESSION, PARLIAMENT, AND RELIGIOUS TOLERATION

Essex defined his rising as an intervention in matters of state—especially the succession—for the health, even the survival, of the English realm. As Essex had written to James, 'now am I summoned of all sides to stop the malice, the wickedness and madness of these men and to releeve my poore country that grones under hir burthen'.[124] Cuffe explained that Mountjoy involved himself in Essex's schemes because he believed the 'publicke to suffer with his private'.[125]

Once again, Bacon argued that this very language of virtue and public service in fact showed evidence of underlying hypocrisy and treason: the rebels posed that 'they would be Common wealths-men'.[126] Camden relates that Essex had been warned by moderate friends in advance of the rising that 'he should not conceal his private wounds with the grievances of the commonwealth'.[127]

From the mid-1590s Essex had been noisily associated with the rhetoric of public service, celebrated as an Atlas, shouldering the welfare of England within the broader sphere of Christendom. Exuberant tribute to Essex's virtues, his military prowess, his wisdom, and his (over-estimated) political influence was lavished on the earl by admirers, followers, and would-be clients. But the post-rising propaganda reflected a swelling critique of Essex's sense of political entitlement that had emerged for some years previously, as a growing body of detractors had censured the earl's belief in his indispensability to the 'commonwealth'.[128] To these critics, Essex's actions proved the danger of subjects who fostered the appearance of excessive greatness: Robert Cecil's historical memorials on the rising note the Latin epithet *'perniciosissima vitia quae virtutis specie fruantur'*: the worst vices are nourished with the appearance of virtue.[129]

As will be argued in Chapter 4, the earl's rhetoric of public service—though largely and self-consciously using the language of 'state' rather than 'commonwealth'—was certainly grounded in self-perception of his

---

[124] BL, Additional MS 31022, f. 107ᵛ.
[125] Bruce, *Correspondence*, 87, 96–102.   [126] Bacon, *Declaration*, sig. E3ʳ.
[127] 'illi . . . praemonerentut . . . privata vulnera Reipublicae malis non obtegeret', Camden, *Annales*, 836.
[128] Discussed in Chapter 5.   [129] TNA, SP 12/278/127, f. 252ʳ.

own virtue and conscience.[130] But the conspirators revealed that the earl
had envisaged wider constitutional means to achieve 'his purpose to alter
the government'.[131] Essex's prosecutors seized on his plans to call a
parliament—'a bloody parliament', as Coke intoned at Essex's trial—as
a vital aspect of the earl's intention to usurp Elizabeth's sovereignty.[132]
These allegations were corroborated by the earl's arrested followers: in
such a parliament—where Cuffe might have been speaker—the realm
would have been reformed and the title of James VI formally declared.[133]
After Essex's death, the earl of Northumberland, writing spitefully to
James of his former brother-in-law, revealed that the earl had planned
for an interregnum between the death of the queen and the succession of
the next monarch, desiring the 'continowall powar of ane army to dispose
of, of being great constable of england, to the end that in an interregnum
he might call parlaments to make laws for owr selwes.'[134] But if Northumberland and Coke described Essex's intentions to call a parliament as
indicative of his treasonable attitudes, others were admiring. The anonymous correspondent of Anthony Bacon was entirely sympathetic to the
'whole end' of Essex's behaviour: the 'settling of the succession by Act of
Parliament on the King of Scotland'.[135]

Northumberland also insinuated that Essex was concerned with the
constitutional power of aristocratic office, when he associated Essex's
interest in parliaments with his ambition of being 'great constable of
England'. The office of lord high constable had lain vacant since the
execution of the duke of Buckingham in 1521. Rather than showing
this alleged desire to be constable, Essex had campaigned bitterly and
successfully in 1597 to be appointed earl marshal, a chivalric civilian office
which ranked subordinate. Historically it was the constable who had been
empowered with the authority to call parliaments when princely government failed.[136]

---

[130] See Introduction and below, Chapter 4.
[131] TNA, SP 12/278/87, f. 142^r.
[132] TNA, SP 12/278/101, f. 169^{r-v}; SP 12/278/102, f. 186^v.
[133] TNA, SP 12/278/125, f. 247^r. Danvers confessed that Essex had planned to call a
parliament; TNA, SP 12/278/89, f. 144^v; Sir Henry Neville also reported in some detail
Cuffe's revelations that a parliament would be called, TNA, SP 12/279/11, f. 17^v; also see
Howell, *State Trials*, I, 1445.
[134] Bruce, *Correspondence*, 66. The possibility of an interregnum in the event of
Elizabeth's death had long taxed Elizabethan minds: see especially Collinson, 'Elizabethan
exclusion crisis'.
[135] Bod, Rawlinson MS D 1175, 207.
[136] See the dispute between Richard C. McCoy, *The rites of knighthood: the literature
and politics of Elizabethan chivalry* (Berkeley, CA and London: University of California Press,
1989), 79–102, and Linda Levy Peck, 'Peers, patronage, and the politics of history', in
Guy, *Reign of Elizabeth I*, 92–3 and *passim*. These issues are discussed further in Chapter 4.

Of the conspirators, Sir Charles Danvers reported that Essex had voiced his intention to 'doe like an Erle Marshall' at Ludgate.[137] Thomas Dove, the dean of Norwich, also claimed that he had challenged the earl in the Tower to state as to under what 'warrant' of authority he had acted: the earl replied that he was 'earl marshal of England', and needed 'no other warrant'.[138] One explanation is that as earl marshal Essex believed that he could use force under martial law. It also seems possible that the earl would have been cognizant of the extraordinary constitutional powers associated with these medieval offices of state—certainly if Northumberland was. Most importantly, though, the marshalship underpinned Essex's own generalized sense of his public authority as a great noble magistrate, separate from an ordinary subject of Elizabeth.[139]

The greatest of all matters of state—which underpinned every anxiety about the succession—was, of course, the confessional identity of the future monarch, and the still uncertain fate of the English church. The earl's rising also threw these knotted tensions into uncomfortable relief, highlighting Essex's own very ambiguous religious politics. At Essex's trial, it was alleged that further proof of his seditious plans for 'reformation' of the government of England rested in promises made about religion—in particular, the promise of toleration to Catholics. These insinuations of popery were vehemently repudiated by Essex, who died a robustly orthodox Protestant death.[140]

Accusations of Catholicism were easy shorthand for sedition, but Essex's religious patronage was famously amorphous. From the winter of 1599, the government had been more worried about the earl's links to networks of Protestant ministers, including prominent Puritans, who looked to Essex's protection.[141] With the possible exception of Southampton, the aristocrats with Essex were staunchly Protestant, as were many of the wider following. On the day of the rising itself, there was mysterious confusion over whether or not Sheriff Smith had promised

<hr/>

[137] TNA, SP 12/278/68, f. 117[r].
[138] Barlow, *A sermon preached at Paules Crosse,* sig. D3[v]. There is confusion as to whether or not Essex *was* earl marshal in 1601. Barlow argued that the marshalship had been sequestered from him 'long before', referring to Essex's being stripped of the office after the York House trial in June 1600; in fact, when Essex sent back his patents of office in response, the queen sent back those of master of the horse and earl marshal, to keep the latter for life: *HMC de L'Isle and Dudley,* II, 422; see letters of Sir Henry Lee and Edward Reynolds addressed to Essex as 'Lorde Marsyal', and 'Earle Marshall of England' sent on 8 and 29 September respectively: Cecil MS 81/74, 83/72.
[139] See Chapter 4.
[140] TNA, SP 12/278/112, f. 220[r].   [141] Discussed below in Chapter 5.

to send Anthony Wotton, the Puritan preacher and a chaplain of Essex, as a sign of his commitment.[142]

Government propaganda, though, did not fabricate the strong Catholic presence in Essex's following: of the Drury House conspirators Sir Christopher Blount, Sir John Davies, and Sir Charles Danvers confessed their Catholicism.[143] Of the wider gentry following involved in the rising, Catholics included Sir Charles and Sir Jocelyn Percy, and the future gunpowder plotters, Robert Catesby and Francis Tresham.[144] Much was made of Blount's admission that the earl 'was wont to say that he liked not that any man shoulde be trobled for his religion'. Davies, too, confessed that Blount had assured him that Essex 'promised lybertye of Catholick religione'.[145] At his trial Essex admitted only to sympathy for individual freedom of conscience: 'did you ever knowe that at such tyme as I had power in the state I was willinge that any man showld be troubled for his conscience?'[146]

This last statement was typically disingenuous, for the earl had been publicly—and consistently—associated with Catholic toleration since the mid-1590s. With the greatest mixture of hope and anxiety, Catholic groups had looked to Essex for promise of a brighter future. But by the final years of Essex's career, the earl's support for toleration, intended to deepen his political gravitas, had become an inky stain on his character. Toleration of Roman Catholicism was one of the audacious demands made by Tyrone following Essex's return to England in September 1599, as a prerequisite for a negotiated peace.[147] In July 1600 the authorities, searching for evidence that Essex had acted treasonably, had investigated his close association with the ex-Jesuit priest Thomas Wright, and the earl's former chaplain and Catholic convert, William Alabaster. After 8 February, Wright's testimony was sought again, revealing the extent to which Catholic hopes about the future 'reformation' of government blurred damningly with admiration of Essex's own character and courses. Wright admitted that he believed the earl to be sympathetic to conversion.

---

[142] TNA, SP 12/278/57, f. 94^v, examination of John Smith, sheriff Smith's brother.

[143] Discussed below in Chapter 3.

[144] The Cholmleys of Yorkshire were Catholic, another gentry family involved in the rising; Sir William Constable, a military captain close to Essex was also known as a Catholic: Hutson, 'Military following', 140–2; James, 'At a crossroads', 435–6.

[145] TNA, SP 12/278/86, f. 141^v; SP 12/278/93, f. 150^r, examination of Sir John Davies.

[146] TNA, SP 12/278/101, f. 177^r.

[147] Essex's dealings with Catholics are discussed in Chapters 3 and 5. Different versions of Tyrone's terms are TNA, SP 63/206/55, ff. 152^r–153^v and SP 63/206/56, f. 154^r: the restoration of Catholic worship tops the list.

He also confessed his own seditious daydream for the kingdom of Robert I:
'if the Earle of Essex were kynge it would be a glorious kingedome, and that
it would be better for us ['Catholiques' is crossed out] for he could not be so
inhumane as but to free us all'.[148]

The bitterest taint of Catholic sedition was also the most ironic. It turned
the earl's own condemnation of the corrupt Elizabethan commonwealth on
its head, designating Essex—not Robert Cecil—as the dangerous reader of
Parsons' *Conference*. In his post-execution sermon, William Barlow solemnly
informed his audience/readers that this treatise—which had been, of course,
dedicated to Essex—was 'a principal, if not the originall poyson of the late
Earles hart', furnishing the earl with the dangerous ambition and ungodly
political theories that had catalyzed his rebellion: justification of the legality
of resistance and the deposition and murder of princes.[149]

THE MALIGNANT INFLUENCE OF SCHOLARSHIP

Thomas Arundel, writing to Sir Robert Cecil on 18 February 1601, had a
different explanation for the origins of the Essex circle's seditious political
thinking. The earl of Southampton had come under the dangerous
influence of Cuffe, when in Paris in the autumn of 1598 Essex's secretary
had 'redd Aristotles polyticks to hym with sutch expositions as, I doubt
did hym but lyttle good'.[150] Clearly, Essex's scholarly friends had a
reputation for reading and debating political texts in a way that Cecil
might understand as subversive.

If the veracity of the abstract of the earl's confession can be trusted,
Essex himself singled out Cuffe as the turbulent spirit who spurred him on
to treasonous courses.[151] Cuffe was denounced at trial as the 'cunning
coiner of all plots'; he is the chief villain of Camden's account of the rising,
egging Essex on by invoking his honour and courage.[152] Sir Henry
Neville's evidence described Cuffe's restless agitation for decisive action
most vividly: prosecuting Cuffe, Coke made much out of Neville's remembrance that Cuffe, with 'wordes of heate and impatience' had quoted

---

[148] TNA, SP 12/278/65, f. 112[r]. The earl's relationship with Wright and Alabaster is
discussed in Chapters 3 and 5.
[149] Barlow, *A sermon preached at Paules Crosse*, sig. [B5[v]].
[150] Bod, Ashmole MS 1729, f. 190[r]. Southampton was in Paris having come to France
in the train of Robert Cecil's embassy to Henry IV in February.
[151] TNA, SP 12/278/104, f. 207[f].
[152] Compare Coke's notes for the trial, TNA, SP 12/278/98 with the account in
Howell, *State Trials*, 1439 and Camden, *Annales*, 833–4.

from Lucan's *Pharsalia—'arma tenenti, omnia dat qui iusta negat'* [he who refuses what is just yields all to one who is armed].[153] This quotation is a statement of the legitimacy of armed resistance in the state. The phrase is directly echoed in Gorges' description of the earl's vision of proposed actions, 'imagininge himself and his ffreindes better able to answer what they had don by armes then by lawe'.[154]

Again, it is Camden, in a typically understated way, who suggests that political theories played a vital role in catalyzing the rising. As he describes the infection of Essex's judgment by Cuffe's poisonous counsel, Camden alleges that the earl consulted with Oxford divines, while preachers at Essex House delivered sermons imputing that 'superior magistrates of the realm had the right to restrain kings'.[155]

The only Oxford man to be investigated who did not have an obvious connection to the rising was not a preacher but Henry Savile, warden of Merton College, and provost of Eton, Cuffe's former colleague and patron. Savile's Oxford study was searched and his servants were interrogated; while no incriminating documentary evidence turned up, there is a whiff of uncertainty about his behaviour. Savile had spent an hour with Cuffe on Thursday before the rising, who then walked in the garden of his lodgings. This was the Thursday when the privy council gained scent of Essex's plots. It was unlikely that Cuffe, who had also been canvassing Neville's support, had visited Savile for a purely social call, particularly as Savile's academic studies might have made him sympathetic to Cuffe's vision of Essex's situation and intentions.[156]

The blame heaped particularly on Cuffe, though, is deliberately misleading. Though the scholar was heavily involved in the plotting before the rising, and played a key role in Essex's negotiations with James VI, his primary influence over Essex is not borne out by the confessions of the other conspirators (who did not make anything of the notable importance of Cuffe's role when it might have suited them to do so), or even the earl's own behaviour. The first plans that Essex hatched to launch an attack on the court were made at Dublin Castle in the presence of Blount and Southampton only; Cuffe's own confessions reveal that he was privy to some but not all of the earl's schemes.[157] The particular desire to make a scapegoat of the former Oxford professor is significant in two ways. First, it shows the developing desire of the privy council to shift the blame for

---

[153] TNA, SP 12/279/11, f. 16ʳ; Howell, *State Trials*, 1439.

[154] BL, Cotton MS Julius F VI, f. 450ᵛ.

[155] 'superiores Regni magistratus jus coërcendi Reges habeant', Camden, *Annales*, 835, 839.

[156] Cecil MS104/26, 27, interrogations of Anne Philipson.

[157] Bruce, *Correspondence*, 85–90.

Essex's actions away from the earl, as public pity for Essex's plight began to surface. An unspoken compromise to be struck with the earl and his sympathizers was to fashion Essex *himself* as the victim of evil advice, delivered by a quarrelsome scholar rather than an aristocratic earl of Southampton. Second, it demonstrated the particular association made between Essex and political ideas, and an anxiety about the scholarly attitudes that shaped Essex's mentality.

FRIENDSHIP, VIRTUE, AND POPULARITY

With some justification Bacon, and Camden after him, would describe the followers who joined the earl on 8 February as a band of dissident social outcasts: Puritans, Catholics, but above all unemployed military men.[158] Many also experienced financial difficulties and political alienation; but the strongest bond common to all the men was an intensely personal identification with the earl, his welfare, and his fortunes. As Gwynneth Hutson's study has shown, by far the strongest common experience of the military rebels (about a third of those arrested) was service in Ireland, where those soldiers who did not desert the troubled campaign developed an entrenched solidarity with Essex, sharing his conviction that their military fortunes were hindered at the corrupt English court.[159] Any soldier harbouring such suspicions would have found his inclinations hugely magnified after Essex's return, when queen and privy council purged Mountjoy's Irish army of Essex's military clients. In the months preceding the rising, the government and civic authorities were acutely concerned about the unemployed soldiers who swarmed through London, many of whom regarded Essex as their patron and protector, and saw their own predicament both caused by and reflected in Essex's downfall.[160]

Those members of the nobility who responded to Essex's summons had very similar reasons to be aggrieved with the existing regime. All had served the earl in Ireland; virtually none at the time of the rising enjoyed satisfying public employment as privy councillors or (with the exception of Lord Sandys) lords lieutenant, a wider manifestation of Elizabeth's failure to reward the peerage with significant office in the last years of her reign.[161] Edward, 3rd Baron Cromwell, a veteran of the Normandy

---

[158] Bacon, *Declaration*, sig. D3^{r-v}; Camden, *Annales*, 835–9.

[159] See Hutson, 'Military following', and James, 'At a crossroads', 424–7; lists of the imprisoned Essex following can be found in *APC*, XXXI, 159–60; *HMC Salisbury*, XI, 86–8.

[160] See below, Chapter 5, 202.

[161] Peck, 'Peers, Patronage and the Politics of History', 91–2.

and Cadiz campaigns, was ensnared in heavy nets of debt.[162] Essex had been unable to procure for Cromwell the governorship of Brill; although he enjoyed significant victory against the rebels in Ireland in August 1599, he had been deprived of his Irish command. In a bitter petition of April 1600 Cromwell complained wretchedly: 'In theis extremities what shall I do?'[163] William Parker, 1st or 5th Baron Monteagle, and Roger Manners, 5th earl of Rutland, were both knighted by Essex in Ireland, Rutland incurring the extreme anger of Elizabeth by joining the army without her leave.[164] During Essex's disgrace they had floated round the Low Countries between June and October 1600 with Southampton, looking for military employment. Sir Henry Danvers, brother of Sir Charles, gloomily observed to Southampton that the brilliant plaudits showered on the soldiers who participated in the Battle of Nieuwpoort served only 'to increase our misfortunes heare that can never have the like occasione but buried in obscuritye dye like dogges'.[165] Like many of Essex's followers, Southampton himself had found it politic to keep up channels of communication with Sir Robert Cecil, especially after his marriage to Elizabeth Vernon in August 1598 had brought down Elizabeth's thundering wrath on his head. Also ruinously indebted, though, his identification with Essex's alienation was intensified with the queen's apoplectic reaction to his appointment as general of the horse in Ireland—which she insisted was against her express warrant—and by the initiation of his bitter personal feud with Lord Grey.[166]

The careers of the inner circle of plotters also depended largely on the restoration of Essex's fortunes; only Gorges, governor of Plymouth, was not mainly reliant on Essex for employment. Cuffe was Essex's secretary, while Merrick was the earl's steward, and receiver-general of income from Essex's estates, his offices as deputy lieutenant and *custos rotulorum* in Radnorshire dependent on the earl's patronage. Sir Charles Danvers

---

[162] Cromwell petitioned to serve under Essex in Ireland to restore the 'estate of his now decaying house': *HMC Salisbury*, VIII, 421. Cromwell's case 'in relief of his declining estate' was favourably resolved in November 1600: *CSPD, 1598–1601*, 114, 326, 368–9; *HMC Salisbury*, X, 392.

[163] Cecil MS 79/4; McLure, *Letters of John Chamberlain*, I, 43; In July 1596 Cromwell submitted a failed petition to Sir Robert Cecil to be lord lieutenant of Norfolk: Cecil MS 43/5.

[164] *HMC Salisbury*, IX, 149, 160, 217, 246, 359. In July 1599 it was feared that Rutland would be sent to the Fleet for disobedience.

[165] Cecil MS 80/28.

[166] See above, n. 91; Stopes, *Life of Henry, third earl of Southampton*, 163–4; Southampton blamed Grey for provoking Elizabeth's objection to his being general of the horse, *HMC Salisbury*, IX, 341; when Elizabeth, countess of Southampton, was jailed in the Fleet, it was left to Essex to pay for her upkeep: Akrigg, *Shakespeare and the earl of Southampton*, 72.

had spent several years in exile with his brother, Sir Henry, for killing a neighbour in a family feud. He had acted as a go-between for Essex's intelligence agents in 1595 and 1596, although Sir Robert Cecil's intervention had played the crucial role in gaining the queen's pardon for the brothers in 1598.[167] Both Sir Christopher Blount, Essex's stepfather, and Sir John Davies served Essex in Ireland, Blount as marshal—also despite Elizabeth's extreme displeasure—while Davies had been appointed by Essex as surveyor of the ordnance in January 1599. Davies, who accompanied Essex on his return to England, had become embroiled in Sir George Carew's campaign to eject the earl's clients from the ordnance office.[168] Sir Henry Neville, too, was certainly dissatisfied with his own career: Cecil had nominated him ambassador to France in February 1599, against Neville's sore protestations that his fortune was not equal to the position. When it seemed as if Neville would be blamed for the failure of peace negotiations with Spain in May 1600, Essex and Cuffe immediately showered him with attention, hoping to exploit his dissatisfaction with the Cecil-dominated regime.[169]

It is also important to discuss those who did *not* join the earl's rising on 8 February. The confession of William Temple bears out Camden's description of events: two factions had arisen around the earl during his political disgrace; one counselling action, the other 'the course held by the right noble Lord Harry', which focused on the restoration of Essex's access through legitimate and pacific means.[170] Important friends, whose lives had been previously entwined with the earl's—who would defend themselves as 'moderate' counsellors of Essex—were notable by their absence. Francis Bacon had distanced himself from the earl since the autumn of the previous year.[171] Anthony Bacon and Fulke Greville had been ejected from Essex House in March 1600 with Southampton and his wife; unlike Southampton, neither joined the swarms of soldiers, clerics, and minor gentry who crowded round Essex in 1601.[172] Less surprisingly, Howard

---

[167] Danvers insisted that he had entered the conspiracy because he owed his life to Southampton, who had aided their escape in 1594; Bruce, *Correspondence*, 101; LPL MS 660 ff. 12ʳ, 99ʳ, 102ʳ–103ʳ.

[168] Cecil MS 180/57. Davies was a veteran of all of Essex's previous military campaigns, and he had only won his Irish office in the face of significant competition: see BL, Additional MS 6177, f. 55ʳ: R. Ashley, 'War in the Ordnance Office: the Essex connection and Sir John Davis', *Historical Research*, 67 (1994), 337–45.

[169] TNA, SP 12/279/11, ff. 15ʳ–17ʳ.

[170] Cecil MS 83/40.

[171] F. Bacon, *Sir Francis Bacon his apologie in certaine imputations concerning the late earle of Essex* (1604), 65.

[172] Anthony's final correspondence with Essex seems to have been on 19 September 1600: Cecil MS 81/77. There is no extant correspondence between Greville and Essex after September 1599: Rebholz, *Life of Fulke Greville*, 122–3.

had slithered into a silent obscurity, although he would soon strike up his own secret correspondence with James VI.[173]

As Neville related, the Drury House plotters planned to reveal nothing of the nature of their strategies to the wider group of men they hoped to attract to their cause, intent on gulling them by some 'invented' purpose.[174] Although members of Essex's following may have harboured concerns about the succession or hopes for religious toleration, the ostensible justification given by the followers who joined the rising was concern for Essex's personal and political wellbeing, and for how his welfare encompassed their own.[175] Danvers recalled that Essex galvanized the solidarity of his followers, 'protesting that he esteemed them the best frends he had, and would ever runne a common and united course with them touching his owne fortunes.'[176]

Essex's followers defined themselves overwhelmingly as a group of devotees, dedicated to his protection. William Killegrew remembered that Christopher Blount had declared his undying allegiance to the earl, proclaiming that 'he and dyvers more had vowed their lyves for him: and wold spend them for him'.[177] Southampton had 'promised to venture my fortune and life for the earl'; the rising was a conspiracy 'by my best frendes'. On 8 February John Bargar's brief entanglement with the rebels was because he 'loved my Lord of Essex' and believed him to be 'a religious honest gent'.[178] So Essex had framed his appeal to the armourer William Pickering in the language of personal obligation: 'not for me, Pickeringe'?[179]

Friendship, though, implies equality, while Essex's followers exhibited a much stronger appreciation of the earl's superiority of birth, and especially his virtue—infused with an overwhelming understanding of Essex's public importance as an instrument for political reform. As Gorges explained, the cause that 'bound mee so inseperably' to Essex was

> his worthe and virtue...that outwardly made him so bountifull...an excellent benefactor and a faythfull protector, & who was ther that seemed more willingely to expose himselfe...by any meanes hee coulde get for the publick good of his country?[180]

[173] Bruce, *Correspondence*, 38–52.
[174] TNA, SP 12/279/11, f. 15[r–v]; also compare *CSPD, 1598–1601*, 549–50.
[175] TNA, SP 12/281/1, f. 1[r], examination of William Temple, Essex's secretary who had sent messages to Giles Fletcher; SP 12/279/12, f. 19[r–v].
[176] Bruce, *Correspondence*, 105.   [177] TNA, SP 12/279/13, f. 21[r].
[178] Cecil MS 82/97.
[179] Cecil MS 76/91.   [180] BL, Cotton MS Julius F VI, f. 451[v]–452[r].

Essex's support was grounded above all upon his charisma, his cultivation of virtue, his strong and committed obligation as a patron, and his ability to persuade others of his political indispensability in the realm—qualities that Gorges insisted were acknowledged in the 'eyes of the worlde'.

The public image of the earl, though an intangible entity, had a critical impact on the direction of Essex's actions, determining his own resolution 'to depende uppon the giddy multitude', and to appeal to the citizens of London. Essex's confidence in the success of this course of action, apparently misliked by other conspirators, was founded on the strength of his fabled popularity.

The earl's immediate target was the city elite, fuelled by the belief—a deliberate deception?—that Sherriff Smith had promised succour. Smith's own protestations of innocence lack conviction: he was only released from custody on 2 August 1602, and heavily fined.[181] But Essex had hopes of far broader support: Cuffe boasted to Neville that Essex held the hearts of least 20 of the 24 aldermen, and asked Neville to contact a London minister to gauge the measure of the earl's wider support in the city.[182]

Evidence of the further involvement of the civic elite is elusive. William Masham, alderman Masham's son and a former military client of Essex, proved to be one of the most recalcitrant of those arrested, refusing to admit that his part in the rising made him guilty of any crime.[183] Giles Fletcher, remembrancer to the City of London, was the most extensively embroiled with Essex. Interrogated after the rising, he vigorously denied supporting the revolt, but admitted that he had believed that rumours of Essex's impending murder had 'seemed not improbable', and he confessed to deep admiration for Essex's virtue and piety.[184] Fletcher was reprieved of the great debts bequeathed by his brother in 1597, mainly through Essex's intervention; in return, he had sought the appointment of Dr Henry Hawkins, Essex's former intelligent agent, as his assistant, a position confirmed some months before the rising, on 7 October 1600.[185] On a more cynical note, many Londoners had a strong pragmatic interest in the restoration of Essex's fortunes: most of the earl's creditors were London merchants.[186]

---

[181] TNA, SP 12/278/75, f. 126ʳ; SP 12/278/58, f. 96ʳ.

[182] TNA, SP 12/279/11, f. 18ʳ.

[183] TNA, SP 12/278/45, f. 63ᵛ; SP 12/282/13, examination and indictment of William Masham.

[184] TNA, SP 12/279/12, f. 19ʳ.

[185] LPL MS 658, f. 202ʳ, 288ʳ; LPL MS 660, f. 279ʳ; L[ondon] M[etropolitan] A[rchives], Repertories of the Court of Aldermen, 25, f. 157ʳ.

[186] For Essex's debts in October 1600, over £16,000, see Cecil MS 181/29: the sums listed here do not include sums owed to the moneylender, Peter Vanlor: notably, Essex also owed £1000 to alderman Craven.

Most intriguing is a laconic entry in the Repertories of the Court of Aldermen, which notes that on 4 November 1600, three aldermen were ordered to 'repaire to the right honourable the Erle of Essex towching the affaires of this citty'.[187] The reason for the visit is obscure, but probably commercial; on 30 September, Essex had been petitioned by members of the East India Company to support a voyage under the command of the future conspirator, Sir John Davies. Most prominent among the signatories of this letter to the earl was one 'Tho: Smythe', the unfortunate sheriff.[188] Another possible reason is that the civic elites, ever fearful of social unrest, may have wanted to interrogate Essex about the stirs of soldiers and preachers around Essex House. But whatever the purpose of the visit, it seems likely that this delegation may have given substance to Essex's *impression* that the aldermen were friends, who sympathized with his plight.

As well as targeting Smith and acknowledging the likely support of the aldermen, Essex made a general oral and visual appeal to Londoners, the 'giddy multitude', on the strength of his personal magnetism. Despite the abject failure of this course of action, the faith that Essex placed in his popularity was itself far from unfounded; it had been ironically shared by the government in the months, even years, leading up to his rising. After his return from Ireland, London had been awash with libels and rumours concerning the earl's political disgrace, and the privy council itself had been extremely disturbed about the strength of public feeling for Essex.[189]

Essex's reliance on his popularity emphasized again the great ambiguity encompassed in his profession of loyalty to Elizabeth. Once more, it was Francis Bacon who pointed to the inconsistency in Essex's speech in relation to his actions. In the political rhetoric of Elizabethan elites the cultivation of 'popularity' was almost inevitably associated with sedition. As early as 1596, Bacon had warned Essex that his popular fame would be seen by the queen as a dangerous quality, evidence of excessive ambition.[190] Bacon embroidered this theme in his account of the *Declaration of the practises and treasons* of his erstwhile patron: the need for public acclaim, he explained, was inherent in the 'nature of all usurping Rebels, which doe ever trust more in the common people, then in persons of sort or qualitie'.[191]

Most significantly Bacon also argued that Essex's appeal to London mirrored the strategies of Henry, duke of Guise, scourge of Henry III

[187] LMA, Repertories, 25, f. 167ʳ.   [188] Cecil MS 81/83.
[189] Discussed below, in Chapter 5.   [190] Spedding, *L&L*, II, 40–5.
[191] Bacon, *Declaration*, sig. E2ᵛ. Bacon followed up the parallel when criticising Essex's creation of an obligated following: *Apologie*, 15.

and the Huguenots, and a fearful cipher for grotesque, overweening ambition in Elizabethan England. In fact, there were aching similarities between Essex's attempted rising and the famous Day of the Barricades in May 1588, when the duke of Guise, head of the Catholic League, had raised Paris in rebellion, and had forced the king to flee the capital. Like Essex, Guise had great personal popularity with Parisians. Bacon pointed out that Guise also had come into the city seemingly unarmed, with only a handful of followers. His strategy for overwhelming royal forces resided in his 'confidence in the cittie'—in Guise's case the council of Sixteen, representing the sixteen *quartiers* of Paris, who organized the barricades that immobilized the royal troops. This rebellion, too, had been initiated by the spread of rumours that the party of Guise would be arrested. Just as Essex would, Guise had stated that his only intention was to be reconciled with Henry III; but his wider public aim was to prevent an irreligious succession (ironically of the Protestant Henry of Navarre). Although he rejected the offer of the crown, once in possession of Paris, Guise took power in the kingdom, forced the king to make a formal edict for a Catholic succession, and assured his own position as virtual ruler of France.[192]

If the parallel sprang so readily to Francis Bacon's mind, it is highly likely that Essex and his followers would consciously have reflected on this most successful example of the congruence of aristocratic and civic power, cemented by the personal popularity and charisma of an individual noble-man. But for Bacon, Guise was hardly a figure to be emulated: he was the most prominent and villainous recent exemplar of the 'popular traitor', who uses and legitimizes seditious behaviour through appeal to public acclaim. Again, the more distant historical frameworks used to analyse Essex's rising also defined the pursuit of popular support by a nobleman as a paradigmatic form of sedition. The most famous and topical example of a 'popular' aristocratic rebel from England's medieval past was, once more, Henry Bullingbrook, who, legendarily doffing his bonnet to the oyster-wench, had deliberately cultivated the 'common grievances' of the people who revered him as 'the onely man of courage . . . saluting him king'. As Essex could have read in Hayward's *The first parte of the life and raigne of King Henrie IIII*, Bullingbrook's 'seat of the warre'—the site of his popular strength—was London.[193]

Essex's abject failure must not cause us to dismiss the wider issues that the rising raises. To dwell too extensively on his professions of loyalty to Elizabeth is partially to miss the point; the rising planned but not enacted

---

[192] TNA, SP 12/278/101, f. 179^{r-v}.
[193] Manning, *Hayward's life and raigne*, 119–20.

in the Drury House conspiracies was an act of active aristocratic resistance: the intervention of a nobleman to reform a misgoverned state. Essex's example, then, asked searching questions about the legitimacy of certain kinds of political behaviour. How was one to criticize monarchy, if hostility to evil counsel could not be expressed? To what extent did nobles or virtuous men have the authority to make physical interventions for the better good of the commonwealth or state, especially when the most vital political issue—the unsettled succession—was at stake?

The act itself, and the government's response, is demonstrative of a significant fracture in political thinking among the Elizabethan elite. Consider the two narratives of the rising, created by the earl and his followers and the government: the post-rising propaganda framing the earl as a would-be usurper, with long-term designs on the throne; Essex presenting himself as the instrument of political reformation, collapsing the boundaries between his private welfare and the public good. These different accounts of Essex's history are grounded in the same concepts, vocabularies, and definitions of the same events: Essex was condemned for his cultivation of a virtuous public image; the rhetoric of the *vita activa*; his popularity and his self-belief in the role that he deserved to play in political affairs; ideas associated—albeit with a more aristocratic bent—with the 'quasi-republican' languages of Patrick Collinson's *Republica Anglorum*. These were easily described as the characteristics of an ambitious malcontent; differently interpreted they were virtues that Essex deliberately embodied, that had been admired and celebrated by his followers and friends for years.

One of the most difficult challenges is extracting a sense of Essex's own mentality. The habitual duality of Essex's language, his consistent aversion to blame, emerges from accounts of the rising and its aftermath in its most extreme form. As will be demonstrated, Essex's delivery of different explanations of his behaviour was not just the product of a broken mind; throughout his career he had frequently employed divergent accounts of his conduct in different textual and political contexts. This duality, this ability to swear to opposite beliefs with great vehemence, undermines our understanding of all of Essex's descriptions of his own behaviour. It demonstrates how difficult it is to define the relationship between the earl's stated and actual intentions in relation to the rising and the pre-rising plotting.

The slipperiness of Essex's statements might even cause us to question his vehement denial that he had ever entertained thoughts of Elizabeth's deposition. James's formal nomination as Elizabeth's heir was Essex's consistent aim. But, as will be shown throughout the rest of the book, Essex and his followers were fully engaged through their intellectual/

historical interests with theories of more radical courses of action available to subjects. Had Essex been able to bring his petition to the queen, ensuring her enforced 'assent' to the purgation of evil counsel and the calling of a parliament, it is almost impossible to imagine how the relationship of Elizabeth, earl marshal, and heir-elect would have functioned up until the queen's natural death.

2

Justifying war

Essex was insistent that he, England and Elizabeth—in an ambiguously defined relationship—had a seminal role to play in the destiny of Europe, blessed with the glorious opportunity to have 'at once delivered all Christendome' from the 'fearefull usurpation' of the King of Spain.[1] Essex defined the war as a chivalric contest between freedom and tyranny: 'Yow twoo are like mightie champions entered into the listes to fight for the twoo generall quarrels of Christendome . . . he aspiringe to an universall monarchie, your Majestie at relievinge the oppressed.'[2]

Before the decline of his career, war determined Essex's ideological preoccupations. The earl's desire for military glory prompted enunciation of the relationship between militarism, virtue-in-arms, and the strength of the state. Essex's identification with anti-Spanish courses shaped his religious politics too, especially his relationship with Catholics, who also framed their political loyalties in terms of their attitude to Spain. Finally, the 'European' dimension of the thought of Essex and his associates was also inseparable from his growing belief in the diseased corruption of domestic politics: it was against the assumed friend of the Spanish peace—Sir Robert Cecil—and the spectre of the infanta enthroned that Essex defended the true succession in 1601.[3]

The obligations of alliance with the Dutch in particular also provoked strenuous consideration of the duties of kingship, the obedience of subjects, and of responses to tyranny. Simon Adams and Blair Worden have shown that commitment to the 'Protestant cause' in the circle of Sidney, Leicester, and Walsingham brought about engagement with the treatment of these problems in the seminal works of continental and Scottish political theorists.[4] So too, the political thought of Essex's circle developed in the context of the broader ideological issues engendered by justification of the war with Spain.

---

[1] TNA, SP 12/259/12, f. 31ʳ.
[2] TNA, SP 12/45, f. 64ʳ; Hammer, *Polarisation*, 246–7.
[3] Chapter 1, 48.
[4] Worden, *Sound of Virtue*, 219–94; Adams, 'Protestant cause'.

PHILIP SIDNEY'S SWORD

Essex's political legacy was weighted with ideological baggage. In the 1570s and 1580s Leicester, Walsingham, and Sidney himself had urged Elizabeth to intervene in the Low Countries from a fervent sense of duty towards the Protestant Dutch, 'afflicted brethren', in revolt against Spanish rule. For 'forward Protestants', the plight of the Dutch Calvinists and Huguenot communities in France was a confessionalized conflict against militant post-Tridentine Catholicism: the pope and his temporal agents, the king of Spain, and, latterly, the Catholic League allied against an international Protestant community—'a common defence' because 'the churches of all cuntries are the common cities of God'.[5] The urgency of the international situation for 'forward Protestants' was fired by their identification of the pope as Antichrist, while the most powerful secular prince, Philip II, was denounced in the rhetoric of the Leicester/Sidney circle as the sword-bearing limb of the papal tyrant.[6] Elizabeth was warned of the dangers to England should she ignore the international Catholic threat, and shun the strenuous path of intervention for the easy comfort of blind 'security', 'enchantment', and perilous 'sleep'.[7]

In the early 1590s, the Leicester/Sidney circle's ideal of an international Protestant alliance appeared to have been realized. Spain's support for the League's opposition to the accession of the Huguenot Henry of Navarre brought Henry, the Dutch, and Elizabeth into mutual military opposition to Philip II, their common adversary.[8] As Leicester's heir, and armed with Sidney's sword, Essex was naturally fitted to the leadership of the 'forward Protestant' cause in England as it entered its most active phase. In the 1620s, when Elizabeth's war record was heaped with praise to shame the peace-loving James, Essex was hailed as a great Protestant hero, the scourge of popery, and the terror of Catholic Spain. Modern historiography has followed suit, defining Essex's militarism as ardent 'commitment to fighting for the 'Protestant cause'.[9] But the mutable character of international politics, and the developing religious

---

[5] Cited in Adams, 'Protestant cause', 44.
[6] Peter Lake, 'Anti-popery: the structure of a prejudice', in Richard Cust and Ann Hughes eds, *Conflict in early Stuart England: studies in religion and politics, 1603–42* (Harlow: Longman, 1989), 72–106.
[7] Worden, *Sound of virtue*, 60–3.
[8] See Wernham, *Return of the armadas*; Paul Hammer, *Elizabeth's wars: war, government and society in Tudor England, 1544–1604* (Basingstoke: Palgrave Macmillan, 2003); Adams, 'Protestant cause'.
[9] Hammer, *Polarisation*, 241.

and intellectual contexts of the late sixteenth century, gave far greater complexity to the ideological justification of the war in the 1590s as expressed by Essex and his supporters, especially in relation to confessional politics.

This complexity is demonstrated by conflicting modern interpretations of Essex's *Apologie... against those which falsly and maliciously, taxe him to be the onely hinderer of the peace and quiet of his country.*[10] Written in 1598 to oppose proposals that England treat for peace with Spain, the *Apologie* is Essex's most extensive defence of England's role in the war. Simon Adams has read the *Apologie* as proof that Essex inherited the mantle of 'political Puritanism'; in complete contrast, Richard Tuck describes the *Apologie* as couched in 'astonishingly secular tones', which 'justified the war in terms of national interest'. Tuck's reading situates Essex's attitudes to foreign policy in the context of the growing popularity of reason of state in the late sixteenth century, itself borne of the search for political stability in war-wracked Europe. In Essex's prose, Tuck sees an exact correlation with the Venetians in their 'unwillingness to make *religion* an overriding interest of the state'.[11]

In fact, *both* Adams's and Tuck's readings of the *Apologie* can be validated. Essex certainly makes the defence of Protestantism a vital reason for the continuation of alliance with the United Provinces. He warns that the restoration of Spanish authority in the Netherlands would reinstate 'popish religion', and probably an inquisition: if abandoned by the English, the dispirited Dutch Calvinists will eventually 'banish Gods true service, to bring in idolatrie... to win the favour of the most tirannical prince in the erth'.[12] But defence of international Protestantism is not the central plank of Essex's overall argument, which is couched in a generalized opposition to Spanish tyranny. The earlier part of the treatise defines Essex's essential vision of the war as a struggle for survival against the tyrannical ambitions of would-be universal monarchs: 'an insolent, cruell, and usurping nation... that aspired to the conquest of my countrey, and was a generall enemie to the libertie of Christendome'.[13] A reader could interpret this definition of Spanish tyranny as inextricably entwined with popery, but a confessionalized reading is not the only possible interpretation: the most 'tirannical prince in the erth' is Philip II, not the pope. Similarly, a letter written by Essex to the privy

---

[10] I use the 1600 printed version of the text, which I have compared with the 1603 version; minor alterations in the spelling and detail which reflect the changing diplomatic situation will be indicated where significant. I am thankful to Hugh Gazzard for sending me his careful study of the manuscript and printed texts of the *Apologie*.

[11] Adams, 'Protestant cause', 118 and *passim*; Tuck, *Philosophy and government*, 107–8.

[12] *Apologie*, sig. C3ʳ.   [13] Ibid., sig. A3ʳ.

council on the eve of the English expedition to Cadiz in June 1596 is stripped of religious language. In grandiose manner (and invoking rather unfortunate historical precedent), the conflict of England and Spain is compared to Athens's losing struggle 'with that ancient usurping Philippe', Philip of Macedon (an analogy that Essex seems to have borrowed from Francis Bacon). The pope's part in international affairs is irrelevant, unmentioned.[14]

To square this circle Hammer has attempted to clarify the foundations of Essex's ideological commitment to the war, describing the earl as an ardent, conventional 'international Protestant', but recognizing that a straightforwardly confessionalized reading of his attitude to foreign policy is inadequate.[15] In fact, Essex *consciously* expressed his opposition to Spain through differing ideas and languages, as he characteristically strained to appeal to as broad a base of opinion as possible. Essex's justifications for war, as Tuck has observed, adopted ideological frameworks and idioms widely used in the 1590s to interpret international politics, including the interest of states, and the search for genuine political stability in a Europe rent by confessional divisions. Essex and his circle also attempted to widen the appeal of his arguments for war to a spectrum of political and confessional viewpoints, pragmatic and ideological, and, crucially, Protestant and Catholic. As will be shown in this chapter and the next, the arguments framed by Essex in support of the war were partly shaped by the pressing desire to respond to polemical attacks on Elizabeth's foreign policy from Hispanophile Catholics. But the consistent foundation of Essex's ideological militarism was a deepening conviction that the tyrannical monarchs of Spain harboured relentless desire for universal monarchy, and threatened the liberty of Christendom.

'FORWARD PROTESTANTISM' TO THE 'COMMON ENTERPRISE OF CHRISTENDOM'

The ideals of the common enterprise of international alliance were maintained by Essex. The earl cut his military teeth on campaigns in Northern France in 1591–2, and in the early 1590s Essex argued that it was in France that the crucial battles with Spain would be fought. Essex enjoyed a soldierly relationship with Henry IV, who addressed him as 'mon cousin' and a comrade-at-arms.[16] Henry and Anthony Bacon's

---

[14] TNA, SP 12/259/12, f. 30ʳ. Bacon draws the same parallel in *Certain observations made upon a libel*: Spedding, *L&L*, I, 182–3.

[15] Hammer, *Polarisation*, 143, 241, 247, 260–1.

[16] For example, LPL MS 656, f. 115ʳ; Hammer, *Polarisation*, 143–7, 322–3, 365–6.

personal acquaintance had less glamorous foundation: Navarre had commuted a criminal sentence passed against Bacon at Montauban in 1586–7, either for sodomy or for debt.[17] Essex and Bacon's relationship with leading Huguenots was also close: the Duke of Bouillon, like Essex in England, played a vital role in French operations against Spain, both as an agitator and a military leader, and was a correspondent of Essex and Bacon, as were a string of other Protestants who served Henry in a diplomatic capacity;[18] these especially included Robert de La Fontaine, and Jean Castol, ministers of the French church in London, who acted as representatives for Henry; and Nicolas de Harlay, seigneur de Sancy, who conducted the negotiations for the Treaty of Greenwich in May 1596.[19] In particular, Castol was a regular correspondent of Anthony Bacon, sending a constant stream of scholarly books, news pamphlets, and manuscripts.[20] English administrators, soldiers, and agents also kept Essex directly informed of affairs in the Low Countries, as Essex cultivated personal contacts with Dutch grandees and diplomats, including Maurice of Nassau, and Noel de Caron, agent of the United Provinces.[21] In December 1594, Essex gave implacable assurance to Maurice that 'there is nothing more connected with the welfare of England than the prosperity of the United Provinces'.[22]

These bonds were fused by a mutual enemy, and a vocabulary of a common religious cause was often invoked. At risk was the fate of 'those of the religion', a phrase usually used by Huguenots and the English to refer to each other and also to the Dutch. Bouillon described the divisions between 'ceux de la religion', fighting for 'l'eglise de dieu', and 'les Catholiques... [qui] nostre ruyne desirent'.[23] Sancy similarly wrote to Essex claiming association through their mutual concern for the protection of 'ceux de la religion' against an 'ennemy commun'.[24] The language of a 'common' Protestant enterprise was similarly maintained in the vocabulary of English soldiers who had campaigned with Leicester. On 1 January 1597, Sir Francis Vere urged that Calais, taken by the Spanish

---

[17] Jardine and Stewart, *Hostage to fortune*, 108–11. In April 1596 Henry admired Bacon's capacity 'en la conducte des affaires publiques': LPL MS 656, f. 330[r].

[18] Bouillon's full title was Henry de la Tour, d'Auvergne, vicômte de Turenne.

[19] *HMC Salisbury*, V, 21, 113, 178; Ungerer, *Spaniard*, I, 422–3; WRO MI 299, f. 81[r]. See Hammer, *Polarisation*, 74, 77, 93–7, 131–2, 365–9.

[20] See LPL MS 652, ff. 12[r]–13[v], 14[r]–18[v], 31[r].

[21] See below, n. 208. Essex sent gifts to the Dutch contingent at Cadiz: *HMC Salisbury*, VI, 353–4. Thomas Bodley, George Gilpin, Sir Robert Sidney, and Sir Francis Vere all wrote to Essex with intelligence from the United Provinces. Their letters are strewn throughout the Cecil manuscripts and Bacon's archive at Lambeth Palace Library.

[22] Tenison, *Elizabethan England*, X, 356.

[23] Cecil MS, 135/183; also see *HMC Salisbury*, XIII, 525.

[24] Cecil MS, 171/102; also see *HMC Salisbury*, V, 20–1, 113.

the previous spring, should be relieved by siege: 'no action can be ... of more advantage to the common cause'.[25] Lord Willoughby of Eresby, who travelled through Central Europe to Italy in late 1595, wrote to Essex to propose a greater alliance of Protestant powers to combat the forces of Spanish Catholicism, 'the common Enemy'. 'Those of the religion upon the ffrontires of Germany ... are in badd estate ... we might imbrace that prince the king of Denmarke, the rich Duke of *Wirtemburgh*.'[26]

The Spanish threat was, of course, widely expressed in public contexts in the 1590s, especially to justify the military burdens placed on Elizabeth's subjects. In one sense, then, Essex's conceptualization of Elizabeth's wars as the defence of Christendom was entirely conventional. The aggressive proclamation of 1591 'Establishing Commissions against Seminary Priests and Jesuits', drafted by Burghley, denounced the 'violence and malice' of the King of Spain, who waged 'a most unjust and dangerous war for all of Christendom'.[27] In the parliament of 1593, which levied an unprecedented triple subsidy, Burghley condemned Philip's hot desire 'to be gretar, yea greater than any Christian prince hath ben'.[28]

But common hostility to Spain over the necessity of the war, couched in thunderous denunciation of Philip's violent ambition, ultimately concealed different visions and ideals behind the ends of England's military engagement. Essex's conceptualization of Philip's relentless thirst for universal monarchy crystallized into the hard-line argument advanced in his *Apologie*: that safety for the English nation could only be achieved once the threat to the 'liberty of Christendom' had been permanently disarmed. The removal of English troops from Northern France in 1595 coincided with Essex's developing belief that the English state could strike that blow itself, by incursive attacks on Philip's fleets and territories, and the establishment of military bases on the Iberian Peninsula.[29] On the eve of the Cadiz voyage in 1596, the earl wrote a famous strategic document to the privy council, impressing the certain success of an offensive military strategy: 'it hathe ben the wisdome of all tymes rather to attempte and doe something in another contrey, then to attende our enemy & be in danger'.[30] The success of the assault on Cadiz itself (achieved with the assistance of Dutch ships and soldiers) was a manifestation of Essex's

[25] Cecil MS, 37/30.   [26] LPL MS 654, f. 218.
[27] Paul L. Hughes and James F. Larkin eds, *Tudor royal proclamations. Vol. 3. The later Tudors (1553–1603)*, (New Haven, CT and London: Yale University Press, 1969), 86.
[28] T.E. Hartley, *Proceedings in the parliaments of Elizabeth I. Vol. 3, 1593–1601* (London: Leicester University Press, 1995), 23–7.
[29] For Essex's strategic writings see L.W. Henry, 'The Earl of Essex as Strategist and Military Organizer (1596–7)', *EHR*, 68/268 (1953), 363–93; Hammer, *Polarisation*, 244–6.
[30] TNA, SP 12/259/12, f. 30ʳ.

desire to establish a 'thorn sticking in [Philip's] foot', a base that would weaken the body as a whole, cut off the financial lifeblood from the New World, and, ultimately, destroy Spanish power.[31]

While Burghley could invoke the tyrannies and oppressions of the war with equally impassioned language, his attitudes were less ideologically motivated. The lord treasurer and Elizabeth—with other privy councillors, including especially Sir Robert Cecil and Lord Buckhurst—were far more defensive, more sensitive to the material cost of war, and the potential social unrest that extended military intervention would entail, concerns that magnified as the crisis in Ireland deepened.

Both Cecils and Elizabeth were, therefore, consistently sensitive to opportunities for the negotiation of peace. These were avenues that Essex jammed with obstacles—chiefly the 'revelation' of intelligence that proved the alleged consistency of Philip's tyrannical designs on England. In 1593 and 1594, plans to open communication with Rudolph II, Holy Roman Emperor, and the Archduke Ernest, Philip's governor of the Southern Netherlands, were derailed when Essex painfully extracted evidence from intelligence and torture to convince a sceptical queen and council of the existence of the assassination plot of her Portuguese physician, Dr Ruy Lopez, in league with a Spanish secretary of state, Cristobal de Moura, and Pedro Enriquez de Acevedo, count of Fuentes and Esteban de Ibarra, Philip's chief ministers in Brussels.[32]

Francis Bacon, now penning political compositions for Essex, wrote a lurid account of the murderous intentions of Lopez and his conspirators, clearly intended for publication, which fiercely alleged Philip's likely complicity in a matter 'against all Christianity and religion... against nature, the law of nations, the law of arms, the civil law, the rules of morality and policy'.[33] This accusation of Philip's tyranny—which breached of all the laws of nature—was never printed; the official pamphlet, commissioned by Burghley, was more conciliatory, exhorting Philip to declare himself innocent of dastardly plots to be performed in his name.[34]

[31] Ibid.
[32] R.B. Wernham, 'Queen Elizabeth I, the Emperor Rudolf II and the Archduke Ernest in 1593–4', in E.I. Kouri and T. Scott eds, *Politics and society in reformation Europe: essays for Sir Geoffrey Elton on his sixty-fifth birthday* (London: Macmillan, 1986), 437–51; Hammer, *Polarization*, 156–63. In 1594 Essex's intelligence also uncovered plots of Edmund Yorke and Richard Williams, English Catholic exiles, to assassinate Elizabeth.
[33] 'A true report of the detestable treason, intended by Dr Roderigo Lopez': Spedding, *L&L*, I, 274–87.
[34] The official published report, probably written by William Waad and Sir Robert Cecil was *A True report of sundry horrible conspiracies of late time detected to have by barbarous murders taken away the life of the Queen's Most Excellent Majesty* (1594).

Essex had, at least, won major political capital from his 'proof' of the guilt of Lopez and his allies, and negotiations with Habsburg rulers were stymied. But the glassy unity of the privy council could ripple under currents of tension. Those who supported Essex's interventionism there-fore still found use for the languages and rhetorical tropes of 'forward Protestantism' of previous decades—of the necessity of wakefulness, vigi-lance, and positive action, and the avoidance of the dangers of 'security' and 'sleep'. Lord Burgh wrote to Essex on 8 October 1595: 'there is nothing which hurteth states more then securitie . . . to be sodaynly sur-prised arguweth want of counsayle, and bringeth inevitable perill'.[35] On 5 February 1596, Anthony Bacon had written to Henry Hawkins, Essex's agent in Venice, of the obstacles that blocked the path of Essex and England's destiny—the perceived reluctance of Elizabeth and William Cecil to embrace aggressive military strategies:

> Gods infinite mercie & providence doe as it were leade us the way to overthrow & breake the werk of the Spanish Tirannie . . . yett wee are rather therby lulled a sleep in a most deep dangerous securitie then encouraged to imbrace & improve such unlooked for & advantageous opportunities.[36]

Above all, as Machiavelli taught, the *opportunity* to act must be seized. By the mid-1590s, it seemed as this *occasione* might have arisen—there were signs that Philip's empire was overstretched and weakening. As Francis Bacon observed, 'the state of Spain . . . having out-compassed itself in embracing too much . . . is not in breif an enemy to be feared by a nation seated, manned, furnished, and pollicied as is England'.[37] Just as Elizabeth had withdrawn English troops from Northern France, reports of Philip's financial crises—including his third and final bankruptcy, declared in November 1596—were gleefully disseminated, with rumours of rumbling discontent with Spanish rule in Portugal and Italy. On 14 March 1597, when peace between Transylvania, the Holy Roman Emperor, and the Turk was rumoured, Hawkins wrote that the Turk must now be encour-aged to engage Spain in naval warfare: 'Most glorious must the Conquest be of so potent an Ennemy, most Ominous the neglecting of suche an Oportunitye'.[38] Essex insisted 'The oportunitie must be watched and it must appeare that this is it which is nowe taken'.[39]

The necessity of taking direct action against Spain was particularly felt by Antonio Pérez, the notorious Spanish exile, who entered Essex's service in November 1593, and whose powerful charisma and intellect had a

---

[35] Cecil MS, 28/81.   [36] LPL MS 655, f. 98ʳ.
[37] *Certain observations made upon a libel*, Spedding, *L&L*, I, 169.
[38] LPL MS 661, f. 62ʳ.   [39] TNA, SP 12/259/12, f. 30ʳ.

formative impact on Essex, the Bacons, and Howard.[40] As the former secretary of state of Castile to Philip II, Pérez boasted unparalleled knowledge of the king's mind and actions. His political insight, now channelled into violent hostility towards Philip, was expressed in a showy epistolary style which had irresistible appeal to Essex and his close circle. Pérez's relationship with the Bacon brothers, especially Anthony, was particularly thick at first, and wreathed in mutual flattery; his admiration for Essex was expressed in a sickly language of fawning adoration. In his letters to Essex, which were scribally circulated among Essex's friends, he described himself as a wandering pilgrim whose travels had taught him to penetrate the secret nature of the minds of princes and their creatures. Essex was Pérez's *panis*, his daily bread, a Christ-like figure, the salvation of England and Christendom as he was the saviour of Pérez.[41]

Pérez was also the most aggressive and unrealistic advocate of a massive offensive war effort against his tyrannical former master, exhorting Europe's rulers to join common forces to crush the Spanish Tiberius. Pérez also denounced Burghley as a hindrance to Essex's more aggressive martial ambitions. In a lumbering allusion to the *Aeneid*, Pérez warned Essex to be wary of hermits bearing poppy-seed potions, whose soporific qualities would blind his eyes and block his ears.[42] England's flourishing military resources and the valour of her soldiers, so feared by the enemy, would be sure to prevail:[43] Essex's destiny was to be the hammer of tyrants— '*Tyrannum, percute Tyrannum*'.[44]

But as strange a figure as Pérez seems to have cut, with his obsessive admiration for Essex, his wild enthusiasm for vigilant militarism was shared by more sober spirits. Essex appears to have commissioned *The practice, proceedings and lawes of armes* (1593), a work dedicated to him on the necessity of military reform by Matthew Sutcliffe, a Cambridge civil lawyer and anti-Puritan theologian. Sutcliffe also prophesized the evils which befall states that are not strongly armed and vigilant: 'our enemies preparatives against us...their pride and malice' and 'neere' practices

[40] Ungerer, *Spaniard*, I, 152; in James's reign Howard framed a series of political conceits '*mala*' and '*bona*' based around excerpts from Essex and Pérez's correspondence: BL, MS Cotton, Titus C VI, ff. 312^r–325^v.

[41] Ungerer, *Spaniard*, I, 322, 337.

[42] Ibid., 327. The reference is to Burghley's self-presentation as a hermit at entertainments at Theobalds.

[43] Ibid., 366–7. This letter was copied and widely circulated; a copy was intercepted en route for Scotland.

[44] Ibid., 443, 458.

require action. 'Why then doe we not awake?. . . . why are we so slowe in taking armes?'[45]

Essex's vision of the necessity of urgent action against Spain was also shared by the most important theorist of international politics in Europe in the late sixteenth century—Alberico Gentili, regius professor of civil Law at Oxford. Gentili's various commentaries on the laws of war appeared in several editions between 1588 and 1598, all dedicated to Essex. They were completely revised in 1598 in *De iure belli libri tres*, Gentili's seminal treatise on the laws of war, now recognized as a weighty forerunner of Grotius' more famous works of the seventeenth century.[46] Essex and Gentili were closely associated, and Gentili more widely connected with the Leicester/ Sidney network and their outlook on international relations. A client of Leicester, Gentili had dedicated his early work, *De legationibus libri tres* (1585), to Sidney. Essex himself was godfather to Gentili's son, and after the earl's death, rumour circulated that Gentili had been implicated in the rising.[47] Furthermore, Essex had actually *read* Gentili's works. *De iure belli* was published in 1598, the year that Essex wrote his *Apologie*: the penultimate line of Essex's treatise, '*Iustissimum iis bellum, quibus necessarium, copia arma, quibus nulla, nisi in armis, spes est*', is a direct quotation from Gentili's treatise [War is most just to those for whom it is necessary; arms are in abundance for those who have no hope except in arms].[48]

Gentili adopted an eclectic methodological approach drawing his analysis from classical texts, history, and scripture, as well as the civil law codes. His writings were also moulded by political context: in the 1590s, they inevitably invoked the war with Spain.[49] The early editions of the commentaries stressed the need for strong defences against invasion, but the resounding message of the revised edition published in 1598 is the common necessity of a more aggressive pan-European strategy against Philip II. And Gentili, like Essex and Pérez, argued with vehemence against the perils of failing to take positive action against a threatening enemy. The whole thrust of his chapter on wars for 'Necessary Defence' is to warn that an aggressive enemy must be assaulted, and without delay, especially

---

[45] Sutcliffe, *Practice, proceedings and lawes of armes*, sig. A2ʳ⁻ᵛ, Cʳ. The dedication implies that it was commissioned by Essex. It was printed by Christopher Barker, the queen's printer, possibly to strengthen enthusiasm for the triple subsidy levied in the 1593 parliament. Sutcliffe had been a fellow of Trinity College Cambridge, when Essex was a student. Also dedicated to Essex was *Matthaei Sutclivii De Catholica, orthodoxa, et vera Christi ecclesia* (1592).

[46] Diego Panizza, *Alberico Gentili, giurista ideologico nell'inghilterra elisabettiana* (Padua: D. Panizza, 1981).

[47] Van der Molen, *Gentili*, 57.

[48] *Apologie*, sig. Eʳ; Gentili, *De iure belli libri tres*, ed. Coleman Phillipson, trans. John C. Rolfe, 2 vols (Oxford: Clarendon Press, 1933), I, 95, II, 59. The first volume is a facsimile of the 1612 printing (the main text is identical to that printed in Hanau, 1598).

[49] Panizza, *Alberico Gentili*.

when he is vulnerable: 'while your enemy is weak, slay him . . . Unless there is something which can resist Spain, Europe will surely fall'.[50]

The epic interpretation of the conflict with Spain as a cataclysmic struggle for liberty shaped apocalyptic interpretations of the war, which fashioned Essex as a Protestant warrior leading the vanguard against the forces of Antichrist. George Gifford, a radical Puritan preacher from Essex, dedicated to the earl his sermon on the Book of Revelation, declaring the war to be a battle against the 'Romish beast', who determined to 'destroy and to roote out al that professeth the holy gopsel of Iesus Christe'.[51] John Norden, in a sermon also dedicated to Essex, called on soldiers to look to the example of Gideon, Barak, Samson, Jephtha, David, and Samuel.[52]

But Gifford's apocalyptic conception of the war was not the vision predominantly articulated by Essex and his close associates. The phrase 'those of the religion' does not prominently feature in Essex's own correspondence, and many of Essex's intimates did not usually describe their allies in terms of a common *Protestant* religious identity. Pérez, a Catholic, of course, could not. But so too Gentili: 'A common cause for fear unites *even those who are most divided*' [emphasis added].[53] Instead, the earl and his circle more usually defined their opposition to Spain as a struggle against the 'terror to all Christendom', who sought to enlarge the boundaries of his already over-mighty dominions, and to repress the liberty of 'free nations'.

ENGLAND AND THE CONCEPT
OF CHRISTENDOM

When Lord Willoughby described the peril to the 'common weale of the three pryncypall Contryes England, Fraunce & Netherland' in 1596, he heroically glossed over the vital rupture in the shared identity of the allies: Henry IV's conversion to Catholicism in July 1593.[54] Though denounced by Elizabeth, the act secured Henry's throne, removing the League's justification for resistance to a heretical monarch. Although relations between England and France grew strained over Elizabeth's

---

[50] Gentili, *De iure belli*, I, 104–5, II, 61–6 at 65.

[51] Gifford, *Sermons upon the whole booke of the Revelation* (1599), sig. A3ʳ, [A5ᵛ]. Gifford also dedicated to Essex *A treatise of true fortitude* (1594), and *Fifteene sermons, vpon the Song of Salomon* (1598).

[52] John Norden, *The mirror of honor: wherein everie professor of armes . . . may see the necessitie of the feare and service of God . . .* (1597), sig. A3ᵛ. Norden received some patronage from Essex: sig. A2ᵛ.

[53] Gentili, *De iure belli*, I, 104–5, II, 65.   [54] BL, Egerton MS 1943, f. 79ʳ.

failure to relieve the siege of Calais in the spring of 1596, Elizabeth and Henry signed the Triple Alliance with the United Provinces, renewing their commitment to mutual assistance against Spain.[55]

Henry's conversion, though, necessitated the redefinition of the common cause. The idea of Christendom was a supremely useful conceptual tool to plaster over confessional differences, defining the alliance as a mutual defence against the secular tyranny of Philip II. Even before his conversion, propaganda for Henry IV, which reached out to a broad, a-confessional audience, denounced Spain's intervention in the French succession crisis as a foreign invasion, a manifestation of his 'high attempt to become Monarch of the World'.[56] English readers were familiarized with the language of Philip's ambitions of universal monarchy by the swathes of translated French propaganda that poured off the English presses in the late 1580s and early 1590s.[57]

In post-Reformation Europe, the concept of the divided body of Christendom was also invoked by irenic writers, who denounced this legacy of schism, which gave strength and purpose to the encroaching Turk.[58] The legendary soldier François de la Noue, in his *Politicke and militarie discourses*, rallied Christian princes to 'quench' 'warres ... against their Subjects', so that 'Christian Princes well united' might 'expulse the Turkes out of Europe'.[59] That most famous irenicist, James VI of Scotland, wrote a poem in praise of the Spanish defeat of the Turks at Lepanto, and articulated several times a desire to orchestrate a peace between the Christian powers and a league against the Turk.[60]

The divisions of Christendom also shaped developments in writing about the state in late sixteenth-century Europe. Tacitism of the 'black' kind defined by Toffanin—which advocated the political stability provided by the enhanced power and authority of the ruler/state over more participatory forms of government—derived from a deep sense of crisis engulfing Europe. In the 1590s, Justus Lipsius revoked his former hostility to Habsburg tyranny in the Netherlands, invoking the threat of the Turk to call for a new imperial rule, which aspired to the power of the autocratic Roman Empire. Of all European states, Lipsius argued, only

---

[55] The Treaty of Greenwich was signed on 14 May 1596, and was expanded to include the United Provinces on 21 October.

[56] [Vasco Figueiro], H. O. trans. *The Spaniards monarchie, and leaguer's Olygarchie ...* (1592), sig. Diiiᵛ.

[57] Parmelee, *Good newes from Fraunce*.

[58] See Chapter 3.

[59] E[dward] A[ggas] trans., *The politicke and militarie discourses of the Lord de La Nouue* (1588), 245 and *passim*.

[60] Franklin Le Van Baumer, 'The conception of Christendom in Renaissance England', *Journal of the History of Ideas*, 6 (1945), 140.

Spain could approach that *grandezza*. Lipsius also rejected the reverence for the Roman Republic and the idealization of virtuous, active citizenship prized by the advocates of Ciceronean and Machiavellian humanism. He argued that the foundation of stability and security in the modern world was grounded in the fiscal and military authority of the impersonal state, rather than the virtue of its individual citizens.[61]

Despite significant interest in Lipsius in England among Essex's circle and their appropriation of the vocabulary of 'state' when referring to the wider realm or country, the *topos* of Christendom and the encroaching Turk was usually invoked in opposite senses by those who advocated Essex's vision of the war.[62] First, the vulnerability of Christendom was the *fault* of the Spanish, who sought by tyrannical means to outstrip the Roman Empire. Spain's belligerence drained the resources of Christian princes, which might be employed against the infidel: the author of an anonymous treatise warning against English participation in the Franco-Spanish peace of 1598 wailed 'the Spaniarde are the firebrands of contention and warres of Christendome; while they neglecting the common enemie do seeke to subdue true Christians, the Turke triumveth and prevaileth'.[63] Henry Hawkins, Essex's agent in Venice, suggested to Essex that he might publish a relation of the progress of the Turk 'especially inveyaling agaynst the Ambition of Spayne, who hathe spent so many millions in vexing injustly Christian Princes, which should have been imployed agaynst the common Ennemy of Christendom'.[64]

Essex and his associates also lauded England's capacity to play a major role in the defence of Christendom through the strenuous virtue of the English subject and the puissance of the English state. This reflected that sharply developing sense of 'nationhood' that Richard Helgerson has identified as characteristic of political culture after the Armada—but also the more conventional classical–humanist correlation of the active citizenship of the virtuous subject with the health of the realm.[65] Sutcliffe recalled England's glorious military past, especially the reigns of Edward III,

[61] Giuseppe Toffanin, *Machiavelli e il 'tacitismo'* (Padua: A. Drahgi, 1921); Tuck, *Philosophy and government*, 62.

[62] See Justus Lipsius, trans. William Jones, *Sixe bookes of politickes, or civil doctrine...* (1594); Jones dedicated to Essex his translation of Giovanni Battista Nennio's treatise *Nennio, or A Treatise of Nobility* (1595). Castol sent Anthony Bacon a Lipsian treatise in September 1595: LPL MS 652, f. 31ʳ.

[63] ITL, Petyt MS 538/46, f. 40ʳ.

[64] LPL MS 660, f. 251ʳ, 1 November 1596.

[65] Richard Helgerson, *Forms of nationhood: the Elizabethan writing of England* (Chicago and London: University of Chicago Press, 1992).

Henry V, and Henry VIII, 'so victorious in France', 'men of heroical spirits'.[66] These sentiments were enshrined in Essex's *Apologie*: the earl exhorted those who were tempted by peace to remember the 'great conquests in France' achieved by the 'ancient virtue' of 'our nation in those former gallant ages when our countrey was farre poorer then it is now'. In the event of accommodation with Spain, England would 'generally grow unwarlick; in love with the name, and bewitched with the delight of peace'.[67]

This emphasis on the revitalization of strenuous virtue was accompanied by a sense of community between all nations and peoples threatened by Philip. At his least realistic, Pérez harboured unthinkable schemes for grand leagues of all anti-Spanish powers, including even the Muslim forces of the Ottoman Turk and the Spanish Moors.[68] But in English denunciations of Philip's tyranny, identification with 'those of the religion' was often expanded to include a sense (albeit rhetorical) of concern for the fate of the Catholic peoples of other parts of Philip's sprawling empire. Francis Bacon's *Discourse in the praise of his sovereign* (*c.*1592) exemplifies the expression:

> The states of Italy, they be like little quillets of freehold lying intermixed in a great honor or lordship. France is turned upside down... Portugal usurped by no other title than strength and vicinity. The Low Countries warred upon... to plant there an absolute and martial government, and to suppress their liberties. The like at this day attempted upon Aragon.[69]

The anonymous tract, *A treatise paraenetical... Wherein is shewed by good and euident reasons... the right way & true meanes to resist the violence of the Castilian king... and to ruinate his puissance* (1598), exhorts the monarchs of France and England to attack Philip directly, 'to restore unto libertie so many peoples and nations, whoe do crie and call for aide under the yoke and burthen of this tyrannie'. In turn this would entail security for the aggressors, delivering 'your owne subiects from the armes of the enemie'. The likely author of the *Treatise paraenetical* is no Protestant: purporting to be the translation of a treatise by an Aragonese subject of Philip II, the author is almost certainly Pérez.[70] The printed English version is strongly associated with Essex's circle: dedicated to Essex's close friend,

---

[66] Sutcliffe, *Practice, proceeding, and lawes of arms*, sig. B3^r.   [67] *Apologie*, sig. E1^r.

[68] Ungerer, *Spaniard*, I, 130–1, 458–9.   [69] Spedding, *L&L*, I, 136–7.

[70] *Treatise paraenetical*, 56. The treatise was published in France in 1597 (whence Pérez had travelled on leaving England), as the *Traicté paraenetique*, addressed to Henry IV as a warning against making peace with Spain: 'I. D. Dralymont', the purported author, is a pseudonym. A list of books owned by Robert Cecil attributes the treatise unequivocally to Pérez: Tenison, *Elizabethan England*, X, 408. On 12 June 1598, Atye sent 'the enclosed' to William Downhall, Essex's gentleman of the horse, to be shown to Mountjoy; 'of the motion for Mr F. Grevile, you may adde of yourself': Cecil MS 61/76.

Fulke Greville, Essex is described as a 'Prince of the bloud Royall of England... adorned with many morall vertues'. The treatise was probably translated by Arthur Atye, Essex's client, who performed similar important works of Spanish translation for Essex.[71]

Much capital was made in England of the plight of Dom Antonio, the dispossessed 'king' of Portugal and claimant of the Portuguese throne, whose fate was mourned as a particularly poignant example of Philip's injustice and cruelty. After the failure of the Lisbon voyage of 1589 (in which Essex had clandestinely participated), Dom Antonio strenuously massaged Essex's enthusiasm for his cause.[72] Although he never pressed for a similar voyage to restore the dispossessed king, by 1596 Essex's cherished military strategies argued for the feasibility of establishing a base at Lisbon. Most importantly, supporters of interventionist strikes against Spain had to convince that the failure of 1589 would not be repeated. Matthew Sutcliffe berated those who 'doe great wrong to our Generals in the Portugall expedition, when they impute the fault to them', when 'such slender provision' was the cause of the voyage's failure.[73] An anonymous manuscript treatise written in 1595, bound up with a collection of tracts relating to Essex and to foreign policy, agrees that faults of provision and command would be easily rectified in the future, and argues strongly for the strategic desirability of a 'Second Jorneye into Portinggall' and the honour that would accrue to 'herr Majestie to restore an oppressed King to his Kingdome'.[74]

The Portuguese usurpation had particular menace because it sounded a sinister warning about the sincerity of Spanish designs on the English throne, and the likelihood that Philip II would press his own hereditary claim or that of his daughter, the infanta. The author of the *Treatise paraenetical* bluntly asks: 'Because having added unto his Empire the Monarchy of Portugall, who can be able to resist him?'[75] More aggressive warnings are sounded in an English translation of a mysterious treatise, *The Anatomie of Spayne,* written in 1598 and translated the following year, which describes the historical foundations of the Spanish monarch's title to govern all its dominions. The Spanish empire is founded on tyranny, murder, usurpation, and the forceful assertion of false hereditary claims: the titles claimed by the Spanish Habsburgs are founded in 'smal right', 'false pedigrees', and are accompanied by a catalogue of 'oppressions, wronges, agreavances, ynjuries, usurpations, and Tyranies, by which the petite Countie of Castil, hath risen to so greate a monarchie'. Philip II and

[71] *Treatise paraenetical*, sig.*2, [29].   [72] *HMC Salisbury,* V, 348.
[73] Sutcliffe, *Practice, proceedings*, sig. B3ᵛ.
[74] Huntington Library, MS Ellesmere, 1612, ff. 15ʳ–22ᵛ.
[75] *Treatise paraenetical*, 48.

his ancestral tyrants are also guilty of the worst kinds of moral and spiritual depravity: 'yntrusion, perjurye, blood, yncest, adulterie, bastardie, sacriledge, and homicide', as well as the abrogation of divine law.[76] The annexation of Portugal in particular is a 'great oppression which against al right and humanitie he committed in the usurpation of the kingdome': Habsburg designs on the English throne are luridly signalled.[77]

Although the authorship of text and translation is unclear, Ungerer has argued persuasively for the authorship of José Texeira, the chaplain of Dom Antonio, and more importantly, that the treatise was translated by Atye, Essex's client.[78] The *Anatomie* also vigorously endorses Essex's insistence on the necessity of aggressive war: praise is lavished on that 'most magnanimous and puissante Lorde Roberte Erle of Essex', and the English more generally, who of all of Spain's enemies 'deserve to carie awaye the honor, for havinge ben the verie first and onlie invadors of the Spanish monarchie', in the voyages to Portugal and Cadiz.[79]

The desire to stir up grand alliances of Christian princes also appears to explain Essex's and his circle's particular interest in intelligence from Italy and in forging contacts with Italian states.[80] In terms of practical intelligence, Essex desperately needed agents in Spain who could give accurate information about Iberian military and naval preparations. Essex's intelligence, though, seems to have provided little that was useful beyond reports that the Spanish were planning a further attack.[81] In contrast, from the evidence of Anthony Bacon's surviving archive, the earl was extraordinarily well furnished with intelligence from the Italian peninsula, from established agents and reports by gentlemen travellers. In particular Hawkins, Essex's agent in Venice, sent home dense swathes of letters and *gazetti*, which gave extraordinarily detailed relations of Italian politics; Hawkins and another agent, Mons. le Douz, were also instructed to write 'relations' of all the Italian states.[82]

---

[76] *The Anatomie of Spayne, Composed in the Castilian tonge by Don Biud de Haro. Anno, 1598. Translated into Englishe by Harye Bedwod, gent. England, 1599*, Yale Beineicke Library, Osborn MS 20, 2–4, 114. 'Don Biud de Haro' and Harye Bedwod are pseudonyms. I am extremely grateful to Professor Hammer for reminding me of the significance of this text and for allowing me to use his copy.

[77] *Anatomie of Spayne*, 84.

[78] Ungerer, *Spaniard*, II, 275–6. For Atye see above, 80 n. 70; below, 88.

[79] *Anatomie of Spayne*, 96–7.

[80] For the structure and personnel of Essex's intelligence gathering, see Hammer *Polarisation*, Chapter V.

[81] Pauline Croft '"The state of the world is marvellously changed": England, Spain and Europe, 1558–1604', in Doran and Richardson, *Tudor England and its neighbours*, 196.

[82] Hawkins's relation of Ferrara survives: LPL MS 660, ff. 240^r–248^r; Hammer, 'Essex and Europe'. It should be noted that almost none of the intelligence gathered from Central and Eastern Europe still survives: Hammer, *Polarisation*, 183.

There was a wider purpose to this cultivation of Italian intelligence. Philip II's complex diplomatic hegemony over those Italian states that were not formally part of his domain was crucial to the stability of his empire. The 'Spanish Road', connecting Philip's southern and northern European possessions, ran through Italy; the enormous loans that fuelled his military operations were raised through Genoese creditors.[83] Anthony Standen, the Catholic double agent and client of Essex, wrote of Florence, 'I thinke after France and the Low Cuntreys there is noe place amongst Christians where her Majesty had more need of an instrument' to topple 'the Spanish insolencie'.[84] And Hawkins and Thomas Chaloner, Essex's agent in Florence in 1596–7, kept feeding the seductive evidence Essex wanted to hear, of Italian hispanophobia which could be turned to English advantage. 'The joy is great heer, of the Spanishe going backewarde... in the Lowe Cuntries... the expectation of Englandes forces, is hooped heer to revenge the breache of payment to the Italians'.[85] Hawkins, who made heroic efforts to have Essex's version of the Cadiz voyage published, wrote of popular opinion in Venice that 'these... deadly blowes to King Philip is thought will altogether make an ende of him & free Christendom'.[86]

Hawkins had also insisted that Essex must cultivate the friendship of the 'great Duke of Tuskan who is like to swaye most th'estate of Italy & other places', a piece of advice taken seriously by the earl, who dispatched Henry Cuffe to Tuscany in 1597–8, a mission which at least confirmed Grand Duke Ferdinand I's latent hispanophobia.[87] Essex's contacts in Italy made a particular impression on the agents of James VI, also seeking Italian support for his title to the English throne. James's emissary, Sir Michael Balfour, reported that Ferdinand regarded Essex as a future kingmaker, who 'may advance or hinder ony man' with a claim, and must be 'dealt with & large offers maid to him'.[88]

This desire for closer alliance with Catholic Italy, or compassion for Philip's oppressed Portuguese subjects, also demonstrates the irenicism of Essex's international politics. Hammer has brought attention to the description of Italy as 'le jardin de la Chrestienté' in a private letter of

[83] Geoffrey Parker, *The grand strategy of Philip II* (New Haven, CT and London: Yale University Press, 1998), 81–5.

[84] LPL MS 656, f. 81ʳ.

[85] LPL MS 661, f. 170ʳ, 25 March 1597; See similar comments by Hawkins: LPL MS 660, f. 260ʳ; MS 658, f. 65ʳ.

[86] LPL MS 656, f. 239ʳ.

[87] LPL MS 660, f. 260ᵛ, MS 658, f. 65ʳ; Cecil MS 55/106, 140/70, 58/91.

[88] J.D. Mackie, *Negotiations between King James VI and Ferdinand I, Grand Duke of Tuscany* (London: St Andrews University Publications, 1927), 7–8.

travel instruction written to le Douz: as he notes, an 'extraordinary' phrase for a Protestant Englishman to use.[89] Hammer attributes the letter to Essex; but the list of instructions is in the hand of Anthony Bacon's amanuensis, and is not endorsed as by the earl; it is just as likely that the term is Bacon's. But whoever wrote or dictated the phrase, its use by a Protestant is only comprehensible if the author held similarly modish views on the historical legitimacy of the Catholic Church to those of Richard Hooker.

Unsurprisingly, then, this flirtation with Catholic states raised some criticism from those who supported the general thrust of Essex's martial strategies. The author of the tract advocating a 'Second Jorneye into Portinggall' admits that many worry about supporting the restoration of Dom Antonio 'in regard of his Religion'. Will 'he that sheweth himself a papist' 'brooke the Gospell' when restored to the Portuguese throne, or tolerate freedom of Protestant worship? The author suggests, rather desperately, that recent reaction to the dispersal of Protestant bibles promises that the Portuguese are ripe for conversion.[90] Essex's desire to cultivate political alliances with Catholic powers in Italy also troubled Willoughby. From Venice he wrote 'the rest of Italy [are] generally enemies to our profession and nation except *Florence* and this state who rather for feare of Spaines risinge, than care of our falling... stands newtrally affected'. Far more useful and sensible would be an alliance with Protestant princes in Germany 'somewhat nearer to England, knowing Italy to farr of for much good or much hurte'.[91]

WAR AND 'THE CATHOLICS OF CHRISTENDOME'

The denunciation of Philip II as a tyrant was hardly new in the 1590s. The language of condemnation, though, was, as we have seen, couched in broader secular terms: Philip's oppression of Protestants in the Low Countries remained just one proof of his desire for universal domination, while his ambition was more commonly cited as evidence of his irreligion, rather than his ardent Catholicism. The *Treatise paraenetical* even warns of the tendency of Castilians to 'turne altogether Turke and Infidell'.[92] In anti-Spanish polemic, the notion that the papal Antichrist manipulated

---

[89] Hammer, 'Essex and Europe', 380–1: LPL MS 656, f. 186; the endorsement is 'Des instructions pour Monsieur le Douz'. The endorsement of instructions by Essex or in his name would usually specify that they were by the earl.

[90] Huntington Library, MS Ellesmere, 1612, f. 25[r–v].

[91] LPL MS 654, f. 218.   [92] *Treatise paraenetical*, 24.

the puppet King of Spain was reversed.[93] As Francis Bacon warned, 'the Church of Rome, that pretended apostolic see is become but a donative cell of the King of Spain; the Vicar of Christ is become the King of Spain's chaplain'.[94]

Also driving their desire to describe the war with Spain as an assault on the secular tyranny of Philip was the concern of Essex's circle to respond to hostile denunciation of Elizabeth's foreign policy – explosively posed in the printed tracts of Hispanophile English priests – and to win a polemical battle for the loyalty of Elizabethan Catholics.

As Hammer has revealed, Anthony Standen, the Catholic spy whose return to England Bacon and Essex coordinated in 1593, urged Essex to support the cause of toleration: it would 'bynd unto hym all the catholiques of Christendom' if he were to 'enter substantially into the matters of toleration for the catholiques at home'.[95] As will be discussed in Chapter 3, Essex saw substantial merit in Standen's mandate, seeing Catholics as a vital source of information about foreign affairs.[96] By defining the war with Spain as a secular assault on an irreligious tyrant—rather than a confessionalized conflict—essential ideological common ground could be created with 'loyalist' Catholics, who in turn could prove their allegiance to the queen by reviling Spain.

But the circle of the Jesuit Robert Parsons had also appropriated the extremely useful *topos* of the divided body of Christendom and the menace of the Turk to mischievously critique the late Elizabethan state. A cluster of Hispanophile treatises printed in the early 1590s ferociously denounced the Elizabethan regime, reserving particular venom for English foreign policy.[97] The immediate spur for the publication of these tracts was the 1591 proclamation which correlated the tyrannical foreign policy of Philip II with the seditious practices of seminary priests and Jesuits, who attempted to divert the allegiance of Elizabeth's true subjects.[98] From

---

[93] Julian Lock, 'How many Tercios has the pope? The Spanish war and the sublimination of Elizabethan anti-popery', *History*, 81/262 (1996), 197–214; *Treatise paraenetical*, 90–2.

[94] Bacon, '*Discourse in praise of his sovereign*': Spedding, *L&L*, I, 136–7.

[95] LPL MS 648, f. 139ᵛ; Hammer, 'Return of Anthony Standen'.

[96] Hammer, *Polarisation*, 173–81.

[97] Victor Houliston, *Catholic resistance in Elizabethan England. Robert Persons's Jesuit polemic, 1580–1610* (Aldershot: Ashgate, 2007), 47–70; Peter Milward, *Religious controversies of the Elizabethan age: a survey of printed sources* (Lincoln, NE: University of Nebraska Press, 1977), 111–14; Thomas H. Clancy, *Papist pamphleteers: the Allen-Persons party and the political thought of the Counter-Reformation in England, 1572–1615* (Chicago, IL: Loyola University Press, 1964), 14–43.

[98] Adams, 'Favourites and factions', 258; Victor Houliston, 'The Lord Treasurer and the Jesuit: Robert Persons's Satirical *Responsio* to the 1591 Proclamation', *Sixteenth Century Journal*, 32/2 (2001), 383–401.

the pen of Robert Parsons's closest collaborator, Richard Verstegan, appeared *A Declaration of the true causes of the great troubles, presupposed to be intended against the realm of England* (1592), which resurrected the polemical strategy of laying the blame for England's troubles on the Machiavellian counsel of that 'sly Sicophant' William Cecil, deemed responsible for the proclamation. Through Cecil's domination, it is argued, Elizabeth has spurned the friendship of Philip II, fomented rebellion in the Netherlands, and forced the illegitimate attempt to put Dom Antonio on the throne of Portugal: it is Elizabeth's government, not Philip II's, that terrorizes the 'repose of Christendome'.[99] Similar arguments are fired in Verstegan's *Advertisement written to a Secretarie of my L. Treasurers of Ingland, by an Inglishe Intelligencer as he passed through Germanie towards Italie* ... (1592), an English summary of a longer Latin tract by Parsons himself, while Parsons's *Newes from Spayne, and Holland* (1593) makes particularly heavy weather of Elizabeth's ungodly and 'open dealing with the Turke the publique enemye of al christian profession'.[100]

These libels elicited the question of response, a question quickly answered by the combined efforts of the Bacon brothers. Francis is the assumed author of the known direct reply to Verstegan's *Declaration, Certain observations made upon a libel punished this present year* (1592), a tract that yokes a defence of the policies of the regime to an apology for Burghley's character.[101] Francis, waxing ancient at 31, was still angling for the patronage of his uncle, and the tract was probably written at Burghley's behest.[102] But Anthony as well as Francis kept closely abreast of the propaganda of Catholic exiles, and *Certaine observations* draws on the researches of both brothers.[103] Before Standen returned from exile in 1593, Anthony copied choice excerpts from his intelligence, especially relating Parsons's connections with the Spanish court.[104] In November 1592, Edward Jones sent to Anthony Bacon a 'seditious vile booke' to read and send back with all secrecy, meaning Verstegan's *Advertisement*.[105] The pens and minds of the Bacons were also

---

[99] [Verstegan], *Declaration*, 8–9, 22, and *passim*.

[100] [Parsons] *Newes from Spayne and Holland... Written by a Gentleman travelour bourne in the low countries, and brought up from a child in Ingland...* (Antwerp, 1593) 16ʳ–23ᵛ.

[101] Spedding, *L& L*, I, 143–208. The attribution is made certain by a book list of le Douz owned by Anthony Bacon: as well as 'Observacions upon a libel published in ye yeare 1592', are other tracts by the Bacons: LPL MS 656, f. 184ʳ⁻ᵛ.

[102] 'Letter to Lord Burghley', in Vickers, *Francis Bacon*, 20.

[103] Jardine and Stewart argue that we must see many of these productions as jointly authored: *Hostage to fortune*, 132.

[104] See drafts of Standen's letters in Bacon's papers, condensed into a series of extracts: LPL MS 648, ff. 268ʳ–278ʳ.

[105] LPL MS 648, f. 305ʳ.

sharpened by the reprisal in the 'Burghley's Commonwealth' tracts of the slander of their father Nicholas Bacon, also grotesquely caricatured as a Machiavel.[106]

Bacon's tract remained unpublished, but Burghley may have sponsored a printed response. Lewis Lewkenor's *Discourse of the usage of English fugitives, by the Spaniard* and a revised version, *The estate of the English fugitives under the king of Spaine* were published anonymously in four editions in 1595 and 1596; like Bacon's *Certain observations made upon a libel*, Lewkenor defends Elizabeth's regime while warning Hispanophile Catholics about Philip's tyranny. The tracts are presented as the narrative of a Catholic Englishman who defines his loyalty to Elizabeth and his patriotism through hostility to Spain, a 'loyalist' Catholic response to pro-Spanish, 'anti-commonwealth' tracts.[107]

But soon after the composition of *Certain observations made upon a libel*, both Bacons were moving far more closely in Essex's orbit.[108] In the mid-1590s they conjoined their scholarship, knowledge of European politics, and their understanding of the polemical strategies of the Parsons circle to very similar effect—but an effect that was intended to strengthen *Essex's* public association with Catholic loyalism, as well as justifying the earl's vision of the war. When commonplacing Standen's intelligence reports Anthony Bacon noted his remark that 'all the Catholiques of Christendome' attributed the 'rigor now used in England' to the lord treasurer, and vilified him as an 'open declared & professed enemie to their faythe & religion'.[109] Here, Bacon observed, opened a space for Essex to present himself as the focus for the political loyalty of *Hispanophobic* English Catholics, who felt themselves maligned or persecuted by Burghley.

It was almost certainly under the auspices of Essex that the London edition of Antonio Pérez's memoirs, the *Pedaços de Historia ô Relaciones*, was printed under the pseudonym 'Raphael Peregrino' in November or December 1594, as part of a deliberate strategy to strengthen hostility to Philip II.[110] The *Relaciones* was one of the most famous contributions to the 'black legend' of Spanish tyranny: it accused Philip of making Pérez a scapegoat for the murder of Juan de Escobedo, and it contained Pérez's account of the revolt of the Aragonese in 1591–2 in which he

---

[106] [Verstegan], *Declaration*, 9–10. In *Certain observations made upon a libel* Sir Nicholas Bacon is praised as 'a man plain, direct, without all fineness or doubleness': Spedding, *L&L*, I, 202–3.
[107] For Lewkenor's connections to Burghley see Houliston, *Catholic resistance*, 56–7.
[108] In particular, Anthony appears to have become convinced of Burghley's ingratitude for his intelligence very soon after his return from the continent early in 1592: LPL MS 659, f. 25ʳ⁻ᵛ.
[109] LPL MS 648, f. 140ᵛ.   [110] Ungerer, *Spaniard*, II, 249–50.

had played an incendiary role. Pérez circulated copies of his treatise amongst Essex's close associates: Henry Wotton, Lord Mountjoy, the earl of Southampton.[111] Essex's own travel instructions to Robert Naunton advised him to learn Spanish, 'to understande Raphael Peregrinos booke aswell as Bartas did Englishe to understande Sir Philip Sydneys *Arcadia*'.[112] But the printed version of the Spanish text was intended as anti-Habsburg propaganda on the continent; copies were sent abroad for dissemination in the Spanish Netherlands.[113]

Anthony Bacon also discerned the propaganda value of an English version of the *Relaciones*. He commissioned from Arthur Atye a translation intended for print publication, which was completed and sent back in March 1595 to Bacon to edit.[114] The preface to the translation, possibly but not necessarily by Atye, demonstrates that the circulation of a vernacular version of the *Relaciones* was particularly meant to persuade English Catholics of the secular tyranny of Philip II: 'Have we any at home or abroade that discontenting them selves with their owne Prince and Countryes estate, relye their hopes upon this kinge of Spayne?' The preface flags the appalling treatment of Pérez and his own subjects as a dire warning to those English Catholics who might be considering transferring their allegiance to Philip, and who would place false trust in the Spanish king's character. Then follows Pérez's fawning dedication to Essex, whom he exalts as a man of extraordinary qualities, who has 'wrought admiration and envye in nature, to see herselfe overcome by her owne creature'.[115] Through preface and dedication, then, the reader is persuaded to connect a patriotic message aimed at English Catholics with the particular virtues of the earl of Essex.

The preface to Atye's unpublished translation also calls upon the reader to 'enlarge' upon the 'examples of this booke', to explore the tyranny of Philip 'with lyke examples of his dealinge in the Low Countryes, in Portingall' and other places'.[116] This challenge was met in Essex and his associates' most extended response to Parsons's attack on Elizabeth's wars, the anonymous treatise *The state of Christendom*. Written at some point in 1594–5, the treatise was probably a group production by members of the earl's circle, coordinated by Anthony Bacon. Whether or not the treatise, like the translation of the *Relaciones*, was intended for print publication cannot be known for certain, but it

---

[111] Ungerer, *Spaniard*, II, 254–5.
[112] From Hammer's transcription, 'Essex and Europe', 378.
[113] Ungerer, *Spaniard*, II, 254–5.
[114] LPL MS 653, f. 76ʳ. The manuscript of the translation is Bod, Eng. Hist. MS C 239; there is a note to printer at the end, f. 108ʳ.
[115] Ibid., f. 4ᵛ.
[116] Ibid.

received significant scribal publication for a text of its length. As will be shown, it was the counter-response to Essex's engagement in Catholic politics—the dedication of *A conference about the next succession to the crown of Ingland* to the earl—that stopped Bacon's plans to publish the English version of the *Relaciones*; possibly *The state of Christendom* as well.[117]

Through a densely layered and sometimes contradictory set of commentaries on the contemporary state of Europe, *The state of Christendom* is an apology for the policies of Elizabeth's government as viewed through the lens of Essex's political priorities. Among a bewildering range of other political questions, the treatise examines the origins of the Spanish empire, the rise and assassination of the duke of Guise, the condition of the United Provinces, and especially England's role in the wars of Christendom. The Supplement to the treatise, a lengthy exegesis of the *Relaciones*, forms an extended exploration of the tyranny of Philip II.

But the immediate thrust of *The state of Christendom* is the rebuttal of Catholic libels against the Elizabethan regime, as the author(s) apes the literary strategies used in the 'Burghley's Commonwealth' tracts to obfuscate authorial identity. Although the argument of the main treatise and Supplement is antipapal and broadly Protestant, the narrative frame is clearly borrowed from Verstegan's *Advertisement* (copied by Anthony in 1592), presenting the substance of the treatise as an exchange between a loyalist 'exile' of 'conscience' and an English traveller from Italy. The traveller demands that the exile answer the catalogue of attacks launched on the Elizabethan regime by Catholic polemicists, particularly those that vilify English foreign policy. Why has he heard 'our Sovereign in my poor opinion wrongfully blamed for aiding both the *French* and *Flemish* Nations'? Why has Elizabeth been slandered as a friend of the Turk, and excoriated for her succour of Dom Antonio? The 'narrator' then answers point by point all the allegations of recent Catholic polemic; with the notable exception that no attempt is made to counter the vicious slander of Burghley's character.[118]

As in *Certain observations made upon a libel*, the narrator argues that it is Philip, not Elizabeth, who is a monstrous, secular tyrant, the 'common and only perturber of Christian peace and tranquillity', expanding his

[117] *The state of Christendom. Or, a most exact and curious discovery of many secret passages, and hidden mysteries of the time* (1657). Published in 1657, the treatise was originally attributed to Henry Wotton, Essex's secretary, but Wotton's sole authorship is unlikely; the number of known manuscripts copies stands at six; see Alexandra Gajda, '*The State of Christendom*: history, political thought and the Essex circle', *Historical Research*, 81/213 (2008), 423–46.

[118] England is 'plentiful of warlike Captains, and rather over-burthened, then not thoroughly furnished with sufficient Counsellors', an Essexian jibe at Cecilian pen-pushing, *State of Christendom*, 85. Otherwise there is no mention of any living statesmen, as anonymity is sought.

dominions to exceed the size and strength of the Roman Empire.[119] 'No wars of what nature soever, can be held unjust and unlawful, that shall be enterprised and exercised against him'.[120] Not only does *The state of Christendom* refute Catholic polemic by reasserting the tyranny of Philip: it also endorses the continuation of an interventionist English foreign policy that is distinctively Essexian. But England's intervention in the war is also praised in terms of the relative strengths of the English and Spanish states. Elizabeth 'hath far better ability then any other Christian Prince to weaken his power . . . in truth neither is his power greatly to be feared, nor his wealth far exceeding her Majesties and other Princes substance'. Philip is overstretched militarily, his New World treasure sapped by creditors; history and providence demonstrate that imperial power is unsustainable in perpetuity, and must pass from nation to nation.[121]

In contrast, a rather more militaristic destiny is pressed on Elizabeth than the queen desired: *if* Elizabeth had chosen to send greater forces to the Low Countries, 'it lay in her power long sithence to have overthrown him'.[122] In particular, the Portuguese voyage of 1589 is rued as a lost opportunity: it is compared to the near success of Hannibal's attack on Rome, which failed despite Hannibal's great gifts as a general, through 'secret enemies at home' (a reluctant council?), and the neglect of 'many occasions of good fortune'.[123]

The treatise also endorses Essex's vision of a great, pan-European alliance of Christian powers, Catholic and Reformed: between England, France, the Italian Princes, the United Provinces and Portugal (with Dom Antonio restored), which might restore balance to Christendom and unite against the 'common enemy', the Turk.[124] Indeed, Philip's justification of war in the name of religion is likened to the 'feigned and hypocritical zeal of Religion' used by the Roman emperors, oiling their schemes to be 'Monarchs of the universal world'.[125]

This definition of the war as entirely a secular struggle for the liberty of Christendom had a more rigorous intellectual foundation—and more substantial dissemination—in the writings of Gentili. Gentili had arrived in England in 1580, fleeing the Inquisition; between 1582 and 1585, he had written a tract proving the identification of the pope as Antichrist.[126] But he did not bring a similarly apocalyptic lens to the laws of war. The public proclamation of religious motives by aggressors is always 'the

---

[119] *State of Christendom*, 64–5.   [120] Ibid., Supplement, 32.
[121] Ibid., 7–10, 111–12.   [122] Ibid., 110.
[123] Ibid., 69; also see 60–1, 93–4. Compare with similar remarks by Matthew Sutcliffe, above, 75–6.
[124] Ibid., 256.   [125] Ibid., 14.   [126] Panizza, *Alberico Gentili*, 19–27.

invention of the most greedy of men and to be cloaks for their dishonesty', concealing a desire for secular glory, or riches, or power. 'There is no religion so wicked as to order an attack upon men of a different belief'. Although Philip has declared war on infidels and heretics, religion is merely a pretext.[127] In Gentili's thought, the wars for the liberty of Christendom are not wars of religion: the very concept is misconceived.

THE TYRANNY OF PHILIP II

Vivid descriptions of the tyranny of Philip II were therefore articulated in the regime's general justifications of the war, but with particular vigour in texts associated with Essex, Pérez, and Anthony Bacon. As the author(s) of *The state of Christendom* asks—'why should not men sufficiently versed in matters of State ... depict the Spaniard and his tyranny so lively and so truly, that their reasons ... penetrate even to the hearts of his best friends and his most assured Allyes?'[128]

This desire to identify the manifestations of Philip's tyranny over his inherited territories as well as his 'usurpation' of the throne of Portugal, or his designs on the thrones of France and England, necessarily engaged with more searching political debates, which were rarely articulated with clarity in Elizabethan England. Essex conventionally called upon the duty of Elizabeth to succour the oppressed; but denunciation of Philip's tyranny over his own subjects inevitably broached theoretical questions about their potential to resist his authority.

At the heart of England's foreign policy was alliance with the Dutch, which clearly engaged Elizabeth in a war of a people who had abjured the authority of an anointed prince. As the polemic of Parsons and Verstegan recognized, Elizabeth's support of the Dutch 'rebels' was a vulnerable Achilles heel, at odds with the more authoritarian definitions of monarchical power expressed in the 1590s in England. Justifying Elizabeth's entry into the war in the 1580s, her apologists insisted that, far from condoning rebellion, the queen desired merely to restore the Dutch to the liberties and constitution that they had enjoyed under Charles V.[129] Part IV of the *Vindiciae, Contra Tyrannos*, which defended the rights of foreign princes to remove tyrants,

[127] Gentili, *De iure belli*, I, 63, II, 40. See in general Chapters VII–XI.
[128] *State of Christendom*, 242.
[129] *A declaration of the cavses mooving the Queene of England to giue aide to the defence of the People afflicted and oppressed in the lowe Countries* (1585), sigs. B1ʳ, Biiiʳ–; Adams, 'Protestant cause', 1–2, 40–2.

had been published in English translation—but without books 1–3, which treated the rights of subjects to resist their own monarchs.[130]

Thomas Bilson's *The true difference betweene Christian subjection and unchristian rebellion* (1585) tries to medicate the headache of supporting the Dutch while enjoining Elizabeth's own subjects to obedience with some slippery argument. Bilson admits that the laws or constitutions of certain polities and elective monarchies allow that rulers might be resisted/ deposed by subjects: the Holy Roman Empire functions thus, and, so implicitly does the authority of Habsburg rule in the Low Countries. In contrast, the monarchies of Spain, France, Scotland, and England, Bilson insists, are 'absolute' monarchies, where princes inherit by succession and cannot be deprived of their authority by subjects.[131]

Gentili struggles similarly to reconcile theories of obedience to the legitimacy of supporting rebels. Gentili praises the heroic Leicester for recognizing that intervention in the Netherlands was necessary for England's protection. But there is an ideological foundation to this expediency.[132] Succour of the 'Belgians' is defensible for the protection of their liberty: if conquered, the United Provinces will suffer the fate of the Southern states, now ruled by force and arbitrary power.[133]

Gentili also, then, recognizes the need to address the theoretical problem of the legitimacy of resistance of subjects. He denounces both rebellion and the right of the private individual to oppose tyranny, and echoes Bilson's theory of constitutional relativism, arguing that the powers of princes may be more or less absolute or circumscribed in different states.[134] But Gentili's concern is to define international law rather than to grapple with the particular constitutional arrangements of different polities. Therefore he also tackles the abstract question of whether subjects could lawfully resist an oppressive prince in terms of natural—generally applicable—laws, with suggestive, if sibylline, answers. Gentili cites without endorsing the judgement of the fourteenth-century jurist Baldus, that the people lack the authority to deprive a king.[135] But he also emphasizes the reciprocity of the relationship between monarch and subject. A prince might breach ordinary privileges granted to his subjects; but even a prince of 'absolute' power cannot breach privileges that are enshrined in contracts.[136]

What to do, then, when the terms of *contracts* between subjects and princes are broken? Although his argument is indistinct, Gentili admits

---

[130] Stephanus Junius Brutus (pseud.), *A short apologie for Christian souldiours . . .* (1588).
[131] Bilson, *True difference*, 509–10.
[132] Gentili, *De iure belli*, I, 124–5, II, 77–8.   [133] Ibid.
[134] Ibid., I, 32, II, 20.
[135] Ibid., I, 186, II, 115.   [136] Ibid., I, 619, II, 377–8.

that there are men of public authority who may resist oppression by force of arms. He distinguishes between true—or private—subjects and those who hold a public position endowed with some extraordinary authority, who are 'subjects in some particulars, [but] they are not subjects in others'.[137] For clarification Gentili cites the powers of the German princes over the Holy Roman Emperor, and of the ephors of Sparta: both *topoi* commonly found in sixteenth-century resistance theories to argue that the 'magistrate' had a constitutional role to limit the power of monarchs, and even to depose a tyrant. In 1598 (the year of *De iure belli*'s publication), Essex would self-consciously employ this language of public and private power to define himself as a subject of exceptional authority—an earl marshal of England—in his famous letter to Lord Keeper Egerton.[138]

Other justifications of aggressive English interventionism draw attention to the dilemmas faced by the plight of Philip's subjects who must address their natural right to resist tyranny. In particular, there is lengthy theoretical discussion of the origins of the Dutch revolt in *The state of Christendom* that reveals the author's/authors' familiarity with and cautious approbation of sixteenth-century theories of resistance. As with Gentili, rebellion is flatly denounced: 'Not that I approve Rebellion, or allow Subjects to Rebel against their Soveraigns, when, or for what occasions they will'. Nevertheless, in the Netherlands, Philip's subjects were forced to revolt because he had imposed intolerable tribute, government by foreigners, and had repressed their religious freedoms through the Inquisition: 'Such Subjects were freed from all manner of Obedience so soon as these Conditions were broken'.[139] Here a theory of limited monarchy is invoked that defines the relationship between monarchs and subjects as enshrined in contracts: if a prince were to break the conditions imposed on his rule, his subjects would be released from their obligations of obedience, and empowered to resist.[140]

The author of the *Anatomie of Spayne* also approves of the Dutch revolt because their constitution is *'Mistum ymperium and not merum'* (mixed not unlimited monarchy): subjects of any mixed monarchies, it is implied, may reject their monarch. And Philip's authority is seemingly limited or *'mistum'* in *all* of his territories; in Castile, the heartland of his power his subjects might also rebel, because the 'estates have authoritye over their

---

[137] Ibid., I, 81–2, II, 50–1.

[138] See Chapter 4, 159–62. Gentili reversed these conclusions in subsequent works written in James's reign: van der Molen, *Gentili*, 238–40.

[139] *State of Christendom*, 16–19.

[140] The most famous exposition of the theory of monarchy limited by contract was in the anonymous *Vindiciae, Contra Tyrannos*, which the author/s of *The State of Christendom* made use of: see Gajda, *'State of Christendom'*.

king', and 'manie such like liberties do the rest of his kingdomes possesse which are greate ympediments for the kinge'.[141] It is not in the interests of the author to describe and compare the English constitution with that of Castile. Nevertheless, the logic of this argument is that theories of mixed monarchy enshrine the rights of subjects to resist their rulers: there are glaring implications here for the conceptualization, then, of England as a Polybian mixed state, a 'monarchical republic'.

The Aragonese revolt, brought to English attention by Gil de Mesa's expedition to England in 1592, also prompted interest in the secular constitutional issues at stake. The Aragonese rising was a protest against the violation of ancient privileges by a resented, Castilian monarch: Mesa's petition invited Elizabeth to intervene for 'the restoring of them to their former liberties', urging Elizabeth to act as 'the true *Judith* against that *Olofernes*', King Philip.[142] Judith, symbol of republican liberty, had of course beheaded the tyrant Holofernes as he slept; unsurprisingly, the petition, and its intolerably radical imagery, was unheeded by Elizabeth. But discussion of the Aragonese revolt did find resonance in contemporary English texts. A pamphlet translated from the Dutch explained the breach of Philip's Aragonese coronation oaths, 'the formal words and articles which were pronounced at his coronation'.[143] Francis Bacon tellingly compared Philip's attempt to suppress the liberties of his subjects in the Netherlands with 'the like this day attempted upon Aragon'.[144]

The author of Mesa's provocative petition was almost certainly Pérez, who had orchestrated the mission to England. It was through Pérez's influence that Essex's circle was prompted to engage with the more radical solutions for resistance to tyranny. His correspondence with Essex and the Bacons refers to Philip as all manner of tyrants: he is Pharoah, Nebuchadnezzar, Nero, and, of course, Tiberius, an analogy employed in Essex's responses.[145]

Pérez was also a well known Tacitist, bringing his scholarship to a receptive audience in England.[146] His *Relaciones* itself is a self-consciously Tacitean treatment of Philip's kingship, which proposes to uncover the 'affections and naturall inclinacions of Princes'.[147] But Pérez did not interpret Tacitus through the filter of Senecan passivity, nor the 'black' Tacitism of the reason of state authors of the late sixteenth century. Unlike Lipsius (or rather like the earliest manifestations of Lipsius's Tacitism) he

---

[141] *Anatomie of Spayne*, 89–91.
[142] Ungerer, *Spaniard*, I, 37, from an English translation of Mesa's petition.
[143] Anon., H. W. trans., *A Pageant of Spanish Humours*... (1599), sig. B3ᵛ.
[144] *Discourse in the praise of his sovereign*: Spedding, *L&L*, I, 137.
[145] Ungerer, *Spaniard*, I, 327, 424, 366, 393, 466.
[146] He visited Henry Savile, whom he praised with typical rapture: ibid., I, 186.
[147] Bod, MS Eng. Hist. C 239, f. 20ᵛ.

saw Tacitus's revelations of the workings of tyranny as a means of deflating the power of tyrants, by revealing the human corruption of rulers.

Pérez argues that a modern Tacitus would use the matter of his narrative to strip away the mystical charisma of kingship used by princes to enslave their subjects. The 'intent' of a historian 'namely Cornelius Tacitus' was that 'men should not believe [kings] were any thinge ells but men'.[148] In an extraordinarily blunt passage, Pérez explains that the 'principall ende of histories' is that 'men mought deminishe parte of the love and confidence which they have in princes. The parte I meane which is to muche, and draweth menne to Idolatrye'. It is this blind reverence for the sanctity of kings that causes subjects to 'make them selves slaves and are manacled with their owne handes'.[149]

In short, this is an attack on the very concept of divine right monarchy. These passages might have struck a particular chord with the contemporary English courtier, who mused on the baroque excesses of the cult of Elizabeth, and the obligation to reverence the ageing queen as a goddess.

Pérez's *Relaciones* also contains lengthy descriptions of the dangers of arbitrary rule in its protracted exploration of the history of the Aragonese revolt. Offering a potted historical account of the Aragonese constitution, Pérez discusses the reasons for placing constitutional limits on the power of a monarch: princes *naturally* incline to increase their power: 'for there is no love of any thinge on earth that so troubleth suspendeth inflameth or beateth downe mans mynde as to Reigne, to commande and increase commandment'. Laws and magistrates restrain the propensity of princes to misgovernment for their subjects' benefit.[150]

In his discussion of the nature of the legal privileges of Aragon broken by Philip, Pérez provides the first Spanish description of the Aragonese coronation oaths, which were widely used by sixteenth-century resistance theorists as an exemplification of the principle of contractual monarchy, and to justify the deposition of rulers.[151] These were uttered by a kneeling, bareheaded king, and encompassed a range of privileges and immunities, the *fueros*. In return the Aragonese pledged: 'We who are as good as you, do make you our king and lorde, upon condicion that you keape us our lawes & liberties, & yf no, no'. The importance of the oaths is not lost on Pérez, who draws attention to and justifies his digression on the Aragonese constitution: 'it shalbe muche to the purpose to ye intent of my relacion'.[152]

And the author of the Preface to the English translation certainly recognizes the radical implications of Pérez's discussion of the Aragonese

---

[148] Ibid., f. 20^r.   [149] Ibid., f. 24^r.   [150] Ibid., f. 50.

[151] See Ralph E. Giesey, *If not, not. The oath of the Aragonese and the legendary laws of the Sobrarbe* (Princeton, NJ: Princeton University Press, 1968).

[152] Bod, MS Eng. Hist. C 239, ff. 47^r–49^v.

constitution. He indicates that readers might feel unease about the content of the *Relaciones*: 'Lett them consider that the matters are matters of
estate and those very highe... of the manners, customes and judiciall
dealinge of a straunge people'. Nevertheless, the author's wisdom and
gravitas are thoroughly defended: he is 'a man of estate', 'learned in
philosophye, in civile, in canon lawe'.[153]

Not surprisingly, the *Anatomie of Spayne*, though, warmly approves of
the *Relaciones*, and cites the coronation oaths as yet more evidence of the
limitations on Philip's authority in another of his dominions. Representative institutions, such as 'generall estates' of Castile and Aragon also bridle
a monarch: 'the onlie bodie to holde a tyrante yn.'[154]

The *Relaciones* is also analysed at length in *The state of Christendom*, in
the Supplement that concludes the treatise. The character and government of Philip, over his Castilian subjects as well as those under his wider
dominions, are forensically explored to define the attributes of tyranny
and to explore solutions to the government of a tyrant. Drawing on the
jurist Bartolus of Saxoferrato's *On Tyranny*, a tyrant is described as a ruler
who abrogates all forms of laws—divine, natural, and human—in the
interest of protecting his own power, and is suspicious of his subjects'
freedoms. He suppresses and kills his nobility; he keeps his 'doings hidden
and secret from wise men'; he 'suppresses learning' for fear of its destabilizing effects; he has 'spies in ever corner and place'. Tyrants foment
divisions among their subjects to keep them weak. They repress them
with harsh pecuniary exactions. Philip, of course, is found guilty of all of
these crimes.[155]

The author(s) of *The state of Christendom* also discusses the nature of
contractual monarchy in universal rather than particular terms, and in
ways that are directly applicable to England. Princes and subjects, it is
argued, are bound by contracts, which are grounded in a natural law that
is more binding than the positive laws of individual constitutions: 'for
Laws may be repealed, but contracts cannot'.[156] Most importantly for
English readers, the rights of the 'Nobility of Aragon' should their prince
'chance to break this [coronation] oath', are likened exactly to the powers
that the 'Nobility of *England*' might assume if their prince breaks the
'ancient Laws and Liberties of our Realm'—such as if the English
monarch should refuse a nobleman trial by his peers. Here, then, the
author(s) of *The state of Christendom* directly equates the principles
enshrined in Magna Carta with the Aragonese coronation oaths. If

---

[153] Bod, MS Eng. Hist. C 239, ff. 4ᵛ.   [154] *Anatomie of Spayne*, 91.
[155] *State of Christendom*, Supplement, 31–2. This is similar to the 'moral' and 'civil'
attributes of tyranny defined in the *Anatomie of Spayne*, 109–15 and *passim*.
[156] *State of Christendom*, Supplement, 19.

Aragon is a contractual monarchy, so is England. By implication, then, the resistance of the nobility or magistracy allowed in Aragon could be justified in Elizabeth's realm.[157]

When the question of whether it is lawful to kill rather than merely resist a prince is seriously addressed, the author is circumspect: certainly, 'subjects need not obey such a prince'. But may they 'lawfully expel their Prince out of his Country, and from his Crown and Dignity'? The author concludes:

> The best course is, to admonish such a prince of his duty, and pray him to reform, and reform all that is amiss. But who shall admonish him? His *best subjects* and other princes; and if after such admonition he shall still remain incorrigible... it may be lawful to implore, and employ their help and assistance for the speedy suppressing such a manifest and incorrigible oppressor and tyrant [emphasis added].[158]

This delineates a clear constitutional role for the 'best subjects'— the magistrate or the noble—to resist manifest tyranny, when necessity demands the reformation of government.[159]

THE PROBLEM OF PEACE: THE *APOLOGIE* IN CONTEXT

From the spring of 1598, Essex's justification for war assumed a different urgency. On 22 April 1598 (2 May NS), Philip II and Henry IV made peace with the signature of the Treaty of Vervins.[160] According to the terms of the Triple Alliance, Henry was required to negotiate with England and the United Provinces; in February, Sir Robert Cecil had headed an English delegation to France to investigate the possibilities of a peace between all of the allies and Spain. It was soon revealed that Henry, dissembling to the English and Dutch, had already agreed terms with Philip; but the Treaty of Vervins allowed Henry's allies a six-month window to join the French.[161] This, then, was the dilemma that faced Elizabeth and her council in the spring and summer of 1598.

In anticipation of Vervins, delegations from the United Provinces were sent to England in March and May to implore the queen to maintain the

---

[157] Ibid., 24.   [158] Ibid., 26.   [159] Ibid., 26–7.

[160] Wernham, *Return of the armadas*, 191–249 and *passim*; Adams, 'Protestant cause', 145–53; J. C. Grayson, 'From Protectorate to Partnership: Anglo-Dutch relations, 1598–1625', unpublished PhD thesis (London, 1978), 19–47; Paul C. Allen, *Philip III and the pax Hispanica, 1598–1621: the failure of grand strategy* (New Haven, CT and London: Yale University Press, 2000).

[161] *HMC Salisbury*, VIII, 90–9, 104–12, 118–27; for the following discussion see also Alexandra Gajda, 'Debating war and peace in late Elizabethan England', *HJ*, 52 (2009), 851–78.

Anglo–Dutch alliance.[162] The attractions of peace, though, were deepened by growing crisis in Ireland, and the heavy fiscal burdens of the war on a weary population. Elizabeth's decision was also complicated by news of the intentions of Philip II to bestow the sovereignty of the Netherlands on his daughter Isabella and her betrothed Albert.[163] The rejection of the archdukes' sovereignty by the United Provinces, however, crushed Elizabeth's fleeting hopes that the Netherlands problem might be solved by the reincarnation of the old Duchy of Burgundy under dual monarchs, independent of Spain. After several months of negotiations, Elizabeth renewed the Anglo–Dutch alliance on 6 August, the United Provinces conceding to shoulder most of the fiscal burden.

It seems, then, to be no coincidence that several of the aggressively pro-war tracts discussed above—Gentili's *De iure belli*, *The Treatise paraenetical*, *The Anatomie of Spayne*—were written or published this year. The excoriation of Spanish tyranny in these treatises is a damning indictment of the shift towards peace: the 'great and never before hard of tiranies wch his [Philip II's] ambition together with his power and usurpation caused' must compel the princes of Europe to 'bynde yourselfes together' in opposition to Spain.[164] Indeed, there is no more propitious time to strike than when the Spanish feel forced to negotiate: 'March therefore into Spaine and you shall have peace at your pleasure, otherwise you shall have it with shame and dishonour, and you will in the end repent you, that ever you spake of peace'.[165]

Nor is there any coincidence in the connection of these tracts to Essex. For it was now that the latent tensions between Essex and the Cecils could no longer be soothed by a shared rhetoric of hostility to Spanish tyranny. Essex's inclination to believe that his rivals thwarted his military goals swelled into a passionate conviction that the opponents of the war's continuation were more dangerous enemies, foes to the state and Christendom. These convictions were to be made broadly public, asserted vigorously to a wide audience in a variety of texts.

On 24 February Essex had written in friendly tones to Robert Cecil doubting that Spain could offer a secure peace.[166] His position soon hardened, as did his identification with the United Provinces. Unsurprisingly,

---

[162] Wernham, *Return of the armadas*, 234–6; Grayson, 'Protectorate to Partnership', 23–4.

[163] At first Elizabeth was joyful at the prospect: André Hurault, Sieur de Maisse, *A journal of all that was accomplished Monsieur de Maisse, ambassador in England from King Henry IV to Queen Elizabeth, Anno Domini 1597*, ed. and trans. G. B. Harrison and R. A. Jones (London: Nonesuch Press, 1931), 81. On 6 May (NS) Philip confirmed rumours that the infanta would be betrothed to Albert; the marriage was celebrated by proxy in November, and took place on 18 April (NS), 1599.

[164] *Anatomie of Spayne*, 53, 96, 114.   [165] *Treatise paraentical*, 55.

[166] BL, Lansdowne MS, 86, ff. 55ʳ–56ʳ.

the Dutch targeted Essex as their strongest ally.[167] The earl's channels of intelligence from the United Provinces had recently intensified, and, in Cecil's absence on embassy, he also took over his secretarial duties, becoming intimately engaged with the States General's arguments for maintaining the alliance.[168] On 17 May, Essex wrote to a correspondent in disgust at the perfidious French, identifying the Dutch as 'our only constant and able friends'.[169] But from July—the month preceding the renewal of the Dutch alliance—Essex was absent from court, having quarrelled with the queen.[170]

The earl's opposition to the peace was, instead, forcefully expressed in his *Apologie*, which was soon disseminated in manuscript, before its unauthorized print publication in 1600. Essex would later insist that the treatise was never intended to be spread abroad, but here he was, typically, dissimulating.[171] By framing the *Apologie* as a personal letter to Anthony Bacon, Essex employed a genre widely used in the covert publication of political treatises. It seems likely Essex wrote the majority of the *Apologie* in the spring of 1598—a contribution to a vigorous debate about the Dutch alliance, with a wider, semi-public audience in mind.[172]

In a brilliant vignette, Camden's Burghley taxes Essex in the course of these debates as a bloodthirsty warmonger, piously illustrating his admonition with a verse from the psalms.[173] Also in favour of peace on the council were the lord admiral, Charles Howard, and especially Lord Buckhurst; Henry Brooke, 11th Lord Cobham, (though not a councillor), also was noted for his intelligence links with Brussels.[174]

---

[167] Maurice and Louis of Nassau and the States General wrote flatteringly to Essex; Caron and Essex had been intimate since the earl's elevation to the mastership of the ordnance the previous year: *HMC Salisbury*, VIII, 20, 250, 257; Collins, *Letters and memorials*, II, 48, 89.

[168] See the massive correspondence of George Gilpin and Sir Francis Vere to Essex from 1596–8 in *HMC Salisbury*, VII and VIII. In Essex's hand see notes on the peace and the position of the States in French and English, with Essex's own observations: Cecil MS 67/55, 56, 57.

[169] Cecil MS 61/25.

[170] Essex's absences from the privy council date from 2 July–10 September: *APC*, XXVII, 560; *APC*, XXVIII, 153.

[171] Essex claimed that his servant had been instructed that the treatise should be shown to his friends only in his presence: Cecil MS 79/74, 23 May 1600. For Essex's further disavowal of his involvement in the printing of the pamphlet see Chapter 4, 174.

[172] The earl refers to the division of France from the allies: *Apologie*, sigs. C2^r, [C4^r]. As late as July Essex received, in response to his request to Sir Thomas Bodley, printed materials from the Low Countries and a summary of the States' decision to reject the peace, strikingly similar to the arguments used in the *Apologie*: BL, Additional MS, 4125, f. 340.

[173] Camden, *Annales*, 771.

[174] De Maisse, *Journal*, 44–5, 107. On 15 July Sir Thomas Edmondes reported to Sir Robert Sidney that the council had been polarized by 'schismaticall' disagreement over peace: *HMC De L'Isle and Dudley*, II, 356. Buckhurst was described as the most consistent conciliar advocate of peace in 1602: H. S. Scott ed., 'Journal of Sir Roger Wilbraham,

Camden's discussion of conciliar divisions draws directly, though (and without acknowledgement), from a series of manuscript treatises written before the alliance with the Dutch. These position pieces argue either in favour of the peace or conclude, with Essex's *Apologie*, that the war with Spain must be maintained until secure terms can be established. Burghley's manuscripts contain notes on the merits of peace with annotations by Robert Beale, clerk of the privy council, although the rest are anonymous.[175] The large number of surviving manuscripts of these tracts implies that Essex's *Apologie* was just one of a number of texts that conveyed the substance of the debate about foreign policy—that most prized of *arcana imperii*—to a wider audience in court and country.[176]

All of these position papers, Essex's *Apologie* included, propose reasons and arguments *in utramque partem*, before concluding firmly either in favour of peace or war. They weigh up the implications for security, trade, domestic prosperity, and the military crisis in Ireland. The central obstacle, though, is the fate of the Dutch.

Essex employed the language of reason or interest of state to defend the continuation of the war. The earl correctly predicts in the *Apologie* that any peace offered by the Spanish will be on impossible terms; he argues that Madrid will insist that Elizabeth hand over custody of the cautionary towns and allow toleration of religion, terms fit 'only for a conquerour to impose', not to be conceded by an equal treating for peace.[177] When English and Spanish representatives did meet at Boulogne in May 1600, talks dissolved in squabbles over precedence, but primarily because Spanish proposals were unacceptable to Elizabeth.[178] One anonymous pro-war author lists the points of 'honour' that made reconciliation with Spain impossible at present; but also a long list of reasons 'Against Profit',

Master of Requests', *Camden Miscellany*, X, Camden Society, 3rd. ser., 4 (London, 1902), 49–50.

[175] BL, Lansdowne MS 103, ff. 252ʳ–257ʳ. Of the anonymous treatises, in favour of war are 'A resolution of some doubts now cast to move simple men to embrace the conditions of peace', and 'An answer to certain trifling reasons alleaged to perswade her Majestie and the English nation to conclude a peace with the Spaniards', ITL, Petyt MS 538/46, ff. 36ʳ–41ʳ, 42ʳ–46ʳ; 'The suddaine and evill digested opinions of some whoe are comitted to the censure farr more worthie Spirits touching the peace', BL, Stowe MS 161, ff. 37ʳ–64ʳ, and Stowe MS 151, ff.74ʳ–96ʳ. For peace are 'Considerations touching the peace nowe in speache', see four copies in ITL, Petyt MS 538/46, ff. 47ʳ–48ᵛ, 103ʳ–106ᵛ, 130ʳ–134ᵛ, 139ʳ–140ʳ; copies in the British Library, BL, Cotton MS Galba DXII, ffs. 188ʳ–198ʳ and Lansdowne MS 87, ff. 139ʳ–141ᵛ; BL, Cotton MS Caligula EIX, ii, f. 155ʳ–ᵛ; BL, Cotton MS Titus CVII, ff.146ʳ–148ʳ.

[176] Camden, *Annales*, 765–71.

[177] *Apologie*, sig. Dᵛ. The irony, of course, is that Essex was supportive of religious toleration for Catholics; see Chapter 3.

[178] Wernham, *Return of the armadas*, 320–34.

concluding that 'warres are more safe then peace both in regarde of her Majesties person, and the state'.[179]

But arguments against the peace, especially Essex's, are framed primarily in terms of opposition to Philip's tyrannical ambition to overwhelm Christendom. In the *Apologie* Essex warns against the tyrant's practice of deception. No Catholic, he insists, will consider himself bound to terms agreed with heretics: peace feelers snaking from Madrid merely buy time to replenish exhausted treasuries, in order to launch a fresh assault on the free states of Europe. Adopting the argument of the *Treatise paraenetical*, Essex insists that Philip's dangerous pacific overtures are, instead, further evidence of Spain's weakness, and indicate a great *occasione* for the allies to press the war to its climacteric conclusion.[180] Essex also echoes Pérez's earlier warnings about wakeful vigilance: Philip sings a deadly lullaby to 'sing us asleepe with the name of peace, til he may rouse us from sleepe by a thundering warre'.[181]

The anonymous pro-war treatises offer similar justification. If 'the Spaniard giue noe assurance but his oathe, this peace is no more assured then a castell built on sande'.[182] The now ubiquitous definition of Philip as a common threat to Christendom also resonates strongly in these tracts. Elizabeth's wars are honourable as they are undertaken 'for the defence of our countrie and lives, and libertie against the ambition of the Spaniarde'.[183]

The treatises in favour of peace are no less vehemently argued. The war is 'chargeable, uncertayne, fruteless, & endless'.[184] Tyrone's rebellion, dismissed with extraordinary bravado by Essex as that 'miserable beggerly, *Irish* war', grows more nightmarish every day, 'kindled' by Spanish 'fire'.[185] Elizabeth's treasury is exhausted—'a reason unanswerable'.[186] Calling to mind (deliberately?) Essex's own parallel between England and Athens, the author of one pro-peace tract remarks that the Athenians bitterly regretted their initially 'proud' refusal of peace from the Macedonians.[187] The language of reason of state is also used repeatedly to opposite effect. The 'interest', 'commodities', and 'benyfitts' of the peace are 'more of necessitie then the warres'.[188]

In marked contrast to the pro-war treatises, tracts in favour of peace are not saturated with the vocabulary of Spanish tyranny. Philip II is merely the 'enemy', or the king of Spain. In a pale reflection of Lipsius's approval of Spanish imperialism, the Spanish empire is not invoked as evidence of

---

[179] ITL, Petyt MS, 538/46, ff. 37[r–v], 39[r].   [180] *Apologie*, sig. [D4[r–v]]
[181] Ibid., sig. E1[r].   [182] ITL, Petyt MS, 538/46, f. 37[v].
[183] Ibid., f. 39[r].   [184] Ibid., f. 48[v].
[185] BL, Cotton MS Galba DXII, f. 192[r]; Titus CVII, f. 147[r]; *Apologie*, sig. E1[v].
[186] BL, Cotton MS Titus CVII, f. 147[r–v].
[187] Ibid., f. 148[r].   [188] ITL, Petyt MS, ff. 47[r], 48[r].

his insatiable appetite to swallow the liberty of free states, but a reason why England must make peace. Far from weakening, the power and the treasure of the Spanish Habsburgs is so great that this war cannot be won outright: 'our warrs agaynst his provinces weare *opus infinitum*'(an infinite task).[189]

In particular, though, it is the sympathy extended to the United Provinces that stakes out an ideological gulf between the sets of arguments. The pro-peace treatises are far less concerned with the fate of the Dutch, arguing that States General might successfully fight on alone or, more satisfactorily, reach independent accommodation with Spain. While mainly ignoring rumours of the prospective donation of the Low Countries to Isabella and Albert, these authors emphasize the original, limited aims of Elizabeth's intervention in the Dutch Revolt: the restoration of the original constitution and privileges of the Low Countries, including some form of Habsburg rule.[190]

Essex's *Apologie* treats the predicament of the States General most extensively and sympathetically. He argues that an Anglo-Spanish peace will destroy the independence of the United Provinces, because the authority of the virtuous military leadership of the Dutch will be fatally undermined.[191] Accommodation between the United Provinces and Spain will certainly follow, but this will entail no restoration of a constitutional monarchy, or lost privileges and liberties; rather, the dreadful outcome of an English peace with Spain will be the reimposition of 'slaverie upon the Netherlands', either directly, or 'by him that shall claime under [the King of Spain] for their Soveraigne, as the Duke of Burgundie'. Essex describes the inevitable slide of the Dutch into 'voluntary servitude' where the temptations of peace have expunged martial virtue:

> Province will strive with Province, Towne with Towne, & man with man, who shall be most obsequious, and shew themselves most servile; all care of defence neglected by minds bewitched with the name of peace; all memorie of former tirannie blotted out of their harts resolved to accept a Soveraigne.[192]

This description of the awful fate of the Netherlands reflects the reasons proffered by the Dutch themselves for refusing to treat with Spain, or later for rejecting the sovereignty of the archdukes. But the objections fit perfectly within Essex's preoccupation with the despotic tendencies of the Spanish monarchy, which propels the whole of his argument: he

---

[189] ITL, Petyt MS, f. 146ʳ.
[190] See, for example, BL, Lansdowne MS 103, ff. 254ᵛ–255ʳ.
[191] This point was made by Gilpin to Essex on 23 February 1598, *HMC Salisbury*, VIII, 60–2.
[192] *Apologie*, sig. C2ʳ.

cannot countenance the notion that a tyrant will ever stem underlying ambition to expand his power.

Essex's treatment of the peculiar constitutional arrangements of the United Provinces is idiosyncratic and important. Should the Dutch slide back into their previous monarchical allegiances, he warns, their brave new polity will be utterly transformed once again:

> ... the authority of the generall states, and the present forme of government shall be broken and dissolved, a monarchie set up ... there shall nothing limit the princes absolutenesse, but his owne will. The strength of a contract cannot limit it.[193]

Once more, this recycles arguments made by the Dutch.[194] But Essex specifically expects the reader to abhor the transformation of the Dutch polity from one governed by 'generall states' to an unlimited absolute monarchy. Thus he implicitly endorses the representative government of the United Provinces as a legitimate polity. Essex certainly sees weaknesses in the constitutional arrangements of the Dutch: because decision-making in the States General is federated, the virtuous minority who maintain the momentum of the war might be overruled by a fearful, self-preserving majority, who will be tempted by Spain's seductive overtures. But Essex also recognizes that this representative decision-making is at the heart of the Dutch concept of liberty. The sovereignty of the States General is rooted in the grant of a voice to all provinces, 'such libertie being *the true cause of their taking armes*, and standing out against the common enemie'[emphasis added].[195] The Dutch revolt is here described as the defence of secular liberty, which includes free speech and representation: in other words, Essex exhibits a sympathetic understanding of Dutch resistance linked to an appreciation of republican theories of government.

There is a striking difference between Essex's appraisal of the government of the United Provinces and the attitude exhibited towards the rebellious Dutch in the pro-peace treatises. One author excoriates the 'blunt Democraticall weapons by the which these popular estatz impugne a peace with Spayne.'[196] Another argues that the indefinite levy of 'unaccustomed & new devised taxations' might cause the disgruntled English to 'rise in swarme', and 'reduce this Monarchie to a popular state'—like the United Provinces.[197] On 17 August 1599, Sir Robert

---

[193] Ibid.

[194] Robert Cecil had pointed out to Henry IV that the Dutch would never agree to terms of a peace that would impose absolute rule by conquest or contract: *HMC Salisbury*, VIII, 96.

[195] *Apologie*, sig. [C4ᵛ].

[196] BL, Cotton MS Titus CVII, ff. 3ᵛ–4ᵛ.   [197] Ibid., ff. 147ʳ–ᵛ.

Cecil grimly described the 'coldness' of England's Dutch allies: 'there is small friendship in a popularity'.[198] Divisions over foreign policy, then, demarcated similarly divergent attitudes towards political authority, the legitimacy of non-monarchical government, and the response of subjects to tyrants. Essex's views were distinctly less conservative, more sympathetic to republican ideas, and the legitimacy of resistance: his main opposition to peace was on ideological grounds.

PEACE, COURT FACTION, AND SPANISH SUCCESSION

The debate about peace had wider implications for the decline of Essex's career. It hardened his alienation from the politics of the court; but it also framed the earl's incipient suspicions that his rivals were possessed of nefarious designs on the English succession. In July 1597, the earl insisted that Philip II must cease his 'ambitious humour' of pressing the title of the infanta before any peace negotiations could be countenanced.[199] When Essex's intelligence sources first filtered rumours of the impending marriage in December, the union of Isabella and Albert was immediately denounced as a ruse to reunite the seventeen provinces and allow Philip to recover the Low Countries.[200] Now, Essex cried, rather than offering a brilliant solution to England's diplomatic crises through the recreation of the Duchy of Burgundy, the archdukes would be puppets, controlled from Madrid. And could not the peace-lovers see the danger from 'the infant the person whose title to the crown of *England, Parsons* so laboured to prooue? Is not the lowe countries the rise by which hee must leape into *England?'* [201] Friends of the peace, unwittingly or not, would help the infanta's claim to the English throne.

In the *Apologie* Essex also directly correlates his own 'known enemies' with the friends of the peace. The other pro-war tracts also use factional language, denouncing those who 'censure farr more worthie Spirits touching the peace', but it is only Essex who chooses to personalize the debate, framing his political argument within an autobiographical defence of his own war

[198] Sir Ralph Winwood, *Memorials of affairs of state in the reigns of queen Elizabeth and King James I,* 3 vols (1725), I, 92.
[199] TNA, SP 12/45, f. 12ʳ.
[200] Cecil MS 178/65.
[201] *Apologie,* sig. C3ᵛ.

record.[202] As a tract that proudly trumpets its authorship, Essex's *Apologie* is, therefore, unique among the war/peace tracts of 1598. It is typical, though, of the scribal circulation of other texts throughout the 1590s that promoted his public image. The earl's argument perfectly encapsulates his conceptualization of his own fortunes as a synecdoche for the welfare of the realm.

In robustly vituperative language Essex denounces the dangerous peace-mongers as triple foes—enemies to himself, to the queen, and to the realm: 'Iniurious are they to the countrey which bredde them ... Iniurious they are to her to her Majestie who hath ruled them', and 'Inurious and most unthankfull to God himselfe'.[203] A specific target soon emerges, though, as he excoriates those who cite the impoverishment of the realm as an argument for peace, yet lavish exhaustive riches on 'sumptuous buildings, infinite plate, and costly furniture of houses'.[204] A commonplace classical–humanist definition of the relationship between luxury, corruption, and the decline of states is twisted into an obvious attack on the magnificent building projects of the Cecils.[205]

Even as he prepared to leave for Ireland, Essex continued to fear that Robert Cecil's enthusiasm for a peace would bring catastrophe to England.[206] These suspicions were worsened when the archdukes, more enthusiastic than Philip III for settlement with England, reopened negotiations with Elizabeth. Cecil was an obvious ally, the recipient of portraits of Isabella and Albert in the winter of 1599.[207] The envoy Jerome Coomans paid four visits to the English court in 1599; in February the following year, the more formal embassy of Audencier Verreycken was received with elaborate ceremonial and 'roiall feasting', in which Sir Walter Ralegh and Lord Buckhurst played a very prominent role. These diplomatic feelers prompted widespread *rumours* at the court in England—and crucially in Scotland—that peace was 'a thing very much desired' by Elizabeth and most of the council and the court.[208]

---

[202] See above, n. 180.   [203] *Apologie*, sig. D2ᵛ.   [204] Ibid., D3ʳ.
[205] 'Introduction', in Pauline Croft ed., *Patronage, culture and power. The early Cecils* (New Haven, CT and London: Yale University Press, 2002), ix–x.
[206] Essex reported Cecil's enthusiasm for peace in conversation with the French ambassador: Pierre Paul Laffleur de Kermaingant, *L'ambassade de France en Angleterre sous Henri IV. Mission de Jean de Thumery, Sieur de Boissise 1598–1602* (Paris, 1886), 337.
[207] Pauline Croft, '*Rex Pacificus*, Robert Cecil, and the 1604 Peace with Spain', in Glen Burgess, Rowland Wymer, and Jason Lawrence eds, *The accession of James I: historical and cultural consequences* (Basingstoke: Palgrave Macmillan, 2006), 140–54.
[208] Collins, *Letters and memorials*, II, 169–80; Cecil MS 68/40, Cobham to Cecil, 16 February 1600.

Cecil, in fact, was pessimistic about the feasibility of peace before the Irish rebellion had been suppressed.[209] But to Essex, sequestered after Ireland, blaming personal enemies for his political disgrace, the friendliness of the court to diplomatic overtures from the Habsburgs easily consolidated his suspicions of a broader conspiracy focused on the succession and the infanta's title. Nor was Essex alone in harbouring these outlandish expectations of the secretary.

In Spain, the Jesuits Joseph Creswell and Robert Parsons grasped at various strategies to exploit the growing paranoia and factionalism that now gripped the Elizabethan court.[210] The death of Philip II in September 1598, and the accession of his son, Philip III, had given a massive adrenaline boost to the infanta's supporters in Spain. For all the financial weakness of the Spanish monarchy, Philip III was determined to reassert the dignity and authority of his title.[211] In March 1599 it was rumoured that he planned to support the infanta's claim with pensions for influential councillors, courtiers, and nobles in England. And on 12 February 1601 (NS), Philip gave formal endorsement of his support for his sister's title to the throne of England.

All the time, Parsons and Creswell were confidently asserting that a party *could* be bought at the English court. As Father Leo Hicks has shown, Parsons maintained an anonymous agent who claimed to be in direct contact with Robert Cecil and other councillors whom he described as hostile to James VI, and potentially willing to communicate with Spain. The secretary was probably sounding out Philip's position through secret, dangerous feelers. But in February 1601, Philip argued that his sister's title would be supported by powerful figures in England sympathetic to the Catholic cause: he named Cecil, the secretary, and Charles Howard, earl of Nottingham, the lord admiral.[212]

Catholic exiles in Spain, then, founded their hopes for Isabella's queenship on exactly the same suspicions as those of Essex: that a Cecilian court faction, inclined to peace, would inevitably be receptive to approaches from Spain. These must have fuelled Mountjoy's fears about the succession; as will be shown in Chapter 4, they were certainly held north

[209] Scott, 'Journal of Sir Roger Wilbraham', 49–50.

[210] Leaving no avenue untried, Parsons and Creswell also seem to have sounded out the possibility that Essex's desperation could be used to encourage him to support the infanta's title! See Chapter 5, 214.

[211] Leo Hicks, S.I., 'Sir Robert Cecil, Father Persons and the Succession, 1600–1601', *Archivium Historicum Societatis Iesu*, 24 (1955) 95–139.

[212] Henri Lonchay and Joseph Cuvelier eds, *Correspondance de la Cour d'Espagne sur les affaires des Pays-Bas au XVIIe Siècle*, 6 vols (Brussels: Commission Royale d'Histoire, 1923–37), I, 63–4.

of the border, by James VI. Unlike Philip III, though, the archdukes actually exhibited no desire to make good Isabella's dynastic claim to the English throne; as Robert Cecil probably recognized, their pursuit of an Anglo-Spanish peace was driven by a much more immediate priority, the establishment of their authority in the Netherlands. But in light of strengthened channels of communication between Elizabeth, Cecil, and Brussels, and the mounting intensity of anxieties about the succession, it is possible to comprehend how Essex became so easily and unswervingly convinced that a Cecilian faction plotted to divert the succession of the crown to Spain, and was so quick to identify the secretary—with unparalleled access to the queen and power on the council—as England's deadliest enemy.

3

'Profane pollicy'? Religion, toleration, and the politics of succession

In the construction of the earl's treacherous character in post-rising propaganda, Francis Bacon inevitably provided the most memorable definition of the earl as a cynical politique: 'knowing there were no such strong and drawing cordes of popularitie, as religion', Essex pursued 'a profane pollicy to serue his turne (for his owne greatnesse,) of both sorts & factions, both of *Catholicks* and *Puritanes*'.[1]

In more propitious times, some six years earlier in February 1595, the earl, with a crew of nobles and gentlemen in tow, had made an ostentatious appearance at the BA Commencement ceremony in Cambridge. On 26 February, several of his party were invested with the MA degree. After a good dose of college drama, entertainment took the form of 'disputations ... upon philosophical questions which the earl of Essex had previously set down under his hand'.[2] The next day Essex's clique was a glamorous presence when Dr William Whitaker, master of St John's College and an acquaintance of the earl from his student days, preached a notorious sermon denouncing the doctrine of universal grace.[3] The episode would have deep implications for the future unity of English Protestantism: Whitaker was launching a formal assault on the Cambridge anti-Calvinists Peter Baro and William Barrett, which preceded the formulation of the Lambeth Articles later in the year—Whitaker and Whitgift's attempt to give formal endorsement to Calvinist soteriology, and to suppress swelling theological disunity in the English church. Essex's glossy endorsement of Whitaker at this vital moment shored up his public association with the Godly, and with the patronage of orthodox Calvinism in Cambridge.

---

[1] Bacon, *Declaration*, sig. D3^{r-v}.

[2] C. H. Cooper, *Annals of Cambridge*, 5 vols (Cambridge: Warwick and Co., 1842–1908) II, 528–9.

[3] BL, Harleian MS 7038, f. 53^v; Peter Lake, *Moderate Puritans and the Elizabethan church* (Cambridge: Cambridge University Press, 1982), 204–5; Hammer, *Polarisation*, 303–4.

Just a few months later, in June 1595, Essex's patronage and protection were invoked by a completely different source. A Catholic priest made the dangerous crossing to England, and surrendered himself to Anthony Bacon. Thomas Wright was no ordinary priest but a Jesuit, who had left the order to better the condition of Catholics in England, first by procuring individual toleration from the state. Against opposition from Burghley, Wright was protected by Essex, who gained for the priest freedom of personal movement—an astonishing liberty.[4] This episode would be full of later implications for the earl. Wright would be intensively questioned about his relationship with Essex by the authorities before and after the rising, in 1600 and 1601.[5] But in 1595, Essex's protection of Wright was as strong a signal to English Catholics to place their trust in the earl, as his public endorsement of Whitaker offered assurance to the Godly of his Protestant credentials.

Like almost all elements of the polemical attacks on Essex's treasonous ambition made after the failed revolt, Bacon's sneers at Essex's 'profane pollicy' have deep roots. Although historians have long recognized the amorphous nature of his religious patronage, further analysis of the significance of Essex's appeal to both Catholics and Godly Protestants reveals the extremely complicated interplay of religion and politics in Elizabeth's final decade. In the 1590s, Catholics and Puritans alike appraised the earl as Wright did, with a fervent mix of hope and desperation as one who would determine the future of true religion in England. Their expectations, and the flattering idioms in which appeals to the earl were couched, intersected with Essex's own conception of the leading role he deserved to play in domestic and European politics in this reign and—most importantly—the reign to come.

There are striking similarities in the ways that religious groups regarded Essex and the hopes that were projected onto James VI of Scotland, whose religion was as differently interpreted as that of the earl. Before the Hampton Court Conference of 1604, English Puritans had great expectations of James, member of the Scottish Kirk, whose 'thorough' reformation was a galling mirror-for-churches to English Puritans. But in the mid-1590s, English understanding of James's religion was complicated by his troubled relations with the Kirk, the conversion of his wife, Anne of Denmark, and especially his favourable treatment of Catholic nobles who engaged in seditious communication with Spain. James was increasingly convinced that he needed to court

[4] T. A. Stroud, 'Father Thomas Wright: a test case for toleration', *Biographical Studies*, 1 (1951–2), 189–219.
[5] See Chapter 1, 55–6; Chapter 5, 214–5.

Catholic opinion on the continent and in England to secure the crown, dripping fuel onto the endlessly complex range of plots and designs entertained by English and Scottish Catholic exiles which hinged on the succession. Once he ascended the English throne James would, like Essex, bitterly disappoint the more radical elements of both groups, while continuing to make his concern for the reunion of Christendom a perpetual—if unattainable—project.[6]

In fact, it will be argued that both Essex and James played the politics of religion in the same way, and for almost identical reasons, inseparable from the pragmatism of succession politics, but with a fibre of the genuine irenicism that was increasingly prominent in late sixteenth-century religious culture. That Francis Bacon should piously denounce Essex's manipulative religious politics was either ridiculously ironic or exquisitely politique: a wonderfully hypocritical attack on religious hypocrisy. As will be shown, both Bacon brothers were deeply engaged with Essex's gestures to different confessional groups in the middle of the decade; these were intended to shore up his pivotal role as the leading English statesman who would steer the politics of succession to a safe—but as yet unknown—harbour.

The prism of Essex's example also refracts the spectrum of ways that religion continued to shape political discourse in the post-armada period. In the mid-1590s, as Essex associated with both the Godly and Whitgift's Conformist Protestantism, he also deliberately engaged with Catholics willing to express their loyalty to queen and/or the Elizabethan state. Thus Essex established his public role in the midst of fundamental debates about the relationship between political identity and religious conscience. The sharpest bones of this discourse, however, were revealed in the response that Essex provoked within the English Catholic community. Here, Robert Parsons's dedication of *A Conference about the next succession to the crowne of Ingland* to Essex assumes a pivotal significance.[7] This act of dedication—as significant a textual 'event' as any other in Elizabeth's reign—will be re-evaluated in the context of the earl's relationship with religious toleration, and especially with that other (former) Jesuit Thomas Wright, through a set of extraordinary literary materials written by Wright for Essex in 1595. Through the response of Parsons and Wright to Essex can be seen the complex variety of ways that Elizabethan Catholics defined

---

[6] James's lenient treatment of the communication of the Catholic earls of Huntly, Errol and Arran with Philip II, known as the 'Spanish Blanks' affair, caused particular consternation: W. B. Patterson, *King James VI and I and the reunion of Christendom* (Cambridge: Cambridge University Press, 1997), 13–16 and *passim* for James's irenicism.

[7] It is assumed that the attribution of the treatise to Parsons is correct: 'The authorship and early reception of A *Conference about the next succession to the crown of England*', *HJ*, 23/2 (1980), 415–29; also see Houliston, *Robert Persons*.

their own relationship to queen and state; through the earl's own religious politics more generally can be seen the ways that his very public cultivation of political *gravitas* and support outside his immediate client base contributed to his immense political vulnerability later in the decade.

THE IDEA OF RELIGIOUS TOLERATION

The idea of toleration in the sixteenth century is a very distant ancestor of the modern conception of the individual's right to freedom of conscience, or the acceptance of religious variety in the state as inevitable, let alone desirable. In post-Reformation Europe, 'toleration' was a contested term, most often invoked in a positive sense by religious minorities seeking freedom of worship in the confessional state.[8]

Irenic literature from Erasmus onwards invoked the concept of Christendom to exhort the rulers of Europe to reunite divided Christians through the cessation of persecution, based on the ideals of charity and common Christian identity, and an aversion to the forcing of conscience. Politique arguments for religious toleration, which developed during the post-Reformation wars of religion, pressed for the suspension of persecution for reason of state, for civil stability. Unsurprisingly, the most fertile ground for the latter was France, where a form of politique toleration was enshrined (however unsatisfactorily) in the Edict of Nantes in 1598. But irenic thinkers rarely envisaged perpetual pluralism. When persecuted religious groups petitioned for freedom of worship, or writers argued that toleration was an essential condition to restore civil peace, it was often from the perspective that time, education, or providence would abolish the erroneous doctrinal beliefs of the dominant or persecuting church/authorities, or, respectively, misguided heretical subjects. When the English Jesuit Robert Parsons had made the case for the toleration of private Catholic worship in the 1580s, the eventual re-Catholicization of England had been his long-term aim.[9]

[8] W. K. Jordan, *The development of religious toleration in England*, 4 vols (London: Allen and Unwin, 1932–40); Alexandra Walsham, *Charitable hatred: tolerance and intolerance in England, 1500–1700* (Manchester: Manchester University Press, 2006); John Coffey, *Persecution and toleration in Protestant England, 1558–1689* (Harlow: Longman, 2000); Perez Zagorin, *How the idea of religious toleration came to the West* (Princeton, NJ: Princeton University Press, 2003); Ole Peter Grell and Robert Scribner eds, *Tolerance and intolerance in the European reformation* (Cambridge: Cambridge University Press, 1996).
[9] Peter Holmes, *Resistance and compromise: the political thought of Elizabethan Catholics* (Cambridge: Cambridge University Press, 1982), Chapter 3, especially 61–2. Arnold Pritchard, *Catholic loyalism in Elizabethan England* (London: Scholar Press, 1979), 27–8.

A purer irenicism, which denounced religious persecution on philosophical rather than pragmatic grounds, did exist in the sceptical tradition, which inclined to identify a minimal number of knowable Christian truths. In the sixteenth century these arguments were in their infancy, but were expressed in the writings of Sebastian Castellio and Jacopo Acontius, who questioned the certainty of much religious doctrine on grounds of the fallibility of human knowledge, even in interpretation of scripture.[10] There is a reverberation of these views in the thought of Gentili. A fiercely anti-papal Protestant, Gentili nevertheless believed that Christian identity required merely belief in the Trinity; the individual conscience must be free to search out religious truth without fear or legal impediments.[11] As he wrote in *De iure belli*, 'Religion is a matter of the mind and of the will, which is always accompanied by freedom'.[12]

On the one hand, the cessation of punitive measures against religious non-conformity seemed an ever more distant possibility in the 1590s. Penalties for Protestant and Catholic recusancy were toughened in legislation of the parliament of 1593 (35 Eliz. I, c. 1, c. 2), while Whitgift's crackdown on radical Puritanism was mirrored by the continued execution of Catholic priests and laymen.[13] Ironically, though, the intellectual climate became much more responsive to politique and irenic ideas of toleration. Hooker, of course, acknowledged the legitimacy if not the errors of the church of Rome, repudiating the foundations of conventional antipopery.[14] Hooker's pupil, Edwin Sandys, was the author in 1599 of *A relation of the state of religion . . . in the severall states of these westerne parts of the world*, a comparative assessment of the state of religion in Europe, which linked a parallel attitude towards Catholicism with a politique idea of toleration.[15] In this unpublished treatise Sandys argues that, unless providence proves him wrong, religious pluralism will prevail in Europe for the foreseeable future. The longed-for restoration of civil peace will only be possible if confessional divisions are tolerated, and religious violence expunged.

The Elizabethan regime famously insisted that no subject was punished for heresy, rather for civil disobedience. Many Protestant non-conformists

---

[10] Jordan, *Development of toleration*, I, 312–15, 303–65; Zagorin, *Idea of toleration*, 93–144, 210, 258.

[11] Panizza, *Alberico Gentili*, 28.

[12] Gentili, *De iure belli*, I, 61, II, 39.

[13] Between 1580 and 1603, 88 Catholics were executed, including 53 priests: Alan Dures, *English Catholicism, 1558–1642: continuity and change* (Harlow: Longman, 1983), 32.

[14] Lake, *Anglicans and Puritans*, 155–60.

[15] A printed edition of 1605 was unauthorized, and was publicly burned, but the treatise was reprinted in 1622 as *Europae Speculum*, and reissued a further six times in the seventeenth century.

and Catholics decried this as deceitful sophistry, declaring that the punitive measures enacted against those who dissented from the Church of England were indeed religious persecution. But the state's insistence that political loyalty was the touchstone of its demands on individual conscience could be advantageously employed by those who made individual or general appeals for toleration on the grounds of their allegiance. At the end of Elizabeth's reign, the Archpriest Controversy—ostensibly a jurisdictional conflict between secular and Jesuit priests—was framed as a wider dispute about political allegiance and its relationship to freedom of conscience. The Appellant priests attacked the Jesuit espousal of doctrines of resistance, making appeals for toleration in terms of absolute loyalty or 'loyalism' to Elizabeth.[16]

Theoretical appeals for toleration throughout Elizabeth's reign insisted that political loyalty and religious conscience were separable. Of course, the erastian nature of the Elizabethan Church made these politique arguments for toleration in England deeply ambiguous, because the monarch to whom political allegiance was owed was also the Supreme Governor of the Church, an argument frequently emphasized by Conformist opponents of Presbyterian ecclesiology. And Catholics who noisily defined themselves as Elizabeth's loyal subjects harboured a range of more ambiguous attitudes to the queen and state, and often communed with others engaged in more radical solutions to the predicament of English Catholicism.[17] In the 1590s, the unsettled succession may ironically have dampened latent activism: dissatisfied Catholics and Puritans were encouraged to tarry, waiting for the accession of a monarch who would reverse Elizabethan policy.

ESSEX'S RELIGION

At an unspecified date in 1595, Essex wrote to Whitgift in person to recommend that Richard and Anne Godfrey, who 'in matter of Religion . . . be not conformable' might go about their affairs without being 'troubled touching their relligion or conscience'. Despite their not 'repayring to any Churche or Chappell', the earl urged the suspension of the rigours of the recusancy laws, because Godfrey 'hath bene allwayes found to be very

---

[16] Pritchard, *Catholic loyalism*, 146–74; Michael Questier, 'Catholic Loyalism in Early Stuart England', *EHR*, 123 (2008), 1132–65.

[17] Questier, *Catholicism and community*, 124–41 and *passim*; Sandeep Kaushik, 'Resistance, loyalty and recusant politics: Sir Thomas Tresham and the Elizabethan State', *Midland History*, 21 (1996), 37–72.

discreet and dutifull in his carriadge both towards her Majesty and the State'. Notably, he expected Whitgift's sympathetic response.[18]

How seriously did Essex conceptualize his involvement in religious politics? We should begin by considering his attitude toward the penal legislation enacted in the parliament of 1593, when Essex sat first in the Lords as a privy councillor.[19] Although we know very little about Essex's activities, Richard Broughton, his man-of-business, described the earl's complete immersion in 'committees, for the better penning and amendment of matter in bills of importance'.[20] More tellingly, Anthony Bacon wrote to Standen of the 'rigors of the sayd [recusancy] bill whiche of many misliked & namely of us brothers [i.e. himself and Francis] who will do our best agaynst them'.[21] As the parliament itself drew to an end, Essex procured dispensation for Sir Thomas Tresham for three months from his imprisonment for recusancy—a (deliberately?) blatant flaunting of the recent legislation.[22] In Staffordshire, the heartland of his estates, and where Essex informally exercised the office of lord lieutenant after the death of George Talbot, 6th earl of Shrewsbury in 1590, there is no evidence to suggest that Essex enforced the recusancy laws—a sharp contrast to Shrewsbury's activities.[23]

Essex's own pronouncements on religion appear contradictory because his writings were shaped by context and intended audience. In peril and disgrace, the earl was fervent in Protestant devotions. There was much for the Godly to savour in Essex's letter to the earl of Southampton, written in imprisonment in 1599 or 1600, in which he urged his friend to 'make a resolute Covenant with your God to serve him with all your naturall and spirituall inward and outward gifts and abilities... he will give you that inward peace of soule, and true joy of heart... which when you have you shall never be shaken'.[24]

More private writings may reveal different spiritual postures. If Steven May is correct in his attribution of the poem 'The Passion of a

---

[18] LPL MS 652, f. 325.

[19] J. E. Neale, *Elizabeth I and her parliaments, 1584–1601* (London: Jonathan Cape, 1957), 280–97.

[20] Cited in ibid., 295.

[21] LPL MS 648, f. 161[r]. There is no other record of Anthony and Francis Bacon's contribution to religious debates.

[22] TNA, SP 12/244/124, f. 219[r]. Sir Thomas was the father of Francis Tresham, Essex's follower, who participated in the 1601 rising and in the Gunpowder Plot: Chapter 1, 55.

[23] Anthony G. Petti ed., *Roman Catholicism in Elizabethan and Jacobean Staffordshire: documents from the Bagot papers* (Staffordshire: Staffordshire Record Society, 1979), xii and *passim*.

[24] The letter, widely circulated, was printed during the civil war: *The Earle of Essex his letter to the Earle of Southampton in the time of his troubles: containing many pious expressions and very comfortable for such as are in any troubles* (1642), sig. A3[r]; see BL, MS Harleian, 677, ff. 39[r]–40[r].

Discontented Minde' to Essex, the earl wrote a set of religious verses in the Tower in 1601 which revealed his spiritual preparedness for death. The narrator of the poem espouses a conventionally Protestant conception of salvation, fearfully plaining his immersion in the 'cursed custome of sin', and exhorting the 'deepest Searcher of each secret thought' to 'Infuse in me thy all-affecting grace'. But a most un-Protestant invocation to the Virgin for intercession—'faire queene of mercy and of pittye' 'Bee thou attentive to my painefull dittye' and 'further my Sutes' (11: 24–30)—seems to reflect Essex's familiarity with the literary tropes of Catholic devotional poetry.[25]

Nowhere did the earl express an ideal of toleration grounded in Gentili's sceptical conception of the unknowability of religious doctrine. In his *Apologie* the earl even poses a strong argument for the necessity of religious unity: 'where there is not unitie in the Church, there can be no unitie nor order in the state'.[26] But this argument is used to support the wider purpose of this portion of the treatise, which is to demonstrate that the United Provinces will be forcibly reconverted to Catholicism if they are restored to the hegemony of Spain. And by 1598, Essex had a particular need to express religious orthodoxy in his public persona: his reputation had been blisteringly scorched by his earlier association with Catholic toleration.

Also significant is the quality of the earl's public professions of anti-popery. It has been argued in Chapter 2 that Essex tended to denounce the papal monarchy rather than the spiritual authority of the pope, giving him room for ideological association with Catholic states. This inclination to condemn predominantly the *secular* usurpations of the papacy rather than to identify the pope as antichrist was reflected more widely in English texts in the 1590s. For Sandys, the Roman Catholic Church is 'not so corrupt in the very doctrine ... as it is in the practise thereof, and in the usage'.[27] In *The state of Christendom*, the pope is denounced as 'a man, who seeking the preferment of this world and the advancement of his See, endeavoured by all means possible to obtain his purpose'.[28] William Jones's translation of Guicciardini contains the Florentine's notoriously secular analysis of the rise of the papacy: 'by what meanes the bishops of Rome, being appointed, and established only for the pure, and simple administration of spirituall matters are nowe come to the managing of wordlie states, and principalities'.[29]

[25] Stephen W. May, 'The poems of Edward de Vere, seventeenth Earl of Oxford, and of Robert Devereux, second earl of Essex', *Studies in Philology*, 77/5 (1980), 48–59, 94–106.
[26] *Apologie*, sig. C3ʳ.
[27] Sandys, *A relation of the state of religion*, sig. A3ᵛ.   [28] *State of Christendom* rt., 172.
[29] Francesco Guicciardini, William Jones, trans., *Two discourses of Master Frances Guicciardin* (1595), 5. For Jones, see Chapter 2, 79 n. 62, Chapter 4, 178.

Catholic Gallicanism in late sixteenth-century France had also reinvigo-
rated the long tradition of French ecclesiastical independence from the
secular pretensions of papal power. Similar attitudes could be found in
the late 1590s in the writings of English Catholics, who sought accommodation with the state: the Appellants' controversial attempt to distin-
guish between the spiritual and secular authority of the papacy was very
similar to sentiments aired by Lord Henry Howard, that close companion of the Bacons and of Essex, and in the writings of Thomas Wright.[30]

RELIGIOUS PATRONAGE AND PROTESTANT POLITICS

If Essex's wider following was spiritually heterogeneous, so too was his inner
circle of friends and advisors.[31] In James's reign, Sir Henry Wotton, Essex's
former secretary, now ambassador to Venice, would commission a translation of Sandys's *Relation of the state of religion* during the Interdict Crisis of
1606–7. On Wotton's death in 1639, his apparently self-composed epitaph
read 'The Itch of Disputation will prove the Scab of the Church', pointing
to Wotton's theological kinship with Gentili.[32] Essex's sister, Penelope
Rich, had flirted with conversion to Catholicism in the early 1590s.[33]
Meanwhile, the crypto-Catholicism of Henry Howard, brother of the
executed duke of Norfolk, was widely known;[34] while Southampton,
whose religious beliefs remained ambiguous in Elizabeth's reign at least,
was similarly tainted by his father's imprisonment for complicity in Norfolk's schemes to marry Mary Stuart.[35] More conventionally, the correspondence of Henry Cuffe, the 'purytane skoller', contains forceful expressions of
his antipathy to Rome.[36]

---

[30] In the aftermath of the Gunpowder Plot, Howard wrote the tract *A true and perfect relation of the whole proceedings against . . . Garnet* (1606) which attacked the papal usurpation of temporal power and Catholic resistance theorists.
[31] For the mixed religious character of Essex's wider following see Chapter 1, 54–5.
[32] Logan Pearsall Smith, *The life and letters of Sir Henry Wotton*, 2 vols (Oxford: Clarendon Press, 1907), I, 5–6, 216, 219.
[33] Philip Caraman ed., *John Gerard: the autobiography of an Elizabethan*, 2nd edn (London: Longmans, Green, 1956), 34–5.
[34] John Bossy, *Giordano Bruno and the embassy affair* (New Haven, CT and London: Yale University Press, 1991[2002]), 99–104, 117–25; Andersson, *Henry Howard*.
[35] Southampton's father was imprisoned from 1571 to 1573: Akrigg, *Shakespeare and the earl of Southampton*, 177–81; Questier, *Catholicism and community*, 146.
[36] J. W. van Meel ed., *Francisci et Joannis Hotomanorum . . . epistolae . . .* (Amsterdam, 1700), 285–7; Bod, Ashmole MS 1729, f. 190ʳ.

Essex's role as a patron reveals more about his approach to religious politics than his tricky literary remains. Characteristically, the earl's religious patronage was wide-ranging and pursued with vigour. In 1594–5, Lord Keeper Puckering was assaulted with a stream of requests from the earl, suits for benefices and clerical appointments, especially for Essex's chaplains. The thirty or so men who served the earl as chaplain at some point in their careers sported a wide variety of clerical robes: they included moderate Puritans, Samuel Hieron and Anthony Wotton, but also William Alabaster, the poet, who notoriously converted to Catholicism in 1597, as well as a significant number of clerics who would increasingly be known as proponents of strict conformity—Richard Harris, Lionel Sharpe, and John Buckeridge.[37]

Hammer and Collinson have argued that Essex backed away from the open sponsorship of Puritans after the early-1590s, and Whitgift's successful assault on Presbyterianism; in fact, Essex's protection of the Godly was strongly in evidence until his death.[38] In February 1596, Stephen Egerton, the London Puritan minister, was able to solicit, through the forceful agency of Lady Anne Bacon, for Essex's support of his candidate for a Cambridge fellowship.[39] In the winter of 1599, the privy council interrogated several ministers who prayed for Essex's imperilled health, including several known Puritans: Egerton, Anthony Wotton, and Richard Gardiner.[40] In September 1598, Thomas Cartwright wrote to Essex in the most flattering terms, praising his assistance of the hospital at Warwick, and offering congratulations on his appointment as chancellor of Cambridge: 'Let the chronicles of our land be perused, and I thinck it will hardly be found, that there hath bene any such subject . . . clothed with so much honor, and girded with so much authoritie as you are'.[41] On 25 April 1600, Richard Barkley, the custodian of the now captive earl, relayed Essex's urgent request to be allowed conference with 'doctor Reygnolds of Oxford'—John Rainolds, the Puritan president of Corpus Christi.[42]

---

[37] BL, Harleian MS 6996, ff. 114ʳ, 206ʳ, 210ʳ, 239ʳ, 225ʳ·; BL, Harleian MS 6997, ff. 78ʳ, 102ʳ, 168ʳ, 198ʳ; Hammer, 'Robert Devereux', *ODNB*; Gazzard, 'Patronage of Robert Devereux', 125–31.

[38] Patrick Collinson, *The Elizabethan Puritan Movement* (London: Jonathan Cape, 1967), 444–7; Hammer, *Polarisation*, 27, 80–1.

[39] LPL MS 655, ff. 138ʳ, 183ʳ.

[40] The episode is analysed in Chapter 5, 207–9.

[41] Cecil MS 64/69. Early in 1597, at the request of a group of Hampshire gentry, Essex procured the deanery of Winchester for a Dr Heaton, who 'molifyeth the obdurat harts of Irreligious subjects': Cecil MS/186/62.

[42] Cecil MS 78/93. Essex had briefly sponsored Rainolds' lectureship at Queen's College, after the death in 1590 of his patron Francis Walsingham: Mordechai Feingold, 'Rainolds, John (1549–1607)', *ODNB*.

Dedications from the Godly poured off the presses throughout the 1590s, eulogizing Essex's religious credentials. In 1595 Nicholas Bownd, a Puritan minister from Suffolk, acknowledged the earl's previous favours shown to him, and urged his patron to use his exalted position to propagate the message of the *Doctrine of the Sabbath plainely layde forth*.[43] William Hubbock dedicated his treatise on infant baptism to Essex in 1595, hailing the earl's support of London preachers: 'The Lord ripen the good worke he hath begun in your Honour, and increase it with the mightie increasings of God'.[44] Thanking Essex for his 'favour' and 'protection', Robert Linaker prayed that the 'honorable and religious disposition' of the earl would incline him to appreciate his treatise on assurance.[45]

While entertaining the fervent hopes and admiration of the Godly, though, Essex's relationship with Whitgift also intensified. According to Paule, Whitgift's biographer, after the death of Francis Walsingham Essex pledged 'to runne a course for Cleargie causes, according to [Whitgift's] directions'.[46] Whigift reciprocated, maintaining a constant friendship even as Essex's political star began to plummet, which 'drew vpon the Archbishop . . . [the] severest reprehension from her Majestie, that he had ever before vnder-gone in all his life'.[47] The earl's participation in the BA Commencement in 1595 also aligned him with Whigift's attempt to assert the conservative and Calvinist doctrinal position of Conformists. In the same year William Covell, fellow of Queens' College (where Essex and his party had been entertained during the Commencement), dedicated to the earl his treatise *Polimanteia*, which denounced all religious disunity and disobedience as dangerously detrimental to the strength of the common-wealth.[48]

At this moment the doctrinal radar of Essex and Whitgift was ranging beyond the immediate internal tensions in the Elizabethan church. Elizabeth Gilliam and W. J. Tighe have argued that the Lambeth Articles themselves were an act of peace-making born of political as well as theological confusion, determined above all by uncertainty about the

---

[43] Nicholas Bownd, *The doctrine of the Sabbath, plainely layde forth* (1595), sig. A2^{r-v}.

[44] William Hubbock, *An apologie of infants* (1595), sig. A3^v, [A5^r].

[45] Robert Linaker, *A comfortable treatise for the reliefe of such as are afflicted in conscience* (1595), sig. A2^v. Also see Josias Nichols, *Abrahams faith: that is, the olde religion* (1596); L.T., *Babylon is Fallen* (1597).

[46] George Paule, *The life of the most reuerend and religious prelate John Whitgift, Lord Archbishop of Canterbury* (1612), 57.

[47] Ibid., 69.

[48] Covell, *Polimanteia, or, The meanes lawfull and vnlawfull, to iudge of the fall of a common-wealth . . .* (Cambridge, 1595), sigs. Y3^r– Bb4^v.

succession and the religion of James VI.[49] This also seems a likely context for Essex's attitudes. Through Anthony Bacon's channels of intelligence, Essex was better informed than most about the complexity of Scottish religious politics. When Scottish ministers Walter Balcanqu-hall and Robert Bruce, scornful critics of James's religious policies, escaped imprisonment by fleeing to England in December 1596, they appealed to Essex, whose 'religious disposition towards God hath . . . knitt our affections so intirelie towards yor honour'. But although they named Catholics close to the king as agents of their hard fortune, Essex refused to offer protection to dissidents who had incurred James's severe disfavour.[50]

Inevitably, the clienteles of many Elizabethan aristocrats often contained men and women of different religious persuasions.[51] Essex's religious patronage, though, deliberately established him as a figure of mediation between different confessional groups. In return, his offer of protection, as to the Godfreys, was conditional on their being 'very discreet and dutifull', neither disruptive nor disloyal. The need to quell religious dissidence was also crucial because the nature of the government of church and state after the queen's death—which surely now approached?—was unknown. In this respect Essex's religion and religious politics bore a strong and ironic resemblance not only to those of James but also Robert Cecil, who similarly appealed to a spectrum of religious opinion, covertly sponsoring the publication of Appellant literature in 1600–3 for equally politique reasons.[52] The difference, though, was that Essex engaged with religious politics in a far noisier way: his religious patronage and the protection he offered to Catholics in particular were a vital element of his boldly crafted public persona. There was much truth in the allegations made after the rising that Essex affected to be 'the only noble man that cared for religion'.[53]

Essex's desire to be recognized as a significant religious patron became especially marked in 1594–5, when he stepped up the intensity of his clerical patronage, and cemented his alliance with Whitgift. These years were intended to be pivotal to Essex's political career, when the earl and

---

[49] Elizabeth Gilliam and W. J. Tighe, 'To "Run with the Time". Archbishop Whitgift, the Lambeth Articles, and the Politics of Theological Ambiguity in Late Elizabethan England', *Sixteenth Century Journal*, 23/2 (1992), 325–40.

[50] LPL MS 654, f. 256ʳ.

[51] See David L. Smith, 'Catholic, Anglican or Puritan? Edward Sackville, Fourth Earl of Dorset and the Ambiguities of Religion in Early Stuart England', *TRHS*, 6th series, 2 (1992), 105–24.

[52] Pauline Croft, 'The Religion of Robert Cecil', *HJ*, 34 (1991), 773–96.

[53] TNA, SP 12/278/63, f. 108ʳ.

his circle made a concerted effort to enhance his public image as the leading young statesman in England, and the most likely instrument of the succession.[54] The earl's sublimation of religious politics within his broader ambition was already apparent to more critical observers. In Spain, Robert Parsons was aware.

ESSEX, THE BACONS, AND CATHOLIC TOLERATION

Essex's concerted effort to magnetize Catholic loyalism also significantly intensified in the mid-1590s. As he strove to show that he, rather than Burghley, in this most delicate of businesses should be the statesman who engaged successfully with Catholic politics, the earl deliberately established himself as a mediating figure through whom Catholics as well as the Godly could express their devotion to 'her Majesty and the state'.

Both Cecils also recognized the propaganda value of engaging with Catholic loyalists, but Burghley, as we have seen, had been rabidly vilified in Jesuit polemic in the early 1590s as the particular foe of English Catholics, the machiavellian counsellor, the atheistical architect of anti-Catholic legislation.[55] As Standen reported to Anthony Bacon, 'all these rigors now used in England are attributed to my L. Treseror', who was deemed by 'all the catholiques in Christendom . . . an open declared & professed enemie to their faythe and religion'.[56] It was small wonder that Essex's rumoured sympathy for Catholicism would be eagerly tested, especially after his opportune elevation to the privy council in 1593. Had Elizabeth finally availed herself of a 'good' counsellor, sympathetic to Catholic fortunes?

The return of Standen in 1593 was the first significant example of Bacon and Essex working to protect and facilitate the return of an English Catholic exile. On 22 April 1595, just before the return of Thomas Wright in June, Essex directed a petition of the privy council to Whigift (again) that a certain John Gattacre, who had 'lyved some tyme in conversation of ill affected persons and ffugitives', be admitted 'to the chardge of some learned devine . . . [to be] instructed and brought to conformity'. Gattacre protested passionately that 'the cheife occasion of

---

[54] The sermons by Puritan ministers dedicated to Essex discussed above were all published in 1595; the earl was the recipient of more Godly dedications in that year than in any other.

[55] Chapter 2, 85–7.

[56] LPL MS 648, f. 140ʳ; these are excerpts extracted by Bacon from Standen's letters.

his voluntary repayre hether was to lyve in dutyfull obedience to her Majesty'.[57] The return of Catholic exiles like Standen and Gattacre, (as well as the welcome reception of Pérez), could be justified by the intelligence they would provide about the activity of English Catholics, and of affairs in Spain. Because the expression of Hispanophobia was a means of demonstrating loyalty to the patria, Catholic exiles also tended to provide the kind of information about Spain that Essex wanted to hear: Wright's evidence of Philip's intended invasion plans reached Essex as he sought justification for a direct attack on Spain.[58]

Essex and his continental agents also struck up significant acquaintance with those who would later be associated with the Appellant cause. Dr Hawkins, Essex's agent in Venice, maintained contacts with Robert Fisher and Robert Markham, students at the English College at Rome, expelled for their antipathy towards the Jesuits. Fisher, who forged links between the anti-Spanish circles of Charles Paget in Flanders and the secular clergy at Wisbech, boasted acquaintance with the 'better-born followers of the earl of Essex'.[59] In 1599, William Watson, polemicist for the Appellants, claimed that Essex had given him personal assurance of his desire that Catholics should have freedom of conscience.[60]

In response, Essex was also petitioned by 'loyalist' Catholics in continental exile, who yoked their fortunes to his rising star. In the spring of 1599, William Tresham, brother of Sir Thomas, begged Essex—known for his 'singular humanitye to some in the same predicament'—to ease his return to his native country where he might live in 'naturall obedience'.[61] In the autumn of 1597, letters were intercepted from the exiled Francis Dacre to Essex and Lady Warwick, avowing Dacre's loyalty to Elizabeth, and repudiating his association with Philip II. The great-uncle of the young viscount Montague, Dacre was a noisy advocate of James VI's claim to the English throne, and had been embroiled in internal quarrels between Jesuits at the Spanish court over the succession.[62] In the spring of

[57] LPL Fairhurst MS 3470, f. 162ʳ. The letter is signed by the whole privy council, but is directly from Essex: Gattacre was 'by mee the Erle of Essex placed wth Mr Alderman Lee'.

[58] Stroud, 'Thomas Wright', 196–8; Bacon's papers also contain copies of letters passed between Henry Garnet, Superior of the Jesuits in England, and Wright in January 1596: LPL MS 654, ff. 127, 249.

[59] P. Renold ed., *The Wisbech stirs, 1595–1598* (London: Catholic Record Society, 1958), xvi–xvii, 256, 261–2.

[60] T.G. Law ed., *The Archpriest controversy: documents relating to the dissensions of the Roman Catholic clergy, 1597–1601*, 2 vols (London: Camden Society, n.s., 56, 1896) II, 222; Holmes, *Resistance and compromise*, 204.

[61] TNA, SP 15/34/2, ff. 7ʳ, 23ʳ; Tresham wrote also to Henry Howard, SP 12/272/85.

[62] T. M. McCoog, 'Harmony Disrupted: Robert Parsons, S.J., William Crichton, S.J. and the Question of Queen Elizabeth's Successor, 1581–1603', *Archivum Historicum Societatis Iesu*, 73 (2004), 149–220.

1598, it was rumoured that his appearance in Scotland, where he was received and protected by the king, had been mediated by Essex himself.[63]

Catholics close to the earl came to doubt the sincerity of Essex's Protestant faith. Under interrogation on 15 February 1601, Thomas Wright claimed that he had come to 'believe the Earle of Essex a catholique, and that it was a matter of policie for him to conceale it that so both puritans and protestants might be drawn to take his parte'.[64] In 1597, Essex's former chaplain, William Alabaster, was taken into custody when news emerged that he was writing a conversion narrative. Alabaster, who named Wright as the agent of his own spiritual transformation, claimed that he had written the *Seven Motives* with the intention of converting Essex, his former patron.[65]

But many Catholics expected Essex to engage in far grander schemes than protection, or even private conversion. An anonymous and undated petition to the earl directly requested that Essex broker a formal deal for the private toleration of worship in return for a Catholic oath of loyalty.[66] The relations of Essex and Henry Constable, poet and famous Catholic convert, also offer illuminating insight into the earl's association with toleration and loyalism.

In the autumn of 1589, Constable—not yet an open convert—and Jean de Villiers Hotman were employed by Essex and Penelope Rich in the earl's earliest known scheme to open communication with James VI: an opportunity that Constable seized for 'sume reasoning' with James about religion.[67] Joining Essex's expedition to France in 1591, Constable openly repudiated his Protestantism, remaining as a voluntary exile, where he schemed throughout the 1590s to convince Henry IV, James VI, and Essex to support his project for the reconciliation of the churches. Constable was also the author of the irenic treatise, *Examen pacifique de la doctrine des Huguenots* (1589); a response to Robert Bellarmine, the work is narrated by a Catholic

[63] Cecil MS 55/51, 57, 65, 176/34, 140; *HMC Salisbury*, IX, 309; Questier, *Catholicism and community*, 222–6, 243–4.

[64] TNA, SP 12/278/65, f. 112^r.

[65] The substance of the *Seven Motives* is known from replies to it: Roger Fenton, *An answere to William Alablaster [sic] his motives* (1599); dedicated to Essex is John Racster, *William Alablasters [sic] seven motives. Removed and confuted* (1598). For Alabaster, see G. M. Story and Helen Gardner eds, *The sonnets of William Alabaster* (Oxford: English Monographs, 1959); Dana F. Sutton, *Unpublished works by William Alabaster (1568–1640)* (Oxford and Salzburg: Salzburg University Press, 1997), 123–4.

[66] The petition is printed in A. J. Loomie, 'A Catholic petition to the earl of Essex', *Recusant History*, 7 (1963), 33–42. This was the deal that the Appellants would try to strike in 1602.

[67] *HMC Salisbury*, III, 435–6; David Baird Smith, 'Jean de Villiers Hotman' *Scottish Historical Review*, 14 (1916–17), 153–5; Joan Grundy ed., *The poems of Henry Constable* (Liverpool: Liverpool University Press, 1960), 28–30.

persona, who advocates the toleration of Huguenots because the significant confessional divisions between Catholic and Reformed churches are few, and of recent origin.[68] Constable did not idealize pluralism, but he made the core of his irenicism the shared roots of Catholic and Reformed doctrine, adopting the minimalist understanding of fundamentals characteristic of Gentili's beliefs. There was much in Constable's approach to religion that was compatible with the outlook of Essex's inner circle.

In October 1595, Constable renewed his relationship with the earl, expressing his hopes for Catholic toleration in England, and the reunion of Western Christendom. His approach was considered; he dangled in front of Essex the standard tropes of Hispanophobic Catholic loyalism: hostility to Philip II, and the flattering prospect of a great martial role for the earl of a 'mor honorable sort ... against the common fo [foe] of Christendome', the Turk, once peace in religion had been restored.[69] Constable clearly also believed that the political future belonged to Essex—'the worthiest prince which this day liveth'—not the ageing Burghley or his son.[70]

And Constable's 'loyalism' was unabashedly limited. The poet's desire to be 'not unprofitable to my contry' was defined with the express qualification—'though in all other sorts wherein my religion is not prejudiced'.[71] In her excellent analysis of Constable's sonnets, Alison Shell writes that Constable 'is unusual among Catholic loyalists in barbing his praise of Elizabeth'.[72] When he assured Essex that he was 'not in the nomber of those which wish the restitution thereof [of Catholicism] with the servitude of my country to forreine Tiranny', his declaration implied that he objected only to the means, but certainly not the ends, of the restoration of Catholicism in England by Spanish conquest.[73]

Constable did not need to formulate a rhetorically loving relationship with Elizabeth because his own vision, too, was focused north of the border. Having intimate knowledge of Essex's secret channels of communication with James, he wrote a succession tract in 1600 which refuted Parsons's *Conference* and defended the Scottish claim.[74] He would later reveal that he had rejected a surprising invitation from Essex to join the

---

[68] The work was published in England by John Wolfe; a second edition appeared in 1590, with a false Paris imprint: D. Rogers, '"The Catholic Moderator": A French Reply to Bellarmine and its English Author, Henry Constable', *Recusant History*, 5 (1960) 224–35; John Bossy, 'A propos of Henry Constable', *Recusant History*, 6 (1962), 228–37. An English translation was published in 1623 as *The Catholike Moderator: or a moderate examination of the doctrine of the Protestants.*
[69] Cecil MS 175/3.   [70] Cecil MS 35/50.
[71] Ibid.   [72] Shell, *Catholicism, controversy*, 126.
[73] Cecil MS 35/50.
[74] The anonymous *Discoverye of a counterfecte conference...for thaduancement of a counterfecte tytle* (Paris, 1600, imprint Cologne).

Irish expedition of 1599; he had preferred, instead, to travel to Scotland, to sound out the likelihood of James's conversion.[75]

Constable's contiguous correspondence with Anthony Bacon offers a particularly arresting insight into the dynamics of religious politics in Essex's circle. Though the two had never met, he wrote in a far more intimate fashion to Bacon than to Essex, addressing him as a particularly sympathetic intellect. In letters to Bacon written in October 1595 and December the following year, Constable stressed their shared common aims: he was certain that Bacon had weighed up the 'truth of all particular religions', and understood that theological division was a natural and inevitable feature of Christian history. Though differing 'in 'particularytys of religion', they surely agreed on the fundamentals: 'generall beleaf of Christ', mutual 'desier of the union of his church'. In response to Bacon's agent's request for treatises and books, Constable sent to Anthony a manuscript of an unpublished disputation with Huguenot ministers.[76]

The religious outlook of Anthony and Francis Bacon seems to have had a formative impact on Essex's religious posture. Born of a formidably Puritan mother, both were educated under Whitgift's tutelage at Cambridge. Through his travels in the 1580s Anthony had become the friend and correspondent of Theodore Beza and leaders of the Huguenot cause, but he also forged, as Essex's intelligence gatherer, links with Catholics based upon friendship and ideological association.[77] Thomas Wright, on his return to England, knew to surrender specifically to Anthony.[78] In September 1596, Anthony's relations with Wright, Pérez, and his great intimacy with Henry Howard incurred very pointed criticism from Burghley. Bacon wrote up his encounter with Lady Russell, his aunt, who tried to reconcile the breach with his uncle, as a 'relation' or an 'Apologie' that delivers the staunchest defence of his Catholic friendships. Of Wright he declares that the 'infallible arguments of his loyal and dutyfull harte to his Soveraine and Contrie, whatsoever his religion and profession is, I thought it farre from humanitie much more from Christian charretie to barre him my dore and my bord'.[79] In Bacon's papers are also copies of a satirical poem slandering Richard Topcliffe that imagine the

---

[75] Grundy, *Henry Constable*, 37–40. The mission was unsuccessful, but Constable was back in Rome in 1600, seeking papal approval for another approach to James.

[76] LPL MS 652, f. 38; MS 660, f. 161[r].

[77] Anthony's friendships with Catholics, Standen and Pérez in particular, provoked a tirade of admonishment from his mother, Lady Anne Bacon: see, for example, Birch, *Memoirs*, I, 107; Ungerer, *Spaniard*, I, 221.

[78] LPL MS 650, f. 260[r].

[79] LPL MS 659, ff. 21[r], 25v–26[r], 104[r]. Essex approved of Bacon's 'relacion in which I tooke so great pleasure as reeding it att going to my bed I found it ran in my hedd all the night after', LPL MS 659, f. 138[r].

notorious priest-hunter grabbing the 'silken garments' from one of his victims as he twitches on the gibbet.[80]

It was in the writings associated with both Bacons that a politique ideal of toleration and political stability was advocated which is closest to the stance that Essex tried to adopt. In Francis Bacon's early tracts, *An advertisement touching the controversies of the Church of England* (1589) and *Certain observations made upon a libel* (1592), he endorses an orthodox defence of Elizabeth's religious policies, fiercely condemning Catholic attacks on secular power. Bacon argues, though, that the undesirability of religious pluralism must be set against the greater need for stability within the English church, and he places consistent emphasis on the role of preaching and education to correct religious error. In both treatises he admits, not dissimilarly to Constable, that internal conflict is the sign of a true church; after the 'highest mysteries of faith' had been agreed, theological differences of interpretation inevitably emerged. But in response to the Marprelate pamphleteers, Bacon argues that disputation must be reasoned and decorous, never the stuff of common libels, or 'handled in the style of the stage'.[81]

The religious ideas propounded in *The state of Christendom* are broadly similar, but contain a more purposeful endorsement of religious toleration on politique and spiritual grounds. The treatise itself, of course, is framed as the narration of an English Catholic exile who seeks accommodation with the regime. As the narrator's persona fades away, however, the (Protestant) authorial voice compares Elizabeth's policies towards Catholics with Philip II's repression of Protestantism: though Elizabeth has not yet been moved to grant the 'humble petitions' of her 'natural and most loving subjects' for freedom of worship, they enjoy 'liberty of conscience without danger of a Spanish Inquisition'.[82] As in Francis Bacon's tracts, populist intervention is censured: 'unquiet spirits may with a small Pamphlet, or with a simple Sermon do more harm than a number of learned men shall be able to amend or reform with great pains and travail'.[83]

The author, though, returns repeatedly to toleration. While 'there is no straighter tie, No surer stay, no stronger hold to conjoin and knit the hearts of Subjects together, then is the conformitie and unitie of religion', great danger lies in the repression of religious conscience, which can have catastrophic effects on civil stability, as Spain has experienced in the Netherlands.[84] And since 'mens consciences ought to be free and at

---

[80] LPL MS 656, f. 199^r.
[81] Spedding, *L&L*, I, 74–95, 164–5, 177–82.
[82] *State of Christendom*, 128.
[83] Ibid., 227.
[84] Ibid., 19–23, 128–36.

libertie', conversion requires other means—time, toleration, and exposure to the truth—which can only emerge from free discourse: the 'true Christians shall converse with the Schismaticks of the world', just as Christ conversed daily with 'Publicans, with Pharisees, with Sadduces'.[85] Crucially, states that allow religious pluralism are stable and secure: there is 'no straighter League of Amitie amongst them than there is amongst the people of *Poland, Switzerland,* and other Nations which give Friendly entertainment unto a pluralitie of Religions'.[86] Could England grant freedom of worship to Catholics while engaging them in decorous debate? In such an environment, the loyalist Catholic narrator might surely convert to Protestantism.

Antipapal Gallicanism was a model that the Bacons, educated by Whitgift, seem to have admired. Anthony had a copy made of a scurrilous poem libelling Nicholas de Thou, bishop of Chartres, for his rumoured elevation as a cardinal, which dishonoured the liberties of the French church:

> qui pour meriter un Chapeau
> de la boutique vaticane
> a vendu l'honneur de son Roy
> et fait un commerce pour soy
> de la liberté gallicane.[87]

In a letter to Francis from July 1594, Anthony even complained of the 'excessive indiscreet zeale of them of the religion'—i.e. the *Huguenots*—'who not having patience to stay the kings further successe & establishment' had dangerously stirred up the common people against the recently converted king!'[88]

If it is unsurprising that Constable expected Essex and Anthony Bacon to be sympathetic to his irenicism, it is also important to remember that all favoured toleration for opposing ends. When Essex wrote to Whitgift asking that Gattacre be allowed to return from exile, he was to be given learned religious instruction. This condition sweetened the likely success of Essex's petition, but also reflected the irenic commonplace prized by the Bacons: that heresy would be eliminated if toleration were combined with education—but education in the doctrine of the Reformed Church of England. Constable may similarly have emphasized the mutual foundations of Catholic and Reformed belief, but his idealized vision of a post-succession England was ultimately a Catholic state.

---

[85] *State of Christendom*, 130–1.
[86] Ibid., 132.
[87] LPL MS 658, f. 257ʳ.
[88] LPL MS 650, f. 226ʳ.

Strategy, language, and rhetorical tropes common to the discourse of toleration created an illusion of a straight and easy path where Essex could guide Thomases Wright and Cartwright safely towards an irenic future. At close inspection, though, the road to the post-Elizabethan reign forked in divergent routes, to different destinations. These were the hopes and expectations that James VI was bound to disappoint in the early years of his rule.

THOMAS WRIGHT: ESSEX AND THE TEST CASE FOR TOLERATION

These tensions and contradictions were most clearly embodied in the relations of Essex and his circle with Thomas Wright. Essex's succour of Wright was qualitatively different from the protection he offered to Catholic exiles such as Standen and Gattacre. When Wright returned to England in June 1595 he had a clear programme: to achieve personal toleration which would act as a general precedent from which English Catholics would be granted freedom of worship itself. In a letter to the queen, Wright explained that by lenient treatment to 'an irremovable Catholique', other Catholics would be persuaded to abandon 'ther sollicityng of foreyn hostilities, & ther practezyes against your person, and state'.[89] But Wright's scheme was also foolhardy: in February, the Jesuit Robert Southwell had been hanged, drawn, and quartered at Tyburn.

It has been assumed that Wright peddled a particularly authoritarian line on obedience and allegiance to the monarch.[90] Early in 1596, he bitterly complained to Henry Garnet that Jesuits (meaning Parsons) must stop meddling with theories of resistance: '[our] vocation is religion, & not suppressing of princes: for otherwise I am afraid lest all our preests be rather putt to death for matters of state, then religion'.[91] At close inspection, though, Wright's 'loyalism' was as ambivalent as Constable's. His letter to the queen contains a masterly fusion of subjugation to Elizabeth's authority and qualification of his obedience. Wright's expressed desire merely to 'render my life at your feet, & into your power' is contradicted by an audacious threat: if Elizabeth were not to grant him toleration of conscience he would be forced to return to exile, 'Wher according to my calling, I shalbe enforced ether to instruct & prepare preists for England; or my selfe com again and offend yowr lawes . . . and that in a higher degre,

---

[89] BL, Lansdowne MS 109, f. 48ʳ.
[90] Pritchard, *Catholic loyalism*, 61–7; Shell, *Catholicism, conformity*, 126–7.
[91] LPL MS 654, f. 127ᵛ.

then yf I heere resyded privately'.[92] In tone and even vocabulary Wright's letter to the queen is not dissimilar to the epistles that Essex would soon write to Elizabeth when in political disgrace, in which he married expressions of absolute subjection to the queen's mercy and will while qualifying the terms of his devotion. Unlike Essex's letters, it seems doubtful that Wright's reached Elizabeth's eyes.[93]

Despite the ambiguity in Wright's loyalism his political outlook, like that of Constable, was in many senses perfectly Essexian. Wright returned armed with a Latin discourse which discussed that favourite litmus test of the loyalties of an English Catholic—*An lictum sit Catholicis in Anglia arma sumere, & aliis modis Reginam, et regnum defendere contra Hispanos*— whether it should be lawful for English Catholics to bear arms against the king of Spain.[94] The precise date of the composition is unclear, but it seems most likely that the treatise was a manifesto underscoring the purpose of Wright's return in 1595. A version survives in Burghley's papers in the Lansdowne manuscripts, but Burghley, who was overtly hostile to the freedoms granted Wright, cannot have approved of the tract's political messages. The treatise was, however, read by Essex and members of his circle with keen interest, probably with a view to further dissemination. Anthony Bacon wrote to Edward Reynolds on 3 January 1596 to ask him to send 'Wryghtes lattin discourse' back if the earl had finished reading it; Reynolds responded that Essex 'hath not yet had sufficient tyme to peruse Mr Wrights discourse thoroughly', although Anthony could borrow it again for two days.[95]

Wright's view of Anglo-Spanish relations and his concept of the future of Christendom were quintessentially Essexian. Although more circumspect than some later Appellant tracts, Wright's allows that the pope might err in issues that do not pertain to matters of faith, meaning pointedly the case of papal support for Spanish aggression against England. And Wright also presents Philip as a secular and irreligious tyrant, whose 'cruel and insatiable' soldiers would make no distinction between Catholic and Protestant in the 'huge effusion of blood' that would follow a successful Spanish invasion. Against the accusation that Elizabeth pursued an unjust war, made viscerally in Parsons's and Verstegan's anti-commonwealth tracts, Wright insists that it is Philip who is the threat to the 'security' and 'tranquility' of Western Europe, 'the dominion of the Spaniards spreading far and near'. He also invokes that favourite Essexian

---

[92] BL, Lansdowne MS 109, f. 48ʳᵛ.   [93] See Chapter 4.

[94] The treatise can be found in manuscript, BL, Lansdowne MS 115, ff. 95ʳ–101ʳ; I have used this to modify the translation in Strype, *Annals*, III, ii, 583–96.

[95] LPL MS 654, ff. 101ʳ, 109ʳ.

topos, calling on 'all Christian princes', Protestant and Catholic alike, 'France, Scotland, Denmark' to join the common cause and halt the further spread of Spanish tyranny.[96]

The second purpose of Wright's treatise, though, is to address the future of Catholicism in England, in a manner that would have made uncomfortable reading for many English Protestants. There are, Wright insists, 'many other ways of bringing in the Catholic faith into England' than by conquest. If English Catholics are sufficiently loyal and fight for their country, he mischievously suggests, Elizabeth herself might be tempted to convert: 'Who knows she may convert and live?' More likely, she would 'yield to them the liberty of conscience as she has already granted to some' (i.e. himself). But for Wright, too, the succession is the key to Catholic hopes: 'whoever succeeds will certainly be a Catholic, or will permit us to live as Catholics'. Any 'pretenders' to the throne will have to court Catholics, promising 'religious liberty'.[97]

This is a bald and succinct explication of the politique reasons why James VI and Essex both deemed the support of Catholics so essential to the politics of succession. Wright has more radical propositions that might excite the expectations of Catholic readers. The future of Protestantism itself, he argues, is doomed by religious disputation: 'A Protestant being set between Catholics and Puritans, if they must incline to one extreme, will far more probably embrace Catholicism'. It is difficult not to think that Wright imagines Essex as this pliable learned Protestant, whose exposure to Puritan and Catholic arguments would convert him to true faith. Trusting in divine providence, Catholics must 'yield to the time', with confidence that their lot would improve.[98] Wright might have described himself as Elizabeth's loyal subject, and praised the legitimacy of her wars against Spain, but his description of English Catholics is of a subjugated people, enjoined to passive suffering—for the *immediate* future.

The intended audience for the treatise is unclear; it does not appear to have been circulated by Essex. Yet this general exhortation to all Catholics has the quality of public document. Wright, who kept Anthony Bacon abreast of his literary projects, defined the proselytizing role he intended to play through publication, envisaging 'everie 6 monthes to set fourth some thinge' in print, ideally dedicated to Essex and licensed by Whitgift.[99] By

[96] BL, Lansdowne MS, ff. 95ʳ–97ʳ.
[97] Ibid., f. 99ʳ⁻ᵛ. [98] Ibid., f. 99ᵛ.
[99] LPL, MS 654, f. 285ᵛ. Wright did indeed make vigorous use of the press. Treatises that Whitgift refused to license were *The disposition or garnishmente of the soule to receiue worthily the blessed Sacrament*, and *A treatise, shewing the possibilitie, and conueniencie of the reall presence of our Saviour in the blessed Sacrament*, both published secretly in England in 1596 with a false Antwerp imprint, as was Wright's *Certaine articles or forcible Reasons*.

January 1596, when Anthony Bacon was requesting to reread Wright's treatise, the priest had forfeited his boldly claimed freedom: any possibility of publication of this particular treatise through Essex's agents—scribal or otherwise—would be out of the question.

REGNUM ESSEXIANUM

The adoption of Wright by Essex through the immediate agency of Anthony Bacon demonstrated the growing assurance they both had of Essex's political influence, particularly in the sphere of foreign policy.[100] Yet to sponsor and protect a priest such as Wright—still with some affiliation to the Jesuits—was an unprecedented and extraordinary move, not copied after. The archbishop of York, Matthew Hutton, expressed a more conventional apoplexy at the protection of 'a Jesuite a man of State an Archtraitor continuing still in the verie dregges of poperie'.[101] When Essex gained for Wright the liberty to visit his family at York in September, where his notoriously recusant relations lived, Hutton and the earl of Huntingdon, Essex's former guardian, were horrified. Wright apparently soon conformed to type: Archbishop Hutton alleged that he advocated the 'absurd and dangerous oppinion of the killing of a Tirant'.[102] In light of his complaints to Garnet it seems very curious that Wright would have publicly disputed deposition, but Hutton's accusations clearly demonstrate his assumption that all (even former) Jesuits were likely to endorse theories of resistance. It underscores just how controversial were Wright's circumstances.

Essex was forced to demand Wright's return to London, initially to Essex House. In late October, however, Burghley commanded that Wright be sequestered with Gabriel Goodman, dean of Westminster, where he was to be forcibly instructed in Protestantism; a strategy which horribly backfired when instead Wright was accused of converting William Alabaster to Catholicism (a charge that he fiercely denied).[103] From September 1597, Wright spent spells in various prisons, punctuated by a brief escape in February 1600. Although both Bacons and Mountjoy made persistent attempts to intercede for Wright with Essex and the

---

Discouering the palpable absurdities, and most notorious and intricate errors of the Protestants religion, published in 1600. The latter was a strident attack on Protestantism that the authorities hastened to suppress: *HMC Salisbury*, X, 135–6. The less ostensibly Catholic tract *The Passions of the minde* (1601) was published by a London printer. Note the similarity in title to Essex's 'last poem'.

[100] LPL, MS 652, f. 87[r].   [101] Ibid., f. 131[r].
[102] Ibid., f. 131[r–v].   [103] Ibid., f. 115[r].

queen, the earl, preoccupied with his naval campaigns, did nothing that aided the prisoner's predicament.[104] Initially, however, Wright was confident that his patron would release him; while he waited, he whiled away the hours producing the kind of literary compositions generally associated with attempts to glamourize Essex's public reputation.

In the first winter of his discontented captivity, Wright composed a long series of *imprese* (emblems with associated verses) and longer poems which survive in several versions in Anthony Bacon's papers.[105] Three sets were written in November 1595 and another in December, endorsed as 'inventions' or 'conceyts' of 'Monsieur Wright'.[106] The verses appear to have been devised for practical use in some form of public pageantry: the individual descriptions of the *imprese* from November are headed with instructions to 'Painte' each image, and Alison Shell suggests that they were composed for use at the Accession Day Tournaments on 17 November. The verses from December, however, cannot have been written for the Accession Day celebrations: once the imagery of the *imprese* is unpacked, more complex frames of reference emerge.

A first set of the *imprese* from November is addressed directly to Elizabeth, and celebrates the purity and prosperity of her rule. An emblem of the constellation of Leo and Virgo, under fruiting vines, olives, and corn, represents Elizabeth as Astraea, harbinger of prosperity and fertility.[107] A more significant number, though, celebrate England's glorious role in war. The very first image is of a lioness, her paws aloft, swatting the Habsburg eagle. A broken scythe, crowned with a 'circle of glorie' is accompanied by the motto *Frangendo fabricas* (by making you make); it celebrates the renaissance ideal of virtue strengthened by action.[108] Shell has described these *imprese* as 'extravagantly patriotic and pro-monarchical', but this is only true in so far as they reflect Essex's conception of what Elizabeth's foreign policy *should* be: the fertility of Elizabeth's government and the prosperity of

---

[104] Examples of the desperate letters Wright wrote to Essex and Anthony Bacon during his imprisonment are LPL, MS 654, ff. 281ʳ, 285; MS 655, f. 101ʳ; MS 658, ff. 134ʳ, 137–9, 297–8.

[105] The only scholarly attention to date is in Alison Shell's important discussion: Shell, *Catholicism, controversy*, 126–9.

[106] The poems are found in LPL, MS 652 in several copies, out of sequence: 'Des inversions de Mr Wright mois de Novembre 1595', ff. 204ʳ–206ᵛ, 144ʳ–145ᵛ, 214ʳ–215ᵛ. Copies of a second set of *imprese* and a set of emblems libelling the Cecils are ff. 207ʳ, 210ʳ, 212ᵛ, and f. 224ʳ⁻ᵛ. Further emblems that praise Essex's virtues can be found in ff. 217ʳ–218ᵛ, and ff. 327ʳ–332ᵛ. From December are 'Des verses ou inventions de Mr Wright le 20ᵐᵉ Decembre 1595', ff. 335ʳ–336ᵛ, 309ʳ–310ᵛ.

[107] LPL MS 652, f. 205ᵛ.   [108] Ibid., f. 205ʳ⁻ᵛ.

the commonwealth are dependent on the pursuit of a vigorous and interventionist foreign policy that was far from the queen's own ideal.[109]

A further set of *imprese*—longer, and accompanied by Latin and English
verses—completely ignores the queen and focuses entirely on Essex's virtues, which are more numerous, positive, and personal than those of
Elizabeth. The first, an *impresa* of the world, represents Essex: a 'microcos-
mos' of the earth, God's creation, 'who 'lacketh almost no perfectione or
complement in nature'. In Wright's *imprese* Essex rather than Burghley is
Elizabeth's leading statesman, bringing to his role as a councillor 'such
maturitie and deliberatione, I may well attribute unto him the gravitie of
Saturne' (a sneaky appropriation of Burghley's nickname, 'old Saturnus').[110]

Wright's *imprese* also define Essex's greatness in international affairs as
forging political *and religious* peace in Christendom.[111] In text accompanying an *impresa* of a rainbow, Wright describes the 'preparation as it
weare to a diluge for the warres betwixt us and the Spanyiardes' and 'the
dissention of relligion betwixt us at home'. Essex, though, 'doth undoubtedly pronosticate unto us a future peace, bothe at home and abrode, *yf his
noble procedings be not crossed'* [emphasis added]. The English verse describes the wars to come as an Anglo-Spanish conflict: 'Iberus force with
Albion doth contend/Religions haughtie ensignes are displaied'.[112] In the
Latin verse, Essex is described unequivocally as the future *auctor foederis*,
the author of the peace treaty gained by military supremacy; a role that he
would envisage for himself and England in his *Apologie* of 1598.

Through this emblematic imagery Wright creates for Essex a political
identity that brilliantly yokes the earl's vision of the war to his own
manifesto for the politics of religious toleration. The likelihood of 'the
dissention of religion betwixt us at home' could refer to conflict
between Protestant and Catholic, but also conflict between Catholics,
between Hispanophiles of the Parsons camp, or 'loyalists' who oppose a
Spanish invasion. In any case, religious peace will be restored by anti-
Spanish courses, resolved by Essex himself.[113] The final set of Wright's
imprese, those written in December, widens Wright's targets for praise,
depicting Essex as one third of a virtuous triumvirate, with Anthony
Bacon and Henry Howard. The first image is the most provocative: it is
of an altar, in front of which Essex, Howard, and Bacon 'conspire/To
Albions side, eternall peace to bring'. They are a 'triple hierarchy' that

---

[109] Shell, *Catholicism, controversy*, 131.
[110] LPL MS 652, f. 327^{r-v}. These are undated, endorsed 'Conceptions of Mr Wright'.
[111] Ibid., f. 329^r. For similar poems see 'Des inventiones de Mr Wright', f. 217^r and
passim.
[112] Ibid., f. 217^r.   [113] Ibid., f. 329^r.

recalls the Trinity. This charged, religious emblem defines the future of English Catholicism as inseparable from the fortunes of Essex's inner circle of advisors.[114]

One particular *impresa* also speaks more contingently of Wright's vision of England's future. From the set of images addressed to Elizabeth written in November, Wright depicts a 'chariot wherein ar the thre crowns and thre septers', to be drawn by a lion, a mermaid, a unicorn, and a hart. The motto, '*Quis cursus securior*' (what way is more secure) is elaborated in a longer verse, explaining that these creatures can forge a safe passage through sea, land, poisons, and plots.[115] The hart, the emblem of the Devereux family, represents Essex, who is given extraordinary equality if not precedence over Elizabeth, the lion of England; the mermaid seems obscure, but probably refers to the crown of Ireland; the unicorn, though, is the symbol of Scotland. This, then, is an image of succession. Trust placed in Essex, Elizabeth, and James will steer a secure passage through broils and turmoils, and will unite the triple realms of England, Scotland, and Ireland.

But in one final set of verses, Wright envisages England's alternative future—or present? Three sets of the poem survive in Anthony Bacon's papers, more than any other of the verses. Although they take the same emblematic form as the other *imprese*—a verse with accompanying images—they are better described as a libel, or, as Wright himself defines them, a pasquinade, which excoriates the government of England under the Cecils.[116] The first image he instructs the reader to 'Paynte' is of a woman, hanging on a gibbet, as an ass munches the length of straw that suspends her.[117] The verse explains that the 'carefull maide' who 'doth labour to conserve/Her weale and wealth' is starved by 'this old asse'.[118] The second image is of a scorpion embracing and then stinging a bee, a clear reference to Essex, who used the metaphor of himself as a bee in his own poetry. A marginal note explains '*id est cor unum via una*' 'one heart and one way', Burghley's motto, underscoring, if further explanation were necessary, that the lord treasurer is the scorpion whose pretended friendship threatens Essex. In two verses the English lion is fettered in a cage, fed on corn rather than meat. A marginal note points the reader to the Cecilian coat of arms, a sheaf of corn between two lions rampant, to

---

[114] LPL MS 652, ff. 309ʳ–310ᵛ.

[115] '*Cerva, Leo, siren monocornis, ducere possunt/Per mare, per terram, toxica & insidias*', LPL MS 652, f. 206ʳ.

[116] I am using the version of the verse from f. 210ʳ⁻ᵛ, and the emblems from f. 212ʳ⁻ᵛ.

[117] Ibid., f. 212ʳ.   [118] Ibid., f. 210ʳ.

signal Burghley's unquenchable ambition. A subsequent verse warns that the *regnum Cecilianum* spells disaster:

> *That* government cannot endure [emphasis added]
> *That* kingdom must decay
> Wher folie gaming avarice
> And atheisme beare the sway.[119]

The accusation of atheism is developed in the final image and verse, where it is linked to financial rapacity. A bell tolls in a steeple, summoning men to church: again, this represents the lord treasurer, who rings 'dayly bels to subsidies' to 'payeth himself', but 'entreth [church] not at all'.[120]

In these *imprese* Wright is ensnared in a dialogue with English Catholic polemic. Given his Jesuit background, it is hardly surprising that he can luridly realize the nightmarish vision of the *regnum Cecilianum* depicted in the 'Burghley's Commonwealth' tracts. But an alternative future for England is a *regnum Essexianum,* where Essex can be steered to military glory, religious peace, and a safe, Scottish succession, supported by Howard and Bacon. Wright clearly believes that Catholic 'loyalism', such as it is, has far less to do with allegiance to Elizabeth: rather, the agency of Essex.

The emblems in praise of the earl also perfectly capture Essex's public aspiration in 1595 to inherit and surpass Burghley's pre-eminence, and his deliberate association with toleration to bolster his credentials as a future kingmaker. The pasquinade also suggests that Wright passionately believed that Burghley, his own enemy, would continue to threaten Catholic fortunes; but he conflates Burghley's general hostility to Catholics with deadly and concealed antagonism towards Essex, champion of 'religious peace'.

Thus the pasquinade lampoons all the vices that Essex and his circle would later denounce as qualities of the evil counsellors who thrived under Elizabeth: rapacity, atheism, deadly control over the queen's person, masked by hypocritical displays of friendship to the virtuous earl. In substance and tone, Wright's pasquinade is no different from the flurry of pro-Essex libels that emerged later in the decade when the earl was disgraced after Ireland, or even after Essex's death. Wright's emblems, then, demonstrate precisely how most elements of the Essexian complaint about evil counsel derived from or paralleled those Catholic polemical texts that Anthony and Francis Bacon had been keen to internalize and answer in their defence of England's role in the war against Spain.[121]

---

[119] LPL MS 652, the version on f. 207ʳ reads 'Wher follie cardes, dice, avarice,/And Atheism bear the sway'.
[120] Ibid., f. 210ᵛ.   [121] See Chapter 2, 85–7.

As so often, we stumble on Anthony Bacon as the significant link between people, ideas, texts, and the creation of Essex's public political identities. Wright warmly praised Bacon's 'charretie' towards him, recognizing that Anthony, at least, continued vainly to petition Whitgift and the Cecils for his liberty.[122] Anthony Bacon and Wright's sizeable correspondence contains one illuminating reference to the *imprese*: on 15 July 1596, Wright apologized to Bacon for the crude nature of his prose, with the excuse that 'as tyme past hath well declared I left the subtiler *conceits*, and cittie-like *inventions* to your worshipful and such qualified persons' [emphasis added].[123] The *imprese* are labelled in Bacon's papers as 'inventions' or 'conceyts': it would seem that the emblems were written by Wright, if not in conjunction with Bacon, at least with the expectation that Bacon and others—surely Henry Howard—would use and improve them.

Much of the imagery of the *imprese* remains obscure: probably the verses and emblems reflected many an in-joke between Wright, the Bacons, Howard, and Essex. This still leaves the question of why they were written. Had they been adopted at the Accession Day Tilts in 1595, they would have made the most extraordinary public statement about Essex's ambitions, and his correlation of Catholic toleration and the succession. But they were not used on 17 November and none appear to have been widely circulated outside Anthony Bacon's most intimate circle. To understand their meaning we need to look to the text that caused a stunning blow to Essex's relations with Catholics, and his ambitious religious policies more generally: the appearance at the Elizabethan court of Robert Parsons's *Conference* in early November.

'DOLEMAN' AND THE PERILS OF CATHOLIC TOLERATION

On 17 November 1595, Essex's performance at the Accession Day Tilts mixed a typical display of personal aggrandizement with an emphatic demonstration of his absolute devotion to Elizabeth. The earl's appearance to joust was accompanied by a literary device written by Francis Bacon and other close members of the circle, performed both in the tiltyard itself, and after the celebration supper. In the pageant 'Erophilus'—or 'Love'—a representation of the earl is petitioned by the ambassadors of Lady Philautia, or 'Self-Love', a hermit, a soldier, and a secretary of state.

---

[122] LPL MS 658, f. 133ʳ.   [123] Ibid., f. 134ʳ.

Speaking through his squire, Erophilus rejects the temptation to pursue self-fulfilment through contemplation, fame, or 'policy' because he recognizes that the ends of his virtues lie in service to the queen. The device allowed Essex to situate his pressing agenda for the domination of foreign and domestic policy within a framework which emphasized his recognition that the foundation of his virtue and fortune was the bounty of the queen.[124]

At this of all Accession Day performances, Essex had particular need to emphasize his devoted loyalty to Elizabeth, and to *disassociate* himself with literature written by seminary priests. At the start of November, Robert Parsons's *Conference,* published under the pseudonym 'R. Doleman', had been shown to Elizabeth, with its fulsome dedication to Essex. As well as breaking that most explosive Elizabethan taboo, by addressing in print the various claims of Elizabeth's successors, the endorsement of a theory of popular sovereignty in the treatise, of the right of the community to resist and depose tyrannical monarchs, was hardly dissimilar to those ideas being aired and explored in Essex's circle, in Pérez's *Relaciones* and *The state of Christendom.* Essex retired from the court pale-faced until 12 November while the gates of the court were shut.[125]

With devastating solemnity, 'Doleman's' dedication reflects Essex's manner of self-presentation, as a nobleman of unparalleled virtue and great popularity with Elizabeth's subjects:

> ...no man is in more high & eminent place or dignitie at this day in our realme, then your selfe, whether we respecte your nobilitie, or calling, or favour with your prince, or high liking of the people.[126]

And of course the dedication painstakingly highlights the most obvious but unspoken truth: that Essex's pursuit of greatness *was* inseparable from the politics of succession, and his desire to establish political pre-eminence under the next monarch.

Patrick Collinson reads the dedication as a biting 'parody' of the dedicatory epistles of Godly texts dedicated to Essex, highlighting Essex's protection of 'hotter' Protestants.[127] But the dedication also parodies exactly the ways that Catholics such as Wright and Constable attempted to persuade the earl to champion toleration by relentlessly

---

[124] P. E. J. Hammer, 'Upstaging the queen: the earl of Essex, Francis Bacon and the Accession Day celebrations of 1595', in David Bevington and Peter Holbrook eds, *The politics of the Stuart court masque* (Cambridge: Cambridge University Press, 1998), 41–66; for a text of the self-contained literary device 'Of Love and Self-Love' and discussion of the various texts associated with the event, see Spedding, *L&L,* I, 375–91.

[125] Collins, *Letters and memorials,* I, 357–8.

[126] 'Doleman' [i.e. Parsons], *Conference,* sigs. *2–[*3].

[127] Collinson, 'The Religious Factor', in Mayer, *Struggle for the succession,* 249.

flattering his brilliant virtues. See also the reasons given by Essex's former chaplain, William Alabaster, for his designs to convert the earl in 1597 because of

> [Essex's] goode nature, noble disposition and other many giftes and bles-
> singes which almightie god hath bestowed uppon him and in respect of the
> great good or hurt that his good or bad course may woorke unto himself and
> to many others both for this life and for the next by reason of the state and
> place wherein he liveth.[128]

If reading Doleman's dedication through a Catholic lens, one could similarly identify, of course, the Catholics—Standen, Pérez, and most famously and recently Wright—to whom Essex had offered protection. It would not be stretching our appreciation of Parsons's deviousness to suggest that he meant deliberately to draw attention to the *duality* of Essex's attempt to win 'popularity' through 'profane pollicy', by writing a dedication which could obviously be read as a Godly *or* a Catholic appeal to the earl.

The menace of the dedication to Essex also reverses the strategies that Catholics had adopted to attack the tyranny of Leicester or Burghley. Rather than calumny the earl as an evil counsellor, 'Doleman' presents Essex as a potentially over-mighty subject, and bathes the earl in such rapturous praise that it would prick Elizabeth's sensitive nose to a 'popularity' which threatened her own. And through this particular paper grenade, the earl replaced Burghley as Parsons's chief target.

Essex emerged as a particular danger to Parsons in 1595 by his circle's nascent attempts to establish him as the champion of Catholic loyalism. Essex's sympathy to Catholic toleration was also dangerous to the Hispanophile Parsons, because the immediate common ground shared and invoked by Essex and Catholic loyalists was aggression towards Spain and the secular tyranny of Philip II. By writing a book which associated Essex with speculation on the succession, Parsons's dedication threatened his relationship both with Elizabeth and James VI. It aimed also to derail Essex's own inclination to nurture 'loyalists' like Wright.

The *Conference* and Wright's *imprese* also represent a struggle between Parsons and Wright for the political identity of English Catholicism, which would be writ larger in the conflict between the Jesuit and Appellant priests later in the decade, and once again in the aftermath of the Gunpowder Plot. Essentially the different strategies of Wright and Parsons revolved around contrasting attitudes to Spanish invasion and the succession. But in the ideas that underscored the their wider aims, though,

[128] 'Alabaster's Conversion', in Sutton, *Unpublished works*, 123.

Parsons and Wright had more in common than is first apparent: Wright's appeal for personal toleration was conceptualized as the first step towards the reconversion of England—schemes that Parsons had toyed with but rejected by the mid-1580s.[129]

Nor did the 'loyalism' that Wright hoped to promote through the agency of Essex espouse a resounding endorsement of the necessity of total obedience to secular monarchs. Rather, Wright's hostility to Parsons's dabbling in resistance theory, and his expression of allegiance to Elizabeth, were shaped by pragmatism and by reason of state; they were conditioned by his ardent faith in Essex's sympathy to Catholicism, and the certainty that Essex would exert the most important influence over the succession. It is surely no coincidence that the inevitable disappointment that many Catholics felt on James's accession was expressed in plots that involved Catholic supporters of Essex as well as Appellant priests, who had apparently sworn adherence to doctrines of non-resistance and allegiance to Elizabeth.[130]

And it is surely within the context of the explosive appearance of the *Conference* that we should understand the composition of the *imprese*, as well as the involvement of Anthony Bacon in their composition. Written in November and December, just after the appearance of the *Conference* at court, these emblems and verses must have responded to Parsons's succession tract, to repair the damage done to Essex's reputation, by re-establishing Essex's destiny as a military hero and an agent of mediation between conflicting religious positions. Possibly Wright and Bacon intended the devices or conceits to be circulated as an emblem book with the 'Device of Love and Self-Love'; but they seem, too, to be an appeal to Essex himself, an attempt to persuade him to persist in the cause of Catholic toleration. Anthony Bacon also seems to have felt the need to respond to the *Conference*. It was in February 1596 that Bacon urged Essex to reread Wright's Latin treatise; in September, later that year, that he defended his relationship with Catholics in the 'relation' of his meeting with Lady Russell.

The *imprese*, however, had no further public impact than to continue to cement the relationship of Wright with Anthony Bacon. The earl's only offer to Wright was an attempt to persuade him to travel into exile once more, to act as an intelligence agent on the continent—an offer Wright indignantly refused.[131] Meanwhile, Essex moved clearly away from more

---

[129] See above, n. 9.
[130] William Watson, the Appellant priest, devised the failed Bye Plot of 1603; while Francis Tresham and Robert Catesby, who participated in Essex's rising, participated in the Gunpowder Plot two years later.
[131] ITL, Petyt MS 538/46, f. 226[r–v].

public support of Catholic loyalism. The English translation of Pérez's *Relaçiones* was never published, nor was *The state of Christendom*. Wright's *imprese* were not circulated more widely.

The question of whether or not to answer Parsons also seems to have continued to plague Essex's circle. The translation of *The Anatomie of Spayne*, which lacquered the 'black legend' of Philip, is another oblique refutation of Parsons's succession tract: it downgrades the claims of the infanta to the English crown by arguing, through an excruciating amount of historical and genealogical detail, that the authority of the Spanish Habsburgs over every territory in their dominions has been illicitly gained by a mixture of force, deceit, and even more bloody private crimes.[132] And if the testimony of William Watson, the Appellant priest, can be trusted, even queen and privy council urged him to develop a treatise hostile to the Jesuits into a direct response to the *Conference* at some point between 1598 and 1599. The result was a book which 'drew the clayme rather to Yourke than to Lancaster' (refuting Isabella's claim which was through the Lancastrian line). Watson claimed that the council liked his treatise, while Essex and Elizabeth kept their own copies, the earl assuring Watson that he desired that he might have liberty of conscience.[133]

Essex's polymorphous religious persona, as patron of the Godly, friend and ally of Whitgift, and proponent of Catholic toleration, left livid scars, making him easily vulnerable to the accusations of atheistic ambition levelled in the post-rising propaganda. As Parsons's dedication so brilliantly anticipated, he was vulnerable, too, to similar suspicions long before the rising. By the end of the decade, when the earl's ostracism from the regime became known, even Parsons seems to have been willing to entertain the possibility that the earl's domestic ambitions outweighed his fierce ideological hostility to Spain. The council's interrogations of Alabaster and Wright in 1600 revealed the existence of a typically chimerical scheme to draw the disgraced Essex into a plot involving Parsons, the Jesuit Joseph Creswell, and various Spanish dignitaries, to persuade Essex to support the succession of the infanta in return for the restoration of his own power.[134] Although there is no shred of evidence to suggest that Essex was tempted by this design, in the eyes of the government, the confessions of Alabaster and Wright were rendered far more plausible in light of Essex's long-term association with Catholic toleration. But at the same time, the privy council was also intensely concerned about the earl's popularity with

[132] YBL, Osborn MS, 20; see Chapter 2, 82–3.
[133] Law, *Archpriest controversy*, I, 222–3.
[134] TNA, SP 12/275/32, f. 53^{r-v}; discussed further in Chapter 5, 214.

the Godly, arresting London ministers who prayed for Essex's physical and political recovery in the winter of 1599.[135] The regime's correlation of the earl's seditious ambition and irenic religious patronage was a well developed embryo many months before the rising: it was derived from an assessment of the 'secular' ends of Essex's involvement with the politics of religion that was grounded in certain truths.

The self-conscious effort to cut a sympathetic figure to Protestant and Catholic subjects was, as Francis Bacon alleged, an indication of Essex's intense political ambition. And Puritans, Conformists, and Catholics alike responded with enthusiasm, imagining the earl, as Wright did, as a glittering prince who determined policy. Rather than securing his own ambitions of the crown, though, Essex's desire to mediate between religious groups was intended to contain religious tensions and to steer a safe and orderly succession to the reign of the monarch whom he desired to serve. However, Essex was no prince, but a subject: rather than clearing a broad and tolerant path to the reign of the future monarch, the earl walked a precarious tightrope—as he was to discover.

---

[135] See Hunt, 'Tuning the Pulpits'; the sermons are also discussed in Chapter 5, 207–9.

4
Physician of the state: Essex and the Elizabethan polity

The triumph at Cadiz proved to be the ephemeral pinnacle of Essex's achievements. After the failures of the naval campaigns of the summer and autumn of 1597, the fervent expectations reignited by the earl's departure as lord lieutenant of Ireland were humiliatingly shattered by the truce with Tyrone in September 1599—an inglorious end to a disastrous campaign. From his return from Ireland, the rise and fall of Essex's hopes were played out on a vastly diminished stage, as he fought for the rehabilitation of his reputation and career.

Through extremes of expectation and disappointment Essex justified his behaviour by adopting a series of ideological positions towards the structures of the Elizabethan polity. Factionalism consumed the mind of Essex and his followers, who defined his misfortunes as the triumph of evil counsel. Essex's hostility to the politics of the court, however, also reflected his increasingly fractious relationship with Elizabeth herself, which developed similarly portentous dimensions as he struggled to reconcile his personal relationship with the queen with a parallel instinct to identify the manifestations of misgovernment and tyranny.

Essex also defined his vocation in terms of his wider sense of duty to the Elizabethan *patria,* rendering the intricacies of his personal relationship with the queen a parallel frustration. As an educated nobleman, whose scholarly training was rooted at first instance in classical rhetoric, Essex's ideological positions were consciously adopted and artfully expressed in a variety of literary forms, his dexterity especially evident in the ways that he conducted a discursive relationship with the queen. Essex's following also exploited scribal forms of publication in a purposeful way to disseminate his ideas to a wider public audience.[1] His declining career engaged the Elizabethan public sphere in a compelling drama about court politics that

---

[1] Hammer, 'Myth-making' and idem, 'Smiling Crocodile'.

was also a complex and increasingly polarized debate about the nature of obedience, and the legitimacy of different forms of political action; a debate soon to be enshrined in competing definitions of the rising itself.

RIVALS TO EVIL COUNSELLORS

In Henry Cuffe's synopsis of Essex's instructions to be delivered to the earl of Mar in February 1601, Essex believed that he was opposed by a cabal of implacable foes 'principally loved by the principall secretary...for the further strengthening of himself'.[2] Most of the blame for the political divisions of the twilight years of Elizabeth's reign has been laid at Essex's feet. Before the death of Burghley on 4 August 1598, it is argued, Essex and the Cecils enjoyed a fractious but frequently harmonious relationship which disintegrated because of the earl's paranoid jealousies and his oppositional mentality. A Cecilian faction was an entity imagined by Essex and his followers, who viewed routine political disappointment as assaults on the earl's honour.[3] In other words, the earl created so-called factional politics by *anticipating* its existence, as an 'anti-Essex coalition' naturally cohered round Sir Robert Cecil, in response to the earl's bitter enmity.[4]

For many scholars, Essex's dichotomized understanding of politics was a temperamental deficiency, indicating his deeper failure to grasp the complexity of Elizabethan patronage, or the necessity of compromise over the pursuit of particular policies.[5] Without doubt, Essex's ambition, coupled with his lofty estimation of his own worth, warped his relations with any who threatened his goals. But the earl's political vision was shaped by widely shared contemporary expectations of the way that politics operated, which were ubiquitously cast in binary paradigms of polarized virtue and corruption or honest and evil counsel. Historians have paid serious attention to the ideological foundations of 'irrational' popish plots in the seventeenth century, because Catholic conspiracy theories had a powerful agency that affected political history: if we want to play closer attention to the relationship between ideas and action, we

[2] Bruce, *Correspondence*, 83.
[3] Hammer, 'Patronage at court'. See also W. T. MacCaffrey, 'Place and patronage in Elizabethan politics', in Bindoff et al., *Elizabethan government and society*, 95–126; Natalie Mears, '*Regnum Cecilianum*? A Cecilian perspective of the court', in Guy, *Reign of Elizabeth I*, 46–64; typically penetrating insights are in Simon Adams's essay, 'The patronage of the crown in Elizabethan politics: the 1590s in perspective', in ibid., 20–45; also Dickinson, 'Subversion or Supplication', Chapter 4.
[4] Hammer, *Polarisation*, 397.   [5] See Introduction, n. 7.

should look to the foundations of Essex's certainty—rooted in reality or otherwise—that something was rotten in the state of England.

Above all, it was Essex's obsessive protectiveness of his individual pre-eminence that calcified his belief that rivals in court, council, and camp actively undermined his authority. Traditionally this narrative has focused on conflict over patronage: the earl's assertiveness as a patron—reflected also in his aggressive cultivation of a following especially in the Midlands and Wales—was also met by a strong upward momentum from his friends and in the localities, creating a dynamic of demand that he was bound to disappoint. The most notorious cases were Essex's relentless but fruitless pursuit of the positions of attorney general and solicitor general for Francis Bacon, and the elevation of Sir Robert Sidney to a barony, court office, or the wardenship of the Cinque Ports.[6] Scholars have argued that Essex's failure was less the triumph of Cecilian enmity, than that Bacon and Sidney's overly-ambitious suits were bound to be unsuccessful.[7] But for Essex, the ability to reward his clients was synonymous with power as well as a test of his personal honour, and defined by the solemn bonds of *amicitia*.[8] Indeed, the strikingly emotive language of Essex's routine correspondence on behalf of clients, even in pursuit of humble offices, conceptualizes these obligations in intensely personal terms. Typical is his demand that Richard Broughton, a circuit judge in Anglesey, be ap-pointed to the council in the marches of Wales: 'Yow know how farr my affection leades me and my credit tyes me to stand stiffely for him'.[9]

The nest of deadly enemies described by Cuffe wove together Essex's long-standing rivalries with a host of individuals: the lord admiral, Ralegh, Cobham, and Buckhurst. Natalie Mears argues that a conflict between martial and civilian codes of behaviour explain the earl's hostility

---

[6] Jardine and Stewart, *Hostage to Fortune*, Chapters 5 and 6; Hay, *Life of Robert Sidney*, 144–66. A. Wall, '"Points of contact": court favourites and county faction in Elizabethan England', *Parergon*, new ser., 6 (1988), 215–26. On Essex's local following see Introduction, n. 18. The geographical range of Essex's clients spanned Lancashire, Norfolk, Hertfordshire, Yorkshire, and Cornwall: LPL MS 656, f. 253ʳ; BL, Lansdowne MS 82, f. 42ʳ.

[7] Bacon was too inexperienced to be attorney general, and had angered Elizabeth during the 1593 parliament; the wardenship of the Cinque Ports customarily descended to Baron Cobham.

[8] See Essex's requests to Lord Keeper Puckering in 1595: 'I pray your lordships favour this gentlemans cause for he is my very good frend'; 'the want of assistance from them who shold be Mr Francis Bacons frendes makes me... more ernist in soliciting myne owne frendes', BL, Harleian MS 6997, ff. 27ʳ, 205ʳ; David Wootton, 'Francis Bacon: your flexible friend', in Elliot and Brockliss, *World of the favourite*, 195–6.

[9] BL, Harleian MS 6997, f. 203ʳ. Also see Essex's request to Puckering that John Bowen Phillips be made JP in Pembrokeshire: 'I will reckon it for a spetiall curtesie, & add it to manye otheres whereby your Lordship continuallye by satisfying my lik requests doth tye me unto yow': BL, Harleian MS 6996, f. 130ʳ.

to the *regnum Cecilianum*—and Essex certainly adopted a sneering attitude to bureaucratic culture when expressing his frustrations with the secretary.[10] However, it was a rivalry *between martialists* that characterized other friction. A contest for military laurels defined Essex's relations with the lord admiral, Charles Howard of Effingham, who was just as querulous and protective of his honour as Essex. When Elizabeth had planned to reorientate her forces for the relief of Calais prior to the Cadiz voyage in 1596, she addressed the commission of 13 April solely to Essex. Howard's furious letter in response, threatening to quit all 'martial courses', was so choleric that Essex had to urge Cecil to conceal the letter, 'for it is too passionate and it may breake all our actions'.[11] Most serious was the aftermath of the victory itself; Essex was permanently aggrieved at Howard for sabotaging his cherished strategy to hold Cadiz, and then for following Ralegh's counsel to disable his alternative proposal, to use the returning fleet for further raiding.[12]

The competition for honour also spiced the piquancy of Essex's long-standing rivalry with Ralegh. Through the amphibious expeditions of 1596 and 1597, Ralegh rekindled a career ruined by his clandestine marriage to Bess Throckmorton in 1591. Essex was bound to interpret his rival's determination to claw his way back into the queen's favour as a deliberate attempt to undermine his own *gloire*. The earl's disgust at Elizabeth's refusal to allow the publication of an Essexian narrative of the Cadiz expedition, or to sanction a national day of public thanksgiving, was compounded by the composition of competing accounts of the voyage that played up Ralegh's heroic role.[13] Before the Islands Voyage of 1597, relations between the men were uniquely cooperative, Essex bargaining with Ralegh and Cecil to work together for mutual office.[14] Ralegh was reinstated as captain of the guard in June, following Essex's promotion to master of the ordnance on 18 March; Cecil became chancellor

[10] Mears, '*Regnum Cecilianum*', 64.

[11] Kenny, *Elizabeth's admiral*, 175–7; TNA, SP 12/257/30, f. 44ʳ; Cecil MS 40/6.

[12] See Essex's defensive 'Ommissions of the Calez Voyage', in Thomas Lediard ed., *The Naval History of England in all its branches, from the Norman Conquest, 1066, to the conclusion of 1734*, 2 vols (London, 1735), I, 337–42, at 338.

[13] Hammer has identified the first version of 'True relacion of the action at Calez' written by Cuffe as The Queen's College, Oxford University, MS 121, ff. 532–40. Versions praising Ralegh's heroic role were a letter from Ralegh to the earl of Northumberland, and another to Arthur Gorges: W. Oldys and T. Birch eds, *The Works of Sir Walter Ralegh*, 8 vols (Oxford: Oxford University Press, 1829), VIII, 667–75; FSL, MS V.b.14, f. 106ʳ–109ʳ. Sir Anthony Ashley (who seems to have alerted the council to Essex's account) was instructed by the Cecils to draft an official account that did not make it into print: TNA, SP 12/259, ff. 226ʳ–227ʳ. Hammer discusses these accounts in 'Myth-making'.

[14] Collins, *Letters and memorials*, II, 24–5, 42.

of the duchy of Lancaster on 8 October. Few were surprised, though, when with the campaign's failure, conviviality disintegrated into a messy morass of mutual recrimination. Elizabeth's reproach of Essex included a dressing down for his treatment of Ralegh, who with infuriating bravura, had pinned the blame for the voyage's failure onto the earl.[15]

Essex's dislike of Henry Brooke, 11th Baron Cobham, had complex roots.[16] A courtier rather than a soldier, with a blossoming friendship with Ralegh, Brooke was no likely bosom companion of Essex, who railed against his 'slanders and practise' and 'base Villanies... towards me'.[17] Burghley and Cecil used Brooke, married to Burghley's daughter, to liaise with Elizabeth; Essex was jealous of the access that this 'Sycophant' enjoyed, and suspected him of maligning his conduct at Cadiz. Essex's violent objections to Brooke as lord warden of the Cinque Ports, though, were based on more than personal enmity or obligation to Sir Robert Sidney. The office played a crucial strategic role in the organization of coastal defences, and Essex reasonably argued that the post should be filled by a man of martial experience, of which Brooke had none and Sidney plenty, through weary years as governor of Flushing. Essex's practical objections had recent foundation. His loathing of the practice of the previous warden, Brooke's father, of filtering all intelligence from Dover to the Cecils, had been horribly vindicated when the elderly Lord Cobham failed to foresee the imminence of a Spanish attack on Calais in the spring of 1596.[18] It was unthinkable that Essex's isolation from this network should be perpetuated under the directly antagonistic son, who had already ruptured the earl's superior connections with French intelligence when he was used by Elizabeth to liaise with Bouillon and La Fontaine before the Treaty of Greenwich. To amuse Anthony Bacon, whose credit had also been severely dented, Jean Castol wrote a raft of libels attacking La Fontaine, Cecil, Brooke, and Ralegh.[19]

---

[15] Tensions between Essex's followers and Ralegh emerged when Ralegh struck out alone to land at Fayal. See the official account of the commanders, and the longer narration of Sir Arthur Gorges, captain of Ralegh's ship, published in Purchas, *Hakluytus Posthumus*, XX, 24–33, 34–129. Sir Francis Vere apparently soothed these tensions by exculpating Essex from unnecessary blame: William Dillingham ed., *The commentaries of Sir Francis Vere* (1657), 66–7.

[16] Brooke succeeded his father, Sir William, on 6 March 1597: McKeen, *Memory of honour*, II, 669–73.

[17] TNA, SP 12/256/75, f. 172^r, Essex to Sir Robert Sidney, 4 March 1596; Collins, *Letters and memorials*, II, 20; Birch, *Memoirs*, II, 95–6, 100.

[18] TNA, SP 12/256/75, f. 172^r. Sidney complained to Essex that Cobham would be unable to command defence in the instance of an invasion, and remarked 'how slenderly you were assisted by the late warden in the service of Calais': *HMC Salisbury*, VII, 115.

[19] LPL MS 656, ff. 72^r, 274^r, MS 660, f. 134; Birch, *Memoirs*, II, 5–6, 100, 104, 172, 228.

But the grand master of the anti-Essexian faction in the eyes of Essex's followers in 1601 was undoubtedly the 'Principall secretary'. Until Burghley's death, the open level of cooperation between Essex and Robert Cecil persisted, thanks to the semi-patriarchal respect that Burghley could command from his former ward. The spirit of mutual interest of 1597 was rekindled before the secretary's departure on embassy to France in the early months of 1598, when Burghley arranged for Essex to buy up cochineal and indigo at favourable rates in return for an agreement that the earl would work for his son's interests.[20] To cement Essex's goodwill Cecil, a reluctant ambassador, insisted that any 'pety doubts' that had existed between them could be overcome by 'trew friendship, from which nothing shall devyde me but the separation of body and soule'.[21]

But, as Joel Hurstfield recognized decades ago, the deep ambition of both men to inherit Burghley's position in the polity forged the tensions embedded beneath the patina of cooperation.[22] Domestic reaction to the Cadiz voyage was a primary cause of Essex's burgeoning belief that his rivalry with Robert Cecil might be something more malevolent. The humiliating investigation into the whereabouts of the profits of the venture was an incredible slight on his honour, when he had dug so deeply from his own pocket to finance the expedition. That Robert Cecil himself had been formally sworn in, after long delay, as secretary in Essex's absence seemed confirmation to the earl that both Cecils were responsible for the dishonourable 'inquisition' into his finances and more malignant designs to undermine him.[23] As secretary, with unparalleled access to the queen and to government paperwork, Cecil now also seemed ideally positioned to spy on him, and to misrepresent him to Elizabeth. Here Essex's suspicions were egged on by the Bacons: Anthony warned that Cecil's 'ambuscades and interceptions' silenced Essex's Scottish informants, who feared that their missives would be read; Francis urged Essex to seek bureaucratic office himself as lord privy seal, because it had 'superintendence over the Secretary'.[24]

Ironically, Cecil's skittish protestations of friendship deepened Essex's inclination to regard him as a cunning dissembler. And it is easy to see how Robert Cecil often *appeared* to be acting duplicitously to the earl's significant disadvantage. In good faith, Essex looked after Cecil's interests in 1598, and had reaped no notable political advancement while the

[20] Collins, *Letters and memorials*, II, 83–4, 88–9; Cecil MS 49/22.
[21] TNA, SP 12/266/71, f. 98ʳ.
[22] Hurstfield, 'Succession struggle'.
[23] Ungerer, *Spaniard*, I, 445; Birch, *Memoirs*, II, 60–1.
[24] Ibid., 233; Spedding, *L&L*, II, 43.

secretary was abroad. In turn, as Essex reflected on the progress of Cecil's career, he could see that his rival had profited from his every departure from the realm. His friends corroborated these suspicions. Reflecting glumly on his prospects for a barony on 29 January 1598, Robert Sidney complained to Essex of the secretary: 'he doth not, for all his faire words unto me, affect me at all'.[25]

From late 1597, a chain of conflicts deepened the earl's alienation from other courtiers and councillors. Smarting from the failure of the Islands Voyage, Essex condemned the armchair recriminations of non-martial councillors, who 'have set warme at home and descant upon us'.[26] Further slurs on his honour awaited his return. On 23 October lord admiral Howard had been elevated to the earldom of Nottingham for his service at Cadiz. Worse, as lord steward, the admiral became the senior nobleman, with precedence on the council and in parliament. Essex's incandescent response was predictable: he challenged Howard's patent and absented himself from court and council until Elizabeth appointed him earl marshal, restoring his superior conciliar status. In impotent retaliation, Howard staged his own sickbed retreat.[27]

The fault-line between Essex and the rest of the council was then irrevocably demarcated by the debates described in Chapter 2 over the direction of the war. With the death of Burghley in August, a vital brake had been lifted. With Ralegh returned to favour and Brooke, now Lord Cobham, lord warden of the Cinque Ports, conspiracy theories crystallized in Essex's mind.

Essex finally accepted command of the Irish expedition late in 1598 with a mixture of duty and dread: 'the hardest task that any gentleman was ever set about'.[28] If he meditated on his father's miserable and bloody experiences as governor of Ulster, Essex also absorbed the pessimism of treatises on the reform of Irish government, especially Spenser's *View of the present state of Ireland,* which emphasized the violence of the military putsch that would be necessary to crush the rebels, and the huge operational challenge of victualling and provisioning the army.[29] Most of the

---

[25] BI., Additional MS 6177, f. 45ʳ.

[26] Purchas, *Hakluytus Posthumus*, XX, 33.

[27] Collins, *Letters and memorials*, II, 74–7; De Maisse, *Journal*, 28, 48–9, 70–2.

[28] *HMC Salisbury*, IX, 4. Essex's appointment as lord lieutenant is frustratingly under-documented. In October, according to Camden, he opposed the appointment of Mountjoy and proposed himself: Camden, *Annales*, 786–7. By early November Essex's appointment was expected: McLure, *Letters of John Chamberlain*, I, 48–9.

[29] Spenser's plea for a great commander to undertake the project seems to have been addressed to Essex. Written in 1596, the treatise was entered for publication but not printed; Essex owned a copy, as did some followers: Andrew Hadfield, 'Spenser, Edmund, 1552?–1599', *ODNB*; Edmund Spenser, *A view of the state of Ireland*, ed. Andrew Hadfield

earl's gloom sprang from the coherent identity that he had now given to an implacable body of enemies, which he was certain would thrive, like a well-watered weed, in his absence. Over two years previously, Pérez had warned Essex that his rivals would send him to Ireland, a graveyard where no glory could be won.[30] Now Essex reiterated Pérez's warnings to Willoughby: 'I am not ignorant what ar the disadvantages of absence; the opportunityes of practising enemyes'.[31] To Greville, he rued his rampant enemies at court as symptomatic of the 'sick state' of England, in need of its own healing physician.[32]

Was this violent anticipation of evil counsel merely the product of a petulant paranoia? In fact, for several years, the private correspondence of Essex's close circle, of the Bacons, Pérez, and Henry Howard had given Essex every encouragement to see the Cecils as his enemies. For Pérez, Burghley was malign Aeolus, god of the winds, who thwarted Aeneas/ Essex at the antagonistic command of Juno.[33] Robert Cecil was simply *Roberto il Diabolo*—Robert the Devil.[34] Bacon made copies of a letter by Francis Davison (whose travels round Europe Essex sponsored) that described hunchbacked Robert Cecil as the 'Archenemy...made like an arche' and cheerily wished that Essex would 'breake their neckes as nature hathe broken their backes'. The Spenserian animal imagery used in Wright's *pasquinade* to lampoon the Cecils' ambition, avarice, and pretensions to nobility resurfaces in Anthony Bacon and Howard's malicious references to the 'fox' and his 'cub', or the crafty stratagems of the 'dromedarie'.[35]

True virtue, the commonplace ran, was strengthened by adversity. The antagonism of Essex's enemies was explained as the inevitable envy of a virtue deployed for great public deeds that threatened their own accumulation of power and wealth. For Howard, Essex's forebear was the biblical Daniel, 'raised upp...for confusion of a wicked age'.[36] In indignant

---

and Willy Maley (Oxford: Blackwell, 1997), 5; FSL MS v.b. 214, ff. 136ᵛ–193ʳ. I am grateful to Professor Hadfield for directing me to the Folger manuscript.

[30] Ungerer, *Spaniard*, I, 448.

[31] Cecil MS 58/86.

[32] *HMC Salisbury*, IX, 4; John Harington remembered Essex's burst of optimism: 'By God I will beat Tyrowne in the feilde': *Nugae Antiquae*, I, 246.

[33] See Ungerer, *Spaniard*, I, 329, 354, 401–2; Hammer, *Polarisation*, 242–6, 260, 320, 330–1.

[34] LPL MS 660, f. 145ʳ.

[35] LPL MS 652, f. 210ʳ, MS 660, ff. 107ʳ, 220ʳ (abstract of longer letter of Davison to his father, ff. 235ʳ–236ʳ). Davison's father, William, had been the scapegoat for the death of Mary, queen of Scots, dismissed from the clerkship of the privy council for dispatching the execution warrant: Essex tried and failed to have him reinstated.

[36] D[urham] U[niversity] L[ibrary], Howard MS 2, f. 119ʳ.

triumph that Essex had been exonerated from misappropriating the Cadiz booty, Anthony Bacon crowed: 'the bright beames of his valour & virtue scattered the clouds and cleared the mists that malicious envy had stirred up against his matchless meritt'.[37] Willoughby, who had expressed crawling gratitude to Burghley for help with his debts in 1597, invoked a shared language of military virtue to snigger at the Cecils' reputation for peculation: Essex 'satisfieth my covetings more than a horse company or band of ordonnance of my late Lord Treasurer's Angells'. He eschewed the court himself, rarely seeing the queen, 'and for other saints, I am alredy too croked to crepe to them'.[38] The assumptions of Essex's friends were shared by more neutral commentators. In 1597, the French ambassador to England, André Hurault, Seigneur de Maisse, was convinced that decision making was frozen by conciliar struggles between Essex and the coherent opposition of the two Cecils and the lord admiral.[39]

When Essex was advised by more conservative friends to change his behaviour he was not reminded that the normative operation of Elizabethan politics was cooperative and consensual—rather the reverse. Essex's concept of factionalism was a reification of the much wider anti-court discourse so dominant in late sixteenth-century England, which consistently emphasized the cynical motivations of the powerful, the constant struggles of the virtuous political actor.

Typical were Henry Howard's unfinished meditations on the 'meanes to advancement' for a noble courtier, written towards the mid-1590s with Essex in mind, before the divisions that followed Cadiz. As a first principle, Howard assumed that a virtuous nobleman would inevitably be antagonized by powerful enemies (*inimici*), who must be outwitted by 'stratagems', and politic behaviour.[40] In September 1598, Sir William Knollys urged Essex to return to court, lest he be longer 'subject to theyr tonges who will practyse against you'.[41] An anonymous letter of advice to the earl, written on 16 November 1597, warned him of 'a dubble faction verie strong against thee', and, in a melodramatic analogy, counselled Essex to emulate Mordechai, who foiled the plot of the courtier 'proud Hamon [Haman]' to exterminate the Jews in the Persian empire in the

[37] LPL MS 659, f. 238ʳ.
[38] Cecil MS 59/10; BL, Lansdowne MS 84, f. 157ʳ, 86, f. 49ʳ. On 6 May 1598, Willoughby wrote a similarly flattering letter to Robert Cecil: Cecil MS 60/113. Essex and Willoughby had been knighted together by Leicester in the Netherlands in 1586.
[39] De Maisse, *Journal*, 4 and *passim*.
[40] DUL, Howard MS 2, especially ff. 117ʳ–133ʳ; for content and possible dating see Hammer, 'How to become an Elizabethan Statesman'; Andersson, *Lord Henry Howard*, 175.
[41] WRO, MI 229, ff. 45ʳ, 46ʳ.

reign of queen Esther.[42] Most startlingly of all, Elizabeth herself encouraged her courtiers to imagine themselves engaged in this state of perpetual internal rivalry: 'Look to thyself, good Essex, and be wise to help thyself, without giving thy enemies advantage; and my hand shall be readier to help thee than any other'.[43]

Almost inevitably, Essex's Irish campaign permanently fixed the earl's certainty that dark forces worked against him. The campaign was doomed from its inception by the chronic lack of trust that dogged communication between the earl, privy council, and the queen. The runes were cast with Essex's extraordinary determination to secure a warrant for his return should he need to communicate directly with Elizabeth.[44] The months of preparation between his appointment at the end of December and his commission on 12 March were characterized by typically tense negotiations about the scope of his powers, strategy for assaulting Tyrone, and the size of the army, which pitted Essex's military needs against the arguments for fiscal prudence from other councillors.[45] Rumours that the lord admiral opposed the earl's demands for provisions explain Essex's fervent paranoia that his army was under-furnished in numbers, arms, and victuals; an obsession evident even from letters sent before he had disembarked on the Irish coast.[46] Essex's frantic requests for more supply met with consistent rejoinders from the privy council in England that his 'royal' army was larger than any yet sent to Ireland; but the plan to attack Ulster, agreed to in principle by Elizabeth and the council and so famously abandoned by Essex, was dependent on a multi-pronged strategic assault on Lough Foyle and Armagh, requiring pinnaces and carriage-horses that were unavailable when Essex arrived in the spring.[47] On 17 July, Essex

---

[42] TNA, SP 12/265/10, f. 17. The author, 'not daring' to give his name, knows Essex well enough to send greetings to his wife.

[43] Birch, *Memoirs*, I, 181.

[44] As early as 20 October 1598, it was reported that Essex was demanding the freedom to return at will after a year; McClure, *Letters of John Chamberlain*, I, 49. Essex's warrant giving him permission to return under extraordinary circumstances is printed in J. Morrin ed., *Calendar of the patent and close rolls of Chancery in Ireland, of the reigns of Henry VIII, Edward VI, Mary, and Elizabeth*, 3 vols (Dublin and London: A Thorn and Sons, 1861–3), II, 531–2. On 30 July, Elizabeth issued a personal letter commanding that he remain in Ireland without her leave to return: TNA, SP 63/205/121, ff. 236ʳ–237ʳ.

[45] *CSP Spanish, 1587–1603*, 649.

[46] Immediately on his arrival Essex wrote of his strong fears that supplies would not be met; see letters to the privy council between 8 and 11 April, TNA, SP 63/205/20, 21, ff. 29ʳ–31ᵛ.

[47] See TNA, SP 63/205/38, ff. 46ʳ–47ʳ, the earl and the Dublin council's complaints over the lack of supply, and their plan to alter military strategy, written to the privy council on 28 April 1599, annotated by Cecil. For an account sympathetic to Essex's bargaining over supply, and his reasons for putting off the Ulster strategy, see L. W. Henry, 'The Earl of Essex and Ireland, 1599', *BIHR*, 32 (1959), 1–23.

wrote an extraordinary defence of his ill-fated journey through Munster and Leinster that balanced the polite formalities of an administrative epistle with a direct attack on unnamed members of the privy council itself, to whom it was addressed; any credit he had with his own army was undermined by the widespread knowledge that the queen's trust in him was poisoned by 'the malice and practise of myne enemies in England, who ... now in the darke give mee wounde upon wounde'.[48]

It was while Essex was in Ireland that the series of appointments were made that seemed to confirm his dreaded fears: his enemies had become a triumphant faction in his absence. On 15 May, Buckhurst was made lord treasurer; in August, Lord Thomas Cecil, brother of Sir Robert, became president of the council of the north, while, according to Camden, Robert Cecil's appointment as master of the court of wards on 21 May was the final proof to Essex of the coherence of his enemies' designs. This position, an extremely lucrative office, had been widely expected to fall to Essex himself; contemporaries believed that many of the luxurious feathers in Burghley's several comfortable nests had been purchased through the profits of his 37-year tenure of the post.[49] Cecil's control of the court of wards also gave the secretary vital leverage over the nobility.[50]

Conversely, by 1599, there was no Essexian 'faction' with any significant power. On the council only Whitgift, Egerton, and his uncle, Sir William Knollys (hardly uncritical friends), were sympathetic allies, who would be unwilling to plead with Elizabeth for Essex's rehabilitation in 1600. By 1601, the earl's 'faction' such as it was—other than Lord Mountjoy—was composed of followers and friends with little power or political influence. For all his hostile and irreconcilable mentality, Essex should have been a minor irritant for those whom he labelled his enemies. Instead, Essex was a pulsating problem in possession of one extraordinarily powerful trick: the sympathetic ear of James VI.

ESSEX AND ELIZABETH, C.1596–1601

The obvious corollary of the tyranny of evil counsel was the failure of virtuous government. Writing to James in December 1600, Essex shunned any intent of 'disservice of my Soveraigne or of my cuntry'. He

---

[48] TNA, SP 63/205/111, f. 210[r].
[49] Essex was rumoured to get the post on 7 August 1598, and his appointment was expected on 20 October: TNA, SP 12/268/18, f. 33[r]; McClure, *Letters of John Chamberlain*, I, 48.
[50] Camden, *Annales*, 793–4.

and James were both aware that the by terms of the 'Act for the Suretie of the Queen's Majestie's Most Royal Person' (27 Eliz. I, c. 1), an action that threatened Elizabeth's life could render void the claim of the person in whose name it was committed.[51] And James might well have suspected Essex's devotion to his queen: the earl was repressing here the hostility to Elizabeth that had grown in tandem with his opposition to faction.

Essex's personal bond with Elizabeth was the root and the trunk of his career. With a poor landed patrimony, the following that he derived from his military office, wealth, and position on the council was dependent on the queen's continued favour. As Francis Bacon recognized, all of his own advice on the earl's most appropriate political strategizing could be distilled in one fundamental maxim: 'Win the Queen . . . of any other course I see no end'.[52]

Despite the less than rapturous reception from the queen that followed the sea campaigns of 1596 and 1597, Bacon's warnings seemed premature, at least in terms of the earl's ability to win office for himself. The grant of the earl marshalship appeared an enormous concession by Elizabeth; Essex's denunciation of the elevation of Nottingham attacked the queen's free use of her prerogative to make noble creations, while his even more disruptive behaviour over the marshalship was the most extreme manifestation of Essex's inclination to regard military office as his own to exercise, rather than a gift benevolently bestowed. Did the episode indicate weakness from an ageing fond monarch? De Maisse's portrait of Elizabeth from these months depicts a vain eccentric, who indulges in whimsical politicking with her councillors.[53]

In fact, as the decade drew on, control of the earl's behaviour became an almost impossible task for Elizabeth to handle. Essex remained a formidable political figure: with European-wide fame as the foremost soldier in the realm, he promised to be the most vital representation of the Dutch Protestant interest.[54] There was no obvious solution to the earl's growing alienation from other members of the council.

Despite the queen's willingness to accommodate Essex after periods of disfavour, the earl, in turn, was frequently infuriated by Elizabeth's own behaviour, for reasons that invite our understanding if not our sympathy. His martial self-identity collided consistently with the queen's acute sense of the vulnerability of her authority during war, which prompted her attempts to restrict his autonomy, or to reprimand his failings with galling

---

[51] BL, Additional MS 31022, f. 107ᵛ.   [52] Spedding, L& L, II, 40.
[53] De Maisse, Journal, especially 67–8, 70–2.
[54] See the letters of congratulations from the Dutch on the earl's appointment as earl marshal: HMC Salisbury, VIII, 14, 20.

homiletic counsel. The hero of Cadiz was amazed to find the great humiliation inflicted on Philip II *criticized* as an 'Accon of honor and victorie against the Enemy' rather than a venture 'any way profitable to orself'.[55] Success against the Irish rebel, Essex mused to Willoughby in January 1599, would surely enflame 'the constructions of Prince under whome *magna fama* is more dangerous than *mala* and *successus minius quàm nullus*' (under whom great renown is more dangerous than evil deeds and achievement worse than nothing).[56]

Mired in debt, Essex's absolute reliance on Elizabeth's financial patronage also provoked the resentment that inevitably accompanies deep pecuniary obligation. One wonders how funny Essex found Elizabeth's jokey gift of five shillings in May 1596—'because you are poor'—mediated via a letter from Sir Robert Cecil.[57] His lord lieutenancy of Ireland was impossible until the cancellation on 6 March of debts to the crown.[58]

A great breach in Essex and Elizabeth's relationship occurred, however, before the Irish campaign, in early July 1598, when the earl was exiled from the court. Frustratingly, it is the least well documented episode of Essex's career. Our earliest narrative comes from Camden, which historians have gratefully seized on as a primary source.[59] In a heated quarrel over the appointment of the new lord deputy of Ireland, Elizabeth cuffed Essex's ears; Essex grasped the hilt of his sword and shouted that he would brook no such treatment from Henry VIII himself.[60] Francis Bacon confirmed the quarrel if not the famous denouement, writing with wintry hope 'I assure myself that of your eclipses, as this hath been the longest, it shall be the last'.[61] Essex retreated to Wanstead, appearing at Burghley's funeral at the end of August with memorably downcast expression.[62]

Most informative are Essex's own letters which describe a banishment imposed by the queen: 'I had not gone into exile of myselfe if your Majestie had not chaste me from yow as yow did'. Elizabeth had refused to 'indure that my frends should plead for me to yow' as her 'indignation did take hould of all things that might feed yt'. Essex also proved taciturn when summoned to conciliar business by members of the council: of public duty I am 'freed, being dismissed, discharged, and disabled by Her Majesty'.[63] By the end of September Essex was back at court, compelled

[55] BL, Cotton MS Otho E IX, f. 363ʳ.   [56] Cecil MS 58/86.
[57] Devereux, *Lives and letters*, I, 347.
[58] TNA, SP 12/270/52, f. 83ʳ⁻ᵛ; McClure, *Letters of John Chamberlain*, I, 61.
[59] See MacCaffrey, *Elizabeth I: war and politics*, 517.
[60] Camden, *Annales*, 771–2.   [61] Spedding, *L&L*, II, 104.
[62] McClure, *Letters of John Chamberlain*, I, 41.
[63] BL, Additional MS 6177, f. 32ʳ, copy of original. The letter is only dated 1598. See also, BL, Additional MS 74286, f. 110ʳ, Essex to Elizabeth, 20 September (1598?), BL

by the deepening crisis in Ireland. He now played the humble penitent, declaring his faults, and promising to 'depend absolutelie upon your Majesty's *will and pleasure'* [emphasis added].[64]

In pen and speech Essex could be a skilful master of the language of love and fawning supplication that Elizabeth's courtiers and statesmen used to court the queen. With no apparent sense of hypocrisy he also aired bitter frustrations, often in gendered language, charging her with inconsistency, injustice, for letting passion and emotion dictate her judgments. The 'honor of your sex', he lectured Elizabeth, should incline her to 'shew yourself constant in kindness', rather than to carp at his military shortcomings.[65] When the earl exclaimed to Edward Reynolds 'I know I shall never do her service butt against her will' he imagined his Machiavellian *virtù* honed in a struggle with a fickle, arbitrary female—Elizabeth, the blind goddess Fortune.[66] Writing to Elizabeth during the breach of 1598, the placatory tone of his letters could become quickly critical. Elizabeth treated him indiscriminately with 'favours' and 'afflictions', the latter 'unnatural'. Passive submission sits uneasily alongside strong censure of Elizabeth's arbitrary misuse of her powers: *'since your Majesty's will is the lawe...* if you repent you of it hereafter, you must charge yourself & not your Majesty's humblest servant' [emphasis added].[67]

Of course Essex did not use this language of humble service and vassalage before the omnipotent cruel mistress exclusively or originally. He self-consciously employed the hermeneutics of courtly romance, where the desires and frustrations of the subject's career were figured as the pursuit of a changeable mistress—a political relationship styled in personal terms, defined by the emotion of love.

The courting of Elizabeth was thus an *art* discussed by Essex's advisors, who were increasingly concerned that his choleric expression would harm his essential bond with the queen. Henry Howard urged the earl that the best armour against his enemies' slanders was to 'run all your counsels, referre all to the quenes wisdome and iudgment'.[68] Francis Bacon, the circle's unlikely Cassandra, warned Essex in his advice letter of 1596 that his courtly language lacked conviction; he declared his affections *'magis in speciem adornatis verbis, quam ut sentire videaris'* (seeming to use words

---

microfilm 2275 of the 'Hulton Manuscript'. Grace Ioppolo, '"Your Majesty's most faithful servant": the Earl of Essex's construction of Elizabeth in the Hulton Letters' in Peter Beal and Grace Ioppolo eds, *Elizabeth I and the culture of writing* (London: British Library Press, 2007), 43–69.

[64] BL, Additional MS 6177, f. 31[v]. The given date of 1595 seems incorrect.
[65] Devereux, *Lives and letters*, I, 250. The letter was written on 18 October 1591, during Essex's Normandy campaign.
[66] WRO, MI 229, f. 97[r].
[67] Cecil MS 63/97, 5 September 1598.   [68] DUL, Howard MS 2, f. 127[v].

ornamentally rather than to mean them).[69] A cynical summation of Bacon's advice was that Essex was failing to flatter the queen with simulated emotion.

Essex's chivalric ideals, glossed with a Machiavellian edge, meant that the 'winning' of Elizabeth had theoretical appeal; but the earl believed that the queen should reward his public service, rather than ability to frame his affection in suitably oleaginous terms. These tensions reverberate in some of Essex's poetry.[70] The Italianate court verse popularized by Wyatt had proved an exceptionally useful stylistic model for Elizabethan courtiers to express their relationship with a female monarch. In Essex's compositions the misogynistic frustration exhibited by the authorial voice of the loving suitor frequently transgresses into self-righteous indignation. 'Verses made by the Earle of Essex in his Trouble' define the impossible conundrum of a man who cannot plot the unfathomable injustice of his mistress's treatment of him, which conforms to no natural laws: 'Earth, Sea, Heaven, Hell are subject unto lawes/But I, poore I, must suffer and knowe noe cause' (8: 13–14).[71] The narrator of a poem from 1598 is more direct in his hostile criticism of the cruel female who has cast away her lover: 'She in whom my hopes did lye/Now is chang'd, I quite forgotten./She is chang'd but changed base,/Baser in so vile a place'(4: 27–30).[72]

Despite the earl's return to court, Essex's calamitous behaviour in 1598 had caused permanent damage. Elizabeth's wary anxieties about the autonomous powers of her generals were magnified schizophrenically in her attitude to his Irish command. On the surface, the scope of Essex's commission, as well as his title—lord lieutenant, rather than lord deputy—was one final manifestation of the queen's willingness to place extraordinary authority into his hands. With the largest army Elizabeth sent to Ireland, Essex had sweeping powers to convene parliament, grant forfeited land, and to pardon rebels.[73] But the accompanying instructions came laced with those proscriptions typical of Elizabeth, ordering the earl to reduce the army as soon as feasible, and to exercise extreme caution in the granting of knighthoods.[74] The queen's hostility to Essex's attempt to give

[69] Spedding, *L&L*, II, 42.

[70] Steven W. May, *The Elizabethan courtier poets: the poems and their contexts* (Columbia, MO: University of Missouri Press, 1991).

[71] May, 'Poems of Robert Devereux', 47. Chamberlain seems to have sent this poem to Dudley Carleton on 20 October 1599: McClure, *Letters of John Chamberlain*, I, 50.

[72] May, 'Poems of Robert Devereux', 45–6.

[73] The commission is printed in Thomas Rymer et al. eds, *Foedera, conventiones, literae, et cujuscunque generis acta publica, inter reges Angliae . . . ab anno 1101, ad nostra usque tempora, habita aut tractata*, 10 vols (The Hague, 1739–45), 7, 212–15.

[74] *Calendar of Carew Manuscripts, vol. 3, 1589–1600*, 292–5.

office to his closest friends, Blount and Southampton, and her insistence that the earl of Rutland should not be in Ireland at all seemed to Essex to be petty grudges, dangerous to the morale of the campaign; at worst a demonstration that Elizabeth was trying to part him from the support and counsel of his nearest allies.[75]

Meanwhile, the queen's sharp epistolary lectures upbraided the lord lieutenant with the most imperious language that she could wield. Ordering Essex into Ulster to confront Tyrone in the summer, an action that he was certain would fail, and was contrary to the advice of the Irish council and his own captains, Elizabeth crushed all anticipated excuses: 'These are the effects of your own actions, which are contrary to our will . . . We will not tolerate this'.[76]

In July, on his wretched return to Dublin, Essex warned his rivals of the dangerous nature of Elizabeth's changeable attitudes: were they to succeed in destroying him, they must be wary 'that she do not one day resume the saying of Augustus, "Had Maecenas or Agrippa been alive, she should sooner been put in mind of her own danger"'.[77] This heated pessimism was vented even more vigorously in his private letters to Lady Essex: 'The Queenes commaundment may breake my neck, but mine enemies at home shall never break my hart'.[78] As his dark valuation of Elizabeth's attitude towards him intensified, Essex hatched his first abandoned scheme in August to return to England with soldiers and to assert control over the court.[79]

The earl's eventual return from Ireland in September was not an armed assault, but hinged on his much tested ability to exploit the personal relationship he enjoyed with Elizabeth. By forcing his way in person to the queen's bedchamber, he could prevent his enemies inevitably misconstruing the truce agreed with Tyrone, while replenishing the well of affection that had sustained their relationship in previous years. Elizabeth's trust, though, had finally run dry. Placed under house arrest, Essex could only

---

[75] Relenting in her initial opposition to Blount's appointment as marshal of the army Elizabeth continued to refuse his appointment as a full member of the Irish council; she also insisted that Essex had appointed Southampton general of the horse against her command, though Essex complained that he had not interpreted this as a formal order: TNA, SP 63/204, ff. 147^r, 150^r–151^r, 166^{r-v}, 179^{r-v}; SP 63/205/2, 12, 40, 52, 79, ff. 3^r 19^r–20^r, 54^{r-v}, 78^v–79^r, 133^r.

[76] *Calendar of Carew Manuscripts, vol. 3, 1589–1601*, 315–16; see also 'The opinion of the Lords and Colonels of the Army, dissuading the journey northward', signed by 18 captains and sent on 27 August: TNA, SP 63/205/145, f. 269.

[77] *Calendar of Carew Manuscripts, vol. 3, 1589–1601*, 313–14.

[78] This evidence is from extracts taken from copied letters stolen by Lady Essex's servant, John Daniel; our knowledge of their content comes from the declaration of the scrivener, Peter Bales, taken on 31 July and 3 October 1601: TNA, SP 12/281/34, f. 73^r, 282/3, f. 3^r. Daniel asked Bales to copy this letter more than twelve times.

[79] Chapter 1, 36.

wield the pen, now in a manner more ingratiatingly lover-like than he had employed in 1598. On 11 February 1600, desperate to avoid a criminal trial, the earl pleaded with Elizabeth to remember 'how much more it will agree with your princely angel-lik nature' to have 'your mercye blazed by ye tungue of your Majesties once happye but nowe most sorrowfull orratour'.[80] He eschewed all political relationships and ambitions other than his love of the queen: 'Betwene my ruyne, & my Soverains favor, there is no meane'.[81]

Still, Essex's advisors worried about the earl's tendency to lapse in his profession of abject humility. Anticipating Essex's preparations to make a public defence of his actions in Ireland, Edward Reynolds wrote to Henry Cuffe on 29 November 1599 that the earl's fate depended on the *words* that he used:

he may by way of protestation & caution, & with full humble respect to her Majesty mak full aunswere to all objections and so an end of his troubles; whereas if he contest, & speak in a highe stile he shall plunge himself further, & overthrowe his fortune for ever.[82]

The self-conscious conduct of this relationship—the cultivation of a 'show, of great humility of mind' as Camden tellingly describes it—was admitted by Essex himself.[83] In a letter in which he promised to eschew confrontational rhetoric, he swore to 'enjoin myself never to speak in that stile which your Majestie doth not lik to heare'.[84]

To the delight of the court gossips, the earl's epistolary strategy could only function in a fairly haphazard way, with Essex worried that his missives would fail to reach the queen's eyes.[85] The earl's submissive letter from 11 February 1600—apparently passed by Sir Robert Cecil—persuaded her to cancel a hearing in Star Chamber.[86] The earl's supporters, also debarred easy access to the queen, tried similar strategies. A letter by Lady Penelope Rich (one of several written for her brother) had a disastrous impact, completely contrary to its purpose. Lady Rich warned the queen directly that she was smothered by 'evil instruments', and commanded Elizabeth to 'check the course of their unbridled hate', by removing Essex from captivity.[87] The queen's rage at Lady Rich's

[80] TNA, SP 12/274/39, f. 52ʳ.   [81] TNA, SP 12/274/138, f. 232ʳ, 12 May 1600.
[82] TNA, SP 12/273/38, f. 80ʳ.
[83] 'interim singularem animi prae se tulit humilitatem', Camden, *Annales*, 833.
[84] TNA, SP 12/275/85, f. 136ʳ, 4 October 1600.
[85] On 29 April 1600, Sir Richard Barkley conveyed Essex's fears that his letter had not been read by the queen to the intermediary Sir John Stanhope: Cecil MS 79/11.
[86] Collins, *Letters and memorials*, II, 166–7.
[87] *Lady Rich to her Maiestie in the behalfe of the Earle of Essex* (1600), sig. A2ᵛ. Lady Rich was commanded to keep to her house at the end of February to answer for the letter's scribal

presumption was only surpassed when the letter was published with Essex's *Apologie* in May, finally precipitating Essex's formal trial at York House.

More emollient were letters written on Essex's behalf by Francis Bacon. In particular, he penned an 'exchange' between Essex and his brother Anthony, which also meliorated Anthony's public reputation as the addressee of the earl's *Apologie*, and Essex's closest associate. 'Anthony's' letter is sprightly, emphasizing the queen's just nature and rallying Essex not to 'slaken and break of your wise, loyall and seasonable endevors for reintegration to her Majesty's ffavoure'. As Essex's ventriloquist, Francis has the earl declare himself the queen's assured '*re creationis* [own creation]'.[88]

At the eventual trial at York House on 5 June, Essex gave a passionate performance, declaring that he 'wold rather with his owne handes and nayles rent his fleshe and teare fourthe his harte then he would either make confession or aske forgiveness for anie thought of disloilltie'.[89] But even this self-righteous display of loyalism paradoxically enhanced Essex's assessment of the injustice of his predicament. The letters sent during his deepest period of disgrace are suffused with the critical language that Francis Bacon thought so deadly to his cause. Essex's queen is a cold, fierce deity who toys with her creation: 'when your Majestie doth anewe create me, what worldlye thing shall I account affliction?'[90] He appealed, as he would at his trial after the rising, to the queen's natural justice: 'I do humbly crave to heere your . . . naturall voyce of grace or else thatt your Majestie in mercy will send me into an other world'.[91] The frequent dashing of his hopes of reconciliation only enhanced Essex's sense that he was being perpetually baited with false indications of favour: why wait until June to formally charge him?[92] Why acquit him of disloyalty but refuse to receive him at court? The earl's fate would be determined by the exercise of Elizabeth's irrational will rather than reason, mercy, or natural justice: '*Domina dedit, domina abstulit, fiet voluntas Dominae*' (The queen gave, she took away, the will of the queen is done).[93]

---

publication; Penelope also sent expensive presents to the court at Christmas: Collins, *Letters and memorials*, II, 153, 158–9, 172, 194–5.

[88] *HMC Bath*, V, 266–9.

[89] Ibid., 272. Accounts of the trial are discussed in Chapter 5.

[90] TNA, SP 12/275/81, f. 130ʳ, undated 1600.

[91] TNA, SP 12/275/107, f. 167ʳ, undated 1600.

[92] On 20 March Essex was removed to Essex House with keepers; only on 26 August were custodians removed: Collins, *Letters and memorials*, II, 181, 213.

[93] TNA, SP 12/275/107, f. 167ʳ.

A final letter of the earl to the queen was possibly written after Elizabeth's refusal to renew the sweet wines monopoly at Michaelmas. Unsigned, the letter was apparently never sent, but it reveals desperate frustration at the fruitlessness of letter-writing to a mistress who has no desire to listen to the truth:

> ... for to write *freely* to a Lady thatt lyes in weyght for all things that I do say, were too much hazard, to write in a *plausible stile* when I have so discontented a hart were baseness yf nott falsehood. [emphasis added]

Essex palpably recognized that the queen deliberately sought to maintain his political alienation:

> I sometimes thinke of running and then remember whatt yt will be to come in armor triumphing into thatt presence out of which by your owne voyce I was comanded and by your handes thrust out ... It is well that you have that you looked for, and so have I ... in making this conclusion of my fortune you shall please them yow seeme to favor most.[94]

The queen is not a powerless dupe, but the powerful participant in his enemies' plans to ruin him. They are champion and mistress but Essex reverses the power of their roles; her wrongful behaviour towards him will meet with restitution.

PASSIONATE AND ERRANT PRINCES: THE EGERTON LETTERS IN CONTEXT

Essex's description of his relationship with Elizabeth reflects the dilemma felt by any discontented subject who sought to reconcile loyalty with a critical attitude towards a particular monarch. Essex's critiques of Elizabeth's government, though, reveal an awareness of frameworks that reflected on the deeper problems of personal monarchy. In letters to the queen he defines her rule as effeminate and unpredictable, dependent on her emotions. Her actions cannot be predicted, because she governs through *will*, which she equates with the *law* ('since your Majesty's will is the law'). She will listen to counsel only when flattered.

These languages have origins in courtly rhetoric, certainly; but they are also commonly associated with the characteristics of weak tyranny. The Aristotelean definition of a tyrant is a ruler who governs arbitrarily, dispensing with positive or natural laws, guided by will rather than reason, private interest over concern for the public good.[95] In the stoic

---

[94] BL, Additional MS, 74286, f. 133ʳ.
[95] Aristotle, *The Politics*, Book III, 1286a–1288b, Book IV, 1295a, ed. Stephen Everson (Cambridge: Cambridge University Press, 1996), 85–91, 105–6.

tradition, tyrants are governed by their passions, often manifest in fearfulness and suspicion of those whom they rule. Essex's indictment of Elizabeth's government through passion and emotion, her anger and jealousy of his virtue, and her rejection of natural justice are typical of sixteenth-century neo-stoic critiques of tyranny that emphasized the moral qualities of rulers, especially their capacity for emotional self-government.[96]

All of these languages were extensively developed in Essex's most famous epistolary exchange. In the summer of 1598, Lord Keeper Egerton wrote a letter of counsel to the earl, urging him to scrutinize his attitude towards the queen.[97] Essex refuted this unwelcome dressing-down with a platform for the principles of political conduct that he endorsed.

In his letter Egerton endorses a doctrine of monarchical power akin to that held by Elizabeth herself, of the perpetually irresistible authority of the prince. Essex's recent behaviour imperils 'your indissoluble dutye which you owe unto your most gratious soveraigne, a dutie not imposed upon you by nature and pollicie onelye but by religious and sacred bondes'. This is a statement of divinely ordained descending power: the queen's relationship with Essex is not reciprocal; there is 'no equall proportion of dutye' between subject and sovereign. Egerton also condemns Essex's habit of excusing himself from the implications of his actions by using the empty language of loyalty: 'these duties stand not only in [con]templation or inward meditation, theire effects be externall and cannott be performed but by externall actions'.[98]

Essex's reply to Egerton's summary of the theory of obedience develops into an exposition of the intractable problems of performing political duty to an unreasonable prince. Essex complains that the queen's condemnation of him is unlawful because she has passed sentence without trying him: 'in some causes I must appeale from all earthlye Judges . . . when the highest Judge on earthe hath imposed upon me the heviest punishment without triall or hearing'. The complaint of legality had some legitimacy in 1599 and 1600, when Essex was under house arrest without trial, but in the summer of 1598 he had been merely banished from the court! To suggest that Elizabeth could only disgrace her ministers with 'triall or hearing' was an assault on a vital aspect of her prerogative, her right to choose and dismiss counsellors. It underscores vividly the earl's sense of fundamental right to a public role.

---

[96] For neostoicism in England, see Salmon, 'Stoicism and Roman example'.
[97] Sometimes dated to October, the letters were written on 15 and 18 July. I have used the versions in the State Papers: TNA, SP 12/268/43 (44 is a copy) and Essex's reply, SP 12/268/45.
[98] TNA, SP 12/268/43, f. 70^r.

The main thrust of Essex's critique of the queen lies in his condemnation of the 'violente and unseasonable stormes' of Elizabeth's intemperate, emotion-driven government. Essex declares himself the innocent victim of 'the *passionate indignation* of a prince' [emphasis added] whose censure, wrongly imposed, he will bear with 'strength' and 'constancie in oppression'. 'Seneca saith that fortune is both blind and stronge.'

With this name-check to the younger Seneca, Essex most consciously nods to stoic concepts of tyranny: he also raises the problem of how a subject should *respond* to a tyrant. Here his attitude is ambiguous. Neo-stoic doctrine commanded the individual to weather foul political storms through 'constancie' and fortitude. Essex also responds strongly to the lord keeper's counsel on the obedience owed to his sovereign as God's representative. He concedes ground: allegiance is, of course, the 'dutye which I owe to my soveraigne'.

What constitutes this duty, though, is not a blind response to the queen's every command—instead it is defined by service commanded by the public office of 'an Earle Martiall of England: I have bene content to do her Majesty the service of a clarcke, but can never serve her as a villaine or slave'.[99] Essex glosses Egerton's words to be a statement of the infallibility of princely power, which he refutes in his bold statement about the separation of the secular and religious obedience of subjects:

> Doth religion enforce me to serve? Doth god require it is it impietye not to do it? Why, cannot princes erre and cannot subjects receive wronge: Is earthlye power and authoritie infinite: pardon me pardon me my good Lord I can never subscribe to theise principles.

While reluctant to broach squarely the legitimacy of resistance, Essex makes two points clear. First, he distinguishes between private subjects of Elizabeth, and the more public role that he enjoys as 'earl marshal', who cannot be commanded as a 'villaine' or a 'slave'. Second, no subjects must be obedient to ungodly commands. Essex here offers a resounding denunciation of theories of unlimited absolute monarchy. Because princes are mortal, and subject to ordinary passions and errors, they must be answerable to human judgment. The allegiance of subjects is problematized by conscience.

Essex then presents those who *do* subscribe to the principle of passive submission to tyrants as irreligious flatterers:

> Lett Solomons foole laugh when he is stricken, lett those that meane to make theire profitt of princes faulte, shew to have no sense of Princes. Injuries let

---

[99] A reference to his stint as secretary in the early months of 1598.

them acknowledge an infinite absolutenes on earth: that do not beleve an infinite absoluteness in heaven.[100]

Essex argues that rulers are obligated to respond to virtuous, critical counsel from free subjects: the greatest threats to the state are those evil advisors, who will necessarily encourage monarchs to compass their powers as unlimited, fostering their inclination to govern arbitrarily. This has much in common with the 'monarchical republicanism' identified in Elizabethan 'citizens' before 1585.[101] It is through the malign treatment of the virtuous noble individual, the 'earl marshal of England'—i.e. himself—though, that Essex defines the queen's misgovernment; his own fortunes represent wider corruption in the state.

Again, Philip Sidney had been a forerunner with these intellectual interests.[102] The poetry of Sidney's younger brother, Robert—perennially frustrated in Flushing—explores the agonies of unrequited love as a metaphor for political disappointments, while Sidney's commonplace book, compiled *c*.1600, reveals critical reading about monarchy.[103]

Far closer to Essex, though, was Fulke Greville who, unlike Robert Sidney, collaborated in Essex's literary/political projects.[104] Greville's Elizabethan sonnet sequence *Caelica* presents an even bleaker version of the Petrachan ideal, where his male lover is tormented by an indifferent or hostile female.[105] As Greville was a resident of Essex House from September 1596, it seems more than reasonable to imagine that Essex and his friends were the intended audience (or readers) for the neo-Senecan 'closet' drama that he began to write in the middle of the decade. Not meant for public performance but for a private audience, this genre was popularized in England in the circle of Mary Herbert, countess of Pembroke. It made use of historical settings to draw deliberately instructive parallels with the present—so deliberate that Greville had to destroy the final play of his trilogy of tragedies, *Antony and Cleopatra*, after Essex's rising, because it commented too overtly on Essex's recent history.

---

[100] TNA, SP 12/268/45, ff. 73^r–74^r.   [101] See Introduction, 14–19.

[102] Worden, *Sound of Virtue.*

[103] P. J. Croft, *Poems of Robert Sidney* (Oxford: Clarendon Press, 1984); Hay, *Life of Robert Sidney*, 205–6.

[104] Essex and Cuffe considered attaching Greville's name to the printed text of the 'True relacion', while Greville was apparently willing to be blamed for the dissemination of the *Apologie*; *The treatise paraentical*, published in English, was dedicated to Greville: LPL 658, f. 88^r; TNA, SP 12/261/53, f. 114^r; Chapter 2, 80.

[105] Geoffrey Bullough, ed., *The poems and dramas of Fulke Greville, first lord Brooke*, 2 vols (Edinburgh and London: Oliver and Boyd, 1939), I, 33–153; Rebholz, *Life of Greville*, 50–67.

Surviving texts of his earlier dramas, *Mustapha* and *Alaham*, written between 1595 and 1600, would be revised in the seventeenth century.[106]

In both plays Greville explored the Christian stoic themes that would become the abiding focus of his literary works: the struggle of reason and passion, the relationship of mind and will, nature and religion, the pursuit of virtue in a corrupted world. Essentially, though, both were studies of different forms of tyranny, which spoke to the same concerns of Essex, especially in their exploration of the psychology of rulers. If they had been read or performed in front of the earl, he would have found strong thematic parallels in the ways that he conceptualized his own relationship with Elizabeth, borne out in linguistic echoes in his own letters and writings to and about the queen.

The setting of *Mustapha* is the Ottoman court of Soliman (Suleiman) the Magnificent. Mustapha, Soliman's son and heir, is a successful military leader, who enflames the suspicious jealousy of his ageing father. Soliman's wife, Rossa, and her lover, Rosten, manipulate Soliman's vulnerable psychological state, preying on his fear and resentment of his son's popularity, and drawing him to comply in Mustapha's murder so that Zanger, Rossa's natural son, can inherit the throne. The tragedy pits virtuous actors—Mustapha and virtuous advisors (Camena, Rossa and Soliman's daughter, and Achmet, a wise servant)—against evil counsellors (Rossa and Rosten). Virtue emphatically fails to prevail; Mustapha and Camena are destroyed.

The moral and psychological deterioration of Soliman, not immediately evil, prefigures Essex's description of the corruption of Elizabeth's freedom of mind. As Essex warned Elizabeth of the flatterers who would play up the rhetoric of unlimited monarchy, so Rossa makes Soliman jealous of his authority as king: 'he that *Monarch* is,/*Must (like the Sunne) haue no light shine, but his*' (1:1, 37–8).[107] Rossa and Rosten recognize that Mustapha's virtues are his greatest enemies: 'Thinke Innocencie harme; Vertue dishonour;/Wound Truth; and overweigh the scale of Right;/*Sexes have wayes apart; States have their fashions:/The vertues of Authoritie are passions*' (3:1, 30–3).[108]

---

[106] For dating see Bullough, *Poems and dramas*, II, 1–62; Rebholz, *Life of Greville*, 101–8, 124–40, 328–31. Rebholz gives a date for the earliest versions of *Mustapha* of 1594–6. The three variants of the earliest versions are a manuscript in Trinity College, Cambridge (C), a manuscript in the Folger Shakespeare Library (FL), and a version printed in 1609 (Q). The text was again revised *c.*1607–10, surviving in a printed version from the 1633 edition of Greville's *Works*, and a version in Greville's manuscripts at Warwick Castle. Bullough's edition, based on the printed version of 1633, gives textual variants: unless stated, I have only quoted lines used in all versions (though spellings/structure of scenes vary).

[107] Bullough, *Poems and dramas*, II, 64.

[108] Ibid., 99 (C, Q, 2:3 – Q has 'Wound truthe and overthrow the state').

The most ambiguous aspect of the play is Greville's treatment of response to tyranny. Mustapha is the exemplum of stoic fortitude, the mouthpiece for the passive acceptance of the tyrant's rod: 'Our Gods they [princes] are, their God remaines above/ *To thinke against annoynted Power is death*'. A priest, though, complicates these arguments with a persuasive remonstrance: 'To worship Tyrants is no worke of faith' (4:4, 150–3).[109] The dilemma is revisited after Mustapha's death, in the conundrum of Achmet the virtuous counsellor, who must decide whether to join in rebellion against Soliman. Greville's most substantial revisions were to Act V, and variant versions of Achmat's speeches survive. In all, he rejects resistance, trusting in 'God onlye Judge' to punish kings for their sins. Achmat's agonies of counsel, though, are a long exposition of the limited powers of monarchs, which, in one Elizabethan text at least, is highly sympathetic to more radical forms of action: 'dutyes to kinges they be Conditionall/when they from god, we from them then maye fall' (5:2, 202–3).[110]

The fate of Mustapha and the dilemma of Achmat formed the debates at the heart of the earl's circle. Now, Essex and his followers began to identify these literary dilemmas spooling out in real time in Essex's own story, giving sharp, bleak edges to their interpretation of the politics of the court, evil counsel, and the character and actions of Elizabeth.

THE PHYSICIAN OF STATE

Essex's letters to the queen necessarily dwelt on the relationship of two individuals, creature and creator, subject and sovereign. To Egerton, however, he also defined his behaviour in relation to broader ideals of public duty, and towards the wider polity.

In the aftermath of the rising, Essex's use of political rhetoric was attacked with gusto 'as though none had regarded the generall good of the common welth but himself'.[111] Francis Bacon emphasized Essex's dangerous identification with the languages of service both to 'state' and 'commonwealth', describing an occasion when he had chastised Essex for magnifying grievances to serve his own ambition: 'I tooke you for a Phisition that desired to cure the diseases of the State... [Now Essex is] like those Phisitions, which can be content to keepe their patients low, because they would alwaies be in request'.[112]

---

[109] Bullough, *Poems and dramas*, II, 119 (C, Q, 3:5).
[110] Ibid., 276 (5:2 from the C text, printed as Appendix A, 267–78).
[111] TNA, SP 12/278/63, f. 108ʳ; Chapter 1, 52.
[112] Bacon, *Apologie*, 21.

Suspicion of the manipulation of these political languages was deeply engrained in contemporary political culture, marking that shift away from the first three decades of Elizabeth's reign, when the elite had frequently defined their political identity as citizens as well as subjects, informed by Ciceronean ideals of the *vita activa* and godly duty to a distinct concept of the commonwealth that could incorporate or exist separately from the body of the queen. In the 1590s many—Bacon perhaps most self-consciously—were newly wary that these forms of expression forged unwanted divisions in subjects' consciences between their perception of public duty, and the personal loyalty that they owed to Elizabeth as an 'absolute' rather than a 'limited' monarch.[113]

With flamboyance, though, Essex employed the languages of active citizenship to imagine his role in all the political issues of moment that had energized their expression in previous decades: religion, war, and the succession. This is most immediately evidenced in his *Apologie*: Essex draws the superiority of his argument from his understanding of the 'true naturall and healthful temper for all estates', and his service as 'a most faithfull subject, and zealous patriot'. From this lofty moral perch, he hymns a martial ideal of the *vita activa*, praising soldiers for 'their vertues sake, for their greatnesse of minde', who 'shewe they love the publique profite more then themselves'.[114]

Essex did not snatch his 'patriot's' ideals of service from the ether; he was surrounded by friends desperate to fête his public role in a manner identical to that of Wright's gratuitous *imprese*. Anthony Bacon wrote enraptured of Essex's 'noble active minde' working constantly 'for the publique good which stands now in need of all diligent Arquitecks to uphould the happines of her Majestie and the State'.[115] Sparks flew from the pen of Francis Davison: Essex 'hathe so notably beaten ye greatest Monarcke of the worlde' (a rather generous assessment of Cadiz), but faces a more insidious enemy: the 'Pigmey' (Robert Cecil).[116]

In periods of disfavour, Essex easily expressed his embrace of the ideal of stoic retirement. In the dark months of house arrest, he trumpeted the benefits of an untroubled conscience through rejection of 'worldy delights' 'which the Prince of this world will seek to entertain you with'.[117] In a poem sent to Elizabeth, 'Robin' dreams of 'some unhaunted Desart, most Obscure', where he might spend his days 'in Contemplation' and 'Holy Thoughts' (7:2, 7–10).[118] But Essex, with so many authors of

---

[113] Discussed further in Chapter 5.   [114] *Apologie*, sigs. A^{r-v}, B3^r.
[115] LPL MS 654, f. 149^r.   [116] LPL MS 660, f. 220^r.
[117] *The Earle of Essex to Southampton*, sig. A3^v.
[118] May, 'Poems of Robert Devereux', 47.

anti-court poetry, was inexorably drawn to the life that he condemned. Ironically, this presentation of his delight in the spiritual *rus* over the worldly *urbs* was an artificial construction in itself, designed to convince Elizabeth of his reformed character, his preparedness for a return to political life.

But the emphasis placed by Essex and his friends on active virtue was almost exclusively personalized: when they used the languages of civic duty it was usually to emphasize *Essex's* indispensability to *patria* or state, as Parsons exploited so successfully in the dedication of the *Conference*. Thus important elements of the 'quasi-republican' modes of mixed monarchy were bypassed or restructured in Essex's thinking. Most importantly, there was little sense of the corporate identity that previously had underpinned the concept of England as a 'monarchical republic'. The earl consistently defined his loyalty to the 'public', his 'country', or most often, the 'state' or 'state of England' (used interchangeably with 'estate'): never, though, a 'commonwealth' of godly like-thinking men.[119]

This individualism is strikingly apparent in Essex's attitude towards that central element in most Tudor theories of mixed monarchy—the monarch's responsiveness to counsel. In fact, Essex and his followers rarely used the language of counsel to define his relationship with Elizabeth: rather the earl's role was to 'win' the queen or 'alter her mind', through the manipulation of Elizabeth's unreasonable emotions. Crucially, Essex conceived this as a personal interaction, where the queen should be guided by the justice of his argument, and Elizabeth's respect for his virtues. Unlike William Cecil, Essex also exhibited no interest in political theories that enshrined the institutional role of the privy council.[120] Although the earl's political authority in the wider realm was dependent on his membership of this body, the Cecils' dominance of conciliar politics made Essex increasingly inclined to describe his role in the polity outside of it. On the strategy adopted in the Islands Voyage, he explained 'her Maiestie and *her counsell* knowe, what offer of service I made her when I came up post from Plymouth' [emphasis added].[121] Of his initial refusal to advise the council meeting when the Irish crisis summoned him: 'I am sworne to give counsell to your Majestie and not *your Counsell*: so that which I was and am to deliver is fitt to be harde only by yourselfe' [emphasis added].[122]

Despite his preference for the vocabulary of state, Essex was still accused of employing the language of 'commonwealth' to further his ambition,

---

[119] Professor Malcolm Smuts has also noted Essex's use of this language in the *Apologie*, in an unpublished paper delivered at the IHR Midsummer seminar on 16 August 2010. This language is consistent throughout the *Apologie*: see sigs. A^v–A2, B3^r, [B4^r], and *passim*.
[120] Collinson, 'Monarchical republic'.
[121] *Apologie*, sig. B2^r.   [122] BL, Additional MS 6177, f. 32^{r-v}.

especially to cultivate popular support. Bacon's letter of advice in 1596 warned Essex to 'go on in your honourable commonwealth courses as you do', but pretend otherwise to appease the queen, speaking publicly 'against popularity and popular causes vehemently'. Essex must never seek political advantage 'by dealing in monopolies, or any oppressions. Only, if in parliament your Lordship be forward for treasure in respect of the wars, it becometh your person well'.[123] The directions for preachers issued after the rising denounced the earl's conduct of a 'kinde of popular conversation to allure the harts of the simple sorte unto him, especiallie concerning levyinge of money'.[124] These critiques imply that Essex's political identity also encompassed a deliberate strategy to engage with wider socio-economic grievances, Bacon issuing an extremely enigmatic warning about the earl's use of parliament as a forum to protest against prerogative levies and other fiscal exactions.

There were strong paradigmatic precedents for the kind of behaviour that Essex was allegedly striving towards, though they divided opinion. Paternalistic representation of the grievances of the Commons was a venerable requirement of noble behaviour; but the aristocrat who courted popular acclaim through ambition was a bogeyman just as menacing as the evil counsellor in contemporary political thinking. For Elizabethans, the most frequently-invoked *exampla* of noblemen pandering to public fame were Guise and Bullingbrook, both alleged models for Essex's behaviour.[125] The barbs fired at Essex's posture as a 'friend to the commons' drew obvious parallels, too, with the most notorious sixteenth-century aristocratic champion of the grievances of the commons: Edward Seymour, duke of Somerset, whose reputation as the 'Good Duke' in the reign of Edward VI, Ethan Shagan has argued, reflected deliberate efforts to construct a powerbase outside of his landed following through the cultivation of public opinion.[126]

Emphasis, though, on Essex's concern for the economic problems of the lower orders is puzzling. As the 'post-rising' directions for preachers scoffed, his hunger for war made him a most unlikely spokesman for the poor—'he hath ben still the Author of the most of her highness charges and expences'—while his dependence on the sweet wine farm made him an unlikely opponent of monopolies.[127] Hammer remarks: 'Essex did not involve himself in the labyrinthine business of government finance'.[128]

---

[123] Spedding, *L&L*, II, 44.   [124] TNA, SP 12/278/63, f. 108[r].
[125] See Chapter 1, 63–5.
[126] Ethan Shagan, 'Protector Somerset and the 1549 rebellions: new sources and new perspectives', *EHR*, 114 (1999), 32–63.
[127] TNA, SP 12/278/63, f. 108[r].   [128] Hammer, *Polarisation*, 123.

Posthumous presentations of Essex offer clues. Ballads describe their tragic protagonist as the particular friend of the needy: 'He alwayes helpt the poore'. 'The poore he never did reject'.[129] Some imagine alternative texts of Essex's execution speech, ventriloquizing words of affection for the commons: in one the earl protests '[I]neither wisht the Commons ill/In all my life/But lov'd with all my hart/and always tooke their part'; in an 'Elegy on the late earle of Essex', he prays on the scaffold 'for the pore comunalty/that long in peace their weale might stand'.[130] These accounts completely rewrite official narratives of Essex's execution, and refute the record of Essex's alleged reflection immediately prior to his death that 'all popularitie & trust in man was vaine'.[131]

According to Bacon, some of the defining 'points of popularitie which every man tooke notice and note of, [were Essex's] affable gestures, open doores, making his table and his bed popularly places of audience to suters'.[132] The allegation seems borne out in the language of Essex's suits, which certainly reflects the ideals of charitable paternalism. In 1594 and 1595, as Essex made prominent the public face of his ambitions, he besieged Puckering with a stream of requests for suitors ensnared in difficult legal cases: for the 'poore cappers of Litchfield', the 'poore men [who] for my sute found favor'; for a debt owed to Thomas Simpson, a 'poore man' whose plight had been brought to his attention; for a further case brought by friends of 'the poore gentleman', Mr Lawe.[133]

Essex's alleged entanglement with the making of fiscal policy is more difficult to discern. One newsletter writer, gossiping on the eve of his departure for Ireland, provides enigmatic corroboration: 'The favour and affection of the common people still is addicted to therle of Essex, rather as in thoughte, hoeping by his meanes some way to be freed from theire intolerable exactions'.[134] Suggestive evidence comes from the pen of Essex himself: as he prepared for the Islands Voyage, Essex wrote to Cecil on 14 August about the imminent parliament: 'looke about you to provide extraordinarye meanes to maintayne the warres for yf you go the playne way of subsidyes to worke, I feare you will find it was not well forethought of'.[135]

---

[129] Anon., *A lamentable ditty composed upon the death of Robert Lord Devereux, late Earle of Essex* (1603).

[130] W. R. Morfill and F. J. Furnivall eds, *Ballads from manuscripts*, 2 vols (London: The Ballad Society, 1868), II, pt 2, 249.

[131] TNA, SP 12/278/113, f. 222[r].

[132] Bacon, *Declaration*, B[r].

[133] BL, Harleian MS 6997, f. 52[r]; BL, Harleian MS 6996, ff. 183[r]; 36[r], 187[r]. For similar examples see ibid., f. 237[r]; BL, Harleian MS, 6997, ff. 16[r], 38[r], 42[r], 44[r], 46[r], 48[r], 50[r], 52[r], 82[r], 14[r], 154[r].

[134] TNA, SP 12/271/106, f. 171[r].   [135] Cecil MS 54/47.

Essex at least tried to present the war as a feasible burden on the English economy; his argument for establishing a naval base on the Iberian coastline was that it would, theoretically, be low-cost, damaging Spanish power by intercepting New World treasure. In the *Apologie*, Essex thrashes around for an economic argument for the continuation of the war. Venting sympathy for the 'poore husbandmen' who 'these late hard yeres hath now scant means to live', he explains that hostilities can be simply funded: if the Dutch double their contribution and add a (most unlikely) sum from Henry IV, Elizabeth can easily gather £150,000 to fund the war without excessive taxation. The details of this dubiously optimistic budget wash into a polemical attack on the 'expencefull vanities', the houses, the clothes, the plate of the rich that had long been low-hanging fruit to satirists of the *regnum Cecilianum*, but reflected also the under-assessment of the taxation of the Elizabethan nobility.[136]

But did Essex really see parliament as a forum to enhance his reputation for concern for the commonwealth? He was certainly aggressively alive to the importance of parliamentary patronage as a tool to reward his followers. In 1593 and again in 1597 (with less success because of his absence at sea) the earl conducted vigorous campaigns to have his clients elected, exploiting his ties to the significant number of boroughs where he was lord high steward, and the counties in the Midlands and Wales where his influence was strongest.[137] Neale remarks that Essex's parliamentary patronage resembled the tactical organization of the Puritan political movement of the 1570s and 1580s, but without any platform other than the magnification of Essex's personal following.[138]

In the parliament of 1593, though, the performance of several of the earl's friends in the Commons does suggest a shared concern to address the exacerbation of the socio-economic grievances of the realm through taxation. In the troubled passage of the triple subsidy bill, introduced unconstitutionally by Burghley in the Lords, Greville's speech in favour eloquently acknowledged the dangers of social unrest that heavy taxation might provoke. In language that Essex would employ in the *Apologie*, he argued that the obvious wealth of the country was evinced in 'our

---

[136] *Apologie*, sig. D3ʳ (the 1603 text reads 'wastefull', sig. E4r). As lord treasurer, Burghley's own subsidy assessment rated at around 30 times less than its true value: John Guy, *Tudor England* (Oxford: Oxford University Press, 1988), 383–4. His income as master of the court of wards from 1594–8 was three times that of the Crown from fees from private suitors: Joel Hurstfield, *The queen's wards: wardship and marriage under Elizabeth I* (London: Jonathan Cape, 1958), 266–9.

[137] Essex was high steward of at least eleven boroughs: Ipswich, Bristol, Great Yarmouth, St Alban, Andover, Dunwich, Hereford, Leominster, Oxford, Reading, Tamworth: Neale, *Elizabethan House of Commons*, 224–5.

[138] Ibid., 230–1.

sumptuousness in apparel, plate, and all things ells [that] argueth our riches'. The burden for this unprecedented number of subsidies, then, 'must be helped by increasing our owne burthen, for otherwise the weake feet will complaine of too heavie [a] boddie'.[139] Far more surprising was the active opposition of Francis Bacon and Sir Henry Unton (another client of Essex), who imperilled their careers when they objected to Burghley's infringement of the right of the Commons to initiate financial bills. Bacon gave a further impassioned speech, urging that the subsidy be spread over six years to ease the burden on the poor, and issued a further warning about the future implications for English property rights: 'of all nations the English care [not] to be subject, base, and taxeable'.[140] Richard Broughton, Essex's man-of-business, objected to the absolutist implications of the bill's preamble which implied that subjects' property was the queen's to dispose.[141] Finally, Unton accused an unnamed councillor (clearly Sir Robert Cecil) of reporting to Elizabeth those who had objected to the bill in the Commons. Essex replied glumly to his friend that this course had been disastrous: the queen 'startles at your name, chargeth you with popularity, and hath every particular of your speeches in parliament'.[142]

Of Essex's own parliamentary activities, the skeletal information conveyed in the *Lords' Journals* is suggestive. In 1593, in a flurry of committee business, he was appointed with Lord Willoughby to administer a forced donation from the peerage and episcopacy to poor and maimed soldiers.[143] In the 1597–8 parliament Essex was absent during the sessions that saw the passage of the subsidy bill, as well as motions against privileges and monopolies that were suppressed by the crown in December.[144] When he returned on 11 January, though, the new earl marshal played an active role in the remainder of the myriad socio-economic legislation for which this parliament is famous, sitting on or chairing multiple committees, including one for the crucial bill that emerged as the seminal 'Act for the Relief of the Poor' (39 Eliz. I, c. 3).[145] Thomas Cartwright gave gushing thanks for Essex's particular help in the passage of the bill

---

[139] Hartley, *Proceedings*, 102–3.

[140] Ibid., 109–10; the omission of [not] seems to be the scribe's error of transcription; see Simonds D'Ewes, *The Journals of all the Parliaments during the reign of Queen Elizabeth* (1682), 493; Neale, *Elizabeth I and her parliaments*, 298–312.

[141] Hartley, *Proceedings*, 122. The bill was sent back to committee for amendment.

[142] *HMC Salisbury*, IV, 68–9, 452–3; (the first letter is wrongly dated 'October' in the *Calendar*). In 1597, Francis Bacon initiated the tillage bill in the Commons: Neale, *Elizabeth I and her parliaments*, 337–9 and *passim*.

[143] *Journal of the House of Lords. Volume 2. 1578–1614* (London, 1771), 176–7.

[144] Neale, *Elizabeth I and her parliaments*, 352–62.

[145] D'Ewes, *Journal*, 522–47; *Lords' Journal*, 214–24.

that had confirmed leases and lands held by Leicester's hospital at Warwick.[146]

But how else did the earl seek to generate popular acclaim? Essex's popularity in London especially was strongly bound up with his identification as a military hero, shored up by his contacts with civic elites and churches in the capital.[147] Though Essex's attempts to procure a national day of 'publike thanksgeving for this great victory' were scotched, Londoners remembered Cadiz as *his* victory all the same: Stowe describes the day of 'great triumph ... in London' on 8 August for 'the good successe of the earle of Essex, and his company in Spaine', no mention by name of other gallants or even the lord admiral.[148] As well as a sermon preached by William Barlow (then Whitgift's chaplain) at Paul's Cross, Essex's followers may have targeted individual parishes: Robert Bacon, Anthony and Francis's cousin, instructed parishioners at 'St Clements' to assemble for a ceremony of thanksgiving for 'the right honourable & or singular good Lo: the Earle of Essex', encouraging attendance with the mysterious promise of 'some charitable acte'.[149] In the months of his political exile at Essex House, the earl's ostentatious piety would be enacted physically in his attendance at sermons which drew scores of spectators.[150]

But the earl's popular militarism served a wider purpose: to maintain public support for Elizabeth's war in the face of the current experiences of economic deprivation and hardship. After Cadiz, Essex successfully persuaded Giles Fletcher, remembrancer to the city of London, to approach the privy council in the name of the London aldermen, urging that the Cadiz troops might be used for the recovery of Calais with financial contribution from the citizens.[151] The earl's ability to use his personal influence to press for this intervention is even more striking given the frequent expressions of war-weariness that increasingly emanated from the London elite. By December, just months after Fletcher's failed petition, they responded obstructively to the demand for ten ships, protesting the 'great dearth of victual', and the 'public calamity' increased by the interruption of trade.[152]

---

[146] Lord Leycester's Hospital was founded in 1571 to provide particular relief for retired soldiers and their families: Cecil MS 64/69.

[147] See Chapter 1, 62–3; Chapter 5, 207–9.

[148] LPL MS 658, f. 135^r; Stowe, *Chronicles*, 406–7. This reference is more telling because Stowe describes Howard's and Essex's co-command in his previous entry.

[149] LPL MS 658, f. 196^r; the church is most likely St Clements without Temple Bar, where Essex had supporters: LPL Fairhurst MS 3470, f. 217^v, also Chapter 5, 207.

[150] See Chapter 1.

[151] LPL MS 658, ff. 202, 272^r.

[152] *HMC Salisbury*, VI, 534–5; see also BL, Lansdowne MS 81, ff. 78^r–84^r, a list of those Londoners who refused to pay towards the ships and pinnaces in July 1596 for the Cadiz

Essex and his circle made a few attempts to intervene in the public sphere through the shadowy world of covert print publication in ways that aped the Macavity-like use of the press by Burghley.[153] Of the earl's followers Anthony Bacon, Henry Cuffe, and Lord Willoughby had connections to networks of booksellers, printers, and scriveners in London.[154] Plans to print the English translation of Pérez's *Relaciones* and *The state of Christendom* were scotched in 1595; Francis Bacon's robust Philippic on the Lopez conspiracy languished in manuscript, as did Essex's 'True relacion' of the Cadiz voyage. Likewise, the printing of William Barlow's Cadiz sermon, though entered in the Stationers' Register on 29 November 1596, was stalled.[155] Printed ballads and poems in celebration of the earl's martial and chivalric performances may also have been sponsored covertly by Essex's followers at climacteric moments.[156] *A prayer for the prosperous proceedings and good success of the Earle of Essex and his companies, in their present expedition in Ireland against Tyrone* (1599) written by John Norden, a client of the earl, notably defines the venture as *Essex's* heroic moment, in distinct contrast to the official *Prayer for the good success of her Majesties forces in Ireland* (1599), published by the queen's printer, Christopher Barker.[157]

The key point is that none of the texts even abortively planned for print publication could be directly associated with Essex. Our main piece of direct evidence that Essex kicked the sands over his own footprints to the press is from Cuffe's letter detailing the earl's personal instructions for

voyage, complaining of other subsidies. See I. W. Archer, *The pursuit of stability: social relations in Elizabethan London* (Cambridge: Cambridge University Press, 1991), 10–12, 35.

[153] For Burghley's use of the press see Conyers Read, 'William Cecil and Elizabethan Public Relations', in Bindoff et al., *Elizabethan Government and Society*, 21–55; Elizabeth Evenden and Thomas S. Freeman, 'Print, profit and propaganda: the Elizabethan Privy Council and the 1570s edition of Foxe's "Book of Martyrs"', *EHR*, 119 (2004), 1228–307.

[154] Anthony Bacon undertook with all possible 'discretion and secrecy' to deliver Cuffe's 'True relacion' to a printer: LPL MS 658, ff. 259ʳ–260ᵛ, also see f. 88ʳ; Hammer, 'Mythmaking'; above, n. 13. For Cuffe and Norton, see below, 182; Willoughby anonymously published a defence of his service in the Low Countries, *A Short and True Discourse for satisfying all those who speak indiscreetly of her Majesty* (1589).

[155] E. Arber ed., *A transcript of the registers of the Company of Stationers of London, 1554–1640 AD,* 5 vols (London, 1875–1894) III, 75.

[156] No longer extant are: 'Englandes resolution to beate backe the Spaniards', entered on 3 January 1596; Thomas Churchyard's *Welcomme home of the E[a]rle of ESSEX and the Lord Admirall*, entered in October 1596; 'The E[a]rle of ESSEX going to Cales', entered posthumously, in 1603: Arber, *Transcript*, III, 36, 56, 71.

[157] For Norden, see chapter 2, 77. Thomas Churchyard also published *The fortunate farewell to the most forward and noble earle of Essex . . .* (1599). A further ballad was *Londons Loathe to departe' to the noble E[arle of ESSEX*: Arber, *Transcript*, III, 141.

the publication of the 'True relacion'—so that 'no slender guesse may be drawne who was the penneman'.[158]

Essex and his supporters' preferred intervention was through the manuscript publication of texts, especially the ostensibly private 'letter', where accusations of dissemination could be more plausibly denied. Here, the circulation of the *Apologie* and the exchange with Egerton are even more significant. Framed as private epistles, they were circulated contemporaneously, in the late summer of 1598. Certainly Camden insists that the exchange with Egerton was disseminated quite deliberately by Essex's followers; his account is corroborated by allegations levied at Essex at the York House tribunal.[159] In the instances of both of these texts, though, Essex cast off the guise of anonymity that Elizabethans usually employed when making interventions in public debate through a position piece: both proclaimed *Essex's* authorship, thus acting as a kind of textual soapbox whence he could pronounce as the physician of state—through a defence of the war, but also through the propagation of a critique of divine right theories of obedience.

As Essex's career drew more sharply into decline, letters and poems associated with him swept round the court, the city, and even emerged from the press.[160] It becomes even more difficult to judge how widely the earl intended materials defending his behaviour to be read. Francis Bacon is clear: the falsified exchange between Essex and Anthony Bacon was intended to attract the attention of Elizabeth, and, perhaps, courtiers who might have spoken on the earl's behalf to the queen.[161] Contemporaries thought the cause of Elizabeth's anger at Lady Rich's letter was that it had been 'published Abroad'.[162] At the York House trial, a stinging attack was launched on the wide, deliberate circulation of the letter: 'though written to her sacred Majesty...first divulged by copies everywhere (that as it seemeth the newest and finest form of libelling)'.[163] As this quotation indicates, Essex's *Apologie* and Penelope's letter were printed as a slew of anonymous libels simultaneously washed around the court and city, vituperating his enemies in threatening language.[164]

---

[158] LPL MS 658, f. 88ʳ.

[159] Camden, *Annales*, 772–3; corroborated by Fynes Moryson, *An itinerary written by Fynes Moryson Gent.... containing his ten yeeres travell... Divided into III parts...* (1617), II, 71.

[160] Rowland Whyte knew content of Essex's letters to Elizabeth, while Chamberlain sent copies to Dudley Carelton: McClure, *Letters of John Chamberlain*, I, 50, 99.

[161] *Apologie*, 61–2.

[162] Collins, *Letters and memorials*, II, 172.

[163] Spedding, *L&L*, II, 178; for the texts of the York House Trial, see Chapter 5, 198.

[164] See lord chief justice Popham to Cecil on 2 and 3 February 1600, reporting libels: Cecil MS 68/15, 17.

The content of pro-Essex libels will be more searchingly analysed in the following chapter: here, the relevant point is that we have no way of identifying the libelling as a directed campaign from Essex's followers. While certain extant verses suggest an intimate knowledge of political attitudes in Essex's close circle, others may represent the spontaneous efflorescence of texts by more distant admirers, genuine products of the earl's popular appeal.[165]

By February 1601, Essex was well aware that Bacon's prophecy about the perils of popularity had reached unfortunate fruition, and that his scorched reputation was extremely vulnerable to manipulation. Blackmail was the ostensible motivation of John Daniel, Essex's servant, who stole the earl's private letters to Lady Essex from Ireland, and had a selection copied by the scrivener, Peter Bales. Essex spied behind the arras the looming shadows of Ralegh and Cobham.[166] Finally, in early May 1600, Essex was horrified at the unauthorized printing of just under 300 copies of his *Apologie*, together with his sister's disastrous letter. From captivity Essex set Cuffe and Whitgift to suppress the publication 'that the parties may be punyshed'.[167] Those 'pratising libellers' were 'no well wishers to me butt my secreett enemyes':[168]

> The prating tavern hunter speaks of me when he list: the frantick libeller writes of me when he list: already they print me, and mak speak to the world; and shortley they will play me in what forms they list upon the stage.[169]

The earl should have heeded his own warning; as he would find in 1601, the public opinion that he had played with was no tame animal, but a beast with its own instincts and appetites.

---

[165] See Chapter 5, 206–11.

[166] Daniel blackmailed the countess in the spring of 1600, and was found guilty in Star Chamber in June 1601, fined and pilloried. He consistently denied that Ralegh and Cobham had put him up to making the forgeries, insisting that he had only kept hold of particular letters because they contained important matters of state; Bales denied that he inserted any material prejudicial to Essex in his copies: TNA, SP 12/279/124, 125, 126; 281/34, 77, 77I, 77II; TNA, SP 12/282/3, 4; TNA, SP 12/285/22; Geoffrey Chesters, 'John Daniel of Daresbury, 1544–1610', *Proceedings of the Historic Society of Lancashire & Cheshire*, 118 (1966), 1–17.

[167] Cecil MS 79/37, 41, Richard Barkley to Sir Robert Cecil, 9 and 10 May 1600; 79/40, Whitgift to Sir Robert Cecil. Of the 292 copies that he believed had been published, Whitgift claimed to have called in 210.

[168] Cecil MS 80/2, Essex to the council, May 1600.

[169] TNA, SP 12/274/38, f. 232^r 12 May 1600.

THE EARL MARSHAL AND THE
ANCIENT NOBILITY

Of all aspects of Essex's adherence to the reform of the English polity, his association with noble honour is the least surprising. It is often assumed that Essex's hostility to the Cecils and Ralegh stemmed from his desire to assert the rights of the ancient martial nobility against 'bureaucratic' Cecilian parvenus, or Ralegh, the bumptious Devon gentleman.[170]

Oppression of the nobility by upstarts was a centuries-old trope of anti-court complaint. In Elizabethan England, the discourse was exploited with vigour by Catholic polemicists, who argued that the dominance of evil Protestant ministers—particularly Burghley and Leicester—had removed Elizabeth from the influence of her natural counsellors.[171] As we have seen, these *topoi* emerged in Thomas Wright's *pasquinade* on the *regnum Cecilianum*, which makes visual jokes on the Cecilian coat of arms, laughing, as Jesuit polemic had, at Burghley's humble pedigree.[172] But Protestant Elizabethans also exhibited a more general concern that the natural social order was being undermined. As the sixteenth century drew to a close, calls for the regulation and tighter control of the honours system were strongly yoked to wider fear of social unrest. Ironically, the mocking jibes of Catholic polemicists were partly provoked by Burghley's own concern to rejuvenate the decayed estate of the greater nobility.[173]

The Devereux pedigree entitled Essex to claim membership of the 'ancient nobility', although the earl's lineage was rather less distinguished than he might have liked. Robert d'Evreux had settled in England at the time of the Norman Conquest, but Essex's titles were of much more recent creation, and inherited through the female line: the title Viscount Hereford had been bestowed in 1550 on Essex's great-grandfather, Sir Walter, 3rd Baron Ferrers, whose mother, Cecily Bourchier, provided the Devereux claim to the earldom of Essex. Walter, Essex's father, had been elevated by Elizabeth to this higher rank of nobility as recently

---

[170] Mears describes Robert Cecil and Essex embodying the conflict between '*noblesse de robe* and *noblesse d'épée*': '*Regnum Cecilianum?*', 64.

[171] William Allen, *Admonition to the nobility and people of England and Ireland concerninge the present warres made for the execution of his Holines sentence* ... (1588); Verstegan, *An aduertisement written to a secretarie* ..., 14–18.

[172] See Chapter 3.

[173] In 1588, Burghley had made suggestions for elevations to and within the peerage, but had declined the earldom of Northampton, perhaps knowing the vilification that would greet such a title: BL, Lansdowne MS 104, ff. 51ʳ–52ᵛ; Burghley's treatise on the decayed state of the realm, written *c.*1595, deplored the shortage of noblemen on the council: TNA, SP 12/255/84.

as 1572.[174] Nevertheless, Essex's pride in his lineage is reflected in a treatise written for him by the antiquarian scholar, Francis Thynne, in December 1599; a long exposition in dialogue form of the earl's noble ancestry, written when the earl was under house arrest and desperately ill. Thynne's treatise, which also contains a glowing account of Essex's military record, may have been intended as a contribution to Essex's political rehabilitation, or at least as a fitting tribute to the earl's memory, should current rumours of his imminent death prove prophetic.[175]

It was in Essex's earlier pursuit and exercise of the earl marshalship, though, that he yoked his own political ambitions most clearly to ideals of the traditional role of the hereditary nobility. Nevertheless, Essex strongly identified his title to the marshalship as dependent on his *abilities*. Noisily rejecting the draft of his patent, he complained 'I am praysed for too innocent vertues when they are active vertues, and nott negative, thatt should draw on a prince to bestow a marshall's office'.[176]

As well as pre-eminence over the lord admiral, the assumption of the marshalship also gave Essex responsibility over the community of honour, which he briefly pursued with intensity and zeal. Essex commissioned a scholarly investigation into the scope of the earl marshal's duties, intended to inform a programme for the reform of the honours system that had been somewhat fitfully pursued throughout the sixteenth century. Here the silken glove of Henry Howard guided Essex's approach, as the two men endeavoured to restore the earl marshal's prestige and to clarify his jurisdiction over the heralds. Howard's treatise for Essex, finished just before the earl's departure for Ireland, proposed a scrutiny of all titles to arms granted since 1568.[177]

There was considerable irony in making Essex responsible for regulating the honours system: some of Elizabeth's most enraged criticisms had been provoked by the earl's notorious practice of dubbing scores of battlefield knights.[178] Just as startling was the first major role that Essex played as

---

[174] Howell A. Lloyd, 'The Essex inheritance,' *Welsh History Review*, 7 (1974), 13–59.

[175] BL, Harleian MS 305, ff. 150^r–186^r.

[176] Cecil MS 57/109. A draft of the letters patent of creation objected to by Essex, with underlinings and annotations by Cecil, includes the instruction to add 'particular services of ye Erle': Cecil MS 176/10.

[177] Surviving tracts collected for Essex include a fragment of a further treatise by Thynne, BL, Cotton MS Vespasian CXIV, ii, ff. 98^r–101^v; an anonymous tract, ibid., ff. 103r^r–106^v; Howard's tract is, 'A brief discourse of the right use of giving arms ...', FSL, v. b.7; also see Bod, Ashmole MS 862, pp. 63–6, a condensed copy of Howard's notes for Essex. When the marshalship was put into commission in 1601, Howard was authorized to head a review of the honours system: Hammer, 'Lord Henry Howard', 9; Peck, *Northampton*, 104, 156–9.

[178] See Chapter 5, 194.

earl marshal, when, in the late spring of 1598, he chose to make an example of two members of the Suffolk gentry for duelling. The subsequent imprisonment of Anthony Felton and Edmund Withipool was deliberately publicized by the circulation of the record of the trial and judge's verdict, to indicate the intention of the authorities to crack down on unregulated duels among the elite, anticipating the more concerted Jacobean campaign.[179]

Again, there was a terrific paradox in Essex's judicial role. The earl had been a notorious participant in the culture of duelling; in the winter of 1597, angling all the while for the marshalship, Essex had even issued a personal challenge to the lord admiral or one of his sons![180] The trial of Felton and Withipool may have showcased the reformation of the earl's own chivalry; but Essex seems to have turned a blind eye to duelling among his own followers, so long as they conducted their quarrels abroad.[181] The episode illuminates Essex's desire to identify with the broadest possible range of statesmanlike positions: it is no coincidence that Burghley, long preoccupied with reforming the honours system, had exercised the role of the earl marshal in commission before Essex's appointment.[182]

The most important event of Essex's marshalship had a weightier significance when he famously presided over the grandiose revival of the court of chivalry, which had not met since the duke of Norfolk had held the office in the 1560s.[183] The court convened to hear the trial of the disputed Abergavenny peerage at Essex House on 25 November, with the earl presiding in ceremonial robes. The case was referred unresolved, but Essex delivered a speech which is his most extended surviving statement on the role of the hereditary nobility. In many senses this is a conservative rumination on the relationship of crown and the peerage: Essex idealizes a notion of medieval England, when the nobility 'commaunded in warre and weare great housekeepers at home'. The prince's duty to uphold the hereditary

---

[179] BL, Additional MS 6297, f. 13^{r-v}; George Drewry Squibb, *The High Court of Chivalry. A study of the civil law in England* (Oxford: Clarendon Press, 1959) 39 40. I am extremely grateful to Richard Cust for bringing this case to my attention, and for allowing me to read an early draft of his own work on the court of chivalry; Markku Peltonen, *The duel in early modern England: civility, politeness and honour* (Cambridge: Cambridge University Press, 2003).

[180] *HMC De L'Isle and Dudley*, II, 305; Hammer, *Polarisation*, 84–5.

[181] Southampton and Grey pursued their duel in Ireland and on the continent during 1599–1601: Chapter 1, 59. In June 1598 Mountjoy and Sir Melger Leven travelled to duel in Paris after Essex's intervention, although the combat appears not to have taken place: *HMC Salisbury*, VIII, 224–5, 228–31.

[182] The office had lain vacant since 1590, after the death of the earl of Shrewsbury.

[183] Squibb, *Court of Chivalry*, 157–8.

nobility is 'a most necessary and religious care', 'naturall' in respect of Christ's own hereditary divinity. If this is an unremarkable definition of the hierarchy of nature, Essex places significant emphasis on the reciprocity of the relationship of prince and noble. If the nobility, the 'subalterne parts of the prince', is repressed then 'magistrats are contemned, and consequently all government subverted'. 'God hath tyed himselfe to the honour of men and so should the prince doe otherwise'.[184] By the point at which this speech was delivered, of course, Essex was increasingly inclined to think that his *own* honour was unrewarded by Elizabeth.

But Essex did not fly the banner of repressed nobility as often or as vigorously as we might expect. He attempted vainly to procure a barony for Sir Robert Sidney, but unlike Burghley, Essex evinced no particular desire to restore the number of nobles on the privy council, or to affect the composition of the peerage more generally. In his own mind, Essex *himself* (possibly with Southampton) was the noble whose politics were challenged by evil counsellors in 1601: his own fortunes, rather than the restoration of the political role of the ancient nobility *per se* was the position that he sought to restore. A significant plank of Essex's factionalized view of politics was his hostility to Charles Howard, newly created earl of Nottingham, of a family whose lineage Essex could hardly disparage, and the assuredly aristocratic—if loathed—Lord Cobham.

Often the vocabulary of virtue and corruption, though married to chivalric notions of honour, sprang more naturally to Essex's mouth and pen than the language of ancient lineage. Typically, in his anguished letter to James VI from December 1600, 'virtue' and 'nobility' are synonymous: Essex's enemies, it is charged, seek to repress 'all noble vertuous and heroicall spirits', to 'oppress innocencie and cancel merit'.[185]

Here are reflected the influence and long impact of the humanist obsession with Aristotelean debate about the superiority of the nobility of virtue versus the nobility of birth, often invoked by Essex's admirers. In his dedication of Giovanni Battista Nenna's *Treatise of nobility* to the earl, William Jones insists that both kinds 'conjoyned together in your Lord doe make you perfectly Noble'; the treatise itself concludes, though, with a more traditionally humanist resolution, that 'the nobilitie of the minde, is farre more true, and farre more perfect, then the nobility of blood conjoined with riches'.[186]

---

[184] Yale University, Beinecke Library, Osborn MS 370, commonplace book of William Camden. The manuscript is erratically foliated.

[185] BL, Additional MS 31022, f. 107ᵛ.

[186] Nenna, Jones, trans., *Nennio, or A treatise of nobility* (1595), sigs. A2ʳ⁻ᵛ, 96ᵛ. In 1600 the dedication was significantly removed.

Still, Essex clearly attached immense prestige to the public authority invested in the office of earl marshal. Richard McCoy has argued that Essex's determined pursuit of the marshalship had a more significant dimension, reflecting the regeneration of interest in the constitutional powers of the great medieval offices of state—especially of the constable—which had traditionally been endowed with the authority to arrest the king and call parliaments in periods of monarchical incompetence. Anticipating John Adamson's interpretation of the English civil wars (and the role of his own son, the 3rd earl of Essex), Essex's revolt was thus a 'baronial revolt', informed by medieval theories of aristocratic resistance.[187]

McCoy's argument hinges on the premise that one of the treatises on the earl marshalship written for Essex argued that the office should incorporate the power of the lapsed role of the constable, drawing Essex provocatively into contact with constitutional thinking about the powers of the jurisdictions conjoined.[188] In fact, Essex had a stronger hereditary claim to the office of constable, which had been exercised by the Bohun earls of Hereford and Essex (and had also been associated with the mastership of the horse). The author of the anonymous treatise on Essex's new powers recognizes this, expecting Essex's ancestral claim to be constable will be realized 'whensoever it shall please Her Highnes to restore to bloode what in former tymes was houlden'.[189] This author also proposes more specifically that should the office of constable be unfilled, the judicial functions should be absorbed by the earl marshal.[190] But as Linda Levy Peck argues, the treatises written for Essex are solely concerned to define the judicial powers of the earl marshal, for the better ordering of degrees of honour and inheritance disputes. None contains any discussion of the extraordinary political or constitutional authority that might inhere in the combined office of marshal and constable.[191]

In Chapter 1, however, it was shown that at the time of the rising, contemporaries argued that Essex defended his actions as the conduct of an 'Erle Marshall'. The earl of Northumberland further alleged that Essex's ambitions had been stirred by a long-standing desire to be

---

[187] McCoy, *Rites of knighthood*, 91–5; John Adamson, 'The Baronial Context of the English Civil War', *TRHS*, 5th ser., 40 (1990), 93–120.

[188] McCoy, *Rites of knighthood*, 92–3.

[189] BL, Cotton MS Vespasian, CXIV, f. 106ᵛ.

[190] Ibid.

[191] Peck, 'Peers, patronage and the politics of history', 98–104; Peck points out that the roles of constable and earl marshal were collapsed uncontroversially for the earl of Arundel in 1622: ibid., 105–6.

constable of the realm, because this would have invested him with the
power to determine the succession through parliament.[192]

And Essex certainly seems to have identified extraordinary public
authority in the marshalship. In the famous letter to Egerton, the earl
makes clear a distinction between his own duties as a subject and his
public role within the commonwealth, defined by office, and related to the
preservation of virtuous government: 'the dutye of an Earle Martiall of
England'.[193]

ESSEX THE KINGMAKER:
THE SUCCESSION REPRISED

Had James's ambassadors arrived in England before the February rising, they
would have been confronted with the earl's justification of future action:
Essex knew that his enemies, 'will not fayle one daye, if God prevente it not,
to make theyre avantages of the uncertaintie of succession . . . to the evident
hazarde, and almost inevitable ruine, of the whole Iland'.[194]

For the self-defined 'physician' of the realm, the unsettled succession
was the most ancient, festering sore on the English body politic. The
dedication of Parsons's *Conference* to Essex had been so wounding because
it gave voice to this obvious but unarticulated reality: that the earl indeed
had every intention to 'have a greater part or sway in deciding of this great
affaire'.[195] In 1599, the dedicatory epistle of Hayward's *First part of the life
and raigne of King Henrie IIII,* remarkably similar in tone and content to
that of the *Conference,* wreaked similar damage because it appeared to
make a *public* statement about Essex's real ambition to steer the succession: the earl's extraordinary character is famously lauded as 'great indeed,
both in present judgment and in expectation of future time'.[196]

Through Anthony Bacon, contacts were established through Scottish
agents—Dr Thomas Moresin, David Foulis, and James Hudson—that
cemented ties with James's court through the exchange of news and
intelligence. Significantly, Essex struck up a friendly relationship with
the earl of Mar, whom he requested be sent to London in 1601 as
ambassador.[197]

[192] See Chapter 1, 53.   [193] TNA, SP 12/268/45, ff. 73^r–74^r.
[194] Bruce, *Correspondence,* 82.   [195] Parsons, *Conference,* sig.*2^{r-v}.
[196] Manning, *Hayward's Life and raigne,* 61, n. 1., translation from the Latin by the editor.
[197] Essex's earliest attempt to court James, in 1589, had been snubbed: Essex and
Bacon's intelligence with Scotland are documented by Stafford, *James VI and the throne
of England,* 203–20; Hammer, *Polarisation,* 91, 163–73. For Essex's letters to Mar see LPL,
MS 655, f. 218^r, 9 February 1596; LPL MS 656, f. 177, 10 March 1596.

Sporadic rumours had associated Essex with alternative schemes for the succession. Gossip that Essex entertained his own designs on the crown emerged first in Catholic newsletters in the mid-1590s.[198] More plausibly, in his own pro-Scottish succession tract of 1602, Sir John Harington recalled that Essex had followed Leicester in supporting the Puritan earl of Huntingdon's claim, reacting with passion at news of Huntingdon's death in December 1595, 'as if some great designe of his had bene frustrated thereby'.[199] Huntingdon had been one of Essex's guardians, and the two were personally close; it is possible to imagine Essex as the kingmaker of a Hastings succession. After Huntingdon's death, however, Essex's support of James was unequivocal: in an undated letter Essex declared 'such as I am, and all whatsoever I am, . . . I consecrate unto your regal throne'.[200]

Open discussion of the succession, of course, had been prohibited by Elizabeth.[201] The translation of the manuscript treatise the *Anatomie of Spayne* and William Watson's Appellant response to the *Conference* seem to have been textual interventions coordinated by Essex to discredit the claims of the infanta, but they were not published widely. Parsons' *Conference* itself was so electrifying because it did exactly that which Elizabeth's Protestant subjects could not: it presented a forensic debate about the range of claimants—in print.

Once one peers closely at the production of succession literature north of the border, however, more translucent skeins emerge, linking Essex's followers and the Scottish court. First, Essex had shadowy connections to the famous succession treatise of Peter Wentworth, *A pithie exhortation to her Majestie for establishing her successor to the crowne* (1598).[202] Written in 1587, in the aftermath of the execution of Mary, Queen of Scots, the tract was published in Scotland in 1598 with Wentworth's own refutation of the *Conference*, his *Discourse containing the authors opinion of the true and lawfull, successor to her Majestie* (written *c*.1596), which now asserted James's hereditary right. In 1591 Wentworth, most famous for his defence of free speech in the Commons, had presented Essex with a manuscript

---

[198] Hugh Owen to Thomas Phelippes, March? 1594, TNA, SP 12/248/53, f. 125ʳ. It was reported to Essex in August 1599 that James had taken very badly to rumours that Essex sought the throne himself; James's subsequent relations with Essex suggest that these suspicions were quickly quashed: *HMC Salisbury* , IX, 307–9.

[199] Essex reportedly tore his hair: Sir John Harington, *A tract on the succession to the crowne (AD 1602)*, ed. C.R. Markham (London: Roxburghe Club, 1880), 41.

[200] Birch, *Memoirs*, I, 176 (Dated only 17 May).

[201] The so-called 'Statute of Silence' of 1571 forbade discussion of the succession in print.

[202] In fact, the tract may have been published late in 1599; see Nicholas Tyacke 'Puritan politicians and King James VI and I, 1587–1604', in Cogswell et al., *Politics, religion and popularity*, 35 n. 51.

copy of the *Pithie exhortation*, which beseeched Elizabeth to affirm the title of her successor in parliament.[203] In 1593 Wentworth was imprisoned for planning an open parliamentary campaign to force Elizabeth's hand. Jailed temporarily with Wentworth was Sir Henry Bromley, one of the first to acclaim the new king on his accession in 1603. Bromley was also a follower of Essex; playing a shadowy role in the rising of 1601, he was an intimate of Cuffe, his 'dear Brother', and involved in plans to spring Essex from custody in the summer of 1600.[204] Bromley had significant connections to the church of Stephen Egerton, the most notorious of the London Puritans who enjoyed Essex's protection.[205] As Nicholas Tyacke has brilliantly shown, it was almost certainly Bromley and David Foulis who arranged for the publication of Wentworth's tracts in Edinburgh by James's official printer, the English Puritan, Robert Waldegrave.[206] In 1601, Essex intended to secure the Scottish succession through methods identical to the ends that Wentworth had propounded: the formal declaration of Elizabeth's heir in parliament.

Another shadowy link in the Anglo-Scottish book trade was John Norton, a London bookseller. Norton had transmitted English Puritan works for publication in Scotland; he was entrusted by Cuffe, whom he clearly knew personally, with the dispatch of the letter written by Essex on Christmas Day 1600 informing James of his plans to rise.[207] A further author with pens ambidextrously employed to win favour at Essex House and Holyrood was the Irish poet, Walter Quin, who emerged at James's court in December 1595. Quin could not have written any literary offering more appealing to James than his series of verses in Latin, Italian, English, and French, imagining the king as a heroic Arthur and second Caesar who would bring peace to the whole of Britain. He was

---

[203] Peter Wentworth, *A pithie exhortation to her Majestie for establishing her successor to the crowne. Whereunto is added a discourse containing the authors opinion of the true and lawfull successor to her Majestie* (Edinburgh, 1598). Wentworth had previously been unsure about James's claim: the editorial interpolations and marginalia from the printed edition of the *Pithie exhortation* of 1598 reframe the text to imply that it supports the argument of the *Discourse*. J. E. Neale, 'Peter Wentworth (Continued)', *EHR*, 39/154 (1924), 175–205.

[204] Cecil MS 179/131; see Chapter 1, 40.

[205] Bromley promised Lady Rich to turn out, but seems not to have taken part; he was released in 1602: see Chapter 1, 28; Tyacke, 'Puritan politicians', 21–44.

[206] Tyacke, 'Puritan politicians', 35; for Egerton see Chapter 3, 117, Chapter 5, 207.

[207] Verstegan mentioned to Parsons on 1 April 1593 'The Puritanes sent one John Norton into Scotland, ther to print their bookes, who is returned and imprisoned in London': Petti, *Letters and despatches of Richard Verstegan, c.1550–1640* (London: Catholic Record Society, 1959), 114. In his will, Cuffe left forty pounds to Norton, his 'honest friend', apologizing for the trouble he had caused: Bruce, *Correspondence*, 90, 92.

immediately employed by James to write about the succession.[208] As well as an oration, now disappeared, which contained unflattering material on Elizabeth and Burghley, Quin wrote a Latin treatise (also lost) defending James's title for dissemination on the continent, and planned a poetic response to Spenser's offensive allegorical depiction of Mary Stuart as Duessa, personification of falsehood.[209] Quin was also a correspondent of Anthony Bacon, to whom he sent a syrupy sonnet praising his virtues.[210] The poet's verses to James would have been highly regarded in Essex's circle. In a passage identical in tone to Thomas Wright's libel, Quin slandered the *regnum Cecilanum*, drawing on the Spenserian allegory of Burghley as Reynard the fox, hoarding money to strengthen his cubs. Quin exhorted James to be guided to the throne of England by a man of great honour: possibly the poet himself; possibly Bacon or Essex.[211]

Essex's involvement in the politics of succession was not merely driven by his personal ambition, but by the palpable fears shared by many that England would be cast into a crisis of civil war or invasion in the wake of Elizabeth's death. The execution of Mary Stuart had changed the focus but not the intensity of these nightmares. Could Elizabeth not see, prophesized Wentworth, that England would be overwhelmed by 'the rage & furie of hell & hellhounds', inflamed in civil war, laid open to the predations of mighty foreign enemies? 'Oh the rivers of blood, which then by these doleful consequents will overflowe every where this noble Iland'.[212] Wentworth's fears were widely shared: in scores of French pamphlets printed in English translation in the early 1590s, Elizabethans could read of the bloody atrocities of civil war in France.[213] England's own experience of civil war had also left livid scars on the historical memory; it is no coincidence that contemporary poets and dramatists so frequently took topical inspiration from the Barons' Wars of the later Middle Ages.[214]

The unsettled succession also deepened the ambivalent response of the queen's subjects to her government. Wentworth's hellhounds had been snapping at Elizabeth's heels for decades. Repeated attempts from the 1560s to the 1580s to coerce her into providing or designating an heir encompassed a barely-concealed subtext: that failure to preserve the future

---

[208] The verses are published in full in *CSP, 1595–1597*, XII, 79–86.

[209] For the Latin book, oration, and proposal to answer Spenser see *CSP, 1597–1599*, XII, 112, 125; *CSP, 1597–1599*, XIII, i, 167.

[210] LPL MS 656, ff. 192^r–193^v; 657, ff. 173–4^v.

[211] 'Si ne crois en Ce Cil, qui poussé d'avarice,/Et desire d'aggrandir ses petits Renardeaux': *CSP, 1595–1597*, XII, 85.

[212] Wentworth, *Pithie exhortation*, 8, 25–6.

[213] Parmelee, *Good newes from Fraunce*.   [214] Discussed in Chapter 6.

of the nation was a woeful dereliction of duty. The *Pithie exhoration* employs (to inadvertently comic effect) the similar rhetorical strategies used by Essex to address the queen, fluctuating between persuasion and flattery and the stronger impulse to hector, to chastise Elizabeth. Wentworth describes his treatise as an act of textual petition, where he might 'lye prostrate before your Graces feete, most humblie and heartily beseeching your Maiestie', anticipating the physical action that Essex intended to perform in February 1601. Wentworth's grovelling complete, Elizabeth is upbraided with a vision of England's dreadful dystopian future, and a constant reminder of her own imminent demise: 'die most certainlie you shall'. Wentworth even exhorts the queen to imagine the day of judgment itself, when she will stand in front of 'the tribunall seate of God, the revenger of all ungodlines', to answer for the state of the earthly realm that she has departed.[215]

Only marginally less pithy than Wentworth was an extraordinary court sermon preached early in 1596 by Matthew Hutton, archbishop of York, remembered by Sir John Harington. To the amazement of onlookers— which included the queen and 'all the lords of the parliament'—Hutton thundered the dangers that had befallen great monarchies during periods of dynastic change. He reminded his audience that the Conquest of England in 1066, and the imposition of the Norman Yoke, had been the consequence of a succession crisis following the death of Edward the Confessor. So did Spain threaten to enslave the English population: 'onely the uncertainty of succession gave hopes to Forreiners to attempt fresh invasions'. Advice to Elizabeth was bracing indeed: the tyrant Nero had been 'specially hated for wishing to have no Successor'. Harington relates that Hutton's sermon provoked an especially interested response from a 'great peer of the realm'—almost certainly Essex—who badgered him to procure a copy.[216]

This continued perception of Elizabeth's dereliction of duty to the succession coloured further the inclination of Essex's own friends to fear that England was sliding towards catastrophe. Once more, these connections were explored by Greville; *Mustapha*, as Rebholz notes, is a play about a succession struggle.[217] Soliman's descent into tyranny occurs because he fears that his subjects will transfer their love to his son; he is warned by Camena, his virtuous daughter, '*Doubt is Successions foe*'

---

[215] Wentworth, *Pithie exhortation*, 3–4, 99–100.

[216] Elizabeth remained composed, but apparently reprimanded Hutton afterwards: Sir John Harington, *Nugae Antiquae. Being a miscellaneous collection of original papers in prose and verse*, ed. Thomas Park, 2 vols (London: J. Wright, 1804) II, 248–53.

[217] Rebholz, *Life of Greville*, 203.

(2:3, 98).[218] Rossa seeks Mustapha's destruction so that she can instate her own son, Zanger, as Soliman's heir. As she fans Soliman's suspicions of Mustapha's virtue, she speaks Elizabeth's own justification for refusing to name her heir: '*A fatall winding sheet Succession is*' (4:3, 94).[219] As the play ends, Turkey is engulfed in rebellion and anarchy.

As Essex's sensitivity to the deepest dangers and corruptions that faced the Elizabethan polity intensified, a succession plot almost inevitably cohered in his mind as he fell from power. All the elements—danger of Spanish invasion, the tyranny of evil counsel, and the wilful government of the queen herself, who refused to name James her heir—deepened contemporaries' expectations of political crisis on the death of Elizabeth.

The crucial leavening agent, though, was the attitude of James VI. It is often assumed that James's initial hostility to Robert Cecil was driven by biased intelligence from Essex, blackening Cecil's character north of the border.[220] In fact, James was independently hostile to William and Robert Cecil, and easily inclined to believe that both men would oppose his claim. Rather than poisoning Robert Cecil's reputation with the king of Scotland, Essex's attitudes towards a Cecilian faction developed synchronically with those of James.

Throughout the 1590s, James, no less than Essex, had blamed a range of political frustrations on the *regnum Cecilianum*. Not unfairly, he held William Cecil chiefly responsible for the death of his mother, an animosity that he transferred to the lord treasurer's son. This distrust had been enhanced from late 1593, when both Cecils coordinated Elizabeth's support of the Protestant rebel, Francis Hepburn, earl of Bothwell.[221] By October 1595, James wrote furtively to Essex: 'I am glad that he who rules all there [i.e. Burghley] is begun to be loathed at by the best and greatest sort there, since he is my enemy'.[222] In 1596 and 1597, James blamed Burghley for the delay, then the non-payment of his English pension; by early 1598, he was airing his suspicions that Robert Cecil had contacted Bothwell again at Rouen, during his embassy to Henry IV.[223]

By the end of 1597, James also began to make more concrete plans to assert his claim, asking parliament for money to put diplomatic pressure

---

[218] Bullough, *Poems and dramas*, II, 89 (C, Q, 2:1).   [219] Ibid., 114 (C, Q, 4:3).

[220] See comments by J-C Mayer in his introduction to *Breaking the silence*, 19.

[221] James asked Essex to facilitate his envoys' protest to Elizabeth about her support of Bothwell: James VI to Essex, 13 April 1594: Akrigg, *Letters of King James VI and I*, 131.

[222] Ibid., 142–3. For secrecy, this letter was addressed to 'my goode friend SHB'.

[223] Birch, *Memoirs*, I, 175; Stafford, *James VI and the throne of England*, 210.

on Elizabeth to declare his title.[224] Just as Essex used scribal publication to defend his own stance about peace and the perils facing the English polity, James also launched a discursive defence of his claim to the English throne. As well as Wentworth's treatises, James's own *Trew law of free monarchies* was published in 1598 which, as Peter Lake has shown, robustly contradicted the political theories aired in Parsons' *Conference*.[225] Alexander Dickson's *Of the right of the crowne after hir Majesty, Three books where... is refuted a treacherus libel intitling the house of Spagne to the succession...*, written in the same year was never printed, but provides another connection to Essex: Dickson had written an earlier defence of the earl of Leicester, and had probably fought in the Netherlands with Leicester and Sidney when Essex had first blooded his own spurs.[226] A book by Quin about James's title (possibly his Latin treatise) was also in circulation.[227]

As this chronology suggests, James's anxieties about the future of his title were fanned at exactly the same time as Essex began openly to define his courtly rivals as foes of the state. It was argued in Chapter 2 that the development of Essex's notions of a Cecilian plot to support the infanta's claim occured in the context of the foreign policy negotiations that followed the peace of Vervins. Essex made these conspiracy theories public to the readership of the *Apologie*, scaremongering about the schemes of Spanish councillors and spies to pay pensions to members of the council and English noblemen.[228]

James too had long harboured the belief that Burghley would actively oppose his title, and had favoured the claim of the earl of Hertford.[229] But when peace between England and Spain was bruited, James just as eagerly

---

[224] A. I. Cameron ed., *The Warrender papers*, 2 vols (Edinburgh: Scottish History Society, 1931–2), II, 433; *CSP, 1597–1599*, XIII, i, 133. In the spring of 1598 Valentine Thomas, a Catholic horse-thief, alleged that he had been employed by James to murder Elizabeth. Although Elizabeth thought that this was nonsense, James was frantic that his association with an assassination plot would debar him from the throne: Stafford, *James VI and the throne of England*, 194; S, Doran, 'Three late-Elizabethan succession tracts', in Mayer, *Struggle for the succession*, 97.

[225] Peter Lake, 'The King, (the queen) and the Jesuit: James Stuart's *True Law of Free Monarchies* in Context/s', *TRHS* 6th series, 14 (2004), 243–60.

[226] The original is in the National Library of Scotland; extracts are printed in Mayer, *Breaking the silence on the Elizabethan succession*, 157–87. On 12/22 November 1598, Andrew Hunter wrote to Sir Robert Cecil that Dickson was 'ane enemie of your stait', (meaning Cecil rather than England): SP 52/63, f. 57ʳ.

[227] *CSP, 1597–1599*, XIII, i, 216, 219.

[228] See Chapter 2, 104–7; *Apologie*, [B4ᵛ].

[229] In instructions to an ambassador to Denmark, James warned that Lord Zouche, the English ambassador, was 'one of my motheris jurie and enemy to my title, being Burlyis dependar who favoris the house of Hartforde': Cameron, *Warrender Papers*, II, 42–3; Stafford, *James VI and the throne of England*, 117.

shared Essex's deep suspicions of Robert Cecil's friendly relations with the archdukes. On 12 January 1600 George Nicolson reported to Cecil the opinions of Scottish councillors that the English council 'were by Spaine layeinge a bar in the king's way'.[230] In April, before the Anglo-Spanish peace conference at Boulogne, James spelled out to Nicholson that he associated the peace, and Cecil's part in it, with the propagation of the infanta's claim. The endless round of negotiations, James alleged, was to allow the secret diplomatic exchanges for darker purposes 'which wold be to his hurte'. He was more than aware that many of Elizabeth's courtiers would be bought by bribes.[231] On 19 October 1600, James Hamilton, the king's envoy in England, accused Cecil of being 'a practiser for the infant... and now advanser of a Spanish course'.[232] It may be far more than coincidence that Essexian answers to the *Conference*—the *Anatomie of Spayne* and Watson's treatise—were commissioned in 1598 and 1599, when James was overseeing the production of similar literature.[233]

By 1599, the fates of Essex and James seemed utterly entwined. Essex's political disgrace after his return from Ireland was a major blow, depriving James of his foremost supporter in the English court, and confirming the ascendancy of Cecil, whom he had long distrusted. In this context, James was forced to try a series of attempts to raise formal political, fiscal, and military support to assert his claim. The envoys sent by James to the king of Denmark and the Holy Roman Empire in 1598 had sounded out the rulers for military aid.[234] Copies of the General Band of the Scottish nobility, taken in November 1599 to support James' title, circulated in England, one surviving in the commonplace book of an English follower of Essex.[235] The following June (just after Essex's trial at York House), James made a final unsuccessful attempt to levy taxation in the convention of the Scottish estates to raise a domestic army to fight for his title.[236] As we have seen, during these eighteen months, while he

[230] TNA, SP 52/66, f. 3ʳ.
[231] TNA, SP 52/66, f. 21ʳ, Nicolson to Cecil, 20 April 1600.
[232] TNA, SP 52/66, f. 78ᵛ.
[233] Camden juxtaposes the scribal publication of the Egerton letters with James' propaganda effort: *Annales*, 781–2.
[234] The responses he received from all were polite but non-committal: Cameron, *Warrender Papers*, II, 362–79.
[235] *CSP 1597–1600*, XIII, i, 576–9; the text is in the Scott commonplace book: FSL, MS v.b.214, fols. 200ᵛ–201ᵛ, discussed in J. McManaway, 'Elizabeth, Essex, and James', in H. Gardner and H. Davis eds, *Elizabethan and Jacobean Studies* (Oxford: Clarendon Press, 1959), 225–6.
[236] *CSP 1600–1603*, XIII, ii, 661–4.

surveyed negotiations between Brussels and England with deepening dismay, James was convinced by Mountjoy, Southampton, and finally Essex to recognize the urgency of the looming succession crisis, and to give his support to the vital action to which Essex was 'summoned' by his 'reason, honour [and] conscience'.

5

The popular traitor: responses to Essex

In death Essex retained the power to divide and enthral. In response to
government propaganda that forensically analysed the treasons of the
rebellious over-mighty noble sprung up a slew of ballads and libels that
lionized the earl's heroic memory, excoriating his destruction by the
'tongues and pens' of 'thrise double men'.[1] These polarized narratives of
Essex's behaviour had taken root, though, several years before his rising.
Essex triggered a range of responses, from critics of his actions and
character, who offered politic counsel or sterner admonition, to fervent
admirers who expressed hyperbolic admiration for Essex as protector of
the state. These divergent appraisals emerged more acutely in 1598, when
Burghley's death clearly divided the court. Before the earl's departure for
Ireland, he was advised and chastised to temper his attitude towards war,
patronage, and the authority of the queen. After his return and disgrace,
wary criticism was transformed into a much deeper anxiety about the earl's
political designs, as well as his implacable animosity towards central figures
in the government. All the treasonable characteristics that would be used
to describe Essex's fermenting ambition after the rising were invoked in
the growing concern about his future behaviour: self-association with
Henry Bullingbrook and the duke of Guise, the cultivation of the support
of Catholics and Puritans, and, in particular, his popularity. Essex's
detractors self-consciously contrasted their own seemly political attitudes,
employing authoritarian political ideas about sovereignty, obedience, and
adherence to doctrines of divine right monarchy.

But the very qualities condemned by Essex's detractors—in particular his
doggedness in pursuit of virtue and honour—were those most larded with
praise by his supporters, who endorsed Essex's vision of court politics and
denounced his critics as enemies of the realm itself. The strongest declarations of support for Essex often contained the seeds of those political ideas
that were most feared by the privy council and the queen.

---

[1] Pricket, *Honors fame,* sig. A2*.

CRITIQUES OF THE EARL: OBEDIENCE
AND SOVEREIGNTY

The first critiques of the earl's behaviour emanated from his closest advisors and relatives. Henry Howard's instructions for Essex on the 'meanes of advancement' of a young noble courtier, written in the middle of the decade, was one of the earliest of a flurry of letters and tracts offering advice on how the earl should frame his behaviour to suit these most dangerous times.[2] Some, like the author of the anonymous advice letter to Essex, counselled the earl to ape the Machiavellian behaviour of his enemies, to 'dissemble lyke a courtier', so that he might outwit them at their own game.[3]

But other advice to the earl, even from his friends and relatives, cut deeper and more critically, urging Essex to remember that the foundation of power lay in the monarch's bounty. This was, of course, the message of Egerton's famous letter, answered with deliberate defiance by Essex in the summer of 1598. So too, the advice of Sir William Knollys, Essex's uncle: 'ther ys no contestynge betwene soverayntye and obedeyence'.[4]

Criticism directed at Essex particularly queried his hyper-humanist conviction that his magnificent virtue entitled him to a naturally pre-eminent public role, and the fruits of office and patronage. Essex was reproved through definitions of an alternative ethic of service, which crowned personal obedience to the monarch as king of virtues. Writing as a propagandist in 1601, Bacon described Essex's most profound fault as 'supposing that to be his owne mettall which was but her marke and impression'.[5]

Here the comparative attitudes of Henry Howard and Francis Bacon are instructive. Both men warned Essex that he would be the practical victim of a particularly Elizabethan interpretation of *paradiastole*—the rhetorical technique of re-describing moral qualities—so that 'all his vertues [would be] drawne into the nature of vices' by his enemies, but also the queen.[6] Howard's counsels to Essex, lengthier than they are original, contain a vaguely Lipsian endorsement of the use of moderate deception, while emphasizing the utility of patience and constancy as virtues to rank with Essex's more actively brilliant qualities. In Howard's

---

[2] DUL, Howard MS 2 ff. 117^r–133^r. Hammer, 'How to become an Elizabethan Statesman'; Andersson, *Henry Howard*, 173–6.

[3] TNA, SP 12/265/10, f. 17^v 16 November 1597.

[4] WRO, MI 229, f. 55^r August 1598.

[5] Bacon, *Declaration*, sig. [A4^v].

[6] DUL, Howard MS 2, f. 120^v. For *paradiastole* and English rhetoricians see Quentin Skinner, *Reason and rhetoric in the philosophy of Hobbes* (Cambridge: Cambridge University Press, 1996), 161–72.

treatment, though, these are regretfully framed as 'pollicy' or 'strategems' deemed necessary because of the corruption of the times, and the fearful jealousy of the ageing Elizabeth, and he lauds Essex with uncomplicated praise for his military heroics.[7] This was closer in tone to Bacon's more famous advice letter for Essex, written in October 1596, in which he counselled the earl to recognize that his militarism and popular reputation—while intrinsically admirable qualities—irritated Elizabeth's sensitivity to his 'suspected greatness'.[8]

Francis Bacon, however, was also increasingly inclined to criticize Essex's political setbacks as faults of his own character and values. In the first published volume of his *Essays* of 1597 (which he addressed indirectly to Essex through its dedication to his brother Anthony), and his *Apologie* of 1604, which defended his alleged betrayal of the earl, Bacon's censure of Essex's conduct stimulated a much deeper critique of his behaviour, which developed into sceptical analysis of the general application of classical–humanist values in a monarchical state.[9]

Bacon's particular insistence that Essex prioritise the ends over the means of his conduct was most evident in topical redefinitions of honour and chivalry, to suit a Machiavellian servant of an absolute prince. While Howard rather tepidly warned the earl that the 'eies of jealousie' were fixed on feats of greatness,[10] Bacon wrote more radically that the latter must be conceptually divorced from the pursuit of individual fame or glory. In his essay 'Of Honour and Reputation', Bacon argued that the truest form of honour is 'the revealing of a man's virtue and worth *without disadvantage*' (emphasis added). Those who prosper in politics *appear* at least 'rather to seek merit than fame', and attribute success 'rather to divine providence and felicity than to...virtue or policy'.[11] As Essex prepared to go to Ireland, Bacon warned that his pursuit of valiant conduct might completely derail the whole purpose of his mission, if he inclined 'rather to seek the fruition of that honour, than the perfection of the work in hand'.[12]

Essex's adherence to the *vita activa* through martial courses was also challenged by divines, who counselled about the conflict between pagan and Christian virtue. John Norden, cleric and client of Essex, tempered praise with a similar warning: 'there is nothing so powerfull to prostitute the heroicall mind to all vanitie, as an overgood conceit of a mans own worthiness'.[13] In his Ash Wednesday sermon before Essex's departure for

---

[7] DUL, Howard MS 2, ff. 125ᵛ, 129ᵛ and *passim*.   [8] Spedding, *L&L*, II, 40–5.
[9] Anthony, the dedicatee of the 1597 *Essays* immediately redirected the work to the earl, as Francis knew he would: Jardine and Stewart, *Hostage to Fortune*, 187.
[10] DUL, Howard MS 2, f. 129ᵛ.   [11] Vickers, *Francis Bacon*, 86–7.
[12] Spedding, *L&L*, II, 129–33.   [13] Norden, *Mirror of honor*, sig. D4ᵛ.

Ireland, a far less partisan Lancelot Andrewes preached a sermon at court that was obviously critical of militarism: 'War is no matter of sport'.[14]

Other elements of Essex's behaviour prized as manifestations of his virtue were heavily criticized as challenging the necessary bonds of allegiance that subjects owed the queen. As the confessions of Essex's fellow 'rebels' revealed after the rising, they felt bound to follow the earl through the doubly magnetic force of the obligations of friendship, and admiration for the earl's virtue. As has been demonstrated, Essex's determination to procure patronage for his friends was reciprocated by his followers' expressions of slavish devotion.[15] For Essex's critics, though, the rigid loyalty he demanded of his followers was too high-handed and absolute. On 24 May 1595, Sir Thomas Sherley, an officer in the Low Countries under investigation for corruption as well as for the circumstances of his son's marriage to a cousin of Essex, angrily defended himself from the charge of being a dependent of the earl, 'thinkinge yt over base for me that am her highnes servante & officer to depende upon any man livinge but only upon her highness'.[16] Most famously, Lord Grey reported to Cobham on 21 July 1599 that he had told the earl that he would brook 'noe base dependency'; Essex's insistent monopoly of military patronage meant that 'the soveraingty of [the queen's] princely autoritie bee diminished if not extinguished by the participation, or rather alienation of theas royall and essential properties to any save her princely selfe'.[17]

Again, Francis Bacon added pigment to these criticisms. After Essex's death, Bacon insisted that he had counselled his patron on the hierarchy of loyalty, warning him that obedience to the prince would always exceed the demands of friendship: 'for everie honest man will forsake his friend rather than forsake his King'. He explained that he had refused a gift of land which would have made him inappropriately obliged to the earl: 'I must be your homager, and hold land of your gift: but do you know the manner of doing homage in law? alwaies it is with a saving of his faith to the King'.[18] The *Essays* contain the terse, self-regarding aphorism: '*discreet followers* help much to reputation' (emphasis added).[19]

[14] Lancelot Andrewes, *The duty of a nation and its members in time of war. A sermon preached before queen Elizabeth, at Richmond on February 21, 1599*, T. S. Polehampton ed. (London: Joseph Masters, 1854), 17.

[15] See Chapter 4, 148–9.

[16] TNA, SP 12/252/29, f. 60ʳ.

[17] Cecil MS 62/71.

[18] Bacon, *Apologie*, 16; Wootton, 'Francis Bacon: your flexible friend', in Elliott and Brockliss, *World of the favourite*, 195.

[19] Bacon, 'Of Honor and Reputation', in Vickers, *Francis Bacon*, 87.

Even Essex's ostentatious adoption of the language of public service—the fundamental ethic of the 'public man', or the 'monarchical republic'—was challenged.[20] Elizabethans were gripped by the *topos* of the demagogue, whose fervent displays of care for the *respublica* concealed nefarious private ambition. As Sir Robert Sidney scribbled in his edition of Tacitus's *Annals*, 'A conning traitor wil for his treason pretend the care of his contreys good'.[21] The anti-Marprelate campaign further pushed this trope prominently into the public sphere, by sneeringly condemning the illegitimate use of the language of 'commonwealth' by radical Puritans: the queen's response to the speaker's request for freedom of speech in the parliament of 1593 censured 'idle Heads...which will meddle with reforming the Church and transforming the Common-Wealth'.[22]

Similar warnings were fired at Essex. As we have seen, in October 1596 Francis Bacon had urged a public retreat from 'commonwealth courses', lest Essex anger Elizabeth. Defending his participation in the proceedings against the earl at York House, Bacon explained that he had been motivated above all by his desire to have the 'conscience and commendation, first of a *bonus civis*, which with us is a good and honest servant to the queen; and next of a *bonus vir*, that is an honest man'. Here Bacon enunciated the ethic of service that he had constantly used to criticize Essex's conduct by the distinctive definition of the word '*civis*', usually translated as 'citizen', to mean 'subject'. He argued that honesty in friendship was less important than obedience to the queen. Stung by this counsel on semantics, Essex grumpily declared himself 'a stranger to all poetical conceits, or else I should say somewhat of your poetical example'.[23]

ANOTHER GUISE?

Even before Essex departed for Ireland, critical warnings assumed portentous overtones, evincing fears of an inevitable collision wrecked on the earl's intransigence, Elizabeth's growing mistrust. Greater suspicions of Essex's future behaviour and character were articulated by other members of the council and figures at court. When Essex had been thrust from the court in July 1598, Sir William Knollys wrote with bitter exasperation: 'betweene hir Majesties' running into hir princely power,

---

[20] Richard Cust, 'The public man in late Tudor and early Stuart England', in Lake and Pincus, *Politics of the public sphere*, 116–43.

[21] Sidney's copy of Lipsius's edition of Tacitus's *Opera* is in the British Library, C. 142.3.13; the annotation is from the *Annals*, 12.

[22] D'Ewes, *Journals*, 460.   [23] Spedding, *L& L*, II, 191–2.

and your Lordshipps persisting in your settled resolution, I am so con-
founded as I know not how nor what to perswade'.[24]

These tensions between Essex and Elizabeth reached a pointed head as
he prepared to confront Tyrone in the agonizingly protracted arguments
over the scope of his authority as lord lieutenant of Ireland.[25] As Bacon
had predicted, Elizabeth's gnawing dislike of Essex's 'dangerous image'
had magnified with the growing size of his 'military dependence' as master
of the ordnance and earl marshal.[26] As he prepared for Ireland at the head
of that 'royal' army, Essex attracted even thicker swarms of military
clients.[27] Elizabeth's wariness was expressed most acutely in her thunderous reiteration of past strictures on the creation of knights.[28] While Essex
regarded knighthoods as a just reward when he could offer soldiers scant
material gratification, to the queen, his notoriously free hand with dubbing was an impudent challenge to her control of the honours system:
'Confer knighthoods upon none who do not deserve it . . . That order has
been hitherto granted without moderation'.[29]

Elizabeth's sensitivity to Essex's wide delegated powers seems to have
been replicated even more acutely in the attitudes of members of the privy
council, several of whom Essex now openly detested as his enemies. In
Camden's account, the earl's decision to go to Ireland was a decisive
turning point, the prime stimulus to his enemies' increasingly coherent
suspicions that he sought the throne himself.[30] Bacon vainly urged Essex
to 'observe the due limits' of his commission, because if he were to
abrogate them, his foes would take advantage to misconstrue his actions
to the queen: 'the exceeding of them may not only procure in case of
adverse accident a dangerous disavow; but also *in case of prosperous success
be subject to interpretation, as if all were not referred to the right end*'
(emphasis added).[31] These attitudes were anticipated in Sir Robert Markham's warning to Sir John Harington to 'Observe the man who comman-
deth, and yet is commanded himselfe: he goeth not forthe to serve the
Queenes realme, but to humour his own revenge'.[32]

Gossipy speculation about the gulf between Essex and the government was
underscored sensationally in a report from the French ambassador, Jean de

[24] WRO, MI 229, f. 49ʳ.   [25] See also Chapter 4, 150–1.
[26] Spedding, *L&L*, II, 41.
[27] Cecil MS 60/13; *HMC Salisbury*, IX, 6, 70, 77, 88, 434; Hutson, 'Military following',
44 and *passim*.
[28] The queen had tried to restrain Essex's powers to confer knighthoods in Rouen in 1591,
and even more pointedly before Cadiz in 1596: C. G. Cruickshank, *Elizabeth's army*, 2nd edn
(Oxford: Clarendon Press, 1966) 46–7; Hammer, *Polarisation*, 222–5.
[29] *Calendar of Carew manuscripts, vol. 3, 1589–1600*, 295, 25 March 1599.
[30] Camden, *Annales*, 786–7.
[31] Spedding, *L& L*, II, 132.   [32] Harington, *Nugae Antiquae*, I, 288.

Thumery, Seigneur de Boissise: describing the earl's rapturous send-off by London citizens, he noted that queen and leading courtiers were considerably less joyful, and drew explicit comparisons with the favours shown by the people of Paris to the duke of Guise.[33] This vignette describes an extraordinary political predicament: the lord lieutenant of Ireland, with a mandate to crush Tyrone, was compared by the queen herself to a notoriously overweening nobleman, who cultivated popular opinion to dangerous ends.

From the official missives sent to Essex by the council from London, measured and impersonal, none of this direct antagonism can be gleaned. L.W. Henry's suggestions that the council may have deliberately sabotaged the supply chain to Ireland rest on a misleadingly selective reading of some of the extant correspondence about the provision of carriage horses and pinnaces.[34] But further speculation greeted the privy council's massive and panicked attempt to organize the country's defences in August 1599. This was ostensibly a bathetic and embarrassing overreaction to false rumours of another imminent Spanish armada. But Chamberlain speculated that the 'vulgar sort' perceived 'some great misterie in the assembling of these forces', surmising that they were intended to 'shew to some that are absent, that others can be followed as well as they, and that yf occasion be, militarie services can be as well and redily ordered and directed as yf they were present'.[35] As the morale of his armies haemorrhaged through disease and desertion, Essex resorted to the familiar technique of dubbing to unite his men, protesting later that he could offer 'noe ymployement . . . no other treasure or giftes to bestowe upon them'.[36] Immediately, a different interpretation was formed at the court: on 23 August, Chamberlain reported 'Yt is much marvayled that this humor shold so possesse him, that

---

[33] Laffleur de Kermaingant, *Mission de Jean de Thumery, Sieur de Boissise*, 483. For Shakespeare's notorious depiction of Essex's departure see below, 204.

[34] Henry's argument that supplies of pinnaces and carriage horse may have been deliberately delayed by the council derives from his reading of a rather elliptical letter of May 1599, when Sir William Knollys appears to warn Robert Cecil that Essex might be able to prove grounds for complaint that supplies previously agreed to had not been sent: Henry, 'Earl of Essex in Ireland', 8–9. Joel Hurstfield, though, convincingly argues that Henry has misread Knolly's advice; the rest of the letter urges that Cecil *should* endeavour to furnish Essex's demands; indeed, it is very unlikely that Knollys would be complicit in any plot to undermine his nephew: Hurstfield, 'Succession Struggle', 375–6. In fact, Knollys acknowledges that Cecil might have personal grievances against Essex, but urges him, for the redemption of Ireland, to send supplies: 'I beseech you not to looke upon the person but the cause': Cecil MS 70/69.

[35] McClure, *Letters of John Chamberlain*, I, 83, 23 August. The panic in general is described in idem, 80–5; Camden makes this argument: *Annales*, 792; *HMC Salisbury*, IX, 282–3, 291–2, 316–17, 322–3; Collins, *Letters and memorials*, II, 114–17.

[36] From the transcript of the York House trial proceedings, *HMC Bath*, V, 272, 274.

not content with his first dosens and scores, he should thus fall to huddle them up by halfe hundreds'.[37]

And what if Essex's campaign had been gloriously successful? Whatever the depths of their loathing of the Irish rebel, those courtiers and councillors whom Essex now openly condemned could hardly have relished his return in triumph at the head of a great army, to the rekindled admiration of a queen who was susceptible to swingeing changes of affection and opinion.

Of course, the nature of Essex's return was the opposite of heroic, but it created a new kind of problem: the means, form, and length of his disgrace. As the council investigated his conduct in Ireland, they began, from a mixture of necessity and genuine suspicion of his character, to accrue a significant arsenal of ammunition. Cecil scrawled 'Ewtopia' on the record of Tyrone's demands for a more permanent treaty, which prioritized not only freedom of Catholic worship, but envisaged the entire reconstruction of the Catholic church, material and spiritual, in Ireland.[38] If these gave a dark hue to the earl's tainted association with Catholic toleration, the unknown scope of Essex and Tyrone's private conversation at Bellaclinthe Ford was a provocatively unmapped hinterland. In October, the council began to record material that would be reworked into more serious charges of treason against the earl.[39]

Once the queen herself was convinced of Essex's fault, she too indicated her concern to make a stern example of his disobedience. His crimes were publicly condemned by privy councillors in Star Chamber on 29 November, to a gathering of JPs and dignitaries.[40] Each orator spelled out the same version of Essex's misdemeanours: the appointment of Southampton as general of the horse against Elizabeth's explicit order; his refusal to follow the preordained strategy to attack Tyrone; his dubbing of so many knights; and his return against the express command of Elizabeth, all were vituperated as examples of disgraceful dereliction of duty.[41] A secondary

---

[37] McClure, *Letters of John Chamberlain*, I, 84.

[38] There are two lists in the Irish State Papers, both heavily emphasizing freedom of Catholic worship: for the list of 22 demands, see TNA, SP 63/206/55 ff. 152ʳ–153ᵛ; a shorter version is SP 63/206/56, f. 154ʳ. Drawing up a ramist table of the charges that he was likely to face at York House, Essex recognized that one of the chief charges was likely to be the making of a treaty 'upon equal terms, the conditions, [and] toleration of Popery': *Calendar of Carew manuscripts, vol. 3, 1589–1600*, 517.

[39] See Cecil's 'Memorial of certain points which the Earl of Essex is to deliver his Opinion' before the council on 3 October, which focus almost exclusively on the deal struck with Tyrone: TNA, SP 12/63/205/192, ff. 365ʳ–366ʳ.

[40] See the two accounts from eyewitnesses, TNA, SP 12/273/35 and 36, and a different account of Cecil's speech, 37. They are consistent in detail, but the first is longer.

[41] The charges that were levelled at Essex were consistent with Elizabeth's longstanding criticism of the campaign, brutally articulated in her letter to Essex on 14 September: *CSPI*,

leitmotif was Essex's magnificent incompetence, despite being furnished, as Lord Admiral Howard related with relish, with such an army as 'it had bene easie to have passed thorough all the kingdome of Spayne'.

More ominously, the speakers also mused on the strangeness of the truce with Tyrone. Nottingham denounced the contemptible conditions: majestice 'her Majestie would rather goe in her own person and undertake the warre agaynst them then to allowe of such a dishonourable composition'. Cecil in particular recalled the report of Captain William Warren on his meeting with Tyrone in late September, when the rebel earl had warned him to expect the 'greatest alteration' in Anglo-Irish affairs, and that he, Tyrone, would have a 'good share in Englande'; the implication being that the famous parley had entailed a more dangerous pact. Warren's account had been significantly distorted: Tyrone was predicting a Spanish invasion, and had made no mention of Essex at all. His words were twisted by the council into a latent charge of disloyalty aimed at Essex—a forerunner of similar strategies to be adopted in the future.[42]

Elizabeth also felt that the occasion was necessary to strike a message about her own authority, determined, as Whyte reported, to 'make the World see, that her Power here is sovraign, that Greatnes in any can no longer be, then during her Pleasure'. The Star Chamber speeches were accompanied by religious homily. A royal chaplain 'in open Pulpitt, spoke much of the Misgovernment in *Ireland,* and used many Words of the Duty of Subjects to their Princes'.[43]

The dilemma for Essex's denounced enemies was markedly different. Essex was still alive, and, although under house arrest, he had not been formally tried or condemned. The earl had always previously grovelled back to favour, with the exuberant penitence that he now exhibited in his stream of overwrought letters. The rage shown by Elizabeth towards her council following the execution of Mary Stuart in 1587 would have haunted every councillor. A decade later, Elizabeth was no less changeable in her opinions; while the untried prisoner who threatened the stability of the existing regime was no Catholic female claimant to the throne unifying the Protestant political nation in hostility, but a former favourite, a privy councillor, the popular hero of Cadiz.

1599–1600, 150–3; the charges that Essex was called to answer by the Privy Council in October, ibid., 169–70; and the charges that would be made at the York House trial.

[42] TNA, SP 12/273/35, ff., 67^v, 68^r, 72^v. See Captain William Warren's account of his first meeting with Tyrone after Essex's departure on 29 September, sent on by the council of Ireland in early October: NA, SP 63/205/218, ff. 417^r–418^r.

[43] Collins, *Letters and memorials,* II, 141, 143.

Yet to leave the earl to fester unrestrained was also a daunting gamble. Robert Cecil might have wanted to be seen passing Essex's letters to Elizabeth, but after the drubbing of the earl's reputation in Star Chamber, it was even more difficult to imagine that Essex would ever be reconciled to his 'enemies' on the council. Cecil seems seriously to have considered retirement in the event of Elizabeth's demise.[44] The other path was to encourage the destruction—or self-destruction—of Essex in a manner that Elizabeth could not possibly regret, and quickly, before her death.

Elizabeth retracted plans to try Essex in Star Chamber in February 1600 only at the very last minute; the earl was sternly warned that such a trial would have resulted in a significant fine, possibly a spell of imprisonment.[45] The trial at York House on 5 June was a compromise, giving formal legitimacy to Essex's removal from political office, while reprieving him from accusations of outright disloyalty.[46] The court was a substantial gathering of nobles, ministers, and crown lawyers, as well as an audience of 200 gentlemen, summoned to spread the news of the proceedings in the country.[47] Despite discrepancies in accounts of the trial, it is clear that the five main charges of misconduct levelled at Essex were consistent with the allegations made in Star Chamber the previous November. The rumour that Essex had sent Captain Thomas Lee for secret conference with Tyrone before his journey into Ulster was invoked to imply that the earl had never intended to fight.[48] In Fynes Moryson's report, an excited Coke threatened Essex with *praemunire*.[49]

Significant queries about Essex's loyalty—'many faults of contempt and disobedience'—were also alleged far more generally, from circulated letters that emphasized his dangerously critical attitudes to court and queen. The lengthiest manuscript account confirms that Essex was challenged with disobedient political attitudes, enshrined in the immortal line 'What, cannot princes err? Cannot Subjectes receyve wronge?'[50] Camden

---

[44] Pauline Croft points out that Cecil was buying up land, probably in the event that he might have to retire as a country gentleman: 'Sir Robert Cecil, first earl of Salisbury (1563–1612)', *ODNB*. For Ralegh's rallying letter to Cecil, see below, 212.

[45] Collins, *Letters and memorials*, II, 166–7.

[46] The fullest description is a transcript printed in *HMC Bath*, V, 269–76; compare with the account of Fynes Moryson, *Itinerary*, II, 69–74; the first part of an incomplete manuscript account of the trial is printed in Spedding, *L & L*, II, 175–89; see also Collins, *Letters and memorials*, II, 199–200, and Camden, *Annales*, 827–30.

[47] *APC*, XXX, 351.

[48] *HMC Bath*, V, 271; Moryson, *Itinerary*, II, 70.

[49] Moryson, *Itinerary*, II, 70; Francis Bacon later indignantly denied that *he* had charged Essex with *praemunire* at the trial: Spedding, *L & L*, II, 161.

[50] *HMC Bath*, V, 272. Other charges included Essex's expression of the following: 'Is yt treason for the Earle of Southampton to marry my kingeswoman? [sic] I cannot doe that

makes the circulation of the letter to Egerton the centrepiece of the
allegations, while Moryson's report confirms that the task of charging
the earl with writing the letter 'very boldly and presumptuously, in
derogation to her Majesty' was given to Francis Bacon.[51] Camden, Moryson, and Bacon's own account also verify that Bacon was charged with
imputing Essex's shadowy association with 'a certaine dangerous seditious
Pamphlet': Hayward's *The first parte of the life and raigne of King
Henrie IIII.*[52]

Essex easily outshone the prosecution.[53] Kneeling in humble contri-
tion, he passionately declared his desire to 'signifie . . . his confession of his
faultles and contricon with protestacon of his loyalltie and fedelitie to her
highnes', tempering admission of his errors with 'amazement and mellan-
choly concerning his obedience'.[54] Despite their lengthy descriptions of
the earl's scene-stealing response to the five main charges of misconduct in
Ireland, none of the extant accounts describe his reply to the allegations of
seditious letter writing or association with Hayward's *Life and raigne*.
Essex violently denied, though, the charges of a sinister pact with Tyrone,
and insisted with equal fervour (responding to a question fed by a
sympathetic Whitgift) that he had been sneeringly dismissive of Tyrone's
demand for liberty of conscience.[55]

There are strong parallels between the York House proceedings and
Essex's treason trial in 1601. In both events, Essex vigorously contested
the definition of his disobedience using the distinction between errant
conduct and personal loyalty. In June 1600 Essex won a partial victory of
definition. He was cleared of charges of disloyalty, and the peers who were
not councillors seem to have spoken with far greater sympathy, mitigating
the fierceness of the lawyers' assaults.[56] When an official report of the trial
was delivered by Egerton in Star Chamber on 12 June, Essex's strident
defence of his honour and loyalty was broadcast sympathetically.[57] It was a

which will overthrowe me and the accon that yf Misenas and Agrippa had lived they would
have said *O tempora, O mores'*.

[51] Camden, *Annales*, 828; Moryson, *Itinerary*, II, 71: in this account, Coke also
denounced Lady Rich's letter. Bacon's autobiographical account does not mention the
Egerton letter, but he is mainly concerned to describe his involvement in the exposition of
Essex's association with Hayward's *Life and raigne*: Bacon, *Apologie*, 49–50.
[52] Moryson, *Itinerary*, II, 71.
[53] Essex was thoroughly prepared for the substance of the accusations against him; see
above, n. 38.
[54] *HMC Bath*, V, 275.
[55] Ibid., 274–5; see also Moryson, *Itinerary*, II, 73.
[56] Moryson, *Itinerary*, II, 73–4; see also Sir Gelly Merrick's account of the trial on
Monday 11 June, Cecil MS 80/20.
[57] Cecil MS 80/29–32; John Chamberlain (naturally) was present: McClure, *Letters of
John Chamberlain*, I, 97.

defence, though, that would only work once. In February 1601, when Essex insisted that he was innocent of treasonous conduct and disloyalty to Elizabeth, there would be no such reprieve.

THE PROBLEM OF POPULARITY

Politics at the turn of the seventeenth century, then, was a game shaped by this curious dynamic between the earl, the queen, the council, and the court, contested on a board fringed by Spain, Scotland, and Ireland, with the minds of the players tuned to the fundamental question of succession. Essex's future, though, was also determined by another player of intangible but forceful agency: the strength of public opinion, and the *perception* of its force by the main political actors in the drama.

Essex may have been bereft of leading courtiers willing to speak for his rehabilitation before and after the York House trial, but rumours that flooded through court and city indicated widespread popular indignation about his downfall. The trial itself was a response to public sympathy for Essex: the queen and council attempted to legitimize the earl's disgrace to appease public criticism of his ongoing imprisonment.

In late Elizabethan and early Stuart England, 'popularity' was most frequently invoked as a buzzword for sedition.[58] The harsh socio-economic conditions of the 1590s, exacerbated by war, caused morbid fear among elites of the latent power of the many-headed multitude. For Conformist clerics, 'popularity' was pejorative shorthand for the proselytizing methods of radical Puritans and their endorsement of theories of mixed government.[59] In Essex's case, as we have seen, his cultivation of popularity—so strongly affiliated to his identification with 'commonwealth causes'—was associated with the strategies of overreaching subjects, Bullingbrook and Guise.[60]

This intensified fear of 'popular politics' occurred, paradoxically, because of the steady growth of an increasingly complex news culture, especially in the capital. The scurrilous manuscript libel, the brash staple of Jacobean political commentary, survives in significant numbers from the 1590s onwards, while the print campaigns conducted by the Marprelate pamphleteers, and the government-sponsored response, presaged the

---

[58] Cust, 'Charles I and Popularity', 235–58.
[59] Lake, *Anglicans and Puritans*, 53–64; Jim Sharpe, 'Social strain and social dislocation, 1585–1603', in Guy, *Reign of Elizabeth I*, 203–4 and *passim*.
[60] See chapter 1, 62–4.

future uses of the popular press for polemical debate.[61] The government's increased sensitivity to popular opinion at the end of the decade was expressed in one of its sporadic attempts to intensify censorship. The Bishops' Ban of 1 June 1599 called in satires and epigrams that were mordantly critical of the broader political culture. The publication of John Hayward's *First parte of the life and raigne of King Henrie IIII*, the prose history of the deposition of Richard II, was clear stimulation to the proclamation that plays and histories should, in future, be subject to conciliar licence.[62] The home-grown newsmongering of the late-1590s was overwhelmingly catalyzed by Essex's example, stimulated by his own appeal to public opinion, but also by unprompted fascination with his real-life drama.[63]

As subsequent Stuart governments would reluctantly acknowledge, the privy council's main weapon to combat the political gossip that surged through London in the form of rumour and libels was response in kind, through speeches and the dissemination of texts. The very purpose of the florid performances by senior council luminaries in Star Chamber on 29 November 1599 was to stem a relentless tide of public sympathy for Essex. First to charge was Egerton, railing against 'traitorous persons (Monsters of men), that without regard of dutie or conscience ... traduce her Majestie and her direction and Counsells and do sclander her Counsellors and Ministers'.[64] This slander spread from the pulpit, where 'Preachers ... have used such particular designations, as their malicious meaning hath appeared to their simplest Auditory'. Elsewhere, the lowly frequenter of 'Ordinarie and Common tables, where they have scarce mony to paye for their dyner, enter politique discourses of Princes, Kingdoms, and Estates, and of Counsells and Counsellors'. Most dangerous of

---

[61] See in particular Alastair Bellany, *The politics of court scandal in early modern England: news, culture and the Overbury affair, 1603–1660* (Cambridge: Cambridge University Press, 2002); Joad Raymond ed., *News, newspapers, and society in early modern Britain* (London: F. Cass, 1999); Adam Fox, *Oral and literate culture in England, 1500–1700* (Oxford: Oxford University Press, 2000); Mears, *Queenship and political discourse*; Lake, 'Fall of Grindal'; Hammer, 'Smiling Crocodile'. For political libels in the late Tudor period, see Pauline Croft, 'Libels, popular literacy and public opinion in Early Modern England', *Historical Research*, 68 (1995), 269–73.

[62] Cyndia Susan Clegg, *Press censorship in Elizabethan England* (Cambridge: Cambridge University Press, 1997), 198–217.

[63] See Chamberlain's account: 'Here hath ben much descanting about yt, why such a storie should come out at this time, and many exceptions taken, especially to the epistle which was a short thinge in Latin dedicated to the erle of Essex': McClure, *Letters of John Chamberlain*, I, 70; Richard Dutton, 'Buggeswords: Samuel Harsnett and the licensing, suppression and afterlife of Dr John Hayward's 'The first part of the life and reign of Henry IV', *Criticism*, 35/3 (1993), 305–40.

[64] TNA, SP 12/273/35, ff. 60ʳ–73ʳ.

all, though, were those who 'doe contrive and publish false and sedicious libells, scattering the same in many parts of the Cittie of London, Yea and in her Majesties Court itself'. Gilding an already gaudy lily, Egerton denounced the spreaders of news and rumour as 'traytors' according to the 'auncient Lawes of England' (which had, as he and other councillors admitted, been refined by the treason act of Edward III). Cecil joined the rhetorical fray with hardly less enthusiasm. In one account of his speech, he made a needling social distinction between the decorum of gentlemen, such as those in attendance at Star Chamber, and the 'base sorts of people' who spread seditious rumour: 'fewe gentlemen of quallitie, Professors of Lawes or Armes but Jack Caad and Jack Straw have bene authors and Capteyenes of those'.

The council faced, of course, the eternally frustrating dilemma of an authoritative body trying to suppress viral rumours. If Bacon can be believed, Elizabeth herself rued the Star Chamber proceedings, believing that they had rather 'kindled factious bruites...then quenched them'.[65] This attempt to jam the lid on popular speculation in such a bombastic way was only bound to churn up further fascination with Essex's plight, sharpening the certain opinion of the earl's admirers that the councillors were his enemies. Meanwhile London swarmed with unemployed soldiers, liable to conflate their own predicament with Essex's disgrace. In Star Chamber, Cecil condemned those who complained that Elizabeth made 'small accompt of men of martiall condition'; but the following July he made it well known that he had moved swiftly to suppress a proclamation of the queen for the unmaking of Essex's Irish knights.[66]

The circulation of Lady Rich's letter and Essex's own compositions, in manuscript and then in print, merely dripped fuel onto the smouldering ashes of rumour and popular indignation. So too did the appearance of an engraving of Essex by Thomas Cockson in January 1600, depicting the earl on horseback with the slogan 'Vertues honor Wisdomes valure, Graces servaunt, Mercies love, Gods elected, Truths beloved, Heavens affected'. There is no evidence to associate the engraving's circulation with Essex himself, or even any of the earl's personal acquaintance, and its iconography was not innately seditious. Although the equestrian portrait is strongly associated with imperial kingship, the image itself was one of a series of similar images of military commanders, which included Lord

---

[65] Bacon, of course, claimed that he had advised against the speeches in the first place, *Apologie*, 42–4.
[66] TNA, SP12/273/35, f. 69ᵛ; McClure, *Letters of John Chamberlain*, I, 104–5. The proclamation itself, which would have nullified 38 knighthoods, was endorsed with the sign manual; it is printed in *CSPI, 1599–1600*, 218.

Admiral Howard. In the context of the anxieties that clouded round Essex, though, any praise for the earl as a military hero was interpreted as subversive by an intensely sensitive and anxious privy council. Whitgift was ordered to subject the individual responsible for dissemination of the image to 'very strong punishment inflycted very hard as his lewd offence in this matter shall deserve'.[67]

THE ANATOMY OF ESSEX'S POPULARITY

Hysteria over the political temperament of London widened the chasm between Essex and the court. For the government, it enforced stereotyped suspicions that he would act as a demagogue, harnessing the power of the mob. Essex's confidence in London's support in 1601 was, ironically, based on a shared *and wrong* expectation that the commons would conform to the polemical type, responding to personal supplication from respect for his noble virtue, and his much famed love of the commonwealth. In February 1601, Essex also expected that his understanding of the tyranny of evil counsel had a wide currency: in the first instance, he expected the citizens to believe his revelation of a court-based plot to kill him; then that his enemies were embroiled in a Spanish succession plot.

According to Mervyn James, the failure of the earl's appeal in 1601 proved the supremacy of the doctrine of obedience over other claims on the loyalty of the subject.[68] But widespread sympathy for Essex after his disgrace, expressed in libels and sermons, evinces the successful penetration of his ideological position: the earl's virtuous heroism was contrasted with a deeply critical appraisal of court corruption, and even the character of Elizabeth. It was the agency rather than the quality of Essex's popular appeal that he would misjudge so spectacularly in 1601.

There was, however, no homogenous 'popular' response to Essex, if literary sources can be trusted. Some writers outside the court clearly shared Elizabeth's suspicious view of Essex's heroic image. One of the most well-known pieces of contemporary commentary on Essex's 'popularity' is the satirist Everard Guilpin's lampoon of the earl as 'great *Foelix*', a popular demagogue who emulates the behaviour of '*Cateline* or *Alcibiades/*to seeme a Cato, or a Socrates', a critique of the earl's very public embrace

---

[67] LPL MS 3470, f. 222^r; see Arthur M. Hind, *Engraving in England in the sixteenth and seventeenth centuries. Part I: The Tudor period* (Cambridge: Cambridge University Press, 1952), 245–6 and Plate 126.
[68] James, 'At a crossroads'.

of arms and letters. With a deliberate echo of Shakespeare's Bullingbrook, Foelix, 'passing through the streete/Vayleth his cap to each one he doth meet', his humble demeanour concealing a vaunting ambition: 'he is the devill/Brightly accostumed to bemist his evill', whose 'thoughts swell/With yeastie ambition'. There is also a reference to Essex as a type of Guise: this *'Signior Machiavell'*, with the 'mumming trick, with curtesie/T'entrench himselfe in popularitie/....Be Barricadode in the peoples love'. Guilpin essentially anticipates the post-rising propaganda, implying in a satire published in 1598, a year *before* Essex's Irish debacle, that the earl bears the characteristics of a usurping nobleman.[69]

Most famously, the only direct reference in the whole of Shakespeare's canon to a living historical figure refers to Essex's popularity in London:

> But now behold,
> In the quick forge and working-house of thought,
> How London doth pour out her citizens.
> The Mayor and all his brethren in best sort,
> Like to the senators of th'antique Rome
> With the plebeians swarming at their heels,
> Go forth and fetch their conquering Caesar in[70]

This verse from *Henry V*, recalling the rain-soaked crowds that cheered Essex's departure for Ireland, is far from directly critical; but the ambiguity of the praise brilliantly captures the fearful edge of expectation that characterized attitudes at court towards an Essexian victory over Tyrone. The return of 'conquering Caesar' from Gaul, of course, initiated the chapter of civil war that heralded the end of the Republic, while the regal comparison of Essex with Henry V was hardly more comfortable.[71] Popular acclamation, as Bacon had sternly warned, was the province of the monarch, not the subject.

[69] Everard Guilpin, *Skialetheia: Or, A shadowe of truth, in certaine epigrams and satyres* (1598), sig. C3ᵛ; for a discussion of other satires that might comment unfavourably on Essex's court career and his militarism, see Clegg, *Press Censorship*, 213–15.

[70] *King Henry V*, 5:0, 22–35, ed. T. W. Craik (London: Routledge, 1995), 334–6. Essex's departure was accompanied by cheering crowds: John Nichols, *The progresses and public processions of queen Elizabeth...*, 3 vols (London, 1823) III, 432–3. Richard Dutton has argued that the passage refers to Mountjoy rather than Essex, and that the play was revised after the Battle of Kinsale. Though Dutton's readings of the reflection of debates about foreign policy and succession politics in the play are illuminating, evidence for the re-dating does not convince, while the similarities with contemporary reports of London's response to Essex's departure are so acute that the parallel seems undeniable: Dutton, 'The dating and contexts of *Henry V*', in Paulina Kewes ed., *The uses of history in early modern England* (San Marino, CA: Huntington Library, 2006), 162–99.

[71] For contemporary interest in Roman history, see Chapter 6.

Much other material, though, was resolutely partisan, reflecting the gloomier attitudes of Essex's intimates. Cecil vituperated the libellous speech of those soldiers who had taken 'the Alarum of a Pacification nowe in speech', suggesting the widespread impact of the manuscript treatises on the peace even before the print publication of the earl's *Apologie* the following May.[72] The threat by Essex's enemies to his glorious militarism was captured in another visual image of the earl printed in 1599, before the controversy over Cockson's equestrian portrait. The hysterical atmosphere that surrounded Essex's Irish campaign bred a ready market for a souvenir, and there is no reason to suspect that William Rogers's depiction of Essex as lord lieutenant of Ireland was produced at the behest of a member of the earl's circle. The half-portrait of Essex is flanked by the figure of Constancy, holding a crown of laurels over his head, while Envy tears sprigs from the wreath. The image is explicated with the earl's personal motto: *Virtutis comes invidia* (virtue is accompanied by envy).[73]

The depiction of Envy refers to previous attempts to dampen the glorification of Essex's role after Cadiz, and is probably intended to warn against a similar outcome, when Essex triumphs over Tyrone. But the image develops a very different meaning when read in the context of the fortunes of Essex's Irish expedition, reflecting the earl's conviction that his enemies would—and did—shackle and thwart the success of his mission.[74] Any partisan of Essex who had bought this engraving in a spirit of expectant celebration would, after his ignominious return, have read its symbolism in this way.

The privy council tried fervently to define the discourse of evil counsel expressed by Essex's supporters as inherently anti-monarchical, just as they would in 1601. Egerton denounced libels against 'good and faythfull servants and ministers' as a direct assault on 'her sacred Maiestie, as tho shee had neglected, or not sufficiently provided for the troubled and dangerous state of the Realme of Ireland'. Cecil was more subtle, claiming that libellers deliberately attacked the queen through her counsellors because 'it was to grosse and perilous a presumption to take particular exception against her Majesties royall person'. Nevertheless, 'all those that spurne at Soveraigntie have ever colored their practises by taxing those that are in authoritie'.[75]

---

[72] TNA, SP 12/273/35, f. 69ᵛ. This seems to refer to 'Considerations of the Peace now in Speech', one of the peace treatises discussed in Chapter 2.
[73] Hind, *Engraving in England*, 267–8, Plate 138.
[74] See Hammer, 'Myth-making', 639–42.
[75] TNA, SP 12/273/35, ff. 61ʳ, 69ʳ⁻ᵛ.

In libels written after Essex's return from Ireland, the earl's admirers exploited the anonymous manuscript form to vent their bilious spleens with vigour. 'Here Lieth the Toad' was scribbled on Cecil's door at court.[76] Disseminated in a more public setting was a verse that vituperates Cecil as a 'Crookeback spider', a 'Proude and ambitious wretch that feedest on nought but Faction' and 'vile detraction'.[77] A further verse, written in December 1599, typically mourns the inversion of virtue and honour and the triumph of 'the machivilians of this lande'. Cobham 'worketh ill', but Cecil, again, is the hellish villain, a 'bussarde' 'Dipt in water from Limbo springe', who has usurped the rightful place of 'nobleness'.[78]

These squibs echo the arguments of Essex's *Apologie*, denouncing the earl's personal rivals as enemies of the state and commonwealth. The arachnid Cecil is a 'foe to Vertue', 'frend to rapine', 'Poison to the state and Commons'.[79] Even closer to the message of the *Apologie* are two connected libels about war and military valour. The first mourns the impossible plight of military virtue in England: who 'seekes to gayne the lawrell crowne' and 'hath a mynde that would aspire' 'Let hym his native soyle eshewe/Let hym goe raunge, & seeke anewe'.[80] The second verse rails against peace with 'bastard Spayne', and ringingly confirms Essex's argument that the continuation of war 'is the onlye waye to strengthen state'.[81]

A libel with more complex literary aspirations adopts the popular form of the beast fable. The poet/narrator allegorizes Essex as a 'stately *Hart*', 'comelie, and of couradge bold', who enjoys 'love of young and old' for his famous exploits against the 'Romish wolfe [and] Spaine' on behalf of his mistress, the '*Lion*' of England. His adversary is the hunchbacked Robert Cecil, a '*Cammel*', who feeds upon the nourishment of Cobham (a 'muddye *Brooke*') and Ralegh ('meate blood *Rawe*'). An addition to this triumvirate of usual suspects is Sir Edward Coke (whose prosecution of Essex at the York House trial of 1600 was particularly fierce), here represented by a tree, adding leaves to a potion concocted by the camel. Enchanted by this potion, the lion is persuaded that the hart is an overmighty subject, 'to great' and embraced by the 'Peoples Love'. Ruined

---

[76] HMC *Salisbury*, XIV, 162; see Pauline Croft, 'The reputation of Robert Cecil: libels, political opinion and popular awareness in the early seventeenth century', *TRHS*, 6th series, 1 (1991), 47.

[77] Bod, Don MS C 54, f. 20ʳ; the final line indicates the public dissemination of the verse: 'Good Gentlemen let this bill stand'.

[78] BL, Additional MS 5956, f. 23ʳ; also see copies in Bod, Rawlinson MS Poet. 26, f. 20 and Bod, Don MS C 54, f. 7ʳ.

[79] Bod, Don MS C 54, f. 20ʳ.

[80] BL, Additional MS 4129, ff. 15ᵛ–16ʳ.   [81] Ibid., ff. 16ᵛ–17ᵛ.

in Ireland by his enemies' schemes, the hart now lies in a 'dampie doungeon'; meanwhile the camel holds 'kingdomes sterne' 'by sleight', and controls 'the sceptres staie'.[82]

If Essex's enemies are thoroughly slandered, Elizabeth herself is the weakest of monarchs. None of these poems overtly challenges her authority; the final line of the most vituperative anti-Cecilian libel declares its loyalism—'God save the queene'. But they all insist that Elizabeth is grievously blinded or drugged by the earl's foes. 'Ffactions actions' are so overt that 'They that see not are verye blynde'.[83]

Similar attitudes—deeply critical of the politics of the court—can be discerned in more godly contexts. During the winter of 1599, when Essex had fallen ill, rumours of his imminent death spawned an alarming display of public sympathy from London pulpits. A series of preachers at Paul's Cross prayed for Essex's health, while a number of ministers throughout the city gave 'publicke touches' in their parish services. The privy council and ecclesiastical authorities immediately investigated, apparently discerning the ghostly hand of Puritan organizational tactics. At first, the evidence was less worrying.[84] The preachers at Paul's Cross were found either to be Cambridge men, bound to pray for their chancellor, or Essex's own chaplains, and nearly all insisted that they had prayed only for Essex's physical well-being. But where the texts of sermons were made available the content was more damning. David Roberts, bachelor of divinity at St Andrews in the Wardrobe, was 'committed' for hailing Essex as a 'noble Barak', his enemies foes of the queen and 'the glorie, the good of this churche and kingdome'. Roberts had stormily prayed for 'the greefe and discouragement of all wicked Edomites, that beare evill will to Sion'.[85]

A deeper analysis of the politics of court faction was made in the Paul's Cross sermon of the Cambridge divine, John Richardson, on 23 November, which triggered the authorities' initial anxiety.[86] Richardson's performance was especially controversial because he made political obedience itself his

[82] Bod, Don MS C 54, ff. 19ʳ–20ʳ.   [83] BL, Additional MS 5956, f. 23ʳ.

[84] See Arnold Hunt's discussion, 'Tuning the Pulpits', 91–94. Sir Edward Stanhope describes the outbreak of preaching: TNA, SP 12/273/59, ff. 111ʳ–112ʳ; the record of the preachers' interrogation is LPL Fairhurst MS 3470, ff. 216ʳ–219ʳ; Anthony Wotton, Stephen Egerton, Richard Gardiner, and George Downham were well-known Puritans, Wotton one of Essex's chaplains. At St Clements without Temple Barr the sexton had tolled the bell on 18 December for Essex at the request of one 'Captain Parrye of Bristoll'.

[85] TNA, SP 12/274/1, f. 1ʳ, Roberts's signed confession; also LPL Fairhurst MS 3470, f. 218ʳ: Roberts describes Essex as his 'good Lord and master'—he had probably been one of the earl's chaplains.

[86] Richardson was a former fellow of Emmanuel College and a protégé of Whitgift, 'my master of many years', which might explain his adherence to Essex: LPL Fairhurst MS 3470, f. 221ʳ.

wider thematic frame, basing his sermon on Matthew 22:21 'Give unto Caesar that which is Ceasar's and unto God that which is God's', the supremely flexible biblical injunction that was widely used in sixteenth-century Europe to justify absolute loyalty to the secular powers *or* to legitimize resistance. Under interrogation, Richardson insisted that he had intended his sermon merely 'to stirre upp the affections of the Auditors, to most loyall dutie unto her Majesties most sacred person'. His blustering protestation shows that he was charged with opposite sentiments.[87]

Richardson's sermon had condemned the views of the Pharisees, who claimed that nothing was due to Caesar, *and* the Herodians, 'whoe held that all was Caesars', as two extremes of ungodly attitudes towards political authority. It was the Herodians, however, who held his interest. Richardson's particular inventiveness was to define these ungodly absolutists as evil counsellors, exulting obedience to secular powers for nefarious purposes. This parallels precisely Essex's excoriation of Solomon's dangerous fools who 'acknowledge an infinite absoluteness on earth' in his famous letter to Egerton.[88]

Richardson continued to explore a range of historical examples of the triumphs of Herodians—'rats of the palace'—and the fall of virtuous men. Seneca, Nero's former tutor, cited prominently in the earl's answer to Egerton, 'to [sic] populare', was driven from court to 'lyve as a private man in the contrye' and hounded to suicide by the 'depraving speeches' of his enemies. Pietro della Vigna, chancellor to the Holy Roman Emperor Frederick II in the thirteenth century, had been 'calumnied and drawn in on suspicion of disloyalty'.[89] Most startling of all was a parallel drawn between the Herodians and the evil faction that had slandered St Ambrose, bishop of Milan in the fourth century. St Ambrose, who had famously threatened the

---

[87] LPL Fairhurst MS 2004, f. 9ʳ, 'The aunsweres or examination of John Richardson', 15 December 1599. Before 8 December Richardson had been fined £100 and banned from public preaching other than in his parish: ibid., f. 10ʳ. He was still under arrest in January.

[88] Two sets of notes from Richardson's sermon survive, TNA, SP 12/276/106, f. 180ʳ⁻ᵛ, endorsed 'Notes of Dr Richardson his Sarmon' and SP 12/276/107, f. 181ᵛ, 'Contents of Dr Richardson his Sarmon'.

[89] TNA, SP 12/276/106, 107, ff. 180ʳ–181ᵛ. On 12 January 1600, Richardson argued 'For my Lord of Essex, their is no attribute given to Seneca yt may agree to him. For the one was togatus, the other armartus, the one a philosopher, the other a man of employment . . . one a writer of books, the other not', LPL Fairhurst MS 3470, f. 219ʳ; of course, Essex's image combined robe and sword, as he was keen to demonstrate in his *Apologie*, itself a book of sorts. The other analogies—of popularity and retirement—clearly indicate that the analogy reflected on Essex; also see Hunt, 'Tuning the Pulpits', 91 and *passim*.

emperor Theodosius I with excommunication, was not predominantly remembered as a victim of evil counsel in Elizabethan England, but for his defence of the principle that duty to God overrode obedience to secular powers. Ambrose's example had been notoriously and disastrously invoked by Edmund Grindal, archbishop of Canterbury, to justify his opposition to Elizabeth's suppression of prophesying in 1577.[90]

Richardson's definition of the methods of evil counsellors was a lacerating attack on the manipulation of the language of absolute monarchy to condemn the wronged, popular, and virtuous subject. From this most public of pulpits, the sermon posed a direct challenge to the authoritarian doctrine of obedience established in the Star Chamber speeches, and in wider critiques of Essex's behaviour.

CROWNING ESSEX

These libels and sermons go some way towards explaining the nervy authoritarianism of the government's response to the 'popular' reaction to Essex's disgrace. The anti-court culture of Essex's supporters provoked a destabilizing critique of the whole of the government, the queen's powers included, that energized the late Elizabethan public sphere.

For the most daring and provocative treatment of Essex's downfall, though, we must return to the anonymous verse. Two companion poems written by a supporter of Essex explore the tensions in his relationship with his enemies—but also with Elizabeth—in a particularly subversive way.[91] 'Verses upon the report of the death of the right honourable the Lord of Essex' were written in the winter of 1599/1600, at the time of the censored sermons, when rumours of Essex's mortal sickness swept prematurely through the city. Although only one copy of the verses exists in a commonplace book of 1599–1600, they were not transcribed in the hand of the author, suggesting that the poems received at least a limited manuscript circulation.

The verses are elegies written prematurely for Essex's death. The first poem, narrated by an anonymous speaker, moves between an earthly and a heavenly setting, described in images of the natural world; the second between imagined visions of heaven and Hades, before mutating into a

---

[90] TNA, SP 12/276/107, f. 181^r. This parallel comes from the second set of notes only, but the first notes mention 'other example out of the ecclesiastical history'.

[91] BL, Harleian MS 6910, ff. 177^r–189^v. The dating of the commonplace book is described in K, Gottschalk, 'Discoveries concerning British Library MS Harley 6910', *Modern Philology*, 77 (1979), 121–31. The poems are printed (and wrongly dated) in Morfill and Furnivall, *Ballads from manuscripts*, II, pt 2, 217–39.

pastoral dialogue between two shepherds, Viator and Menalcas. The poems are loaded with knowing references that demonstrate familiarity with the writing of Spenser, Sidney, and Essex. The speaker of the first poem describes his retirement to a shady wood with 'Philomel', where 'The prickly Briers shall be my centinell' (121–6). Essex had referred to Philomela, the tongueless princess, in an earlier poem to Elizabeth, and in a verse from 1599 or 1600 described his own desire to hide in an 'unhaunted Desert' amongst the 'Hipps, Hawes and Brambleberry' (7:2, 6).[92]

The speaker of the first poem expresses an intensely personal closeness to the earl—'my Essex'—to whom 'I made a vow' (144).[93] Viator and Menalcas bemoan the exposure of their flocks to the appetites of preying beasts now that Essex, their friend and protector, is dead: 'Now he is gon, the wolfe is waxen bould/The Fox doth dare molest my tender lambes' (685–6).[94] But the verses have a public message. Essex's heroic deeds are likened to those of Achilles, Hector, Ajax, Pompey, Phyrrus, Caesar, and especially Scipio the Elder, the saviour of Rome from Hannibal, who was driven from the city to live an exemplary retired life, just as Essex had retreated from the court.[95]

The poems also draw strange and audacious parallels between the 'death' of the earl and Christ's redemption of mankind. Essex is taken to heaven 'to cleare the counts' and 'to make all reckonings even' (105–6).[96] Furies carry him to the underworld, washing his feet and wrapping him in a winding sheet, in a strange ceremony fusing classical and Christian imagery. They dance around the corpse: 'Haile, ESSEX! Hayle to thee! All haile, our King!' (270).[97]

The poems are also saturated with imagery associated with monarchical power, particularly crowns. Essex's ghost is mistaken for 'Some Prince's Spirit, some mightie monarchs ghost' (315) (an echo of *Hamlet*, thought to have been written between 1599 and 1601?).[98] The speaker rues opportunities lost to honour this hero: 'our dutie was t'have crown'd his head with bay' (194), the laurel crown worn by generals and poets. But if Essex has been deprived of due recognition in his lifetime, he has certainly earned a crown of fame that excels any temporal bauble:

> Though hee hast lost his life, yet hath he wonne
> A Crowne of Glorie in the highest sphere,
> A Crowne that far excells the midday Sunne. (199–201)[99]

---

[92] Morfill, *Ballads from manuscripts*; May, 'Poems of Robert Devereux', 44, 47.
[93] Morfill, *Ballads from manuscripts*, 221.   [94] Ibid., 236.
[95] Ibid., 222, 227.   [96] Ibid., 220.   [97] Ibid., 224.
[98] Ibid., 226.   [99] Ibid., 223.

The poet confirms Elizabeth's suspicion that admiration for Essex's virtues could exceed the reverence that her subjects felt for her: 'His Crowne excells an earthly Crowne as farr/As doth the Sunne excell a lesser Starre'. These images of monarchy develop into an explicit discussion of the relationship between Essex's and Elizabeth's authority:

> That head that was more fitt a crowne to weare,
> Nor must, nor dare, I say, a Crowne of Gold:
> A Crowne of Gould alas! it were to deare:
> T'were deare to gett, but dearer farre to hould. (211–14)[100]

This is hugely, if trickily, provocative. The poet shrinks back with self-conscious artifice from the suggestion, deliberately posed, that Essex was 'more fitt' to be a monarch. But this situation would be too 'deare' to get or 'hould'; crucially, not immoral. Having drawn the reader into such controversial territory the author briefly restores Tudor homily:

> Nor do I wish more crownes to see than one
> And none to rainge, but faire ELIS' alone
> And let her raigne, Good God, as long as I
> Or any other drawes his vitall breath. (215–18)[101]

But the author persists with the theme of crowns, addressing a rhetorical question to the queen:

> Is't not an honoure, is't not a grace in thee,
> To governe those that like Kings Crowned be? (233–4)[102]

If Essex cannot be a king in his own right then Elizabeth must acknowledge that her own glory depends on his. Elizabeth's crown is inherited, but Essex's is deserved through his own merit. In other words a form of mixed monarchy is described, where princes are dependent on their great subjects whom they are obligated to honour. In the context of the political situation in 1599 and 1600, this is subversive in a clear and sensational way; but the sentiments articulated here are essentially those consistently expressed throughout Essex's career by his followers, in the *imprese* of Wright, the praise of Pérez.

The poem finishes with an extraordinary and menacing twist. Essex's death, Menalcas triumphantly announces, has been prematurely mourned. The earl is gloriously alive, resurrected to bring Christ-like redemption: 'to helpe his freendes and make his foes afraid'.[103]

---

[100] Ibid.   [101] Ibid.   [102] Ibid.   [103] Ibid., 238.

HAYWARD, TREASON, AND THE
CONDEMNATION OF KING ESSEX

The York House trial, and Essex's subsequent release from house arrest in August, gave no resolution to either party. As Cecil's intelligence burrowed more deeply into communications between Essex and James, Essex's bombastic expressions of loyalty at York House did not restore confidence in his behaviour more deeply any more than his alleged determination to live a private life.[104]

As a succession crisis loomed, it became an urgent necessity that Essex's enemies un-claw this threat. The argument was made with ferocity by Ralegh, who wrote to Robert Cecil in February or March 1600 urging him not to 'relent towards this tyrant': his 'malice is fixt'. Were Essex to be given liberty, 'he wilbe able to break the branches and pull up the tree, root and all', condemning not only Cecil, but threatening his entire family.[105] This is surely an appeal for Essex's death.

The government's wariness of public sympathy for Essex crystallized in the extensive investigation into John Hayward's *First parte of the life and raigne of King Henrie IIII*, which revealed acute concerns about the dissemination of plausible theories of noble resistance. Although the second edition of the history, printed in May 1599, had been called in following Essex's earlier complaint, the *Life and raigne* was sensationally politicized by the earl's disgrace. Francis Bacon's investigation of Essex's connection to the printing of the history at the York House trial initiated interrogation of the text and its author that was ongoing at the time of the rising itself.[106] In July 1600, Hayward was arrested and examined with John Wolfe, the printer, and Samuel Harsnett, the

---

[104] In April 1600, the privy council arrested Henry Lee, used as a messenger between Mountjoy and James; in October, Sir William Eure was arrested for similar reasons, and only released after the earl's rising: see Chapter 1, n. 67. Essex's communication with Mountjoy may also have been intercepted: his letter to Sir Charles Danvers, written on 28 July 1600, is heavily annotated: Cecil MS 80/93.

[105] Agnes Latham and Joyce Youings eds, *The letters of Sir Walter Ralegh* (Exeter: Exeter University Press, 1999), 185–7.

[106] No connection has been proved between Essex and Hayward, who insisted that he began the work twelve years previously; Essex ordered the dedication cut out, and may have initiated the suppression of the second edition: see Hayward's confession on 11 July 1600, TNA, SP 12/275/25 and 25I, ff. 41ʳ–42ᵛ; Wolfe's examination on 13 July, TNA, SP 12/275/28, ff. 45ʳ–46ʳ. See the account of Hayward's editor: Manning, *Hayward's Life and raigne*, 1–39, discussed further in Chapter 6.

unfortunate licensor. Remaining in the Tower, the hapless Hayward was questioned again on 22 January 1601.[107]

In his *Apologie*, Bacon later claimed that it was Elizabeth who pounced upon treason in a book that he regarded as innocuous.[108] The investigation of the history and author by lord chief justice Popham and Sir Edward Coke followed the queen's lines of thought. Hayward was required to defend his choice of such a topical story which chronicled 'deformities of the state', and was acutely redolent of Elizabeth's financial policies, her childlessness, and her difficulties in Ireland.[109]

Just as worrying were the similarities between the mentalities of Essex, the notorious dedicatee, and Bullingbrook, the usurping rebel, whose 'ancient' nobility and valour were contrasted with accounts of Richard's courtiers, 'base harted parasites to whome military vertue ys *lege*'.[110] The subversive character of Bullingbrook's popularity was a persistent concern: 'the chiefest confidence of this earle the favour & resistance of the people of the realme'.[111] Certainly aware of his own reputation amongst Essex's followers, Coke laconically recorded the immediate act performed by Bullingbrook on his return from exile: 'The erle . . . cutt of the heades of corrupt councellors and hatefull favourites'.[112]

Popham and Coke also made an especially authoritarian reading of speeches in defence of Bullingbrook's rebellion.[113] As well as being asked 'what moved him to mayntyn . . . that it might be lawful for the subject to depose the kyng for any cause', Hayward was commanded to define 'what moved hym to sett down that the subjects were bownd for ther obedyens to the state and not to the person of the kyng?'[114] The last question in particular demonstrates the great sensitivity of Hayward's interrogators towards the tension embedded in concepts of political allegiance. The subtle rephrasing of the statement in the revised version of Coke's notes—'subjects rather bownde to the crowne and state of the realme, then to the person of the prince'—yokes together crown *and* state, defining the inseparably 'monarchical' nature of the polity;

---

[107] Popham's questions for Hayward are TNA, SP 12/274/58, f. 100[r-v]; notes, mainly by Coke and another unknown hand are SP 12/274/61, f. 107[r-v] and 62, f. 108[r]. For Hayward's examination on 22 January 1601, see TNA, SP 12/278/17, ff. 20[r]–21[r].

[108] Bacon, *Apologie*, 34–5.

[109] TNA, SP 12/274/61, f. 107[r].

[110] Ibid.

[111] TNA, SP 12/274/62, f. 108[r]; '& resistance' is added by the second hand.

[112] TNA, SP 12/274 61, f. 107[r].

[113] The reading misinterpreted the complexity of arguments articulated by different characters, as will be discussed in Chapter 6. The important point here is the interpretation by Coke and Popham, rather than Hayward's intended meaning.

[114] TNA, SP 12/274/58, f. 100[r].

even this description, though, voices particular concern at the exposition of a theory of kingship that separates the body politic from the
monarch's natural body.[115] Popham, meanwhile, was most concerned
about the widespread propagation of these ideas through the medium
of print: 'Myght he thynke that this hystory sett first in such as yt ys
wold not be very daungerous for to come amongst the common sort
of peoples?'[116]

This interrogation of Hayward and his history, a month after the York
House trial, was part of a quiet and continued accretion of evidence
against Essex, developed from his greatest vulnerabilities: the succession,
his connections with Catholics, sinister glosses on his dealings with
Tyrone, and his association with a subversive interpretation of history in
printed text and performance.

William Alabaster and Thomas Wright were formally examined about
their relations with Essex, Robert Parsons, and Madrid. Both had been
recaptured after recent escapes from prison, Alabaster in August, Wright
in June; they may have been particularly susceptible to pressures from the
council.[117] Trying to lay blame onto Wright, Alabaster confessed on 22
July that he had been embroiled in Rome in one of Parsons' more baroque
plots to encourage Essex to support the Spanish succession.[118] Wright,
examined on 24 July, absolutely denied communing with Parsons in
Rome or in Spain since coming to England, but gave clear indication in
his confession that he believed Essex to be a crypto-Catholic.[119]

Information from Irish sources honed the project to draw up a plausible charge of treason against the earl. In January 1600, Essex and
Sir Christopher Blount's involvement in Thomas Lee's missions to
Tyrone were reinvestigated, and new attention paid to gossip about
Essex's desire for the crowns of England and Ireland.[120] On 20 January,
the confession of Thomas Wood revealed most damningly a spreading
rumour that Tyrone had promised to send 8000 soldiers to help Essex
seize the English throne on Elizabeth's death. It seems most likely that
Wood repeated a lie deliberately spread by Tyrone to panic the authorities in England. An unusual postscript in Cecil's handwriting, though,
reveals the significance of this confession to the council: the examinee

[115] TNA, SP 12/274/62, f. 108ʳ.   [116] TNA, SP 12/274/58, f. 100ᵛ.
[117] See McClure, *Letters of John Chamberlain*, I, 34, 85, 99.
[118] TNA, SP 12/275/32, f. 53ʳ⁻ᵛ.
[119] TNA, SP 12/275/35, f. 58ʳ⁻ᵛ.
[120] Interrogation and declaration of David Hetherington, 8 January, taken and confirmed by English privy councillors on 13 January, TNA, SP 63/207/1, pt 6, ff. 10ʳ–11ʳ;
incriminating passages are underlined; also see ibid., pt 13, ff. 32ʳ–33ʳ.

had sworn that he told the truth upon the pain of damnation, 'uppon his sowle and conscience as he wold answer it, at the later day'.[121]

When in February 1601 Essex suspected that he would be charged with treason if he answered the privy council's summons, he was almost certainly correct. Cecil and the council clearly anticipated some imminent action from Essex, and were making preparations to destroy their enemy. All of the evidence collected in 1600 was to be bound up into a long formal charge of treason 'that he [Essex] plotted and practised with the pope and king of spaine for the disposing and settling to himself aswell the Crowne of England, as of the kingdome of Ireland'.[122] In January 1601, the council reopened the case against Hayward.

The charges were an unwieldy amalgamation of all of the potentially treasonous material collected in 1600 and early 1601: the confessions of Wright and Alabaster; Essex's 'underhand permitting of that most treasonous booke of Henry the fourth to be printed and published'; and his approval of a dramatic representation of the history, 'being so often present at the playing thereof, and with great applause geiving countenance and lyking to the same'. Worst of all, Essex had plotted with Tyrone directly to make himself king of England—to make the crown of gold a physical as well as a poetic reality.

Forged in the crucible of long-standing anxieties about Essex's political attitudes, the unsettled succession, and the perception of London's volatile sympathy, this treason charge was part of a deliberate burgeoning plot to destroy the earl. But the motivations of Essex's enemies were not entirely cynical. It was known that Essex was in some form of contact with James VI; that he was drawing crowds to Essex House with sermons, fostering further his legendary popularity. The construction of the earl's treasons was grounded in a real fear of his ambitions, and a correct if imprecise perception of his plans to take action to 'reform' the state. By summoning Essex to appear before them on 7 February 1601, the earl's enemies moved urgently to save themselves and the commonwealth from a more calamitous reckoning.

---

[121] TNA, SP 12/274/22, f. 34^r.

[122] TNA, SP 12/275/33, ff. 55^r–57^r endorsed by Cecil, 'An Abstract of the Erl of Essex his Treasons'. The date suggested is 22 July, but it appears to have been compiled over the course of 1600 and early 1601 because of the variety of material included, and the promise that 'a number of other matters' may be further added.

6

Scholars and martialists: the politics of history and scholarship

'... poore Pollitiques, that looke only fore right before them, having read in some ould scrowles ... [as] yf they weare capable of the constitution of her Majesties affayres'.[1]

'Among all sortes of humane writers, there is none that have done more profit, or deserved greater prayse, then they who have committed to faithfull records of histories'.[2] This conventional commendation of history, expressed in the preface to John Hayward's *First parte of the life and raigne of King Henrie IIII* was emphatically endorsed by Essex and his friends. One of the letters of travel advice written in Essex's name advised the young earl of Rutland: 'Above all other books be conversant in the Histories ... by which and in which you must ripen and settle your judgment'.[3] But Essex's scholarly interests were also deemed a cryptic key to his treason. According to Camden, the earl's decision to rebel was nourished by Sir Gelly Merrick, who pointed his master towards the prophetic overtones of the dedication of the *Life and raigne* 'in great hope and expectation of future times'. After the rising, it was Merrick who bore the blame for commissioning the Richard II play.[4]

Elizabethans viewed their world through a mesh of historical paradigms and narratives. Linda Levy Peck notes that references to Richard II's reign 'swirled' around the Essex revolt; the imprecision of her carefully chosen verb indicates how difficult it remains to connect particular texts/performances and political events, and to discern the historical patterns that gave shape to thought and action.[5] Recent scholarship, though, has given much clearer definition to the important intellectual influences on Essex—the fascination of his circle with Tacitus, as well as the history of England's late

---

[1] TNA, SP 12/273/35, f. 70ʳ, Sir Robert Cecil in Star Chamber, 29 November 1599.
[2] 'A. P. to the Reader', in Manning, *Hayward's Life and raigne*, 62.
[3] Vickers, *Francis Bacon*, 73.
[4] Camden, *Annales*, 867–8.
[5] Peck, 'Peers, patronage and the politics of history', in Guy, *Reign of Elizabeth I*, 100.

medieval past, which so distinctively characterized the literature of the 1590s.[6] We must also remember that the historical separateness of classical, medieval, and 'contemporary' history and the distinction between history and literature itself were often blurred; or rather, similar ideas about politics and history were interrogated and derived from the plethora of historical texts that engaged late Elizabethan readers.[7] As Francis Bacon wittily noted, most of Hayward's *Life and raigne of King Henrie IIII* itself was constructed from quotations mined from Sir Henry Savile's translation of Tacitus's *Histories*.[8]

Most importantly, the literary culture of the 1590s emphasized recurring political themes that were particularly pertinent to Essex's vision. Interest in history encouraged searching reflection on political obedience, the role of counsel in a monarchy, and the nature of kingship and tyranny. How did Essex's faith in strenuous scholarship, conventionally but forcefully expressed, come to shape his understanding of Elizabeth's rule? And what are we to make of Camden's assertion that ideas about resistance, central to the European politics of Essex's circle, shaped the events of 1599–1601, and Essex's plans—if muddily conceived—to reform the state?[9]

ELIZABETHAN MAECENAS

In his *Apologie* Essex claimed to have been drawn in youth to a life of scholarly retirement, before realizing that his duty lay in public service. Whether literary trope or biographical fact, these scholarly credentials show a conscious assumption of *gravitas*: according to Tacitus, the young Agricola, later a great general and governor of Britain, had planned to be a

---

[6] Smuts, 'Court-Centred Historians'; Womersley, 'Sir Henry Savile's Translation'; Salmon, 'Stoicism and Roman Example'; L. J. Richardson, 'Sir John Hayward and early Stuart historiography', unpublished PhD thesis 2 vols (University of Cambridge, 1999).

[7] There is a large body of work on sixteenth-century historiography: see in particular F. J. Levy, *Tudor historical thought* (San Marino, CA: Huntington Library, 1967); D. R. Woolf, *The idea of history in early Stuart England: erudition, ideology and 'The light of truth' from the accession of James I to the Civil War* (Toronto and London: University of Toronto Press, 1990); Kewes, *Uses of History*; Annabel Patterson, *Reading Holinshed's Chronicles* (Chicago and London: University of Chicago Press, 1994); Henry Savile himself produced an edition of medieval chronicles, *Rerum Anglicarum scriptores post Bedam praecipui, ex vetustissimis codicibus manuscriptis* (1596); May McKisack, *Medieval history in the Tudor age* (Oxford: Clarendon Press, 1971), 64–5.

[8] Bacon, *Apologie*, 36–7.   [9] Chapter 1, 67.

philosopher before realizing, as a Roman should, that his talents must be employed in the *vita activa*.[10]

Essex's commitment to scholarship was no empty boast. In emulation of Leicester, who had been chancellor of Oxford, Essex developed strong connections with the universities.[11] In December 1591, a campaign to become chancellor of Oxford failed; not yet a privy councillor, Essex was too junior for the post, but Elizabeth's duly elected nominee, Lord Buckhurst, found the strength of Essex's influence as steward of the borough of Oxford challenging to his authority.[12] Following the death of Burghley in 1598, a different opportunity arose; Essex was unanimously elected chancellor of Cambridge. Whitgift had given emphatic direction to the vice chancellor—'knowing the disposition of the Earle of Essex towards learning and learned men I doe not think any man in England so fitt for that office, as he is'.[13]

Henry Cuffe, regius professor of Greek at Oxford, was just the most highly qualified of a group of men of scholarly background recruited to Essex's secretariat, which at various times included Thomas Smith, formerly the university orator and fellow of Christ Church; Edward Reynolds, former fellow of All Souls; the ramist scholar William Temple; and Henry Wotton.[14] In addition to the more informal relations that he enjoyed with the Bacon brothers, Pérez, Fulke Greville, and Henry Howard (who had lectured in rhetoric at Cambridge in the 1560s), Essex paid solemn tribute in his *Apologie* to one particular academic, whom he claimed as an intellectual mentor: Sir Henry Savile, warden of Merton, provost of Eton, and translator of the first English edition of works by Tacitus, four books of the *Histories* and *Agricola*, published in 1591.[15]

---

[10]   *Apologie*, sig Aᵛ; 'being young hee had addicted himself to the study of philosophy in earnester sorte, and beyonde the measure of a Roman and Senatour': Tacitus, *Agricola*, in Henry Savile *The ende of Nero and the beginning of Galba*, idem ed. and trans., *Fower bookes of the Histories of Cornelius Tacitus. The life of Agricola* (1591), 239; hereafter Savile, *Ende of Nero*.

[11]   Hammer, 'Uses of Scholarship', 43, 49.

[12]   Penry Williams, 'Elizabethan Oxford: State, Church and University, 1558–1603', in James McConica, ed., *The history of the University of Oxford, vol. 3, The collegiate University* (Oxford: Clarendon Press, 1986) 437–8. On 27 May 1596 Buckhurst complained that if Essex was successful in procuring the deanery of Christ Church for his own client he would be 'utterly disgraced in the University of Oxford': HMC *Salisbury*, VI, 197. Buckhurst prevailed.

[13]   Cooper, *Annals of Cambridge*, II, 592–3. For Essex's education and his patronage of Cambridge scholars see Hammer, *Polarisation*, 303–4;

[14]   Smith, probably Essex's secretary from 1585, was made a clerk of the privy council in 1595, when he was replaced by Wotton; Temple studied at King's College Cambridge, while Wotton had studied at New College: Hammer, 'Uses of Scholarship', 26–51.

[15]   *Apologie*, sig. Aᵛ.

Essex's well publicized encouragement of scholarship was also reflected in the range of literary dedications from eminent scholars who energetically sought his patronage.[16] 'The sober and devout student [is]...fortunate to be tearmed your schollar', effused William Covell in the dedication to his *Polimanteia,* a strange meditation on the health of the commonwealth and the state of its education, literature, and religion.[17] Richard Harvey, brother of the more famous Gabriel, claimed that Essex's 'most honourable munificence' encouraged him to publish his defence of Geoffrey of Monmouth's *History of the Kings of Britain.*[18] Richard Greneway's edition of Tacitus' *Annals* and *Germania* was published in 1598 with a dedication to Essex because 'the worthines of this Author well knowen vnto your honor, putteth me in some hope of pardon for my presumption'.[19] George Chapman's first printed translations of Homer, also published in 1598, were dedicated to the new earl marshal: 'the most honoured now living Instance of the Achilleian vertues'.[20]

It is a more difficult task to gauge how Essex's mindset was shaped by his encouragement of scholarship. No personal library list of works belonging to the earl survives, nor books scribbled with leading marginal annotations. Essex's undeniable erudition is borne out by the more elegant of his letters, which reach a particular level of sophistication in his Latin correspondence with Antonio Pérez.[21] Then there are the earl's own meditations on the importance of scholarship, which reveal the kinds of ideas that appealed to him.

Most often, and most stridently, Essex claimed to exercise the ideal of the *vita activa,* the congruence of skill in arms and letters that befitted the virtuous citizen of his country. A letter on scholarship to Fulke Greville, differently attributed by Hammer and Vickers to Essex and Francis Bacon, reveals more about the insights that both men expected to be gained from strenuous scholarship. For practical political guidance, Tacitus is 'simply the best', Livy a close second, Thucydides the worthiest Greek, while Curtius and Plutarch are most useful for military commanders. Notably, scholars are particularly recommended to study 'periods or revolutions of state'; the causes of these climacteric transitions of political societies are

---

[16] Fox, 'Complaint of poetry'; Gazzard, 'Patronage of Robert Devereux'.
[17] Covell, *Polimanteia,* sig. 2ᵛ.
[18] Richard Harvey, *Philadelphus, or a defence of Brutes, and the Brutans history* (1593), sig. A2ʳ.
[19] Tacitus, Richard Greneway trans., *The annales of Cornelius Tacitus. Germania* (1598), [unpaginated].
[20] George Chapman, *Seauen bookes of the Iliades of Homere, prince of poets...* (1598) sig. A3ʳ; also, *Achilles shield Translated as the other seuen bookes of Homer, out of his eighteenth booke of Iliades* (1598).
[21] Ungerer, *Spaniard,* I, 353–4, 360–1, and *passim.*

'the uncertainty of succession', 'the equal greatness of divers grandees', or the improper maintenance of hierarchy and nobility; calamities sufficient to 'ruin the greatest monarchy'.[22]

We know also that the earl wrote a commentary on Tacitus which survived the cull of books and manuscripts at Essex House on the day of the rising, only to disappear in the seventeenth century, while Ben Jonson famously attributed to Essex the anonymous 'A.B.' introductory preface to Savile's edition of Tacitus.[23] Evidence of Essex's interest in English history is more elusive. According to Annabel Patterson, he owned an expensive copy of the 1577 edition of Holinshed's *Chronicles*, while Gabriel Harvey alleged that Essex 'much commendes' William Warner's historical poem, *Albions England*, an ambitious romp in clattering rhyme through the pre-history and history of England from the Flood until the present day, indiscriminately woven from a ragbag of scripture, classical mythology, chronicles, and legends.[24] Notably, the 1595 and 1599 editions of Samuel Daniel's historical poem *The civile wars*, which spanned the reigns of Richard II to Henry VI, are addressed to Lord Mountjoy, but contain encomium of '*worthy Essex* whose deare blood/Reserv'd from these sad times to honour ours/Shouldst have conducted Armies and now stood/Against the strength of all the *Easterne Powres*'.[25]

ENGLAND'S SCIPIO: THE *VITA ACTIVA* IN THE 1590S

Essex and Pérez revelled in the conceptualization of the earl as a latter-day Aeneas, drawing parallels between the divine mission of the ancestor of the founders of Rome and Essex's own historic destiny.[26] Essex's enthusiasm for *Albion's England* may well have been fired by the prose synopsis of the *Aeneid* appended to Warner's verse history, which drew attention to the

---

[22] Vickers, *Francis Bacon*, 102–6; Paul E. J. Hammer, 'The Earl of Essex, Fulke Greville, and the employment of Scholars', *Studies in Philology*, 91/2 (1994), 167–80.

[23] Cobham asked to borrow the 'paper boke of my Lord of Essex notations of Cornelius Tacitus' from Robert Cotton: BL, Cotton Vespasian MS F XIII, f. 290ʳ; Ben Jonson, *Conversations with Drummond of Hawthornden*, in C. H. Herford and Percy Simpson eds, *Ben Jonson*, 11 vols (Oxford: Clarendon Press, 1925–52), I, 142.

[24] Patterson, *Reading Holinshed's Chronicles*, 16; C. G. Moore Smith, *Gabriel Harvey's marginalia* (Stratford-upon-Avon: Shakespeare Head Press, 1913), 232.

[25] Samuel Daniel, *The first fowre bookes of the civile wars betweene the two houses of Lancaster and Yorke* (1595), 2.126,1–4. The commendatory verse is at 1.5,1–8. Material added to the 1599, 1601, and 1609 editions took the narrative as far as the reign of Edward IV. For a note on texts and editions see below.

[26] See Chapter 2, 75.

connected foundation myths of Rome and Britain, and lavished praise on Elizabeth's own 'valiant Warriors, whose Laudes might special Pens allure'.[27]

Others concurred. The relentless gilding of Essex's reputation drew especially gratuitous parallels with classical heroes, in analogies inevitably relating to the earl's martial deeds, but often to his greatness of mind and, in literary dedications, his intellectual gifts.[28] To Pérez alone Essex was Alexander, 'Achilles *alter*', Scipio Aemilianus and especially Aeneas.[29] To Francis Purefey, who sent a treatise on northern recusants to the earl in 1598, Essex was 'the Scipio and sworde of Englande'.[30] For William Covell too, 'England's Scipio' was the embodiment of military vigilance in a polity imperilled by the corruption of other subjects. If Roy Strong's identification of Essex as the *Young man among roses* in the famous Hillyard miniature is correct, then Essex was also seen—and saw himself—as another Pompey, a great soldier at a tender age, and a Roman hero notorious for his popularity.[31]

This celebration of the earl's martial and intellectual virtues matched Essex's own endorsement of the wider ideal of the *vita activa*, and the theory, so common in Renaissance political thought, that the health of a polity and the virtues of its citizens were directly proportional. Several authors centred their praise of Essex's embodiment of active virtue in a broadly Polybian framework of the rise and fall of states, which Machiavelli had employed so influentially to explain the historical trajectory of the Florentine republic. When the queen visited Oxford in September 1592, she listened to a Latin oration by Henry Savile on the thesis *Rei Miltaris & Philosophiae studia in Republicâ unà vigere* [sic] (on the study of arms and philosophy in a flourishing commonwealth). Savile conventionally exhorted Elizabeth to surpass her medieval forebears in military glory and patronage of learning; but he also defined at some length a cyclical vision of historical change where corruption would tip once-great states into decline.[32]

A dual dynamic emerged in texts that focused on martial and intellectual virtue. On one hand, the militaristic culture of a nation at war

---

[27] Warner, *Albions England... revised and newly inlarged* (1596), 317–35, 268; first written in 1586, it was reissued and expanded in 1589, 1591, 1596, 1597, 1602, and 1612. According to Geoffrey of Monmouth, Warner's source, Britain was founded by Aeneas's descendant, Brutus.

[28] See Chapter 5, 209–11.

[29] Ungerer, *Spaniard*, I, 329, 354, 357, 368.

[30] Cecil MS 178/85.

[31] Covell, *Polimanteia*, sig. Q3ʳ; Strong, *Cult of Elizabeth*, 77–8.

[32] Charles Plummer, *Elizabethan Oxford. Reprints of rare tracts* (Oxford: Clarendon Press, 1887), 265–6 and *passim*.

produced rapturous celebration of the puissant nation, and the strength (potential or realized) of England's soldiery. Many writers, though, increasingly meditated on the corrosion rather than the flourishing of English virtue, and its wider implications for the state. This was a *topos* well established in the classical and Renaissance works of history that were increasingly popular in the late-Elizabethan period. Machiavelli's *Florentine historie* was published in Thomas Bedingfield's English translation in 1595, while Sallust's *War with Catiline* (soon to be available in Thomas Heywood's vernacular translation of 1608) lucidly relates the degeneration of the Roman Republic to the growth of luxury and corruption, peace, and unmanliness.[33]

Tacitus also draws an explicit connection between virtue and the state in his brilliantly succinct account of the transition of Rome from republic to empire in the opening sections of the *Annals*. Here he describes the inclination of the Romans to corruption as a weakness deliberately exploited by Augustus, the emperor, to diminish the institutions and the laws of the republic by stealth.

> After he [Augustus] had wound into the favour of the soldier by giftes; of the people by provision of sustenance; and of all in generall with the sweetnes of ease and repose...he drew to himselfe the affaires of Senate; the dutie of magistrates and lawes, without contradiction of any; the stowtest by war or proscriptions already spent, and the rest of the nobilitie, by how much the more serviceable, by so much the more bettered in wealth, and advanced in honors: seeing their preferment to growe by new government, did rather choose the present estate with securitie, than strive to recover their olde with danger.[34]

As the martial virtue of the citizens—especially the nobility—that had fuelled their capacity for self-government was eroded by wealth and comfort, so Augustus could draw the powers of the senate and the laws to himself; meanwhile, the people were unwittingly complicit in their own enslavement.

In his *Apologie* Essex had violently condemned the 'iniurious' spirits, who threatened English martial virtue by following dangerous peaceful courses.[35] For several Elizabethan authors, their own extravagant praise of Essex's qualities also had a sharp polemical edge, wielded to shame the unvirtuous spirits of the wider political nation. William Covell contrasted

---

[33] See Quentin Skinner, 'Classical liberty, renaissance translation and the English civil war', in *Visions of politics. II. Renaissance virtues* (Cambridge: Cambridge University Press, 2002), 316 and *passim*.

[34] Tacitus, trans. Greneway, *Annales*, 1.

[35] *Apologie*, sig. A^r, B3^r. sigs. D2^v–D3^r; Chapter 2, 97–107.

the friendship that Essex showed to scholars with the general neglect of scholarship and religion in England. For Richard Crompton, who dedicated his treatise on the military virtues of England's ruling elites to Essex, those who 'lightly esteeme' valour and virtue, or 'live idly and daintily afore them, are enemies to the Common-wealth', who 'lay open their Countrey to the force of the enemie'.[36] The dichotomy between the virtues of Essex and the corruption of the Elizabethan state obsessed the earl's scholarly admirers as well as his military following: in particular it dominated the political thinking of the most erudite of Essex's secretaries, the former Oxford scholar, Henry Cuffe.

FROM COLLEGE TO SCAFFOLD: HENRY CUFFE

No direct evidence survives to prove or disprove Camden's allegation that Essex consulted Oxford divines on the legitimacy of armed resistance before the rising. Blame instead was heaped on Cuffe, the 'cunning coiner of plots', for inciting Essex to rise. It is in Cuffe's biography that the world of the university, court, and scaffold most obviously, and dramatically, overlap.[37]

Cuffe's troubled academic career indicates a restless combative character, possessed of an energetic and challenging intellect. He too featured prominently in Elizabeth's visit to Oxford in 1592, presenting his own oration to the queen.[38] At a dinner hosted by Savile at Merton for the council (but not the queen), Cuffe led a disputation on the Machiavellian *topos* '*An Dissentiones Civium sint Reipublicae utiles*': the proposition that civil disturbances were beneficial to the commonwealth. The disputations formally ended with prayers for individual councillors, and the 'commendation of the Earl of Essex' (not yet a councillor) 'his honourable, valiant service in the Low Countries, in Portugall, and in France'.[39]

Of the executed rebels, only Cuffe was accused of theorizing the legitimacy of armed resistance, in his alleged quotation from Lucan's *Pharsalia*: '*arma tenenti, omnia dat qui iusta negat*' (he who denies what is wrong yields all to one who is armed, 1, 348–9).[40] The popularity of

---

[36] Richard Crompton, *The Mansion of magnanimitie. Wherein is shewed the most high and honourable acts of sundrie English Kings, Princes, Dukes, Earles, Lords, Knights and Gentlemen* ... (1599), sig. A3^{r-v}.

[37] A.L. Rowse, 'The Tragic Career of Henry Cuffe', in *Court and country: studies in Tudor social history* (Brighton: Harvester, 1987), 211–41.

[38] Plummer, *Elizabethan Oxford*, 251. As university orator, Thomas Smith played a prominent role in the visit.

[39] Ibid., 256; cf. Fletcher, *Registrum*, 288.   [40] See Chapter 1, 56–7.

Lucan's account of the conflict between Caesar and Pompey reflected Elizabethans' deep-seated fear of the horrors of civil war.[41] Other than this achingly suggestive quotation from Lucan, Cuffe has left a very small evidential trace that would allow us to illuminate this reputation for the subversive interpretation of classical texts.[42] Before he left to join Essex's secretariat, however, the academic circles that Cuffe inhabited had certainly encouraged strenuous meditation on political philosophy. The library at Merton, amplified by the additions of Thomas Savile, Henry's brother, was rich in historical and literary texts; both Cuffe and Henry Savile appear to have been keen students of Machiavelli.[43] Henry Savile's own interest in different kinds of political structures had been furthered during his travels abroad from 1578–85, when he had made comparative studies of the constitutions of European and Persian kingdoms. He paid particular attention to the elective monarchy of Poland, where in 1572, as a result of a succession crisis, the nobility had imposed a new and limiting constitution on the autonomous powers of its king.[44]

The disputations taken by students as part of the BA degree also often required undergraduates to relate philosophical problems to contemporary events.[45] In 1602, students were required to debate the character of Alcibaiades and the dangers of popular understanding of political ideas, obviously inspired by Essex's rising.[46] Disputations within colleges also focused the minds of students and fellows on politics. As Henry and Thomas Savile had grown in influence at Merton, intra-collegiate debates sharply inclined towards political themes. In 1572, Henry Savile's *variationes* included a disputation on the proposition that democracy was the best state of a commonwealth.[47] In 1588, Savile, now warden of the

[41] Marlowe's posthumous translation of the first book of *Pharsalia* was published in 1600. For the significance of Lucan see David Norbrook, *Writing the English republic: poetry, rhetoric and politics, 1627–1660* (Cambridge: Cambridge University Press, 1999), 23–62; Andrew Hadfield, *Shakespeare and republicanism* (Cambridge: Cambridge University Press, 2005).

[42] Cuffe's one known treatise, *The differences of the ages of mans life*, published posthumously in 1607, does not have a political theme.

[43] R. B. Todd, 'Henry and Thomas Savile in Italy', *Bibliothèque d'Humanisme et Renaissance*, 58 (1996), 439–44; Womersley, 'Henry Savile's Translation'.

[44] J. R. Highfield, 'An autograph commonplace book of Sir Henry Savile', *Bodleian Library Record*, 7 (1963), 73–83; see Savile's commonplace book: Merton College Library, University of Oxford, MS Q. 1. 10, especially ff. 32^r–33^v.

[45] James Fletcher, 'The Faculty of the Arts' and James McConica, 'Elizabethan Oxford: the collegiate society', in McConica, *History of the University of Oxford*, 188, 693–702.

[46] A. Clark ed., *Register of the University of Oxford*, 5 vols (Oxford: Clarendon Press, 1877), I, 175.

[47] Fletcher, *Registrum*, 50, '*Democratia est optimus status reipublicae*'.

college, disputed whether or not a mixed monarchy was the best form of government.[48] In 1591, Cuffe debated whether man was born to contemplation or political life, and whether or not the law must be superior to all magistrates.[49] By joining Essex's secretariat, Cuffe clearly believed that his own vocation was public service, rather than cloistered academic contemplation. His exposition of Lucan in 1601 endorsed the theory that magistrates might indeed have a duty to override positive laws in exceptional circumstances.

Unfortunately, the next significant evidence of his political thinking comes from his final oration, made on the scaffold. Typically with Cuffe, the textual evidence is controversial. Two different accounts of the secretary's execution speech survive; both versions, though, give a strong impression of aggressive reasoning, and confirm his Machiavellian understanding of the relationship of virtue and the state, and the weight he placed on asserting the superiority of the law of nature over positive law.

In both surviving versions Cuffe, in shocking contradiction of the conventions of scaffold etiquette, squabbles with the justice of his imminent execution. In the first account, he makes a logistical distinction between the common and natural laws that condemn him.[50] In the second, Cuffe uses the language of the *vita activa* to denounce the state that would destroy its virtuous inhabitants:

> Schollars and Martialists (thoughe learning & vallour should have the prehemynence yet) in England must dye like doggs and be hanged. To mislike this were but folly; to dispute of it, but tyme lost; to alter it impossible; but to endure it manlye, and to scorne it magnanimitye.[51]

This is a damning summation of the health of the Elizabethan polity, and of its political culture. The state that should be sustained by the valour and learning of its population has condemned to death its most virtuous citizens on fabricated pretexts. Rather than the puissant polity celebrated in Savile's 1592 oration to Elizabeth, this commonwealth is cankered and corrupt, a state in decline. How should we judge the princely ruler who has suppressed—or allowed the suppression—of learning and valour?

[48] '*Mistam rempublicam esse prestantissimam*', ibid., 234.
[49] '*Homo natus est ad contemplandum solum non ad vitam politicam; Lex omni magistratu superior esse debet*': ibid., 277.
[50] TNA, SP 12/279/25, f. 35^{r-v}; also see Bod, Rawlinson MS C 744, ff. 30^r–31^r.
[51] TNA, SP 12/279/26, f. 36^r; BL, Harleian MS 1327, f. 55^v; Richard Corbett used this text in his poetic account of Cuffe's death, 'Cuffe's speech at his Execution', J. A. W. Bennett and H. R. Trevor-Roper eds, *The poems of Richard Corbett* (Oxford: Clarendon Press, 1955), 94–5. I am indebted to Martin Ingram for this reference.

'HEROICAL VERTUES PROPERLY BELONGING, OR CHIEFLY BESEEMING THE PRINCES PERSON': ESSEX AND AGRICOLA

As the author of the 'A.B.' introduction to Savile's *Histories* explained,

> For Historie, since we are easlier taught by example then by the precept, what studie can profit us so much, as that which gives us patternes either to follow or to flye, of the best and worst men of all estates, cuntries, and times that ever were?[52]

But Tacitus, Essex's preferred historian, was also the most inscrutable of authors, famous for his supremely opaque attitude towards the constitutional change of Rome from republic to empire, and his refusal to comment on the *solutions* to rather than the *manifestations* of tyranny. European readers were far from unified in their response to Tacitus, discovering in his dark chronicles of Imperial Rome a spectrum of 'patternes' of politics to shun or emulate.

While Justus Lipsius's supremely influential interpretation filleted quotation from Tacitus to argue that princely or state power might be strengthened at the expense of mixed or participatory forms of government, other sixteenth-century readers did not find positive images of monarchy in Tacitus's brilliant psychological portraits of the tyrants Tiberius, Nero, or Domitian in the *Annals* and the *Histories*.[53] In England, Salmon has argued, readers approached Tacitus's dark depiction of the imperial court more usually through the lens of Senecan stoicism, exploring how an individual might balance self-preservation with personal integrity and accommodation to the government of a tyrant; the themes explored in Ben Jonson's censored play *Sejanus*.[54] These readings, it is observed, also tended to enforce a conservative approach to political obedience; perhaps the most frequently cited Tacitean quotation in contemporary political writing was the injunction of Marcus Eprius, that men living under tyranny must tolerate the prince, and pray to God for good rulers in the future.[55] But the more radical edge of Tacitism also prevailed in Elizabethan England, and among Essex's associates. Pérez, as we have

---

[52] 'A.B. Introduction' from Savile, *Ende of Nero*, sig. ¶3ʳ.

[53] Tuck, *Philosophy and government*.

[54] Salmon 'Seneca and Tacitus'; Lake, 'From *Leicester his Commonwealth* to *Sejanus his Fall*'.

[55] '...he praied & wished indeed for good Princes: but if it were otherwise, would tolerate such as they were': *Histories*, IV, in Savile, *Ende of Nero*, 174.

seen, harnessed his own Tacitean study of the tyranny of Philip II to a theory of contractual monarchy which legitimized deposition.[56]

Tacitus's influence on early modern historiography also enhanced a more general feature of contemporary political culture. 'Politic' histories modelled after Tacitus offered not a metaphysical or providential explanation for political change, but probed the secular psychological motivations of historical actors. Above all, Tacitus, as far as he possessed a theory of historical causation, described the passage of events overwhelmingly in moral languages, in terms of the individual and collective virtues and vices of men and women, which had broader implications for the health of the state. It was this particular outlook that shaped Essex's own political mentality.

Although the earl's own treatise is lost, Henry Savile's 1591 edition of the *Histories* and *Agricola* offers striking insights into the ways that Essex might have applied the lessons of Roman history. Savile's reading of and response to Tacitus can be excavated from materials supplementary to his edition. Most importantly, he prefaced his translation with his own original account of the death of the emperor Nero, *The Ende of Nero and the beginning of Galba*, no account of which by Tacitus survives.[57] Although this narrative was forged from other classical sources, David Womersley has brilliantly shown how Savile exploited the creative freedom from direct translation to emphasize particular political themes in his treatment of Nero's death.[58] The work is also supplemented with extensive notes through which Savile guides the reader's interpretation. Again, these commentaries are revelatory of Savile's own thinking: but they also portend with extraordinary accuracy the frameworks through which Essex would interpret court politics, especially his relationship with Elizabeth.

Tacitus's *Histories* had a particular relevance to Elizabethan concerns about the succession. The subject matter is AD 69, the 'Year of the Four Emperors', when Nero's suicide was followed by a wave of bloody civil wars contested over the imperial title; Savile's decision to translate this work, rather than the *Annals*, which were more popular and famous, is a striking one.[59] The author of the 'A.B.' introduction to Savile's translation invokes the reader to draw direct parallels between Rome and England: 'see the calamities that follow civill warres', and 'love and

---

[56] See Chapter 2.
[57] The extant text of the *Annales* breaks off in Book 16, two years before Nero's death in AD 68. The *Histories*, though written earlier, commences the following year; Savile's translation bridged the gap between the two.
[58] Womersley, 'Sir Henry Savile's Translation'.
[59] See Smuts, 'Court-centred historians', 27.

reverence thine owne wise, just and excellent Prince'.[60] This (ironic?) flattery of the queen, to whom the edition is dedicated, encourages particular reflection on anxieties that this wise and just prince exacerbates by failing to settle the succession, and on the related fear of civil war on English shores.

Despite its dedication to Elizabeth, Savile's translation was not intended as a handbook for princes to learn the darker arts of strong government. Indeed, his appreciation of Tacitus has much in common with that of Pérez, who insisted that the historian must disclose to readers the artificial uses of ceremonial and religion wielded by rulers to secure power over their subjects. Savile notes *arcana imperii* that would have had particular resonance for Elizabethan readers. When Galba describes a momentous 'secret of state'—'that a Prince might bee made elsewhere then at Rome'—Savile explains that he divulges a truth long concealed by emperors to serve their own interests: that legitimacy to rule is predominantly dependent on military force and acclamation rather than lineage or title. Subsequent to Galba's revelation, many emperors were made outside Rome.[61]

The edition is bookended with character studies of imperial subjects of outstanding virtue. In the *Ende of Nero*, Savile gives great weight to the role of Julius Vindex, an aristocrat from Gaul whose rebellion 'first stirred the stone, which rowling along, tumbled Nero out of his seat'.[62] *Agricola* is Tacitus's great tribute to the virtues of his father-in-law, a mighty general and governor of Britain. Structurally, then, Savile signals that the predominant experience of reading his edition from end to end would be to explore the searching questions that Tacitus raises about the extraordinarily sensitive relationship between the militaristic subject and the prince, the role of active virtue in a monarchical state.

In each case, the state in question is endangered by the government of a weak tyrant. In the final days of Nero's rule, Savile delineates the extreme fragility of order in a declining state: 'as in a bodie corrupt, & full of ill humours ... so in a state universally disliked, the first disorder dissolveth the whole'.[63] The tyranny of Nero, as Womersley has shown, is evinced in his fearfulness, his suspicion and effeminacy, rather than outrageous acts of cruelty. He is especially unmartial: when faced with rebellion, he responds with fear rather than ferocity, trusting, as Shakespeare's *Richard II* would do similarly, that his mere presence among the people will 'with silence and teares mooue them to compassion' and 'former obedience

---

[60] Savile, *Ende of Nero*, sig. ¶3[r–v].
[61] Tacitus, trans., Savile, *Histories*, I, 3; Savile, 'Annotations upon the first book of Tacitus', in *Ende of Nero*, 6.
[62] Savile, *Ende of Nero*, 6–7; Smuts, 'Court-centred Politics', 26.
[63] Savile, *Ende of Nero*, 1.

without much adoe'.[64] This dithering precipitates Nero's downfall: he is declared an 'enemie of the state' by the Senate, committing suicide before he can be taken prisoner.[65] In deliberate contrast Vindex shows the agency of a man possessed of Machiavellian *virtù*, 'more vertuous than fortunate', who excels in military ability and mental strength.[66] He grasps this *occasione* to renovate the state and restore Rome's freedom by aiming to replace the tyrant Nero with the commander Galba, who, he argues, will be a ruler of honour and virtue.[67]

Vindex acts specifically to restore freedom and civic virtue, which he sees as inseparably linked. He also addresses the grievances of the repressed nobility. In a blood-stirring speech Vindex mourns 'our broken state, and age voide of vertue, not bearing a free common wealth', and he galvanizes the Gallican nobility with militaristic rhetoric: 'let us (quoth he) sell him our lives in the fielde with honour, seeing wee cannot possesse them with safetie'.[68] It is also the nobility who gain most obviously from Nero's suicide: 'Nero beeing slaine, the people and gentlemen, but principallie the nobilitie, the *principall obiect of tyrannie*' [emphasis added] sacrifice to the gods, and wear bonnets 'as beeing newlie enfranchised'.[69] Nowhere in Savile's description of the rebellion of Vindex and Galba are we directed to disapprove of this act of resistance. Vindex kills himself after being taken by a surprise assault by German forces under Verginius Rufus, but Savile painstakingly defines the virtuous ends of his conflagration of rebellion, undertaken for the public good: 'not upon private dispaire to set in combustion the state, not to revenge disgrace or dishonour, not to establish his own soveraignety ... but to redeeme his country from tyranny and bondage'.[70] But there is a darker side to Vindex's success: the new emperor, Galba, will not become a strong, virtuous new prince, but yet another weak ruler, dominated by evil counsellors and deposed himself by Otho, who will prove even more capricious. A rebellion to renovate the state cannot be successful unless a new prince who is capable and virtuous will assume imperial power.

Savile's exploration of resistance through the character of Vindex cannot, of course, be projected onto Essex's actions in 1601. But here, the earl's self-proclaimed mentor described sympathetically the rising of an honourable noble subject against a weak, indecisive, and tyrannical ruler. And as agents that shaped *expectations* and the languages used to describe politics, texts had a powerful agency.

---

[64] Ibid., 8. [65] Ibid., 11. [66] Ibid., 10.
[67] Womersley, 'Sir Henry Savile's Translation'.
[68] Savile, *Ende of Nero*, 2. [69] Ibid., 11. [70] Ibid., 6.

Savile's analysis of his own translation of *Agricola* had an even more acutely charged relevance to the way that Essex would choose to interpret his own career and his relationship with the queen. Tacitus's Agricola embodies a more conventional picture of classical virtues. He is a great military commander, as well as a just and moderate statesman, and he is impeccably loyal; he is Tacitus's supreme *exemplum* of the success of virtuous action in the imperial age and under the government of corrupt rulers, his career proof 'that great men may be found even under bad Princes'.[71] But Agricola's virtues are also actively contrasted with Domitian's burgeoning tyranny. Tacitus strongly insinuates that Domitian has Agricola poisoned when the loyal hero returns to Rome. The implication is that the active exercise of virtue under this 'bad prince' was only possible as long as Agricola was outside the corrupt imperial court.

And it is this sensitivity of princes to virtue in their subjects that fascinates Savile. Calgacus, leader of the rebellious Britons whom Agricola defeats, states with bleak clarity: 'the manhood and fierce courage of the subject pleaseth not much the jelous Souerayne'.[72] The theme is explored further in Savile's own notes. A powerful, confident and virtuous prince, he argues, will recognize that the success of their government is dependent on the might of their greatest subjects:

> Vespasian & other great Princes, standing upon their owne might, & the strength of their vertues, could easily digest, that one should be said, for example to have *imperatoriam genesim* [the qualities of an emperor].[73]

Indeed, this is the ideal model of successful monarchical rule, the orderly functioning of the hierarchical polity. But overall, princes do not emulate Vespasian; instead, they are strongly inclined to distrust and fear their greatest subjects. The tyrant Domitian is 'umbrageous & fearefull' of Agricola.[74] As Savile has Titus Vinius explain: '*Even good Princes* are jelous of soveraine points, and that string being touched, have a quicke eare' (emphasis added).[75]

Savile's categorization of the qualities most likely to arouse the animosity of the 'jelous Soverayne' towards greater subjects fits precisely with Essex's understanding of his deteriorating relationship with Elizabeth in the later 1590s. He dwells at particular length on the dislike exhibited by princes towards subjects' military achievements. Again in his notes, Savile

---

[71] Tacitus, *Agricola,* in Savile, *Ende of Nero,* 264.   [72] Ibid., 256.
[73] Savile, 'Annotations upon the life of Agricola', 47 in *Ende of Nero*. Also noted by Blair Worden, 'Historians and Poets', in Kewes, *Uses of History,* 83.
[74] Savile, 'Annotations upon the life of Agricola', 47.
[75] Savile, *Ende of Nero,* 3,

explores the ways that the emperor Augustus, intent on eradicating the martial virtue of his subjects, refused to allow his generals to celebrate triumphs:

> ... to Augustus who of the old state left nothing standing but names, & hardly that, the pompe triumphall seemed a thing too full of majesty for any subject, & therefore seeking every way to cut the sinews of liberty and yet to retaine a shew of ancienty, hee cunningly converted the solemnity of a triumph into *Triumphalia insignia*; onely the Princes themselves, or their children ... solemnly triumphed.[76]

Savile raises the wider issue at stake: Augustus is not merely fearful of his greater subjects; he thinks that the recognition of martial virtue is a threat to monarchical power itself, and must be 'cunningly' abandoned. This would be a theme with particular resonance, of course, for Essex, who came to believe that Elizabeth was constantly ungrateful for his military exploits.

Libellous/commendatory poetry produced during and after Essex's political demise was similarly critical of Elizabeth's ingratitude. Indeed, Robert Pricket's eulogy for Essex, *Honors fame in triumph riding*, defines itself as a literary manifestation of the triumph that Essex had deserved— but had been denied—during his lifetime by his queen.[77]

Virtuous subjects in Tacitean Rome were also particularly vulnerable to the envy of evil courtiers, who preyed on princes' suspicions of their abilities. Again, Savile's notes on *Agricola* forensically analyse this characteristic feature of the politics of monarchical states, and in ways that would be directly applicable to Essex's situation. Although envious courtiers sometimes destroy their more virtuous rivals in the arena of the court itself

> in later times the contrary example hath bene more usuall in courts, by way of commendation to remove one from about the Prince and send him out of the way under pretence that he is the only fitte man for such and such a service.

This is a direct precedent of Essex's attitude to his Irish command.[78]

Even perceptions of Elizabeth's suspicion of Essex's 'popularity' were foretold by Savile, and defined as a mark of weak tyranny. Tacitus's

---

[76] Savile, 'Annotations upon the first booke of Tacitus', 25.

[77] 'From forth the dust, my lines desire to rayse/bright honours fame, in triumphs state to ride', Pricket, *Honors Fame*, sig. A4ʳ.

[78] Savile, 'Annotations upon the life of Agricola', 46–8.

Agricola has great popularity with ordinary Romans, but this is entirely innocent, a by-product of his brilliant achievements. The hero enters Rome at night to avoid being hailed by cheering crowds. In an especially long leading note Savile admits that of all qualities that attend virtuous conduct, popularity is the most dangerous for a subject: it 'worketh most danger, where the quality commended breedeth not onely love, but admiration also generally among the meane people'. The virtues that the Romans admire in Agricola are also strikingly those that would soon be ascribed to Essex: 'military renowne, magnanimity, patronage of justice against oppressions & wronges, magnificence, & other Heroical vertues properly belonging, or *chiefly beseeming the Princes person*' (emphasis added).[79]

Savile here acknowledges an almost insurmountable problem in the relationship between subjects and princes, which gives a dark shadow to the hyperbolic praise for Essex as a classical hero reborn. How is a ruler to respond to a subject who embodies princely virtues, especially when those virtues, notably ones associated with the masculine conduct of war, are lacking in a prince who is weak and fearful? And how is such a subject to react to a prince who significantly resents the exercise of virtue? As Bacon would explore in his own *Essays* in 1597, the ultimate question is implicitly posed: can the ideal of active virtue, the dominant creed of the Elizabethan counsellor or public citizen, really be sustained in a monarchy?[80]

Less than a month after Essex's execution, Abraham Colfe, an unfortunate scholar at Christ Church, made a speech in praise of the earl in which he unwittingly exhumed this conundrum. Colfe commended 'a Great Generall of the warres lately deade, whom he called *Veri Dux*', renowned for 'his embracing of learned men and warrioures . . . Hee was *pater patriae*.'[81] Languishing in Newgate prison, Colfe wrote to Cecil that he had 'thought to prayse the vertues of the Earle . . . & darkely to poynte at his death under the historie of Cicero'.[82] But if Colfe had studied the notes to Savile's *Histories*, he would have read that the title *pater patriae* itself was an honour 'usually annext to the Princes place'.[83] Francis Bacon's 1597 essay, 'Of Honour and Reputation', also defines *pater patriae* as the last degree of '*sovereign* honour', distinguished from the honours to which subjects could aspire.[84] Or, as James VI and I wrote

---

[79] Savile, 'Annotations upon the life of Agricola', 47.
[80] See Chapter 5, 191.
[81] TNA, SP 12/279/67I, f. 120ʳ, notes from Colfe's speech, 23 April 1601.
[82] TNA, SP 12/279/89, f. 167ʳ, 21 May 1601.
[83] Savile, 'Annotations upon the first booke of Tacitus', 15.
[84] Vickers, *Francis Bacon*, 87.

succinctly in the *Trew law of free monarchies*, 'the style of *pater patriae* was ever, and is commonly used to Kings'.[85]

In 1591 the young earl had barely begun his public career. But Tacitus gave Essex particular interpretive frameworks to explain the later failure of his ambitions, especially his perception of the injustice of Elizabeth's attitude towards the services that he had performed. Essex would certainly come to believe that Elizabeth failed to match the virtuous magnanimity of Vespasian '& other great Princes'. Instead, it appeared that she exhibited all the characteristics that the tyrant Domitian displayed towards Agricola: denying military honours, fearing his popularity, and being willingly manipulated by his envious enemies.[86]

COUNSEL AND THE PROBLEM OF TYRANNY

Abraham Colfe condemned the execution of the earl as the work of three great enemies, a Piso, a Catiline, and an Anthony.[87] Though his analogy pointed so obviously to Cecil, Ralegh, and Cobham, Colfe wrote desperately from prison to the secretary of his innocent intent: he had not meant to 'greive at the sentence of his condemnation, proposed by our most just and wise prince'.[88] As Essex had done, Colfe employed the crucial distinction between his attacks on Elizabeth's counsellors and the inviolable authority of Elizabeth. Here lies perhaps the most important aspect of the Essex circle's readings of Tacitus: the Roman historian deeply probed this triangular relationship of virtuous subjects, 'evil' ministers, and the prince, in a manner that severely challenged or undermined loyalist uses of the language of evil counsel.

The grotesque caricatures in Catholic anti-commonwealth polemic of Leicester and William Cecil as grasping Machiavels shared much in common with Tacitus's famous portrait of the archetypal evil favourite and counsellor Aelius Sejanus, the prefect of the praetorian guard, whose moral depravity mirrored his lust for power. Catholic discourse, though, conventionally presented Elizabeth as a passive and pathetic victim of the ambitions of her Protestant ministers.[89] Tacitus's Tiberius remains more powerful than his dreadful favourite; Sejanus is destroyed by the emperor for conspiring to usurp the imperial throne. Tiberius is a fearful tyrant,

---

[85] *The trew lawe of free monarchies* in Johann Sommerville ed., *King James VI and I: political writings* (Cambridge: Cambridge University Press, 1994), 76.
[86] Savile, 'Annotations upon the Life of Agricola', 47.
[87] TNA, SP 12/279/67, f. 120[r–v]; NA, SP 12/279/89, f. 167[r].
[88] Ibid. [89] Questier, 'Elizabeth and the Catholics', 76–82.

ever-watchful of threats to his power and reliant on flatterers and spies. Republican virtues are banished in Tiberian Rome. But Tiberius's reliance on evil favourites is, in Tacitus's portrait, a manifestation as well as a cause of tyranny, and generally representative of the ways that despotic rulers jealously protect their power. By inviting readers to ponder the dependence of the fearful prince on evil counsellors, Tacitus throws the spotlight back onto the moral character, psychology, and culpability of the monarch.

This emphasis is clearly understood by the author of the 'A. B.' introduction to Savile's *Histories*, who bluntly states 'In Galba thou maiest learne that a good Prince governed by evill ministers is as dangerous as if hee were evill himselfe'. Savile describes Galba similarly:

> To private men it is sufficient if themselves do no wrong: a Prince must provide that none doe it about him, or els he may looke when the first occasion is offered him to be charged with all the whole reckoning togither... though innocent of much harme which passed under his name, yet because he permitted them to commit it, whom he ought to have bridled... [Galba] lost reputation, and opened the way to his owne destruction.[90]

The logical extension of this position is that the government of a prince who rules through evil counsellors is itself a tyranny: certainly his subjects will believe this, and the monarch will suffer the consequences.

A scholar who believed that a reading of Tacitus could illuminate the contours of Essex's career and fate could not ignore the role and responsibility of the queen. Here, a set of Tacitean aphorisms reflecting on Essex's life is extremely revealing. A version in the British Library is attributed to Cuffe himself but the other copy is not, and the date of the text, written after Essex's rising, argues strongly against his authorship.[91] The aphorisms, though, were clearly written by a close partisan of Essex. All of the themes raised by Savile are directly applied to the earl's recent fate. Most importantly, the blame for Essex's death is laid squarely at the feet of Elizabeth.

According to Savile, Nero's Rome was 'a bodie corrupt, & full of ill humours'. This author applies the same familiar metaphor of the ailing body politic to the English state at this particular historical moment: 'politique bodyes are as often sicke, as naturall, and both of them subject to irregular diseases'; the following aphorisms 'were made for the Meridian

[90] Savile, *Ende of Nero*, ¶3ʳ 17.
[91] The quotations are from BL, Harleian MS 1327, ff. 58ʳ–60ᵛ. Tenison has published a slightly different version of the same text with an attribution to one Thomas Donne from a commonplace book in Gonville and Caius College, Cambridge: *Elizabethan England*, XI, 590–1.

of the court of England; And at such a tyme'.[92] The aphorisms themselves are far less focused on the agency of corrupt counsellors than on Elizabeth's arbitrary government. In particular, Essex had been the victim of Elizabeth's fluctuating emotions: the 'Will' of princes 'will change ether accidentally by jealousy or naturally, by the variety of the object'. Essex's failure to regain Elizabeth's favour after Ireland is explained in terms of her implacable resentment of his virtue: 'the settled jealousy of a prince is uncurable'.

Echoing Savile, the aphorisms also discuss the means that corrupt courtiers use to damage the careers of the virtuous, which all had obvious application to Essex, especially concerning his posting to Ireland: 'There are certain rules of state, like ridels: (1) As to hurt with praise; (2) To impoverish with offices of honor; (3) To banish with offices of imployment.'[93]

And inevitably Essex's fate is related to the problems faced by subjects who are popular with the commons: 'Generall love to a private person in a popular state is banishment, in a monarchy death'.[94]

The criticism of the queen, though, is also direct: 'Old princes are more daungerously offended then younger because feeling the declination of nature they apprehend the declination of Majesty'.[95] Although corrupt counsellors are features of a sick polity, it is *Elizabeth* who determines the climate of the political culture: when 'a pollitick prince warne his favouritt of his enemyes, himself is the greatest of them'.[96]

Finally, the aphorisms discuss active resistance to a tyrannical ruler. Aphorism 17 insists that '*except the Prince be odious* it is not pollicy of state to move against odious counsellors' (emphasis added). Resistance to evil counsellors, it is implied, is justified in circumstances of extreme necessity, but only if the prince is thoroughly corrupt. This is not a criticism of Essex's rising, though; the preceding aphorisms demonstrate clearly that the prince in mind is certainly sufficiently 'odious': jealous, suspicious, counselled by flatterers and guided by will, a weak tyrant. Aphorism 18 directly criticizes the rising of 8 February 1601: 'In stirring the bodye of state, it is madness to begin with the wealthyest'.[97] Recourse to the 'wealthiest' is rather obscure, but it appears to mean the trust that Essex placed in noblemen or possibly the London aldermen. It could also be a slip of the pen; in the second copy of these aphorisms it is an appeal to the commons that is specifically condemned: 'in stirring the body of the people, to begin with the weakest is infirmity of Counsel'.[98] The

---

[92] BL, Harleian MS 1327, f. 58^r. This formula is also typical of Tacitean aphorisms in contemporary Europe.
[93] Ibid., f. 58^v. [94] Ibid. [95] Ibid. [96] Ibid.
[97] Ibid. [98] Tenison, *Elizabethan England*, XI, 591.

important point is that in neither version does the author criticize the ends of the action: physical resistance itself is legitimized by criticism of the failure of the *method* of this 'stirring'. Savile's Vindex, who galvanized an aristocratic rebellion, provides a better example of how to 'move a state' successfully, when a prince has become 'odious' to her subjects.

WEAK MONARCHS, CIVIL WARS

The past spoke most notoriously to the present in the interest that Essex allegedly showed in the history of the depositions of English kings— especially, of course, Richard II. From the late 1570s onwards, Elizabethan statesmen and courtiers had drawn comparisons between the Ricardian and the Elizabethan courts. The most infamous parallel of all (if it is not a later invention) was allegedly by Elizabeth herself, in her rebuke to the keeper of the rolls, William Lambarde, on 4 August 1601: 'I am Richard II, know ye not that?' [99]

The evidence that connects Essex to these historical narratives is infuriatingly vague. That the earl and his followers exhibited a sensitive awareness of the history of the reigns of Richard II and Henry IV seems undeniable. On 6 July 1597, Ralegh wrote to Robert Cecil that the earl was 'wonderfull merry att the consait of Richard the 2'. Just a shared joke?[100]

Then, eighteen months after Ralegh's needling letter, Hayward's *The first parte of the life and raigne of King Henrie IIII* was published, with its dedication explosively praising Essex: 'you are great indeed, both in present judgment and in expectation of future time'.[101] The draft charge of treason drawn up against Essex in 1600 alleged that the earl had allowed the work to circulate before requesting Whitgift to remove the troublesome dedication, but no personal connection between Hayward and Essex

---

[99] See the transcript of the conversation from an eighteenth-century manuscript printed in Nichols, *Progresses*, III, 552. In 1578 Sir Francis Knollys had denounced favourites as 'Richard the Secondes men': Thomas Wright, *Queen Elizabeth and her times*, 2 vols (London: H. Colburn, 1838), II, 75. One of the best discussions of the parallels drawn between Richard II's reign and Elizabeth's is Lily B. Campbell, *Shakespeare's 'Histories': Mirrors of Elizabethan policy* (San Marino, CA: Huntington Library, 1947), 168–212.

[100] Latham and Youings, *Letters of Walter Ralegh*, 160. It is argued that parallels between Falstaff (originally Oldcastle) and the elder Lord Cobham in the *Henry IV* plays were a joke enjoyed by Essex's friends: E. A. J. Honnigmann, 'Sir John Oldcastle: Shakespeare's martyr', in John W. Mahon and Thomas A. Pendleton eds, *'Fanned and winnowed opinions': Shakespearean essays presented to Harold Jenkins* (London: Methuen, 1987), 127–8.

[101] Manning, Hayward's *Life and raigne*, 61.

was proven. It was John Wolfe, the most commercially savvy of London publishers, who suggested the dedication that ensured magnificent sales for the book, Wolfe who fruitlessly visited the court to try to procure Essex's approval for the first and second editions.[102]

The post-rising claims that Essex had avidly read his personal copy of Hayward's history, plotting 'how he might become another Hen[ry] the 4th', were rooted in the treason charge of the previous year.[103] The cryptic allegation in the charge that Essex was 'so often present at the playing thereof' has given rise to speculation that Hayward's prose had been dramatized, probably into the very play watched by the rebels on the eve of the rising.[104] Paul Hammer, though, has reasserted with confidence that the play watched by Essex and his followers was probably Shakespeare's *Richard II*, commissioned from Shakespeare's own company, the Lord Chamberlain's Men.[105] While certain attribution will remain impossible, the salient point is that in dedicating the *Life and raigne* to Essex, Hayward and Wolfe were counting on his known enjoyment of histories of Richard's reign, in the form of drama, poetry, or chronicle.

It seems likely that Essex and members of his inner circle had also read the 1595 version of Daniel's *The civile wars*. With its lavish commendatory verses in praise of Essex and Mountjoy, this poem of the baronial conflicts of the fourteenth and fifteenth centuries was an important source for Shakespeare's *Richard II*.[106] Daniel would show himself sympathetically

[102] The second edition was burned in early June by Whitgift and Bancroft; no copies survive other than an epistle to the reader by Hayward, denying parallels with the present: TNA, SP 12/275/28, ff. 45ʳ–46ʳ. A manuscript of Hayward's unpublished continuation of the history, the 'Second Part' is published in the modern edition; Manning, *Hayward's Life and raigne*, 177–258. For the textual history see Manning's excellent introduction to ibid., 17–34; Margaret Dowling, 'Sir John Hayward's troubles over his Life of Henry IV', *The Library*, 4th ser., 11 (1930–31), 212–24; Evelyn May Albright, 'Shakespeare's *Richard II*, Hayward's History of Henry IV, and the Essex Conspiracy', *PMLA*, 46 (1931), 694–719; eadem, 'Reply to Ray Heffner' s Shakespeare, Hayward, and Essex again', *PMLA* 47 (1932), 899–901; Ray Heffner, 'Shakespeare, Hayward, and Essex', *PMLA* 45 (1930), 754–80; idem, 'Shakespeare, Hayward, and Essex Again', *PMLA* 47 (1932), 898–99; Dutton, 'Buggeswords'; Clegg, *Press censorship*, 203–8.
[103] TNA 12/278/63, ff. 108ʳ–110ᵛ. See Chapter 5, 212–15.
[104] TNA, SP 12/275/33, ff. 55ʳ–57ʳ.
[105] Hammer ('Shakespeare's *Richard II*') and Worden ('Which play was performed') are adding to the debate between Albright and Heffner cited above. Also see Leeds Barroll, 'A New History for Shakespeare and His Time', *Shakespeare Quarterly*, 39 (1988), 441–64.
[106] The modern edition of this much revised poem is L. Michel ed., *'The civil wars' by Samuel Daniel* (1958), which reproduces the 1609 text. I am using the 1595 edition, which was reprinted in 1599 in *The poeticall essays of Sam. Danyel*, with an additional fifth book; the commendatory verses to Essex were removed from the 1601 edition in *The works of Samuel Daniel newly augmented*. For Daniel and literary history see especially F.J. Levy, 'Hayward, Daniel, and the Beginning of Politic History in England', *HLQ*, 50 (1987), 1–34. Excellent recent studies of *The civile wars* are Gillian Wright, 'Samuel

engaged with Essex's fall in his censored play *The tragedy of Philotas* (1600–4/5), and in 1595, when the first version of *The civile wars* was published, his second major patron was that other literary friend of Essex, Fulke Greville.[107] Others close to Essex also showed a keen interest in the purposeful reading of England's post-conquest history. In the early 1580s, Anthony Bacon compiled a long collection of notes on English kings from William I to Henry IV.[108] Some of the most complicated arguments about the authority of subjects and monarchs in *The state of Christendom* are derived from a comparative reading of English chronicles alongside the histories of other European states.[109]

Most importantly, the wider literary culture shaped the impulse of Elizabethans to explain contemporary politics through the lens of the past few centuries of England's history, as well as that of classical Rome. The 1590s were famously the heyday of the chronicle play and historical verse. Rivalling Daniel as a poet of civil wars was Michael Drayton: from the reign of Edward II alone, he found material for the historical poems *Peirs Gaveston Earle of Cornwall. His life, death, and fortune* (1594), and the *Mortimeriados. The lamentable ciuell warres of Edward the second and the barrons* (1596) (revised in 1603 as *The Barrons wars in the raigne of Edward the Second*).[110] A major cause of anxiety about Hayward's *Life and raigne* was its sheer popularity: as Wolfe acknowledged, 'never anye book was better sould'.[111]

The writing of English history added deeper meaning to the same ideological preoccupations that Essex's associates exhibited in their study of classical texts. The histories of the disastrous government and depositions of Edward II, Richard II, and Henry VI, spanned a sad chronicle of

---

Daniel's use of sources in *The Civil Wars*', *Studies in Philology*, 101/1 (2004), 233–42; eadem, 'What Daniel Really Did with the *Pharsalia*: *The Civil Wars*, Lucan and King James', *Review of English Studies*, 55/219 (2004), 210–32; eadem, 'The Politics of Revision in Samuel Daniel's *The Civil Wars*', *English Literary Renaissance*, 38/3 (2008), 461–82.

[107] Gazzard, 'Graue presentments of antiquity'. Daniel's poem *Musophilus* (1599) was published with the encouragement of Greville, its dedicatee, who also sought for him the reversion of a parsonage in 1595: John Pitcher, 'Daniel, Samuel. 1562/3–1619', *ODNB*.

[108] University of Edinburgh Library, Laing MS Div. III/193, ff. 3ʳ–105ᵛ.

[109] Gajda, '*State of Christendom*'; below, 252–3.

[110] A second edition of *Peirs Gaveston* was printed in 1595 as *The legend of Piers Gaveston*, which was reprinted in 1596 with *The tragicall legend of Robert, Duke of Normandy*...There were two editions of the *Mortimeriados* in 1596. Drayton's highly popular *England's Heroicall Epistles* (1597), imaginary verse letters by famous historical characters, also contained an exchange between Edward II's queen, Isabel, and her lover, Mortimer, as well as a similar exchange between Richard II and his wife, queen Isabel. This went through editions in 1598, 1599, 1600, and 1602, and was printed with the revised *Barrons Wars* in 1603.

[111] TNA, SP 12/275/28, f. 45ʳ.

civil wars, 'tumultuous broyles/And bloudy factions of a mighty land'.[112] The interest of late sixteenth-century writers in the late medieval past was once assumed to reflect complacent providentialism, of satisfaction with the dynasty of Henry VII.[113] Many scholars now argue the reverse: while writers strived to reconcile metaphysical frameworks with a profound interest in the human causes of historical events, many exhibited deep anxieties that these turbulent troubled times could reoccur.[114] Samuel Daniel's narrator argues that his poetic history has a vital *didactic* lesson for readers: 'that we maie with better profit knowe:/Tell how the world fell into this disease'.[115]

That preoccupation with the corruption of martial virtue in declining states, so resonant in Essexian readings of Roman historians, was also strongly represented in new literary renderings of English history. The reigns of Edward II, Richard II, and Henry VI followed the kingship of England's most successful warrior kings: Edward I, Edward III, and Henry V all expanded the boundaries of the crown's dominions, while their deposed successors ruled over the swift contraction of England's military dominance in the British Isles and on the continent.

This convenient demonstration of these cycles of virtue and corruption was grimly charted by writers, who depicted military decline as a major cause of domestic political crisis. Drayton's Gaveston remembers that Edward I had fostered a court culture that embodied the chivalric ideal praised by Essex, Cuffe, and Savile. Edward I's chief 'counsaylors' of the realm were learned *and* soldierly: 'Schollers his captaines, captaines *Senators*'.[116] Gaveston's ghost freely admits that he was the antithesis of the virtuous martial scholarly counsellor; he was an effete power-hungry upstart, who snared Edward II with physical beauty. In *Richard II*, Shakespeare's Gaunt implores his nephew to emulate his glorious ancestors, 'Renownèd for their deeds as far from home/For Christian service and true chivalry'.[117] Hayward's Ricardian England borrows from Tacitus's account of the corruption of republican virtue during Augustus's

---

[112] Daniel, *Civile wars*, 1.1.1–2.

[113] The classic statement is F. M. W. Tillyard, *The Elizabethan world picture: a study of idea and order in the age of Shakespeare, Donne and Milton* (London: Chatto and Windus, 1943).

[114] See Andrew Hadfield, 'The political significance of the First Tetralogy', in McDiarmid, *Monarchical Republic*, 149–64, especially at 149–50; R. Malcolm Smuts, *Culture and power in England, 1585–1686* (Basingstoke: Macmillan, 1999), 70–6.

[115] Daniel, *Civile wars*, 1.7.4–5.

[116] Drayton, *Peirs Gaveston*, B2r.

[117] Shakespeare, *Richard II*, 2.1.53–4, ed. Andrew Gurr (Cambridge: Cambridge University Press, 1984). The martial achievements of Richard's ancestors and the theme of crusading permeate the play.

principate: king and subjects 'gave over themselves to delicacie and ease, whereby cowardise crepte in, and shipwracke was made both of manhood and glorie'.[118] Echoing Sallust, Tacitus, and Lucan, Daniel also contrasts the dark nature of his own 'sadder Subject' with England's more glorious past. His narrator blames 'peace with Fraunce' enjoyed under Richard II for bottling up the baser energies of his subjects, which has allowed their 'ouergrowing humours' to fester and multiply. In contrast, Henry V reforms the state through the revival of English militarism; his French wars purge the realm of 'languishing luxuriousnes' that has allowed the 'canker-eating mischiefes of the state' to flourish.[119]

Just as Tacitus's historical narratives revolve round psychological character studies, the histories of Daniel and Hayward, as well as the less self-consciously didactic rendering of 'barons' wars' by Drayton, Marlowe, Shakespeare and in other significant chronicle plays, such as the anonymous *Thomas of Woodstock* (1591–5), also explore historical causation in terms of the moral qualities of rulers and political actors.[120] And these plays and poems exhibit a particular fascination with weak tyrants: Richard II and Edward II are portrayed as rulers governed by passion rather than reason, placing their private desires over the needs of the commonwealth, abrogating the natural as well as the customary law.

When Daniel's young Richard assumes the reins of government from his uncles, he is 'transported in this sensuall course'; the country grieves that it is ruled by a 'wanton young effeminate'.[121] In the anonymous *Thomas of Woodstock*, Richard is frequently described as 'wanton', even by his own minions, his obsession with gorgeous clothing contrasted with the masculine plain-dressing of his virtuous uncle, Gloucester. Hayward is at pains to stress that Richard, 'naturally of no cruell disposition', was guided by 'intemperate affection'. Utterly 'plunged in pleasure and sloath', Richard is drawn to 'violent and indirect courses', while his feminine fear for his own life prevents him from taking positive military action to thwart Bullingbrook's rebellion: 'the kings eares were stopped against all impression of manhood'. Like Savile's Nero and Greville's Soliman, the cruelties of Hayward's Richard are driven by 'vaine and needlesse fear'.[122]

Even in letters intended to flatter Elizabeth and to restore her good opinion of him, Essex usually described Elizabeth's political methods in

[118] Manning, *Hayward's Life and raigne*, 106.
[119] Daniel, *Civile wars*, 1.83.1–8, 1.5.6., 4.18.3–4, 4.20.1–2.
[120] Anon., *Thomas of Woodstock, or, Richard the Second, part one*, ed. Peter Corbin and Douglas Sedge (Manchester: Manchester University Press, 2002).
[121] Daniel, *Civile wars*, 1.35.8, 1.60.1, 1.70.4.
[122] Manning, *Hayward's Life and raigne*, 72–4, 106, 129. Bushnell, *Tragedies of tyrants*, 5–38.

terms of the operation of the queen's *will*. In the famous letter to Egerton, Essex linked the queen's 'passionate' indignation, her 'violente' emotional treatment of him, with her arbitrariness and the doctrine of 'absolute-ness'.[123] Curtis Perry persuasively argues that from the late 1580s, literary representations of the moral failings of England's historical rulers exhib-ited a profound unease about the autonomous agency of the royal will that was associated with concerns about the monarch's prerogative powers.[124] Certainly, Ricardian England was highly relevant to Elizabethans who were sensitive, as had been Essex in his response to Egerton, to the increasingly strident articulation of absolutist ideas from the court and clerical establishment.

In the anonymous *Thomas of Woodstock*, Richard assumes his majori-ty intending to take vengeance on the nobles who would restrict the exercise of his will and his *imperial* power. 'Thus like an emperor shall King Richard reign...Let no man enter to disturb our pleasures!'[125] Hayward makes the starkest correlation between absolute power, the exercise of the royal will, and the ruler's moral failings. As Richard's final epigraph, Hayward warns: 'thus doe these and the like accidents dayly happen to such princes as will be absolute in power, resolute in will, and dissolute in life'.[126]

The exercise of royal will, guided by affection rather than reason, en-genders the most distinctive feature of accounts of the misgovernment of both Edward II and Richard II: their reliance on evil counsel, and their propensity to listen to the poisonous advice of flatterers at the expense of advisers of virtue, or of ancient noble lineage. At roughly the same time that Burghley was pilloried by Richard Verstegan as 'farr more noysome and pernitious to the realme, than ever were the *Spencers*, [or] *Peeter of Gaver-stone*', the stock character of the evil favourite emerged in Elizabethan drama, in Robert Greene's *The Scottish history of James the fourth* (*c*.1590) and Marlowe's *Edward II* (*c*.1591).[127] The theme of counsel permeated writing about the reign of Richard II. Daniel suggests that Richard's youthful reliance on evil counsellors was an almost inevitable response to being dominated by his uncles: 'Minions too great, argue a king too weake'.[128]

The theme is less interesting to Shakespeare. Certainly, Richard's England is overgrown with 'noisome weeds which without profit suck/

---

[123] Chapter 4, 159–62.
[124] Perry, *Literature and favouritism*, at 187, and *passim*.
[125] Anon., *Woodstock*, 3.1.1–5.
[126] Manning, *Hayward's Life and raigne*, 107–8, 167.
[127] Verstegan, *Declaration*, 68; Blair Worden, 'Favourites on the English stage', in Elliott and Brockliss, *World of the favourite*, 159–83.
[128] Daniel, *Civile wars*, 1.43.5–8.

The soil's fertility from wholesome flowers'.[129] Compared, though, with the treatments of other writers, we do not see Bushy, Bagot, and Greene exercise poisonous influence over Richard's decision making: the king's seminal action, the confiscation of the Lancastrian estates on Gaunt's death, is a decision sprung from his own uncounselled *will*, making Shakespeare's Richard directly and singularly culpable for the acts that precipitate Bullingbrook's rebellion. (Richard does, of course, *reject* the virtuous and prophetic counsel of Gaunt on his deathbed.)

Unsurprisingly Hayward, who fashioned so much of his prose history from Tacitean quotation, drew on the most probing critique of the reciprocity of the relationship between tyrannical monarchs and evil counsellors. The maxim from the 'A. B.' introduction to Savile's *Histories* is recycled *twice* as his own aphorism: 'it is oftentimes as daungerous to a prince to have evil and odious adherents as to bee evill and odious himselfe'; 'it falleth out to be as dangerous to a prince to have hurtfull and hatefull officers in place and services of weight, as to be hurtfull and hatefull himselfe'.[130]

Inevitably, the theme of the repression of virtue by jealous monarchs also features prominently in representations of Richard II's reign. In the anonymous *Woodstock*, Richard's dislike of his uncle, the duke of Glou-cester, is coupled with a suspicion of his homely and well beloved virtues; ultimately Richard is complicit, if not directly responsible, for the events that lead to his uncle's death. Hayward, as we might expect, borrows tellingly from Savile's Tacitus to dwell on the theme of jealousy using exactly the same tropes that seemed precisely applicable to Essex. At Richard's court, military conduct is not honoured, especially when 'a cunning kinde of enemies, commenders' *persuade* the king 'that to be a discreet and valiant commander in the fielde was a virtue peculiar to a prince'. Once Bullingbrook has been exiled by Richard, the archbishop of Canterbury warns him of royal envy: 'even good princes are nice in points of sovereignty, & beare a nimble eare to the touch of that string'. Bullingbrook's popularity, of course, is also a crucial cause of the king's 'eternall jelousy': the 'generall favour & love the people beareth you hath bereaved you of your liberty'.[131]

The sensitive parallels that contemporaries clearly drew between Richard's reign and that of Elizabeth touched Essex's political pulse points in other key ways. In the hands of Peter Wentworth, Richard II's deposition was invoked as a direct threat to Elizabeth of the most appalling outcome

[129]   Shakespeare, *Richard II*, 3.4.38–9.
[130]   Manning, *Hayward's Life and raigne*, 70, 121.
[131]   Ibid., 107, 116.

of her refusal to settle the succession: Richard's subjects showed that 'they liked rather to have an usurper to raigne over them, that would preserve the crowne and them, then a rightful king, that would peril the crowne and state'.[132] Unsurprisingly, succession crisis is a persistent leitmotif in the literary accounts of Shakespeare, Daniel, and Hayward. In a deliberate distortion, Shakespeare ages Richard II's child-queen Isabel into fertile womanhood to emphasize the couple's barrenness. Isabel's progeny is misery: 'Bullingbroke my sorrow's dismal heir'.[133] The opening paragraphs of Hayward's *Life and raigne* contain an aphorism hardly less blunt than Wentworth's harangue: 'For neither armies nor strong holdes are so great defences to a prince as the multitude of children'.[134]

REMEDIES FOR MISGOVERNMENT?

If, as Essex and his associates argued, the past afforded conceptual frameworks through which the present could be interpreted, literary accounts of England's medieval history must have sharpened their sensitivity to the misgovernment of Elizabeth, increasing their inclination to associate the expression of theories of absolute and divine-right monarchy with fearful monarchs, goaded by ambitious counsellors. Histories quickened their impulse to imagine the likely failure of the ideals of the *vita activa* in a personal monarchy governed by a weak, effeminate (in this case female) ruler, more inclined to peace than war, and suspicious of the virtue and popularity of greater subjects. In short, these frameworks, as with the histories of Tacitus, shaped and deepened that distinctive tendency of Essex and his circle to define the earl's personal misfortunes as representative of the wider corruption and decline of the state, and the government of the queen as a weak tyranny. The historical past foretold the likelihood that these misfortunes would be linked to an imminent succession crisis and to civil war, if evil counsellors could control the translation of the crown to Spain.

But what could the student of history learn about the reform of a declining commonwealth? Should subjects accept misgovernment as God's providential scourge for the sinful nation? Or could the patterns of history teach its students to act as well as to know, offering not only an image of the 'abuses being now in this Realme that were in Richard the

---

[132] Wentworth, *Pithie exhortation*, 79–80.
[133] Shakespeare, *Richard II*, 2.2.62–6.
[134] Manning, *Hayward's Life and raigne*, 67.

second his daies' but also the 'like course [that] might be taken that then was for the redressinge of them'?[135]

Once again, the parameters of this debate about legitimate action were sensationally energized by Parsons. The fulcrum of the theory of the *Conference*—that the English monarchy is contractual and elective, and that English subjects, through representative institutions, can depose a tyrannical monarch—is illustrated by comparative material drawn from the depositions of Richard II, Edward II, and Henry VI.[136] In Parsons's argument, Henry of Lancaster returned from exile with a small band of men. He took the reins of government, and effected the entirely lawful parliamentary deposition of Richard II. Parsons thus demonstrates the legitimacy of the House of Lancaster, from which the hereditary title of the infanta derived.[137]

In fact, as would be argued in post-rising propaganda, there are striking similarities with Essex's planned coup. As Essex aimed to do, Bullingbrook came 'wholy (in a manner) un-armed', at the head of only 'three-score men in al'; by meeting with such great 'concourse of al people' he was able to effect his rising 'without any battaile or bloodshed at al'. To James VI, Essex had insisted that he was 'summoned of all sides' to remedy the grievances of the state; Parsons's Bullingbrook returned at the invitation of 'the more and better part of al the realme'.[138] Small wonder that William Barlow would allege in his funeral sermon that Essex had imbibed the theory of legitimate rebellion from the *Conference*. Essex might have been sensitized to the successful means of Bullingbrook's actions, even while deploring Parsons's arguments for the infanta's title.[139]

Paul Hammer argues that the opposite interpretation was made by Essex and his followers. Bullingbrook's deposition of Richard II was important to Essex and his supporters as a warning *against* the perils of outright rebellion.[140] According to this argument, Hayward's *Life and raigne* and the dramatic performance watched by Essex's supporters on the eve of the rebellion were traditional mirrors-for-princes, reflecting the evils of misgovernment, but placing close limits on the legitimate actions that subjects might take to remedy abuse of power.

---

[135] TNA, SP 12/278/63, f. 108ᵛ.

[136] Doleman [i.e. Parsons], *Conference*, Book I, III, 58–63.

[137] It has been argued that Parsons's *Conference* caused the censorship of Act 4, Scene 1, the so-called 'Parliament scene', from the printed Elizabethan editions of *Richard II*. It is just as likely, though, that the scene was only written after 1601: Bate, *Soul of the Age*, 257.

[138] Doleman [i.e. Parsons], *Conference*, Book II, IV, 66–7.

[139] Barlow, *Sermon preached at Paules Crosse*, sig. B5ᵛ.

[140] Hammer, 'Shakespeare's *Richard II*'; also see Worden, 'Which play was performed?'.

Essentially this restates an older historicist reading of Shakespeare's *Richard II* as a drama enshrining sixteenth-century homily while reflecting contemporary fears of a succession crisis. If Richard is a tyrant, then Henry's own government, effected through Machiavellian *virtù*, has no moral legitimacy. By the end of the play, Henry is complicit in Richard's murder: the tensions that presage revolt against his own government are already present in the foiled plot of Aumerle. Providentialist readings of *Richard II* that assume the ideological coherence of the second tertralogy are resurrected: the appalling difficulties that threaten the king's grasp on power in *Henry IV* parts 1 and 2 derive from the stain of this illegal usurpation of the crown.

This is certainly the position adopted by Daniel. Wise heads, predicting catastrophe, murmur the famous injunction to obedience from Tacitus's *Histories*: aggrieved subjects must 'admire times past, follow the present will/Wish for good Princes, but t'indure the ill'.[141] Scholars have also recently argued that the seditious theory that the government found in the *Life and raigne* was a fundamental misinterpretation of Hayward's entirely orthodox warning about the perils of kingship exercised by unlawful usurpers.[142] Lisa Richardson's brilliant analysis of Hayward's borrowings from Tacitus shows that the description of Henry's character before his rebellion is literally taken from the portrait of Agricola as translated by Savile. After Henry's assumption of the crown, his character is crafted with phrases hewn from Tacitus's portrait of Domitian. Virtuous as a subject, Henry is a fearful, jealous, and tyrannical prince. Hayward's unpublished continuation of the history, 'The Second Year of King Henrie the Fourth', is even less ambiguous than Shakespeare that the political turbulence of the fifteenth century resulted from Henry's unrighteous act: the kingdom 'being gotten with bloud, it was held with horror'.[143]

This thoroughly orthodox interpretation of these representations of Richard II and Henry IV's reigns as mirrors-for-princes and sedatives-for-vexed-subjects entirely refutes, of course, the use made of the same historical episode by Parsons. Once again, this was not coincidental. Peter Lake's forthcoming work will demonstrate that Shakespeare's *Richard II*

---

[141] Daniel, *Civile wars*, 1.71–3.

[142] Richardson, 'Sir John Hayward', I, 46–7, 68; also see Manning's introduction to *Hayward's Life and raigne*, 40–3; Rebecca Lemon, 'The faulty verdict in "The Crown v. John Hayward"', *Studies in English Literature, 1500–1900*, 41/1 (2001), 109–32 and eadem, *Treason by words: literature, law, and rebellion in Shakespeare's England* (Ithaca, NY and London: Cornell University Press, 2006), 23–51; Clegg, *Press Censorship*, 201–4 and *passim*; Dutton, 'Buggeswords'.

[143] Manning, *Hayward's Life and raigne*, 177.

refutes, possibly deliberately, Parsons's account of Richard II's deposition.[144]

We also know that Hayward was engaged with the pernicious doctrines of the *Conference*, because he wrote a direct refutation, *An answer to the first part of a certaine conference concerning succession* (1603). Published just after the accession of James to the throne, Hayward may have composed the treatise contiguously with the *Life and raigne*; certainly his dedication of the *Answer* describes *both* works as written in defence of the principle of hereditary monarchy, and in defence of James's title. Both books condemn the central theory of Parsons's *Conference*, that the deposition of Richard II was lawful:

> I here present unto your majesty this defence ... wherein is maintained that the people have no lawfull power, to remove the one, or repell the other: In which two points I have also heretofore declared my opinion, by publishing the tragicall events which ensued the deposition of King *Richard*, and usurpation of King *Henrie* the Fourth.[145]

In the *Life and raigne*, Hayward fleshes out the fundamentals of this theoretical debate about obedience and resistance in arguments pro- and contra- the legitimacy of rebellion in speeches made by Thomas Arundel, archbishop of Canterbury, and Thomas Merks, bishop of Carlisle (the latter performing the same role in Shakespeare's play). In his entreaty to Henry to restore the freedom of the English, Canterbury articulates a doctrine of resistance similar to that found in the *Conference*: kings of Denmark, Sweden, and the Holy Roman Empire have been deposed by their subjects; while in England 'since the victorie of the Normaines, the lords endeavoured to expel King Henry the third', and succeeded in deposing Edward II, examples 'enough to cleare this action of rarenesse in other countries, & noveltie in our'.[146]

This is not the most convincing justification. In Hayward's hands, Carlisle's blistering denunciation of rebellion is far more powerful, as he hurls biblical injunction and proofs from the law of nature to thunder home 'the generall precept ... not onely our actions, but our speeches also, & our very thoughtes are strictly charged with duety and obedience unto princes, whether they be good or evill'. Carlisle also employs arguments common to English theories of non-resistance, that contrasted mixed states such as Holy Roman Empire or Poland with an 'absolute' monarchy such as

---

[144] I am very grateful to Professor Lake for sharing his work with me. A similar argument is tentatively advanced in Campbell, *Shakespeare's* 'Histories', 173–211.

[145] Hayward, *Answer to the first part of a certaine conference*, sig. A3[r–v], K[v].

[146] Hayward, *Life and raigne*, 116.

England, where no subject whatsoever can 'hazard [a prince] his power, whether by judgement, or els by force', and where 'neyther one nor all magistrates have any authority over the prince from whome all authority is derived'. Carlisle's England is not Parsons's elective monarchy: this passage borrows directly from Bodin's distinction between elective and hereditary states from the *Six books of the commonwealth* (2.5).[147] Nor is this a limited monarchy: resistance cannot be hazarded by 'judgment' or 'force', while the notion that all authority derives from the monarch encapsulates Bodin's famous theory of unlimited sovereignty. Importantly, even our *thoughts* must be always obedient to the monarch, good or evil. Thus the Lancastrian title is rendered an unlawful usurpation; Parsons's claims for the superior claim of the infanta are similarly redundant.[148]

This reading offers a more plausible interpretation of the function of the troublesome dedication of the *Life and raigne* to Essex, which, as has often been noted, is couched in a language practically identical to that of the dedication of the *Conference*. The dedicatory epistle to Hayward's history imagines that the virtues of the 'most illustrious Earl... Should it shine on our Henry's forehead, he would more happily and more safely go forth among the people'.[149] Essex, here defined as a more virtuous type of nobleman than Henry, is designated as the recipient of a history that contains a covert endorsement of James's title, through a repudiation of Lancastrian succession. Wolfe and/or Hayward may have been convinced, therefore, that Essex would look favourably on the dedication of the *Life and raigne* because it was a work that could counter his association with the *Conference*. If Essex did make this connection, it would explain his interest in the history, but also his decision to have the epistle removed, to distance himself from the continuation of a debate about the succession conducted in the all-too-public medium of print.

If Hayward's history was a type of off-shoot of the mirrors-for-princes genre, it was intended for an audience of subjects. *Reading* about contrasting theories of government as propounded in his book, or seeing them enacted on the stage, would have thrust debate about the difference between elective and hereditary succession and limited and absolute monarchy, as well as the characteristics of tyranny, prominently into the reader/audience's mind. Certainly Coke, Popham, and the queen

---

[147] cf. Jean Bodin, Richard Knolles trans., *The six bookes of a common-weale* (1606), Book II, Cap. 5.
[148] Hayward, *Life and raigne*, 142–9.   [149] Ibid., 61, n. 1.

interpreted the *Life and raigne* as a seditious text.[150] Ironically, the doctrine of passive obedience presented in all of these histories is set within gratuitous explorations of the transformation of absolute government into tyranny, with prophetic warnings about the dangers of weak kings, and the bleak assumption that royal courts are fetid, dangerous environments, where virtue will struggle to thrive.

And our concern must lie still with Essex and his followers'*interpretation* of the deposition of Richard II in the context of the earl's deepening crisis. As we have seen, Francis Bacon could plausibly declare after the rising that Essex had followed the 'beaten path of traitors'. Like Bullingbrook, Essex initially proclaimed his sole ends to be political reformation and the purgation of the realm of toxic counsellors. Like Bullingbrook, Essex attempted a bloodless coup, led by a small band of nobles sworn by oaths, capitalizing on his popularity in London. Above all, Essex's rhetoric of loyalism aped that of Bullingbrook precisely: Daniel's Bullingbrook defends his actions: 'Dear Country ô I have not hither brought/These Armes to spoile but for thy liberties: . . . I am thy Champion and I seeke my right,/Provokt I am to this by others spight'.[151] Such a justification was to be found on the lips of Essex and Southampton on 8 February 1601.

Hammer argues that Essex and his circle did indeed connect the blinkered misgovernment of Richard and Elizabeth, but in the face of these portentous parallels Essex sought to avoid the sinful path taken by Bullingbrook that resulted in the enforced abdication or deposition of the king. Essex did not conceptualize his rising (planned or enacted) as an act of resistance: any action taken meant to restore the state and the queen's role within it, as Bullingbrook should have done—and initially intended to do—in 1399.[152]

Hammer also argues that it is the treatise *The state of Christendom* which underpins the ideological justifications of Essex's rising.[153] In a long meditation on the ways that the tyranny of rulers might be restrained, the author/s invoke precedent for action through a paralleled reading of histories; although England is defined as an 'absolute' monarchy, in the extreme instances of misgovernment the 'Peers and Nobility' might *force* the ruler to call parliament, where reform of the polity will follow. Baronial restraints were placed upon Henry III after the battle of Lewes, which decreed that 'by the whole twelve both the Court and the Realm should be governed'; secular and spiritual peers made 'Ordinances for the

---

[150] See Chapter 5, 212–15.   [151] Daniel, *Civile wars*, 1.91.3–4, 7–8.
[152] Hammer, 'Shakespeare's *Richard II*'; also see Chapter 1, 50–2.
[153] Hammer, 'Shakespeare's *Richard II*', 12–13.

State and Government of the Realm' in the reign of Edward II. Parliaments can also be used to bring princes to account for their actions:

> Thus it appeareth that if princes offend, they may be challenged according to their nature and the quality of their offences... [in the] high court of Parliament, from whence all or most Laws have their beginning, their foundation, their strength.[154]

Here is a sensible framework reflecting Essex and his followers' intentions immediately prior to the rising itself: as they insisted, their sole aims were to purge the realm of counsellors and procure a formal declaration of the succession in parliament. Fundamentally Essex would have sought a constitutional remedy, albeit one precipitated by his own rights as a virtuous aristocrat, rather than conciliar initiative. In literary texts a sympathetic model of this course is found in the anonymous *Woodstock*. When the Duke of Lancaster exhorts his brothers to 'Take open arms' Gloucester restrains the choleric nobles, channelling his brother's grievances into a pacific course of action: 'We presently will call a parliament' where the deeds of Richard's minions will be examined by 'fair means'.[155]

But Gloucester's remedy fails miserably. Richard's hatred of his uncles is sealed, and his inclination for tyranny is actually increased, as he strives to cast off these attempts to shackle his authority. Throughout the sixteenth century, the monarchy crushed uprisings of subjects as rebellions, despite their participants' protestations of loyalty. Essex may not have aimed to usurp the throne, but his plans to compel Elizabeth to settle the succession and to be an instrument for political reformation was a pattern of aristocratic interventionism at odds with prevailing definitions of legitimate behaviour within the English monarchy. A peer's public intervention, as defined in *The state of Christendom*, encroached on a prince's prerogative powers. Even if the queen ostensibly consented to call a parliament, this would have been an action inevitably forced by the earl's physical hold of Elizabeth's body and court.[156]

This very concept of a subject's intervention was severely and searchingly critiqued in the historical discourse of the 1590s, along with the doctrine of absolute obedience propounded by the regime. Parsons aside, literary accounts of the rebellion of Bullingbrook were used to undermine the very notion of a loyalist rising, by demonstrating that *any form of autonomous action*—even if undertaken with limited or virtuous intentions—inevitably, unstoppably, set in motion the most radical of events.

---

[154] *State of Christendom*, 207.
[155] Anon., *Woodstock*, 1.3.247–68.
[156] See Chapter 1, 52–4.

Samuel Daniel shows most sympathy towards Bullingbrook's initial motivations. He presents as sincere his oath 'In th'eie of heaven' that he initially hopes only to act 'to'reforme th'abused kingdome here', and claim his birthright: 'And this was all, thou would'st attempt no more'.[157] In a famous conceit modelled on Lucan, Bullingbrook is warned in a dream by the 'Genius of England' that this action, though ostensibly undertaken for the *salus populi*, will have disastrous consequences: 'What bloudshead, ô what broyles dost thou commence/To last for many wofull ages hence?' When Bullingbrook protests his public, virtuous motivations, the Genius warns him that he tricks himself with this rhetoric of limited ambition: 'Thou dost not know what then will be thy mind/ When thou shalt see thy selfe advanc'd and strong/When thou hast shak'd off that which others binde'. But when Bullingbrook wakes the Genius disappears, the warning forgotten: propelled by the dark current of the agitated nobles and commons, and the strong hand of Fortune, Bullingbrook fatefully decides to act.[158]

In giving Bullingbrook no soliloquies, Shakespeare does not allow us to read his character's intentions, or pinpoint the moment when he decides to 'ascend the regal throne'.[159] Nevertheless, Bullingbrook attracts the vital support of the Duke of York with the rhetoric of loyalism, promising that he comes only to claim his inheritance: 'But as I come, I come for Lancaster'.[160] Hayward's Bullingbrook, following closest the account in the chronicles, is more cynically knowing. He realizes that his return from exile will instigate a climacteric confrontation with Richard. Canterbury's invitation to return to England to reform the realm cites the depositions of previous kings in justification, while Bullingbrook himself tells his co-conspirators 'they that deliberate only to rebel, have rebelled already'.[161] Despite their different emphases, all three writers present Bullingbrook's decision to act—his return from exile, his gathering of noble support, the actions that he takes to destroy Richard's 'evil counsellors', as well as taking the body of the king into his own hands—as usurpations of sovereignty before Richard has been forced to abdicate, or has been formally deposed. Bullingbrook's physical intervention, even justified by the rhetoric of the revenge of private grievances and the reformation of the abused commonwealth, establishes an inevitable trajectory towards deposition.

In Daniel's hands, Richard's fate actually hinges around the trust that the king places in Bullingbrook's *misleading* protestations of loyalty. In a

---

[157] Daniel, *Civile Wars*, 1.96.1–8.   [158] Ibid. 1.89.7–8, 92.3–6.
[159] Shakespeare, *Richard II*, 4.1.113.   [160] Ibid., 2.3.113.
[161] Manning, *Hayward's Life and raigne*, 117.

passage that Gillian Wright reminds us shows Daniel's invention, Carlisle persuades Richard to place himself into his cousin's hands because Henry would not dare to lay illegal claim to power.[162] Carlisle is fiercely opposed by Lord Montague, who entertains no such illusions. Montague argues that Bullingbrook has crossed his own Rubicon; there can be no restoration of the relationship between monarch and subject now that the political order has been thus ruptured: 'What hope have you that ever *Bullingbrooke*/Will live a subiect that hath tride his fate?/Or what good reconcilement can you looke/Where he must alwaies feare, and you must hate?'.[163] Richard trusts Carlisle, and surrenders his body meekly; Montague, of course, is right.

As Daniel and Hayward state explicitly and Shakespeare implies, an extraordinary attempt by a virtuous nobleman to reform the state cannot have limited aims. It is impossible for a subject who undertakes such a course of action to re-establish a hierarchical relationship with the monarch, either because this action itself is illegitimate, or simply because, as Montague argues, the existing political structures have been broken. These accounts of Richard's reign, in poem, play, and prose exploded the loyalist justification that Essex would employ, long before he had uttered it.

After Essex's rising, these same *exempla* were invoked. The fates of Richard II and Edward II demonstrated just what happened to 'lame duck' monarchs whose autonomy had been shackled by noble risings: enforced abdication/deposition, later followed by their murder.[164] If this was the scenario that Essex wanted to avoid he would have to *rewrite* the patterns of history, rather than follow them.

None of this is meant to suggest that Essex aimed at the crown; but the rebels must have been aware of other potential fates for Elizabeth had their plans succeeded. They must also have known more generally about the relationship between autonomous acts by public magistrates to reform a misgoverned commonwealth and the eventual removal of tyrannical rulers from power, as they were articulated in the sixteenth-century resistance theories of Protestant and Catholic authors, including Parsons. The virtuous action of Vindex had, after all, set in motion the events that 'toppled' Nero from the throne.[165]

---

[162] Wright, 'Samuel Daniel's use of sources', 75–7.
[163] Daniel, *Civile wars*, 2.36.1–6.
[164] See Chapter 1, 49–50.
[165] Womersley argues that Savile reflects the arguments of Huguenot resistance theorists; 'Henry Savile's Translation', 326–9.

Associates of Essex had certainly thought about the constitutional role of the nobility in ways that were closer to the theories endorsed in the *Conference* than to the doctrine of passive obedience articulated by Daniel's narrator, or by Hayward and Shakespeare's Carlisle. Gentili, as we have seen, gave very cautious endorsement to the agency of public magistrates to restrain princes. During his travels, Savile had made studies of the constitution of Poland, where the aristocracy held the balance of power.[166] In the early 1580s, Anthony Bacon had made his own reading of post-conquest English history, especially the reigns of Edward II and Richard II, which connected the constitutional restraints that might be placed on royal authority to theories of deposition.[167] Also illuminating are Bacon's notes on studying chronicles: the 'reader of histories' must examine the difference between princes illegitimately 'slayn by treason' or reasonably 'deposed voluntary by their subjects or others'.[168]

Anthony Bacon made these notes many years before the earl's revolt. But in *The state of Christendom,* these ideas are also explored in a manner that is more searching and radical than Hammer suggests. It is true that the method for restraining monarchs advocated in the main body of the treatise is through parliament or baronial councils. Hammer implies that these aristocratic buffers against tyranny are a conservative measure that would prevent popular rebellion.[169] But the agency of nobles is here separated from that of ordinary subjects: it is conceptualized as a kind of magistracy, with extraordinary powers vis-à-vis misgoverning monarchs. In the section cited by Hammer, which discusses the prohibitive fetters placed on royal tyranny by peers and parliaments, the author is engaging with the habitual *topoi* of sixteenth-century resistance theorists, used when they endorsed active opposition to tyrants through the agency of representative institutions or subordinate magistrates.[170] Parallels drawn in *The state of Christendom* between the actions taken against Henry III after the Battle of Lewes and the conciliar authority of the cardinals over the pope, or the rights of German electors over the Holy Roman Emperor, were examples cited even by Protestant theorists to condone the eventual removal of tyrannical monarchs by institutions/magistrates representative

---

[166] See above, 224.
[167] University of Edinburgh Library, Laing MS Div. III/193, ff. 57^r–64^v, 80^r–99^v.
[168] Ibid., ff. 124^r–125^v.
[169] *State of Christendom*, 207; Hammer, 'Shakespeare's *Richard II*', 12–13.
[170] Quentin Skinner, *The foundations of modern political thought*, 2 vols (Cambridge: Cambridge University Press, 1978), II, 36–7, 227–8, 235, 344; Robert Kingdon, 'Calvinism and resistance theory, 1550–1580', in J. H. Burns and Mark Goldie eds, *The Cambridge history of political thought, 1450–1700* (Cambridge: Cambridge University Press, 1991), 193–218; J. H. M. Salmon, 'James I, the oath of allegiance, the Venetian interdict, and the reappearance of French ultramontanism', in *idem*, 247–53.

of the will of the people.[171] As we have seen, the Supplement contains the argument, from analysis of Pérez's radical Tacitean memoir, that nobles might legitimately suppress tyrants, because the relationship between monarch and subjects is grounded in contract.

After his release from custody in the summer of 1600, Essex was faced with a choice. Counselled by Francis Bacon and Henry Howard to weather Elizabeth's disfavour, Essex made the decision to ignore moderate courses—to take the more radical step of intervention, 'summoned of all sides . . . to releeve my poore country that grones under hir burthen'.[172] It is surely not inconceivable that Essex and his associates, as they plotted forcing access to Elizabeth, envisaged a worst case scenario, where the queen would be compelled to abdicate, and James would be guided to the throne?

More important than Essex's intentions, opaque as they must remain, are the ways that study of the ancient and medieval world established frameworks that subjected princely government to negative critique. The languages of history exposed in particular the problems inherent in conceptualizing monarch and subject as bound by the mutual obligations to receive and deliver counsel which, as John Guy has so persuasively argued, was the normative language of political legitimation in sixteenth-century England for subjects and princes alike.[173] The historical paradigms through which contemporaries discussed the problem of counsel asked deeper questions about the propensity of monarchs to suppress virtue and to govern wilfully, and they queried the prerogative of monarchs to choose their servants. Could virtuous subjects dictate the king's choice of advisors? Attempts by noblemen to control the ruler's selection of counsellors had precipitated the deposition of weak English monarchs in centuries past. When the Long Parliament would claim authority to choose the counsellors of Charles I in the 1640s, the consequences would be graver still.

Historical thinking also intensified the inclination of Elizabethans to seek out contemporary parallels with the reigns of notorious tyrants and weak monarchs; to be alert to the features of misgovernment; and to frame their own frustrations with Elizabeth's rule within the broader languages of corruption and virtue, freedom and servility. Andrew Hadfield, David Norbrook, and Markku Peltonen have argued with varying emphases that these are the languages and attitudes that would be forged by the experience of the civil wars of the mid-seventeenth century into coherent

---

[171] *State of Christendom*, 206.
[172] BL, Additional MS 31200, f. 107[v].
[173] Guy, 'Tudor monarchy and its critiques'.

republicanism.[174] In the 1590s—a time of great anxiety that there would *be* a civil war if the succession crisis were not resolved—Essex and his followers fixated on the problem of the exercise of the ruler's will, believing that princes were inclined to govern arbitrarily, ultimately tyrannically, fearful of their power, repressing virtue.

This acute sensitivity to the problems of personal monarchy, which had developed over the course of Elizabeth's reign in the context of a great range of frustrations with the queen over matters of church, succession, and foreign policy, would have a long ideological legacy for the reigns of the Stuarts.

[174] Hadfield, *Shakespeare and republicanism*; Norbrook, *Writing the English republic*; Peltonen, *Classical humanism*.

Conclusion

Though strange and anti-climacteric, the rising of 1601 was a 'crossroads' of many paths. The most immediate impact of Essex's death ironically reflected one of its major causes: the spectre of succession crisis that had haunted all the decades of Elizabeth's long reign was exorcized with a scuffle on the London streets, rather than a civil war or foreign conquest. With Essex permanently removed, Sir Robert Cecil was able to strike up his own 'secret correspondence' with James VI, affiliating himself unequivocally with the Scottish succession. To prove his goodwill, Cecil—aided by Essex's own discretion at trial—smothered public revelations of James's deep involvement in Essex's scheming, and ensured that only the most insignificant (mainly Catholic) rebels were arraigned with the earl. Cecil moved in tandem with Henry Howard, Essex's erstwhile friend, for whom the secret negotiations over the succession were a final opportunity to ignite the political career that he had been denied under Elizabeth.

James's relieved response to Essex's rising facilitated outcomes that the earl had staunchly supported, but also consequences that he had relentlessly opposed: the accession of a Protestant king, but a ruler who had no interest in being the militant monarch of Essex's idealized imagining, and who would come to boast his greatest virtues as synonymous with the Spanish peace of 1604. Counterfactual history may be a dangerous indulgence; but had Elizabeth died while Essex still lived, one wonders about the stability of a polity ruled by a Scottish king who owed his crown to Robert Devereux.

Instead, Essex was dead when James was faced with the most dangerous consequences of the manner in which he and the earl had strategized for power in anticipation of Elizabeth's death. The wooing of a broad confessional base of opinion in which both men indulged with the succession in mind came to a head in the resigned disappointment of the Puritans at Hampton Court in 1604, and in the more bitter and deadly alienation of those Catholics who had placed their hopes in ambiguous messages of sympathy from Essex and from James himself. One crossroads of Elizabethan politics, if signposted by aspects of the earl's messy rising in 1601, was traversed in 1605, in the aftermath of the Gunpowder Plot.

The life, rising, and death of Essex are redolent of wider aspects of political culture in Elizabeth's twilight years, but have important implications also for our understanding of the seventeenth century. Isaac Casaubon's assessment of the ideological causes of Essex's rising was roughly correct: the decline and fall of Essex from 1597 occurred when the anxieties caused by religion, patronage, war, and succession were understood by the earl *and his rivals* within paradigms derived from contemporary literary and scholarly culture. Essex was a trusting product of his educational environment; a militarized ideal of active citizenship shaped his mentality, which emphasized the rewards of honour won through virtuous service. Essex believed too his own press (or dedications) that showered him with praise for his virtues, and hailed him as a *pater patriae*, one of the 'physicians' of the state and indispensible to the public good. As he was warned by certain friends and critics, Essex declared his loyalties to the wider Elizabethan state and to Christendom in ways that frequently appeared to problematize his personal allegiance to the queen.

But a simultaneous strand in the political culture of the *late*-Elizabethan polity defined the virtuous citizen as consistently embattled. The historians whom Essex most admired, the writers whose work entertained him, emphasized the dire struggle of the virtuous individual to maintain integrity in the world of courts, which were dominated by flatterers, and presided over by monarchs who were inclined to think the worst of their greatest subjects. We see too the tropes of the Catholic polemicists that exerted such a long reach on the political discourse of Elizabeth's later reign turned inwards upon the Protestant regime *by* a leading Protestant member of the regime itself. For Essex, the perpetuation of the *regnum Cecilianum* under the younger Cecil seemed to become a reality; the idea of faction created the factions that he expected to find in a court. He, in turn, was encouraged to see himself as an anomaly, a virtuous military hero in a Tacitean world; a would-be Agricola not triumphing in Britain, but languishing in Domitian's Rome. That particular sensitivity exhibited by the subjects of James VI and I and Charles I to corruption and misgovernment, and the polarized discourses and media used to debate the politics of the court under the early Stuart kings, were the legacy of the political culture of Elizabeth's later years.[1]

Essex's vocational sense of his deserved destiny was fatally imagined in dichotomized languages of virtue and vice to which he repeatedly turned

---

[1] Bellany, *Court Scandal*.

when analysing his relationship with those who appeared to hinder his ambitions. Of Essex's closest followers, only Francis Bacon, with a fuller appreciation of Machiavelli and Lipsius, would become critical of the earl's understanding of virtue and corruption as moral absolutes in a monarchical state. But Bacon's attempts to persuade Essex to rethink his ethical certainties and to adopt more cynical forms of public behaviour had an even more profoundly negative effect on the earl, increasing his conviction that only evil conduct would triumph at the Elizabethan court.

Ironically, though, Essex also provoked a parallel trend, prompting critiques of his behaviour that would cohere into an authoritarian condemnation of his character and his values. The historical forerunners of Catiline, Guise, and Bullingbrook were also a perfect fit for describing Essex's behaviour, because the earl *was* an ambitious and malcontented aristocrat, with a flickering inclination to seek popular support.

The earl's rising was the product of two colliding narratives of conspiracy: one, significantly believed by James VI, was a kind of 'popish plot' that emphasized the corruption of the court of a weak and ineffectual monarch who listened only to the counsel of dangerous, self-serving flatterers who favoured a perilous peace, and would countenance the perpetuation of their power by supporting a Spanish succession. The other defined the realm as endangered by an over-mighty noble, whose huge political ambitions turned to the usurpation of power. The deep-seated fears about civil conflict over the succession, so lucidly foretold in *A conference about the next succession to the crowne of Ingland*, turned the pitch of these suspicions into certain enmities, which in turn shaped the plots of each side, by Essex and his rivals, to take action to destroy the other.

Another significance of the application of these cynical paradigms of the operation of politics is that in the language of Essex's rivals, concepts of autonomous action and of critical attitudes towards the present government were defined as seditious in themselves. This authoritarian thrust had been anticipated in the response to radical Puritan attempts to popularize Presbyterian ecclesiology. If the Essex rising was the product of political 'polarisation', his career also exemplifies the divisions in political mentality that came to the fore within the elite itself in the 1590s. Essex was not a constitutional or legal thinker. But the new authoritarianism noted by Guy is emphatically apparent in critical responses to Essex's career, in condemnation of the use of the rhetoric of public authority and virtue which was praised by Essex's followers and friends, but defined by his detractors as a political language used to mask dangerous ambitions. In his letter to Egerton, semi-publicly circulated, Essex struggled to reconcile his allegiance to the queen with his own deep displeasure at Elizabeth's treatment of him. To disassociate themselves from the earl's example, prominent privy councillors distanced themselves from the languages that Essex cultivated, of public service to the wider polity or state, and fetishized instead the doctine of absolute obedience. In his Jacobean treatise on the role of the secretary, Sir Robert Cecil would emphasize his political creed in opposition to that of Essex, imagining his role as a creature of the monarch, buttressed by bonds of absolute loyalty and dependency.[2] The self-defined political mentality of this Cecil bears little resemblance to that of his father, as described by Patrick Collinson and Stephen Alford.

But Essex's intellectual associates were also interested in the relationship of these moral languages to notions of wider structures of state, the flourishing and declining commonwealth, and the rights and duties of subjects to remedy tyranny and misgovernment. These interests had been forged in their appraisal of continental politics, which especially evinced sympathy for the Dutch abjuration of the sovereignty of Philip II, and demonstrated more widely a sympathetic understanding of theories of resistance that defined the contractual relationship of subjects and mon-archs, and the duties that were incumbent on superior magistrates—noblemen, or public officers of particular virtue—to bridle misgoverning princes. When looking inwardly on the politics of the Elizabethan state in the later 1590s, Essex attacked his rivals as evil counsellors and presented himself as the true, maligned servant of the queen, who was unable to comprehend the corruption of her own court. In doing so Essex repeatedly turned to the languages of weak tyranny that so fascinated his contempor-aries, emphasizing the inconsistency of Elizabeth's 'passionate' response to matters of state, her love of flattery, and her government through will rather than reason and respect for the good of the realm.

'Summoned of all sides', as Essex insisted to James, the earl acted in 1601 to save the state, the Scottish succession, and himself, the fates of all inseparable in his own mind. He justified his actions to James and to the wider public by his insistence that Elizabeth would come to no harm, and by his refutation of any design on the throne. While Essex insisted on his loyalty to the queen, the theoretical underpinnings of this action could be termed a form of noble resistance to the existing government. For all his protestations of allegiance to Elizabeth, Essex claimed public authority to act for the safety of the realm; he intended to dictate to Elizabeth who her counsellors should be, and how the succession should be settled. He acted in the name of the queen, but to effect his own vision of how he thought

---

[2] See Cecil's treatise: *The state and dignitie of a secretarie of estates place, with the care and perill thereof* (1642). The treatise was written soon after the accession of James.

Elizabeth should govern, and to determine how she wielded her prerogative powers. Parallels loom with the actions of the earl's son, the third earl of Essex, in the English civil war, especially as defined by John Adamson.[3]

Also important is the response of the government. Both before and after the rising, the authorities denounced slander of the queen's ministers as disloyalty in itself, and an attack on Elizabeth's sovereignty. Many poets and playwrights (and of course Parsons) had anticipated this, describing noble insurrection against evil counsellors as an inevitable forerunner of deposition. There was no ideological room in this political outlook for any subject, nobleman or otherwise, to make an autonomous intervention in public affairs that would not be interpreted as rebellious, and that did not have a radical end. Even the discourse of hostility to evil counsel was decreed seditious. In a very different political context, of course, these incompatible understandings of the duties and obedience of subjects and monarchs would reoccur in the early years of the 1640s.

The earl's career, and especially his downfall, also have great significance for the evidence that they reveal about the texture and variety of more public attitudes towards the court and the queen. Mervyn James argued that Essex's failure to mobilize the support of the citizens of London represented the supremacy of the ideology of the sixteenth-century crown, which allowed no alternative *loci* of power or protest. The appeal to London on 7 and 8 February was a dismal failure. Essex's public profile did not have sufficient magnetism to galvanize Londoners or citizens into an adequate force to allow the earl to press his way to the court, and his following was no bastard feudal army. The earl's most dangerous military strategies had involved suborning forces in Ireland (albeit swelled with his own military clientele) that had been entrusted to Essex or Mountjoy as the queen's representatives, raised through the structures of the Elizabethan state.

But the reaction of contemporaries to the arrest of the earl in 1599, as with the response to his execution in 1601, belies a pervasive explanation of the ubiquity and uniformity of political attitudes. Even before Essex's trial, the privy council and London authorities were faced with a rash of libels, defending the earl's character, and attacking those enemies that had engineered his downfall. After Essex's death, sympathy for the hero of Cadiz would overwhelmingly crush attempts to define the earl as a traitor who sought to usurp the throne himself. The positive and nostalgic remembrance of Essex's heroism in early Stuart England bears witness to the strength and independence of public opinion. His fate and character would teach political lessons to future generations.

---

[3] John Adamson, *The noble revolt: the overthrow of Charles I* (London: Weidenfeld & Nicolson, 2007).

Bibliography

MANUSCRIPTS

Bodleian Library
Ashmole Manuscripts
862, 1729
Miscellaneous Manuscripts
Casaubon 28
Don. C 54
Eng. Hist. C 239
Smith 17
Rawlinson Manuscripts
A 122
C 744
D 1175

British Library
Additional Manuscripts
4125, 4129, 5956, 6177, 6297, 31022, 7038, 74286 (can be read on BL
  microfilm 2275)
Cotton Manuscripts
Julius F VI
Galba D XII
Vespasian CIV
Titus C VI
Egerton Manuscripts
1943, 2006, 2026
Harleian Manuscripts
305, 677, 1327, 7021, 6910, 6997
Lansdowne Manuscripts
64, 81, 82, 84, 103, 109
Stowe Manuscripts
151, 161

Durham University Library
Howard MS 2

Folger Shakespeare Library
v. b. 214, v. b. 7

Hatfield House
Cecil Manuscripts

Henry E. Huntington Library
Ellesmere, 1612

Inner Temple Library
Petyt 538

Lambeth Palace Library
648–660 (Anthony Bacon's papers), 2004, 3470

London Metropolitan Archives
Repertories of the Court of Aldermen, 25

Merton College, Oxford University
Q. 1. 10

The National Archives
SP 9, 12, 14, 59, 63

The Queen's College, Oxford University
121

University of Edinburgh Library
Laing MS III/193

Warwick Record Office
WRO, MI 229

Yale University Beinecke Library
370
Osborn MS, 20

PRINTED PRIMARY SOURCES

Akrigg, G. P. V. ed., *Letters of King James VI and I* (Berkeley, CA: University of California Press, 1984).
Andrewes, Lancelot, *The duty of a nation and its members in time of war. A sermon preached before Queen Elizabeth at Richmond on February 21, 1599,* ed. T. S. Polehampton (London: Joseph Masters, 1854).
Anon., *A True report of sundry horrible conspiracies of late time detected to have by barbarous murders taken away the life of the Queen's Most Excellent Majesty* (1594).
——, *A pageant of Spanish humours . . . ,* trans. H. W. (1599).
Anon., (i.e. Henry Constable), *Discoverye of a counterfecte conference . . . for thaduancement of a counterfecte tytle* (Paris, 1600, imprint Cologne).

Anon., *A lamentable ditty composed upon the death of Robert Lord Devereux, late Earle of Essex* (1603).

——, (attr. Henry Wotton), *The state of Christendom. Or, a most exact and curious discovery of many secret passages, and hidden mysteries of the times* (1657).

——, *Thomas of Woodstock, or, Richard the Second, part one*, ed. Peter Corbin and Douglas Sedge (Manchester: Manchester University Press, 2002).

Arber, E. ed. *A transcript of the registers of the Company of Stationers of London, 1554–1640 AD*, 5 vols (London: privately printed, 1875–1894).

Aristotle, *The Politics*, ed. Stephen Everson (Cambridge: Cambridge University Press, 1996).

Bacon, Francis, *A declaration of the practices & treasons attempted and committed by Robert late Earle of Essex and his complices...* (1601).

——, *Sir Francis Bacon his apologie, in certaine imputations concerning the late earle of Essex* (1604).

Barlow, William, *A sermon preached at Paules Crosse, on the first Sunday in Lent...* (1601).

Bilson, Thomas, *The true difference betweene Christian subjection and unchristian rebellion* (Oxford, 1585).

Bodin, Jean, *The six bookes of a common weale*, trans. Richard Knolles (1606).

Bownd, Nicholas, *The doctrine of the Sabbath, plainely layde forth* (1595).

Bruce, John ed., *Correspondence of James VI with Sir Robert Cecil and others in England, during the reign of Queen Elizabeth...*, (London: Camden Society, 1861).

Brutus, Stephanus Junius (pseud.), *A short apologie for Christian Souldiours...* (1588).

Calendar of the Carew Manuscripts, preserved in the Archiepiscopal Library at Lambeth. (1515–1624), eds J. S. Brewer and W. Bullen, 6 vols (London, 1867–73).

Calendar of letters and state papers, relating to English affairs, preserved principally in the archives of Simancas, Elizabeth, eds M. A. S. Hume, 4 vols (London, 1896–99).

Calendar of the Patent and Close Rolls of Chancery in Ireland, of the reigns of Henry VIII, Edward VI, Mary, and Elizabeth, eds J. Morrin, 3 vols (Dublin and London: A Thorn and Sons, 1861–63).

Calendar of state papers, domestic series, preserved in Her Majesty's Public Record Office, Edward VI, Mary I, Elizabeth, James I, eds R. Lemon and M. A. E. Green, 12 vols (London, 1865–72).

Calendar of state papers, relating to Ireland, of the reign of Elizabeth, eds J Stevenson, A. J. Crosby et al., 23 vols (London, 1863–1950).

Calendar of state papers, relating to Scotland and Mary, Queen of Scots, 1547–1603, preserved in the Public Record Office, and elsewhere in England, eds J. Bain, W. K. Boyd et al., 13 vols in 14 (Edinburgh and Glasgow, 1898–1969).

Cameron, A. I. ed., *The Warrender papers*, 2 vols (Edinburgh: Scottish History Society, 1931–2).

Caraman, Philip ed., *John Gerard: the autobiography of an Elizabethan*, 2nd edn (London: Longmans, Green, 1956).

Cecil, Robert, earl of Salisbury, *The state and dignitie of a secretarie of estates place, with the care and perill thereof* (1642).

Chapman, George, *Achilles shield Translated as the other seuen bookes of Homer, out of his eighteenth booke of Iliades* (1598).

——, *Seauen bookes of the Iliades of Homere, prince of poets* . . . (1598).

Churchyard, Thomas, *The fortunate farewell to the most forward and noble earle of Essex* (1599).

Clark, A. ed., *Register of the University of Oxford*, 5 vols (Oxford: Clarendon Press, 1877).

Collins, A., *Letters and memorials of state* . . . *[of the Sidney family]* . . . *from the originals at* Penshurst Place *in* Kent, 2 vols (London, 1746).

Cooper, C. H., *Annals of Cambridge*, 5 vols (Cambridge: Warwick and Co., 1842–1908).

Covell, William, *Polimanteia, or, The meanes lawfull and vnlawfull, to judge of the fall of a common-wealth* . . . (Cambridge, 1595).

Crinó, A., 'Trenta lettere inedite di Sir Henry Wotton, nell'archivio di Stato di Firenze', *Rivista di letterature moderne e comparate* (1955).

Croft, P. J. ed., *The poems of Robert Sidney* (Oxford: Clarendon Press, 1984).

Crompton, Richard, *The Mansion of magnanimitie. Wherein is shewed the most high and honourable acts of sundrie english kings, princes, dukes, earles, lords, knights and gentlemen* . . . (1599).

Daniel, Samuel, *The first fowre bookes of the civile wars betweene the two houses of Lancaster and Yorke*, (1595).

Devereux, Robert, 2nd earl of Essex, *To Maister Anthonie Bacon. An apologie of the Earle of Essex, against those which falsly and maliciously taxe him to be the onely hinderer of the peace, and quiet of his countrey* (1600).

—— *The Earle of Essex his letter to the Earle of Southampton in the time of his troubles. Containing many pious expressions and very comfortable for such as are in any troubles* (1642).

Devereux, W. B. ed., *Lives and letters of the Devereux, earls of Essex, in the reigns of Elizabeth, James I and Charles I, 1540–1646*, 2 vols (London: John Murray, 1853).

D'Ewes, Simonds, *The Journals of all the Parliaments during the reign of Queen Elizabeth* (1682).

Dillingham, William ed., *The commentaries of Sir Francis Vere* (1657).

Doleman R. (i.e. Robert Parsons), *A conference about the next succession to the crowne of Ingland* (Antwerp, 1594/5).

Dralymont, I. D. (pseud.), *A treatise pareanetical* . . . *Wherein is shewed by good and euident reasons* . . . *the right way & true meanes to resist the violence of the Castilian king* . . . *and to ruinate his puissance* (1598).

Drayton, Michael, *Peirs Gaveston Earle of Cornwall. His life, death, and fortune* (1594).

——, *Mortimeriados. The lamentable ciuell warres of Edward the second and the barrons* (1596).

Fenton, Roger, *An answere to William Alablaster his motiues* (1599).

Bibliography

Figueiro, Vasco, *The Spaniards monarchie, and leaguer's olygarchie,...* trans. H. O. (1592).

Fletcher, John M. ed., *Registrum annalium Collegii Mertonensis 1567–1603* (Oxford: Clarendon Press, 1976).

Gentili, Alberico, *De iure belli libri tres*, ed. Coleman Phillipson, trans. John C. Rolfe, 2 vols (Oxford: Clarendon Press, 1933).

Gifford, George, *A treatise of true fortitude* (1594).

——, *Fifteene sermons, vpon the Song of Salomon* (1598).

——, *Sermons upon the whole booke of the revelation* (1599).

Guicciardini, Francesco, *Two discourses of Master Frances Guicciardin*, trans. William Jones (1595).

Guilpin, Everard, *Skialetheia. Or, A shadowe of truth, in certaine epigrams and satyres* (1598).

Harington, John, *The most elegant and witty epigrams of Sir John Harington, Knight* (1618).

——, *A tract on the succession to the crowne (AD 1602)*, ed. C. R. Markham (London: Roxburghe Club, 1880), 41.

Hartley, T. E., *Proceedings in the parliaments of Elizabeth I. Vol. 3, 1593–1601* (London: Leicester University Press, 1995).

Harkey, Richard, *Philadelphus, or a defence of Brutes, and the Brutans history* (1593).

Hayward, John, *An answer to the first part of a certaine conference concerning succession* (1603).

Herford, C. H. and Simpson, Percy, eds, *Ben Jonson*, 11 vols (Oxford: Clarendon Press, 1925–52).

Historical Manuscripts Commission, Calendar of the manuscripts of the Most Honourable the Marquis of Salisbury, K.G., etc., preserved at Hatfield House, Hertfordshire, 24 vols (London, 1883–1976).

Historical Manuscripts Commission, Calendar of the manuscripts of the Most Honourable the Marquis of Bath, preserved at Longleat, Wiltshire, 5 vols (London, 1904–80).

Historical Manuscripts Commission, Report on the manuscripts of Lord de L'Isle and Dudley, preserved at Penshurst Place, 6 vols (London, 1925–66).

Howard, Henry, *A true and perfect relation of the whole proceedings against... Garnet* (1606).

Howell, Thomas Bayley ed., *Cobbett's complete collection of state trials and proceedings for high treason and other crimes and misdemeanours...*, 33 vols (London: T.C. Hansard, 1809–26).

Hubbock, William, *An apologie of infants* (1595).

Hughes, Paul L. and Larkin, James F. eds, *Tudor royal proclamations, vol. 3. The later Tudors (1553–1603)* (New Haven, CT and London: Yale University Press, 1969).

Hurault, André, Sieur de Maisse, *A journal of all that was accomplished by Monsieur de Maisse, ambassador in England from King Henry IV to Queen*

Elizabeth, Anno Domini 1597, ed. and trans. G. B. Harrison and R. A. Jones (London: Nonesuch Press, 1931).

Journal of the House of Lords. Volume 2. 1578–1619 (London, 1771).

L., T., *Babylon is fallen* (1597).

Laffleur de Kermaingant, Pierre Paul ed., *L'ambassade de France en Angleterre sous Henri IV. Mission de Jean de Thumery, Sieur de Boissise, 1598–1602* (Paris, 1886).

La Noue, François de. *The politicke and militarie discourses of the Lord de La Noue*, trans. E. A. (1588).

Latham, Agnes and Youings, Joyce eds, *The letters of Sir Walter Ralegh* (Exeter: University of Exeter Press, 1999).

Law, T. G. ed., *The Archpriest controversy: documents relating to the dissensions of the Roman Catholic clergy, 1597–1601*, 2 vols (London: Camden Society, n.s., 56, 1896).

Lediard, Thomas, *The Naval History of England in all its branches, from the Norman Conquest, 1066, to the conclusion of 1734*, 2 vols (London, 1735).

Linaker, Robert, *A comfortable treatise for the reliefe of such as are afflicted in conscience* (1595).

Lipsius, Iustus, *Sixe bookes of politickes or ciuil doctrine*, trans. William Jones (1594).

Lonchay, Henri and Cuvelier, Joseph eds, *Correspondance de la Cour d'Espagne sur les affaires des Pays-Bas au XVIIe siècle*, 6 vols (Brussels: Commission Royale d'Histoire, 1923–37).

Loomie, A. J., 'A Catholic petition to the earl of Essex', *Recusant History* 7 (1963), 33–42.

Mackie, J. D., *Negotiations between King James VI and Ferdinand I, Grand Duke of Tuscany* (London: St Andrews University, 1927).

McClure, N. E., *The letters of John Chamberlain*, 2 vols (Philadelphia, PA: American Philosophical Society, 1939).

Manning, John ed., *The first and second parts of John Hayward's 'The life and raigne of King Henrie IIII'*, Camden Society, 4th ser., 42, (London, 1991).

Mayer, J. C. ed., *Breaking the silence on the Elizabethan succession: a sourcebook of manuscripts and rare Elizabethan texts (c.1587–1603)* (Montpellier: Université Paul-Valéry, 2003).

Moore Smith, G. C. ed., *Gabriel Harvey's marginalia* (Stratford-upon-Avon: Shakespeare Head Press, 1913).

Morfill, W. R. and Furnivall, F. J. eds, *Ballads from manuscripts*, 2 vols (London: Ballad Society, 1868).

Moryson, Fynes, *An itinerary written by Fynes Moryson Gent... containing his ten yeeres travell... Divided into III parts...* (1617).

Nenna, Giovanni Battista, *Nennio, or, A treatise of nobility*, trans. William Jones (1595).

Nichols, John, *The progresses and public processions of Queen Elizabeth...* 3 vols (London, 1823).

Nichols, Josias, *Abrahams faith: that is, the olde religion* (1596).

Norden, John, *The mirror of honor: wherein everie professor of armes... may see the necessitie of the feare and service of God...* (1597).

Oldys, W. and Birch, T. eds, *The works of Sir Walter Ralegh*, 8 vols (Oxford: Oxford University Press, 1829).

Park, Thomas ed., *Nugae Antiquae. Being a miscellaneous collection of original papers in prose and verse...* 2 vols (London: J. Wright, 1804).

[Parsons, Robert] *Newes from Spayne and Holland... Written by a Gentleman travelour bourne in the low countries, and brought up from a child in Ingland...* (Antwerp, 1593).

Paule, George, *The life of the most reuerend and religious prelate John Whitgift, Lord Archbishop of Canterbury* (1612).

Petti, Anthony G. ed., *The letters and despatches of Richard Verstegan, c.1550–1640* (London: Catholic Record Society, 1959).

——, *Roman Catholicism in Elizabethan and Jacobean Staffordshire: documents from the Bagot papers* (Staffordshire: Staffordshire Record Society, 1979).

Plummer, Charles, *Elizabethan Oxford. Reprints of rare tracts* (Oxford: Clarendon Press, 1887).

Pricket, Robert, *Honors fame in triumph riding. Or, the life and death of the late honourable Earle of Essex* (1604).

Purchas, Samuel, *Hakluytus posthumus or purchas his pilgrimes*, 20 vols (Glasgow, 1905–7).

Racster, John, *William Alablasters seven motiues. Removed and confuted* (1598).

Renold, P. ed., *The Wisbech stirs, 1595-1598* (London: Catholic Record Society, 1958).

Rymer, Thomas et alia eds, *Foedera, conventiones, literae, et cujuscunque generis acta publica, inter reges Angliae... ab anno 1101, ad nostra usque tempora, habita aut tractata*, 10 vols (The Hague, 1739–45), 7, 212–15.

Sallust, *The two most worthy and notable histories... the conspiracie of Cateline, undertaken against the Senate of Rome, and the warre which Iugurth for many yeares maintained against the same state*, trans. Thomas Heywood (1608).

Sandys, Edwin, *A relation of the state of religion... in the severall states of these westerne parts of the world* (1605).

Savile, Henry, *The ende of Nero and the beginning of Galba*, from idem ed. and trans., *Fower bookes of the Histories of Cornelius Tacitus. The life of Agricola* (1591).

Scott, H. S. ed., 'Journal of Sir Roger Wilbraham, Master of Requests', *Camden Miscellany*, X, Camden Society, 3rd. ser., 4, (London, 1902), 79–84.

Shakespeare, William, *King Richard II*, ed. Andrew Gurr (Cambridge: Cambridge University Press, 1992).

——, *King Henry V*, ed. T. W. Craik (London: Routledge, 1995).

Smith, Logan Pearsall, *The life and letters of Sir Henry Wotton*, 2 vols (Oxford: Clarendon Press, 1907).

Sommerville, Johann ed., *King James VI and I. Political writings* (Cambridge: Cambridge University Press, 1994).

Spedding, James ed., *The letters and the life of Francis Bacon... set forth in chronological order, with a commentary...*, 7 vols (London: Longmans, Green, Reader, and Dyer, 1861–74).

Spenser, Edmund, *The shorter poems*, ed. Richard A. Mac Cabe (London and New York: Penguin, 1999).

——*A view of the state of Ireland*, ed. Andrew Hadfield and Willy Maley (Oxford: Blackwell, 1997).

Stowe, John, *A summarie of the chronicles of England* (1604).

Strype, John, *Annals of the reformation and establishment of religion, and other various occurrences in the Church of England, during Queen Elizabeth's happy reign... 4 vols. in 7 (1829).

Sutcliffe, Matthew, *The practice, proceedings, and lawes of armes* (1593).

Tacitus, *The Annales of Cornelius Tacitus. The description of Germanie*, trans. Richard Greneway (1598).

Tenison, E. M., *Elizabethan England: being the history of this country 'in relation to all foreign princes'*, 12 vols in 13 (Leamington Spa: Griffin Press, 1933–61).

Ungerer, Gustav, *A Spaniard in Elizabethan England. The correspondence of Antonio Pérez's exile*, 2 vols (London: Tamesis Books, 1974–6).

van Meel, J. W. ed., *Franciscii et Joannis Hotomanorum epistolae... et clarorum ad eos...* (Amstel, 1700).

[Verstegan, Richard], *An aduertisement written to a secretarie of my L. Treasurers of Ingland, by an Inglishe intelligencer as he passed throughe Germanie towardes Italie* (1592).

——, *A declaration of the true causes of the great troubles presupposed to be intended against the realme of England...* (1592).

Vickers, Brian ed., *Francis Bacon* (Oxford: Oxford University Press, 1996).

Wall, A., 'An account of the Essex revolt, February 1601', *BIHR*, 54 (1981), 131–3.

Warner, William, *Albions England... revised and newly inlarged* (1596).

Wentworth, Peter, *A pithie exhortation to her Majestie for establishing her successor to the crowne. Whereunto is added a discourse containing the authors opinion of the true and lawfull successor to her Majestie* (Edinburgh, 1598).

Winwood, Sir Ralph, *Memorials of affairs of state in the reigns of Queen Elizabeth and King James I*, 3 vols (1725).

Wootton, David ed., *Divine right and democracy: an anthology of political writing in Stuart England* (Harmondsworth: Penguin, 1986).

Wotton, Henry, *A parallel betweene Robert late Earle of Essex, and George late Duke of Buckingham* (1641).

Wright, T., *Queen Elizabeth and her times*, 2 vols (London: H. Colburn, 1838).

PRINTED SECONDARY SOURCES

Abbott, E. A., *Bacon and Essex: a sketch of Bacon's earlier life* (London, 1877).

Adams, Simon, 'Eliza enthroned? The court and its politics', in C. Haigh ed., *The reign of Elizabeth I* (Basingstoke: Macmillan, 1984), 55–77.

Adams, Simon, 'The patronage of the crown in Elizabethan politics: the 1590s in perspective', in Guy, *Reign of Elizabeth I*, 20–45.

——, 'Favourites, and factions at the Elizabethan court', in idem, *Leicester and the court* (2002), 46–67.

——, *Leicester and the court: essays on Elizabethan politics* (Manchester: Manchester University Press, 2002).

——, 'Elizabeth I and the Sovereignty of the Netherlands 1576–1585', *TRHS*, 6/14 (2004), 309–19.

Adamson, J. S. A., 'The Baronial Context of the English Civil War', *TRHS*, 5/40 (1990), 93–120.

——, *The noble revolt: the overthrow of Charles I* (London: Weidenfeld & Nicolson, 2007).

Akrigg, G. P. V., *Shakespeare and the earl of Southampton* (London: H. Hamilton, 1968).

Albright, Evelyn May, 'Shakespeare's *Richard II*, Hayward's History of Henry IV, and the Essex Conspiracy', *PMLA*, 46 (1931), 694–719.

——, 'Reply to Ray Heffner's Shakespeare, Hayward, and Essex again', *PMLA*, 47 (1932), 899–901.

Alford, Stephen, *The early Elizabethan polity: William Cecil and the British succession crisis, 1558–1569* (Cambridge: Cambridge University Press, 1998).

——, *Burghley: William Cecil at the court of Elizabeth I* (New Haven, CT and London: Yale University Press, 2008).

Allen, Paul C., *Philip III and the Pax Hispanica, 1598–1621: the failure of grand strategy* (New Haven, CT and London: Yale University Press, 2000).

Andersson, D. C., *Lord Henry Howard (1540–1614): an Elizabethan life* (Cambridge: D. S. Brewer, 2009).

Archer, I. W., *The pursuit of stability: social relations in Elizabethan London* (Cambridge: Cambridge University Press, 1991).

——, 'The 1590s: apotheosis or nemesis of the Elizabethan regime?', in Briggs and Snowman, *Fins de siecle: how centuries end* (1996), 65–98.

Ashley, R., 'War in the ordnance office: the Essex connection and Sir John Davis', *Historical Research*, 67 (1994), 337–45.

Axton, Marie, *The queen's two bodies: drama and the Elizabethan succession* (London: Royal Historical Society, 1977).

Ball, Terence, Farr, James, and Hanson, Russell L. eds, *Political innovation and conceptual change* (Cambridge: Cambridge University Press, 1989).

Barroll, Leeds, 'A new history for Shakespeare and his time', *Shakespeare Quarterly*, 39 (1988), 441–64.

Bate, Jonathon, *Soul of the age: the life, mind and world of William Shakespeare* (London: Viking, 2008).

Baumer, Franklin Le Van, 'The conception of Christendom in Renaissance England', *Journal of the History of Ideas*, 6 (1945), 131–56.

Beal, P. and Ioppolo, E. eds, *Elizabeth I and the culture of writing* (London: British Library Press, 2007).

Bellamy, John, *The Tudor law of treason: an introduction* (London: Routledge, 1979).

Bellany, Alastair, 'A poem on the archbishop's hearse: puritanism, libel and sedition after the Hampton Court Conference', *JBS*, 34 (1995), 137–64.

——, *The politics of court scandal in early modern England: news, culture and the Overbury affair, 1603–1660* (Cambridge: Cambridge University Press, 2002).

Bennett, J. A. W. and Trevor-Roper, H. R. eds, *The poems of Richard Corbett* (Oxford: Clarendon Press, 1955).

Bevington, David and Holbrook, Peter eds, *The politics of the Stuart court masque* (Cambridge: Cambridge University Press, 1998).

Bindoff, S. T., Hurstfield, J. and Williams, C. H. eds, *Elizabethan government and society: essays presented to Sir John Neale* (London: Athlone Press, 1961).

Bossy, John, 'A propos of Henry Constable', *Recusant History*, 6/5 (1962), 228–37.

——, *Giordano Bruno and the embassy affair* (New Haven, CT and London: Yale University Press, 1991, repr. 2002).

Brennan, Michael, *The Sidneys of Penshurst and the monarchy, 1500–1700* (Aldershot: Ashgate, 2006).

Briggs, Asa and Snowram, Daniel, *Fins de siecle: how centuries end* (New Haven, CT and London: Yale University Press, 1996).

Bullough, Geoffrey ed., *The poems and dramas of Fulke Greville, first Lord Brooke*, 2 vols (Edinburgh and London: Oliver and Boyd, 1939).

Burgess, Glen, Wymer, Roland and Laurence, Jason eds, *The accession of James I: historical and cultural consequences* (Basingstoke: Palgrave Macmillan, 2006).

Burns, J. H. and Goldie, M. eds, *The Cambridge history of political thought, 1450–1700* (Cambridge: Cambridge University Press, 1991).

Bushnell, Rebecca, *Tragedies of tyrants: political thought and theater in the English Renaissance* (Ithaca, NY: Cornell University Press, 1990).

Campbell, Lily B., *Shakespeare's 'Histories': mirrors of Elizabethan policy* (San Marino, CA: Huntington Library, 1947).

Caro, Robert V., 'William Alabaster: rhetor, mediator, devotional poet Pt.1', *Recusant History*, 19 (1988), 62–79.

Chesters, Geoffrey, 'John Daniel of Daresbury, 1544–1610', *Proceedings of the Historic Society of Lancashire & Cheshire*, 118 (1966), 1–17.

Clancy, Thomas H., *Papist pamphleteers: the Allen-Persons party and the political thought of the counter-reformation in England, 1572–1615* (Chicago, IL: Loyola University Press, 1964).

Clegg, Cyndia Susan, '"By choise and inuitation of al the realme": Richard II and Elizabethan press censorship', *Shakespeare Quarterly*, 48 (1997), 432–48.

——, *Press censorship in Elizabethan England* (Cambridge: Cambridge University Press, 1997).

Coffey, John, *Persecution and toleration in Protestant England, 1558–1689* (Harlow: Longman, 2000).

Cogswell, Thomas, Cust, Richard and Lake, Peter eds, *Politics, religion and popularity in early Stuart Britain: essays in honour of Conrad Russell* (Cambridge: Cambridge University Press, 2002).

Collinson, Patrick, *The Elizabethan puritan movement* (London: Jonathan Cape, 1967).

——, *Archbishop Grindal, 1519–1583: the struggle for a reformed Church* (London: Jonathan Cape, 1979).

——, '*De Republica Anglorum*: or, history with the politics put back', in idem, *Elizabethan essays* (1994), 1–29.

——, *Elizabethan essays* (London: Hambledon, 1994).

——, 'The Elizabethan exclusion crisis and the Elizabethan polity', *Proceedings of the British Academy*, 84 (1994), 51–92.

——, 'The monarchical republic of Queen Elizabeth I', printed in idem, *Elizabethan essays* (1994), 31–57.

——'Ecclesiastical vitriol: religious satire in the 1590s and the invention of puritanism', in Guy, *Reign of Elizabeth I* (1995), 150–70.

——, 'The religious factor', in Mayer, *Struggle for the succession* (2004), 243–72.

Coward, Barry and Swann, Julian eds, *Conspiracies and conspiracy theory in early modern Europe: from the Waldensians to the French Revolution* (Aldershot: Ashgate, 2004).

Croft, Pauline, 'The Religion of Robert Cecil', *HJ*, 34 (1991), 773–96.

——, 'The reputation of Robert Cecil: libels, political opinion and popular awareness in the early seventeenth century', *TRHS*, 6/1 (1991), 43–69.

——, 'Libels, popular literacy and public opinion in Early Modern England', *Historical Research*, 68 (1995), 266–85.

——, ed., *Patronage, culture and power: the early Cecils* (New Haven, CT and London: Yale University Press, 2002).

——, '"The state of the world is marvellously changed": England, Spain and Europe, 1558–1604', in Doran and Richardson, *Tudor England and its neighbours* (2005), 178–202.

——'*Rex Pacificus*, Robert Cecil, and the 1604 Peace with Spain', in Burgess, Wymer, and Laurence, *Accession of James I* (2006), 140–54.

Cruickshank, C. G., *Elizabeth's army*, 2nd edn (Oxford: Clarendon Press, 1966).

Cuddy, Neil, 'The conflicting loyalties of a "vulgar counselor": the third earl of Southampton, 1597–1624', in Morrill, Slack, and Woolf, *Public duty and private conscience*, (1993) 121–50.

Cust, Richard and Hughes, Ann, *Conflict in early Stuart England: studies in religion and politics, 1603–42* (Harlow: Longman, 1989).

——, 'Charles I and popularity', in Cogswell, Cust, and Lake eds, *Politics, religion and popularity* (2002), 235–58.

——, 'The public man in late Tudor and early Stuart England', in Lake and Pincus, *Politics of the public sphere* (2007), 116–43.

Dodd, A. H., 'North Wales in the Essex revolt of 1601', *EHR*, 59 (1944), 348–56.

——, 'The earl of Essex's faction in north Wales, c.1593–1601: supplementary notes', *National Library of Wales Journal*, 6 (1949–59), 190–1.

Doran, S., 'Three late-Elizabethan succession tracts', in Mayer, *Struggle for the succession* (2004), 91–117.

Doran, Susan, 'Loving and affectionate cousins? The relationship between Elizabeth I and James VI of Scotland', in Doran and Richardson, *Tudor England and its neighbours* (2005), 203–34.

Doran, Susan and Richardson, Glenn eds, *Tudor England and its neighbours* (Basingstoke: Palgrave Macmillan, 2005).

Dowling, Margaret, 'Sir John Hayward's troubles over his Life of Henry IV', *The Library*, 4/11 (1930–31), 212–24.

Du Maurier, Daphne, *The golden lads: a study of Anthony Bacon, Francis Bacon and their friends* (London: Gollancz, 1975).

Dures, Alan, *English Catholicism, 1558–1642: continuity and change* (Harlow: Longman, 1983).

Dutton, Richard, 'Buggeswords: Samuel Harsnett and the licensing, suppression and afterlife of Dr John Hayward's "The first part of the life and reign of King Henry IV"', *Criticism*, 35/3 (1993), 305–40.

——, 'The dating and contexts of *Henry V*', in Kewes ed., *Uses of history* (2006), 162–99.

Elliott, J. H. and Brockliss, L. W. B. eds, *The world of the favourite* (New Haven, CT and London: Yale University Press, 1999).

Evenden, Elizabeth and Freeman, Thomas, 'Print, profit and propaganda: the Elizabethan Privy Council and the 1570s edition of Foxe's "Book of Martyrs"', *EHR*, 119 (2004), 1228–307.

Falls, Cyril, *Elizabeth's Irish wars*, 2nd edn (London: Constable, 1996).

Ferrell, Lori-Anne and McCullough, Peter E. eds, *The English sermon revised: religion, literature and history, 1600–1750* (Manchester: Manchester University Press, 2000).

Fletcher, Anthony and MacCulloch, Diarmaid, *Tudor rebellions*, 5th edn (Harlow: Pearson Longman, 2004).

Fletcher, James, 'The faculty of the arts', in McConica, *History of the University of Oxford* (1986), 157–200.

Fox, Adam, *Oral and literate culture in England, 1500–1700* (Oxford: Oxford University Press, 2000).

Fox, Alistair, 'The complaint of poetry for the death of liberality: the decline of literary patronage in the 1590s', in Guy ed., *Reign of Elizabeth I* (1995), 229–57.

Gajda, Alexandra, '*The State of Christendom:* history, political thought and the Essex circle', *Historical Research*, 81/213 (2008), 423–46.

——, 'Debating war and peace in late Elizabethan England', *HJ*, 52 (2009), 851–78.

Gazzard, Hugh, 'Those graue presentments of antiquitie': Samuel Daniel's Philotas and the earl of Essex', *Review of English Studies*, 51/203 (2000), 432–50.

Giesey, Ralph E., *If not, not. The oath of the Aragonese and the legendary laws of the Sobrarbe* (Princeton, NJ: Princeton University Press, 1968).

Gilliam, Elizabeth and Tighe, W. J., 'To "run with the time". Archbishop Whitgift, the Lambeth articles, and the politics of theological ambiguity in late Elizabethan England', *Sixteenth Century Journal*, 23/2 (1992), 325–40.

Gottschalk, K., 'Discoveries concerning British Library MS Harley 6910', *Modern Philology*, 77 (1979), 121–31.

Grell, Ole Peter and Scribner, Robert eds, *Tolerance and intolerance in the European reformation* (Cambridge: Cambridge University Press, 1996).

Grundy, Joan ed., *The poems of Henry Constable* (Liverpool: Liverpool University Press, 1960).

Guy, John, *Tudor England* (Oxford: Oxford University Press, 1988).

—— 'The Elizabethan establishment and the ecclesiastical polity', in Guy, *Reign of Elizabeth I* (1995), 126–49.

——, 'Introduction. The 1590s: the second reign of Elizabeth I?', in Guy, *Reign of Elizabeth I* (1995), 1–19.

——, ed. *The reign of Elizabeth I: court and culture in the last decade* (Cambridge: Cambridge University Press, 1995).

——, 'The rhetoric of counsel in early modern England', in Hoak, *Tudor political culture* (1995), 292–310.

——, ed., *The Tudor monarchy* (London: Arnold, 1997).

——, 'The Tudor monarchy and its critiques', in Guy, *Tudor monarchy* (1997), 78–109.

Hackett, Helen, *Virgin mother, maiden Queen: Elizabeth I and the cult of the virgin Mary* (Basingstoke: Palgrave Macmillan, 1995).

Hadfield, Andrew, *Shakespeare and Renaissance politics* (London: Arden Shakespeare: 2004).

——, *Shakespeare and republicanism* (Cambridge: Cambridge University Press, 2005).

——, 'The political significance of the first Tertralogy', in McDiarmid, *Monarchical republic* (2007), 149–64.

Hammer, P. E. J., 'An Elizabethan spy who came in from the cold: the return of Anthony Standen to England in 1593', *Historical Research*, 65 (1992), 277–95.

——, 'The Earl of Essex, Fulke Greville, and the employment of scholars', *Studies in Philology*, 91/2 (1994), 167–80.

——, 'The uses of scholarship: the secretariat of Robert Devereux, second earl of Essex, c.1585–1601', *EHR*, 109 (1994), 26–51.

——, 'Letters of travel advice from the earl of Essex to the earl of Rutland: some comments', *Philological Quarterly*, 74 (1995), 317–25.

——, 'Patronage at court, faction, and the earl of Essex', in Guy, *Reign of Elizabeth I* (1995), 65–86.

——, 'Essex and Europe: evidence from confidential instructions by the earl of Essex, 1595–6', *EHR*, 111 (1996), 357–81.

——, 'Myth-making: politics, propaganda and the capture of Cadiz in 1596', *HJ*, 40 (1997), 621–42.

——, 'Upstaging the Queen: the earl of Essex, Francis Bacon and the Accession Day celebrations of 1595', in Bevington and Holbrook, *Politics of the Stuart court masque* (1998), 41–66.

——, *The polarisation of Elizabethan politics: the political career of Robert Devereux, 2nd Earl of Essex 1585–1597* (Cambridge: Cambridge University Press, 1999).

——, *Elizabeth's wars: war, government and society in Tudor England, 1544–1604* (Basingstoke: Palgrave Macmillan, 2003).

——, 'How to become an Elizabethan statesman: Lord Henry Howard, the Earl of Essex, and the politics of friendship', *English Manuscript Studies, 1100–1700*, 13 (2007), 1–34.

——, 'The smiling crocodile: the Earl of Essex and late-Elizabethan "popularity"', in Lake and Pincus, *Politics of the public sphere* (2007), 95–115.

——, 'Shakespeare's *Richard II*, the play of February 7 1601, and the Essex Rising', *Shakespeare Quarterly*, 59/1 (2008), 1–35.

Harrison, G. B., *The life and death of Robert Devereux, earl of Essex* (London: Cassell, 1937).

Hay, Millicent V., *The life of Robert Sidney, earl of Leicester (1563–1626)* (Washington, DC: Folger Shakespeare Library, 1984).

Heffner, Ray, 'Shakespeare, Hayward, and Essex', *PMLA*, 45 (1930), 754–80.

——, 'Shakespeare, Hayward, and Essex again', *PMLA*, 47 (1932), 898–99.

Helgerson, Richard, *Forms of nationhood: the Elizabethan writing of England* (Chicago, IL and London: University of Chicago Press, 1992).

Henry, L. W., 'The Earl of Essex as strategist and military organizer (1596–7)', *EHR*, 68 (1953), 363–93.

——, 'The Earl of Essex and Ireland, 1599', *BIHR*, 32 (1959), 1–23.

Hicks, Leo S. I., 'Sir Robert Cecil, Father Persons and the succession, 1600–1601', *Archivum Historicum Societatis Iesu*, 24 (1955), 95–139.

Highfield, J. R., 'An autograph commonplace book of Sir Henry Savile', *Bodleian Library Record*, 7 (1963), 73–83.

Hind, Arthur M., *Engraving and England in the sixteenth and seventeenth centuries: a descriptive catalogue with introductions. Part I: the Tudor period* (Cambridge: Cambridge University Press, 1952).

Hoak, Dale ed., *Tudor political culture* (Cambridge: Cambridge University Press: 1995).

Holmes, Peter 'The authorship and early reception of "A Conference about the Next Succession to the Crown of England"', *HJ*, 23/2 (1980), 415–29.

——, *Resistance and compromise: the political thought of Elizabethan Catholics* (Cambridge: Cambridge University Press, 1982).

Honnigmann, E. A. J., 'Sir John Oldcastle: Shakespeare's martyr', in John W. Mahon and Thomas A. Pendleton eds, *'Fanned and winnowed opinions': Shakespearean essays presented to Harold Jenkins* (London: Methuen, 1987), 127–8.

Houliston, Victor, 'The Lord Treasurer and the Jesuit: Robert Persons's satirical *responsio* to the 1591 proclamation', *Sixteenth Century Journal*, 32/2 (2001), 383–401.

——, *Catholic resistance in Elizabethan England: Robert Person's Jesuit polemic, 1580–1610* (Aldershot: Ashgate, 2007).

Hunt, Arnold, 'Tuning the pulpits: the religious context of the Essex revolt', in Ferrell and McCullough, *English sermon revised* (2000), 86–114.

Hurstfield, Joel, *The Queen's wards: wardship and marriage under Elizabeth I* (London: Jonathan Cape, 1958).

——, 'The succession struggle in late Elizabethan England', in Bindoff, Hurstfield, and Williams, *Elizabethan government and society* (1961), 369–96.

James, Mervyn, 'At a crossroads of the political culture: the Essex revolt, 1601', in idem, *Society, politics and culture: studies in early modern England* (Cambridge: Cambridge University Press, 1986), 416–65.

Jardine, Lisa and Grafton, Anthony, '"Studied for Action": How Gabriel Harvey read his Livy', *Past and Present*, 129 (1990), 30–78.

Jardine, Lisa and Stewart, Alan, *Hostage to fortune: the troubled life of Francis Bacon* (London: Gollancz, 1998).

Jones, F. M. H., *Mountjoy, 1563–1606: the last Elizabethan deputy* (Dublin and London: Clonmore & Reynolds and Burns Oates & Washbourne, 1958).

Jordan, W. K., *The development of religious toleration in England*, 4 vols (London: Allen and Unwin, 1932–40).

Kaushik, Sandeep, 'Resistance, loyalty and recusant politics: Sir Thomas Tresham and the Elizabethan state', *Midland History*, 21 (1996), 37–72.

Kenny, Robert W., *Elizabeth's admiral: the political career of Charles Howard, Earl of Nottingham, 1536–1642* (Baltimore, MD and London: Johns Hopkins Press, 1970).

Kewes, Paulina ed., *The uses of history in early modern England* (San Marino, CA: Huntington Library, 2006).

King, Maureen, 'The Essex myth in Jacobean England', in Burgess, Wymer, and Laurence, *Accession of James I* (2006), 177–86.

Kingdon, Robert, 'Calvinism and resistance theory, 1550–1580', in Burns and Goldie, *Cambridge history of political thought, 1450–1700* (1991), 193–218.

Kouri, E. I. and Scott, T. eds, *Politics and society in reformation Europe: essays for Sir Geoffrey Elton on his sixty-fifth birthday* (London: Macmillan, 1986).

Lacey, Robert, *Robert, Earl of Essex: an Elizabethan Icarus* (London: Weidenfeld & Nicolson, 1971).

Lake, Peter, *Moderate Puritans and the Elizabethan church* (Cambridge: Cambridge University Press, 1982).

——, *Anglicans and Puritans? Presbyterian and English conformist thought from Whitgift to Hooker* (London: Unwin Hyman, 1988).

——, 'Anti-popery: the structure of a prejudice', in Cust and Hughes, *Conflict in early Stuart England* (1989), 72–106.

——, '"The Anglican moment?" Richard Hooker and the ideological watershed of the 1590s', in Platten, *Anglicanism and the Western Christian tradition* (2003), 90–121.

——, 'The king, (the queen) and the Jesuit: James Stuart's *True law of free monarchies* in context/s', *TRHS*, 6/14 (2004), 243–60.

——, '"The monarchical republic of Elizabeth I" revisited (by its victims) as a conspiracy', in Coward and Swann, *Conspiracies and conspiracy theory* (2004), 87–111.

——, 'From *Leicester his Commonwealth* to *Sejanus his fall*: Ben Jonson and the politics of Roman (Catholic) virtue', in Shagan, *Catholics and the 'Protestant nation'* (2005), 128–61.

——, '"The monarchical republic of Queen Elizabeth I" (and the fall of Archbishop Grindal) revisited', in McDiarmid, *Monarchical republic* (2007), 129–47.

Lake, Peter and Pincus, Steven eds, *The politics of the public sphere in early modern England* (Manchester: Manchester University Press, 2007).

Lake, Peter and Questier, Michael, *The Antichrist's lewd hat: Protestants, papists and players in post-Reformation England* (New Haven, CT and London: Yale University Press, 2002).

Langston, Beach, 'Essex and the art of dying', *HLQ*, 13 (1950), 109–29.

Lemmings, David and Walker, Claire eds, *Moral panics, the media and the law in early modern England* (Basingstoke and New York: Palgrave Macmillan, 2009).

Lemon, Rebecca, 'The faulty verdict in "The Crown v. John Hayward"', *Studies in English Literature, 1500–1900*, 41/1 (2001), 109–32.

——, *Treason by words: literature, law, and rebellion in Shakespeare's England* (Ithaca, NY and London: Cornell University Press, 2006).

Levy, F. J., *Tudor historical thought* (San Marino, CA: Huntington Library, 1967).

——, 'Hayward, Daniel, and the beginning of politic history in England', *HLQ*, 50 (1987), 1–34.

——, 'Theatre and court in the 1590s', in Guy, *Reign of Elizabeth I* (1995), 287–95.

Lloyd, Howell A., *The Rouen campaign 1590–1592: politics, warfare and the early-modern state* (Oxford: Clarendon Press, 1973).

——, 'The Essex inheritance', *Welsh Historical Review*, 7 (1974), 13–59.

Lock, Julian, '"How many Tercios has the Pope?" The Spanish war and the sublimination of Elizabethan anti-popery', *History*, 81/262 (1996), 197–214.

MacCaffrey, Wallace T., 'Place and patronage in Elizabethan politics', in Bindoff, Hurstfield, and Williams, *Elizabethan government and society* (1961), 95–126.

——, *Elizabeth I: war and politics* (Princeton, NJ: Princeton University Press, 1992).

McConica, James, ed., *A History of the University of Oxford, vol. 3. The collegiate university* (Oxford: Clarendon Press, 1986).

——, 'Elizabethan Oxford: the collegiate society', in idem, *History of the University of Oxford* (1986), 693–701.

McCoog, T. M., 'Harmony disrupted: Robert Parsons, S. J., William Crichton, S. J. and the question of Queen Elizabeth's successor, 1581–1603', *Archivum Historicum Societatis Iesu*, 73 (2004), 149–220.

McCoy, Richard C., *The rites of knighthood: the literature and politics of Elizabethan chivalry* (Berkeley, CA and London: University of California Press, 1989).

McDiarmid, John F. ed., *The monarchical republic of early modern England: essays in response to Patrick Collinson* (Aldershot: Ashgate, 2007).

McGurk, J., *The Elizabethan conquest of Ireland: the 1590s crisis* (Manchester: Manchester University Press, 1997).

McKeen, David, *A memory of honour: the life of William Brooke, Lord Cobham*, 2 vols (Salzburg: Institut für Anglistik und Amerikanistik, 1986).

McKisack, May, *Medieval history in the Tudor age* (Oxford: Clarendon Press, 1971).

McLaren, A. N., *Political culture in the reign of Elizabeth I: Queen and commonwealth 1558–1585* (Cambridge: Cambridge University Press, 1999).

Marañón, Gregorio, *Antonio Pérez, 'Spanish traitor'*, trans. Charles David Ley (London: Hollis and Carter, 1954).

May, Steven W., 'The poems of Edward de Vere, seventeenth Earl of Oxford, and of Robert Devereux, second earl of Essex', *Studies in Philology*, 77/5 (1980), 1–132.

——, *The Elizabethan courtier poets: the poems and their contexts* (Columbia, MO: University of Missouri Press, 1991).

Mayer, J. C., *The struggle for the succession in late Elizabethan England: politics, polemics and cultural representations* (Montpellier: Université Paul-Valéry, 2004).

Mears, Natalie, '*Regnum Cecilianum*? A Cecilian perspective of the court', in Guy, *Reign of Elizabeth I* (1995), 46–64.

——, *Queenship and political discourse in the Elizabethan realms* (Cambridge: Cambridge University Press, 2005).

Milward, Peter, *Religious controversies of the Elizabethan age: a survey of printed sources* (Lincoln, NE and London: University of Nebraska Press, 1977).

Molen, G. van der, *Alberico Gentili and the development of international law: his life, work and times*, 2nd edn (Leyden: A.W. Sijthoff, 1968).

Morash, Christopher, *A history of Irish theatre, 1601–2000* (Cambridge: Cambridge University Press, 2002).

Morrill, John, Slack, Paul and Woolf, Daniel eds, *Public duty and private conscience in seventeenth-century England. Essays presented to G. E. Aylmer* (Oxford: Clarendon Press, 1993).

Neale, J. E., 'Peter Wentworth (continued)', *EHR*, 39/154 (1924), 175–205.

——, *Elizabeth I and her Parliaments, 1584–1601* (London: Jonathan Cape, 1957).

——, *The Elizabethan House of Commons* (London: Jonathan Cape, 1949, repr. 1963).

Norbrook, David, *Writing the English republic: poetry, rhetoric and politics, 1627–1660* (Cambridge: Cambridge University Press, 1999).

——, *Poetry and politics in the English Renaissance*, rev. edn (Oxford: Oxford University Press, 2002).

Oestreich, Gerhard, *Neostoicism and the early modern state* (Cambridge: Cambridge University Press, 1982).

Orr, Alan, *Treason and the state: law, politics and ideology in the English Civil War* (Cambridge: Cambridge University Press, 2002).

Panizza, Diego, *Alberico Gentili, giurista ideologico nell'inghilterra elisabettiana* (Padua: D. Panizza, 1981).

Parker, Geoffrey, *The grand strategy of Philip II* (New Haven, CT and London: Yale University Press, 1998).

Parmelee, Lisa Ferraro, *Good newes from Fraunce: French anti-league propaganda in late Elizabethan England* (Rochester, NY: University of Rochester Press, 1996).

Patterson, Annabel, *Reading Holinshed's Chronicles* (Chicago, IL and London: University of Chicago Press, 1994).

Patterson, W. B., *King James VI and I and the reunion of Christendom* (Cambridge: Cambridge University Press, 1997).

Peck, Linda Levy, *Northampton: patronage and policy at the court of James I* (London: Allen and Unwin, 1982).

——, 'Peers, patronage and the politics of history' in Guy, *Reign of Elizabeth I* (1995), 87–108.

Peltonen, Markku, *Classical humanism and republicanism in English political thought, 1570–1640* (Cambridge: Cambridge University Press, 1995).

——, *The duel in early modern England: civility, politeness and honour* (Cambridge: Cambridge University Press, 2003).

Perry, Curtis, *Literature and favouritism in early modern England* (Cambridge: Cambridge University Press, 2006).

Platten, Stephen ed., *Anglicanism and the western Christian tradition: continuity, change and the search for communion* (Norwich: Canterbury Press, 2003).

Pritchard, Arnold, *Catholic loyalism in Elizabethan England* (London: Scolar Press, 1979).

Questier, Michael, 'Elizabeth and the Catholics', in Shagan, *Catholics and the 'Protestant nation'* (2005), 69–94.

——, *Catholicism and community in early modern England: politics, aristocratic patronage, and religion, c.1550–1640* (Cambridge: Cambridge University Press, 2006).

——, 'Catholic loyalism in early Stuart England', *EHR*, 123 (2008), 1132–65.

Rabb, Theodore K., *Jacobean gentleman: Sir Edwin Sandys (1561–1629)* (Princeton NJ: Princeton University Press, 1999).

Raymond, Joad ed., *News, newspapers, and society in early modern Britain* (London: F. Cass, 1999).

Read, Conyers, 'William Cecil and Elizabethan public relations', in Bindoff, Hurstfield, and Williams, *Elizabethan government and society* (1961), 21–55.

Rebholz, Ronald A., *The life of Fulke Greville, first Lord Brooke* (Oxford: Clarendon Press, 1971).

Reid, R., 'The political influence of the "north parts" under the Tudors', in Seton-Watson, *Tudor studies* (1924), 208–30.

Rogers, D., '"The Catholic Moderator": A French reply to Bellarmine and its English author, Henry Constable', *Recusant History*, 5 (1960), 223–35.

Rowse, A. L., 'The Tragic Career of Henry Cuffe', in idem, *Court and country: studies in Tudor social history* (Brighton: Harvester, 1987).

Ruff, L. M. and Wilson, D. A., 'The madrigal, the lute song and Elizabethan politics', *Past and Present*, 44 (1969), 3–51.

Ruff, L. M. and Wilson, D. A., 'Allusion to the Essex downfall in lute song lyrics', *Lute Society Journal*, 12 (1970), 31–6.

Salmon, J. H. M., 'Stoicism and Roman Example: Seneca and Tacitus in Jacobean England', *Journal of the History of Ideas*, 50/2 (1989), 119–225.

——, 'James I, the oath of allegiance, the Venetian interdict, and the reappearance of French Ultramontanism', in Burns and Goldie, *Cambridge History of Political Thought* (1991), 247–53.

Seton-Watson, R. ed., *Tudor studies* (London: Longman, 1924).

Shagan, Ethan H., 'Protector Somerset and the 1549 rebellions: new sources and new perspectives', *EHR*, 114 (1999), 34–63.

——, ed., *Catholics and the 'protestant nation': religious politics and identity in early modern England* (Manchester: Manchester University Press, 2005).

Sharpe, James, 'Social strain and social dislocation, 1585–1603', in Guy, *Reign of Elizabeth I* (1995), 192–211.

Sharpe, Kevin and Lake, Peter, *Culture and politics in early Stuart England* (Basingstoke: Macmillan, 1994).

Shell, Alison, *Catholicism, controversy, and the English literary imagination, 1558–1660* (Cambridge: Cambridge University Press, 1999).

Skinner, Quentin, *The foundations of modern political thought*, 2 vols (Cambridge: Cambridge University Press, 1978).

——, 'The State', in Ball, Farr, and Hanson, *Political innovation and conceptual change* (1989), 90–131.

——, *Reason and rhetoric in the philosophy of Hobbes* (Cambridge: Cambridge University Press, 1996).

——, 'Classical liberty, renaissance translation and the English civil war', in idem, *Visions of politics. II. Renaissance virtues* (Cambridge: Cambridge University Press, 2002), 308–43.

Smith, David Baird, 'Jean de Villiers Hotman', *Scottish Historical Review*, 14 (1916–17), 153–5.

Smith, David L., 'Catholic, Anglican or Puritan? Edward Sackville, Fourth Earl of Dorset and the ambiguities of religion in early Stuart England', *TRHS*, 6/2 (1992), 105–24.

Smith, Lacey Baldwin, 'English treason trials and confessions in the 16th century', *Journal of the History of Ideas*, 15/4 (1954), 471–98.

——, *Treason in Tudor England: politics and paranoia* (London: Jonathan Cape, 1986).

Smuts, R. Malcolm, 'Court-centred politics and the uses of Roman historians c.1590–1630', in Sharpe and Lake eds, *Culture and politics* (1994), 21–43.

—— *Culture and power in England: 1585–1685* (Basingstoke: Macmillan, 1999).

Sommerville, Johann, 'Richard Hooker, Hadrian Saravia, and the advent of the divine right of kings', *History of Political Thought*, 4 (1983), 229–45.

Squibb, George Drewry, *The High Court of Chivalry. A study of the civil law in England* (Oxford: Clarendon Press, 1959).

Stafford, Helen Georgia, *James VI and the throne of England* (New York and London: D. Appleton-Century Company, 1940).

Stopes, C. C., *The life of Henry, third earl of Southampton, Shakespeare's patron* (Cambridge: Cambridge University Press, 1922).

Story, G. M., and Gardner, Helen eds, *The sonnets of William Alabaster* (Oxford: Oxford University Press, 1959).

Strachey, Lytton, *Elizabeth and Essex: a tragic history* (London: Chatto and Windus, 1928).

Stroud, T. A., 'Father Thomas Wright: a test case for toleration', *Biographical Studies*, 1 (1951–2), 189–219.

Sutton, Dana F., *Unpublished works by William Alabaster (1568–1640)* (Oxford and Salzburg: Salzburg University Press, 1997).

Tillyard, E. M. W., *The Elizabethan world picture: a study of idea and order in the age of Shakespeare, Donne and Milton, and Shakespeare's history plays* (London: Chatto and Windus, 1943).

Tipton, Alzada, ' "Lively patterns . . . for affayres of State": Sir John Hayward's *The life and reigne of King Henrie IIII* and the Earl of Essex', *Sixteenth Century Journal*, 33 (2002), 769–94.

Todd, R. B., 'Henry and Thomas Savile in Italy', *Bibliothèque d'Humanisme et Renaissance*, 58 (1996), 439–44.

Toffanin, Giuseppe, *Machiavelli e il 'tacitismo'* (Padua: A. Drahgi, 1921).

Tuck, Richard, *Philosophy and government 1572–1651* (Cambridge: Cambridge University Press, 1993).

Tyacke, Nicholas, 'Puritan politicians and King James VI and I, 1587–1604', in Cogswell, Cust, and Lake, *Politics, religion and popularity* (2002), 21–44.

Vickers, Brian, 'The authenticity of Bacon's earliest writings', *Studies in Philology*, 94 (1997), 248–96.

Walker, Julia M. ed., *Dissing Elizabeth: negative representations of Gloriana* (Durham, NC and London: Duke University Press, 1998).

Wall, A., 'An account of the Essex revolt, February 1601', *BIHR*, 54 (1981), 131–3.

——, ' "Points of contact": court favourites and county faction in Elizabethan England', *Parergon*, n. s./6 (1988), 215–26.

Walsham, Alexandra, *Charitable hatred: tolerance and intolerance in England, 1500–1700* (Manchester: Manchester University Press, 2006).

——, ' "This newe army of Satan": the Jesuit mission and the formation of public opinion in Elizabethan England', in Lemmings and Walter, *Moral panics* (2009), 41–62.

Wernham, R. B., *After the armada: Elizabethan England and the struggle for Western Europe, 1588–1595* (Oxford: Clarendon Press, 1984).

——, 'Queen Elizabeth I, the Emperor Rudolf II and the Archduke Ernest in 1593–4', in Kouri and Scott, *Politics and society in Reformation Europe* (1986), 437–51.

——, *The expedition of Sir John Norris and Sir Francis Drake to Spain and Portugal, 1589* (Navy Records Society, 127: Aldershot, 1988).

——, *The return of the armadas: the last years of the Elizabethan war against Spain, 1595–1603* (Oxford: Oxford University Press, 1994).

Wickes, George, 'Henry Constable: poet and courtier (1562–1613)' *Biographical Studies*, 2/4 (1954), 272–300.

Williams, Penry, *The Council in the Marches of Wales under Elizabeth I* (Cardiff: University of Wales Press, 1958).

——, 'Elizabethan Oxford: state, church and university, 1558–1603', in McConica, *History of the University of Oxford* (1986), 397–440.

——, 'Court and polity under Elizabeth I', in Guy, *Tudor monarchy* (1997), 356–79.

Womersley, David, 'Sir Henry Savile's Translation of Tacitus and the Political Interpretation of Elizabethan Texts', *Review of English Studies*, 171/167 (1991), 313–42.

Woolf, D. R., *The idea of history in early Stuart England: erudition, ideology and 'The light of truth' from the accession of James I to the Civil War* (Toronto and London: University of Toronto Press, 1990).

Wootton, David, 'Francis Bacon: your flexible friend', in Elliott and Brockliss, *World of the favourite* (1999), 184–204.

Worden, Blair, 'English Republicanism', in Burns and Goldie, *Cambridge history of political thought* (1991), 443–75.

—— 'Ben Jonson among the historians', in Sharpe and Lake, *Culture and politics in early Stuart England* (1994), 67–90.

——, *The sound of virtue: Philip Sidney's* Arcadia *and Elizabethan politics* (New Haven, CT and London: Yale University Press, 1996).

——, 'Favourites on the English stage', in Elliot and Brockliss, *World of the favourite* (1999), 159–83.

——, 'Which play was performed at the Globe Theatre on February 7, 1601?', *London Review of Books*, 25/13 (2003), 22–4.

——, 'Historians and poets', in Kewes, *Uses of history* (2006), 69–90.

Wright, G., 'Samuel Daniel's use of sources in *The Civil Wars*, *Studies in Philology*, 101/1 (2004), 59–87.

——, 'What Daniel really did with the *Pharsalia*: *The Civil Wars*, Lucan and King James', *Review of English Studies,* 55/249 (2004), 210–32.

——, 'The politics of revision in Samuel Daniel's *The Civil Wars*', *English Literary Renaissance* 38/3 (2008), 461–82.

Zagorin, Perez, *How the idea of religious toleration came to the West* (Princeton, NJ: Princeton University Press, 2003).

ELECTRONIC RESOURCES

Oxford Dictionary of National Biography (Oxford University Press, 2004); online edn, Oct. 2008.

UNPUBLISHED THESES

Adams, S. L., 'The Protestant cause: religious alliance with the west European Calvinist communities as a political issue in England, 1585–1630', DPhil thesis (Oxford, 1973).

Dickinson, Janet E., 'The Essex rebellion, 1601: subversion or supplication?', PhD thesis (University of Southampton, 2006).

Gazzard, Hugh, 'The patronage of Robert Devereux, second earl of Essex, c.1577–1596', DPhil thesis (University of Oxford, 2000).

Grayson, J. C., 'From protectorate to partnership: Anglo-Dutch relations, 1598–1625', PhD thesis (University of London, 1978).

Hutson, G. L., 'The military following of Robert Devereux, 2nd earl of Essex and the rising of 1601', MLitt thesis (University of Oxford, 1987).

Richardson, L. J., 'Sir John Hayward and early Stuart historiography', PhD thesis, 2 vols (University of Cambridge, 1999).

Index

Lightning Source UK Ltd.
Milton Keynes UK
UKHW040651150223
416664UK00001B/103